VAULT REPORTS GUIDE TO THE TOP 50 MBA EMPLOYERS

VAULT REPORTS™

VAULT REPORTS GUIDE TO THE TOP 50 MBA EMPLOYERS

H.S. HAMADEH, MARCY LERNER, EDWARD SHEN, DOUG CANTOR, ANDREW GILLIES, CHANDRA PRASAD AND NIKKI SCOTT

For information about permission to reproduce selections from this book, contact Vault Reports Inc., P.O. Box 1772, New York, New York 10011-1772, (212) 366-4212.

Library of Congress CIP Data is available.

ISBN 1-58131-040-4

Printed in the United States of America

ACKNOWLEDGEMENTS

Warm thanks to:

Hernie, Glenn Fischer, Carol and Bart Fischer, Lee Black, Jay Oyakawa, Todd Kelleher, Bruce Bland, Celeste and Noelle, Rob Copeland, Muriel and Stephanie, Michael Kalt, Ravi Mhatre, Tom Phillips, Bryan Finkel, Geoff Baum, Gary Mueller, Ted Liang, Brian Fischer, Glen and Dorothy Wilkins, Sarah Griffith, Russ Dubner, Kirsten Fragodt, Aldith and Robert Scott-Asselbergs, C., J. Nilsson, Geoff Vitale, Dana Evans, Jimi Hendrix, Matt "The Weasel" Garbett, Beavis, Chris Vinegra, and Chris "D.P." Amistadi from the Class of '51, Sue and Radha Prasad, Raman, Ravi, Chris Vinegra, Marky Mark, Über, Olympia, The Goat, MC Solaar, Jo Jo Money, Red Head Jen, Ace Bar (5th Street Between Avenue A and B) and our families.

And to:

Amy Wegenaar, Angela Tong, Kofo Anifalaje, Alex Apelbaum, Al Gatling, Kevin Salgado, Candice Mortimer, Samir Shah, Thomas Lee, Joan Lucas, Kelly Guerrier, Sylvia Kovac, and Austin Shau

Special thanks to:

All of the MBAs who took the time to fill out our survey and offer comments on the companies. Special thanks also to all the company human resources and public relations officers who helped with the compilation of entries; we appreciate your patience with our tight deadlines.

And magicians:

Robert Schipano and Jake Wallace

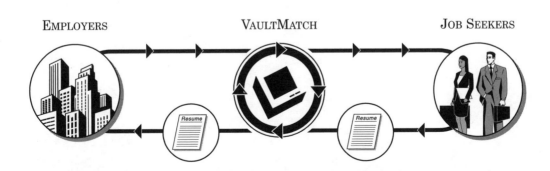

Contents

THE BEST OF THE REST

VAULT REPORTS PROFILES

ARTICLES

VAULT REPORTS RANKINGS OF MBA EMPLOYERS BY CATEGORY

Introduction

Why did Vault Reports produce a guide to the Top 50 MBA Employers? First and foremost, because there was no existing ranking system, or guide to, the nation's most prestigious and sought-after employers for holders of business degrees. For the time being, MBAs and business school students must do their own due diligence, patching together a network of company recruiters, brochures, and word of mouth to form their opinion on a firm – or spend days hunting down relevant articles and magazines. So we at Vault Reports decided to do the legwork for MBAs (and wannabe MBAs) who want to evaluate the nation's top employers.

We surveyed thousands of MBAs throughout the country, business school graduates from some of the nation's top schools, from Wharton to Stanford. We asked them to tell us what they knew and thought of other top MBA employers by asking them to score each company based on its reputation. Based on this information, we ranked and rated the top 50 MBA employers.

Not only did we go to business school graduates and ask them to rank the most prestigious and desirable employers, but we also decided to give you the inside scoop on what those companies are actually like. We asked contacts at each company we ranked to share their impression and opinions of their firm. This information was not used as part of the rankings, but in the detailed profiles of each firm contained in this book. Remember that every quote by a company insider should be considered his or her opinion, and not necessarily representative of what all employees at a company think (much less the company itself).

Why should you care about the reputation of the company you plan to join (or are already with)? Well, for starters, for the same reasons you cared about the reputation of the college and the business school you attended. The most prestigious firms do some of the most interesting work and have some of the most widespread operations. In an unstable economy, you can be sure these firms will stand strong.

Second, if it turns out that your present employer isn't destined to be your home for life, your new job search, whether you're staying in your industry or trying to branch out, will be made much easier if that name on the top of your resume is golden. Insiders at these companies are catnip for recruiters and headhunters.

Those who need to tend their egos (of which there are a few at business schools, we know from experience) will be much happier working for Microsoft or McKinsey than at MBI, Inc.

Which companies pay MBAs the most? What companies will allow you some flexibility in your hours and lifestyle? If you want to work in San Francisco, what firm is your best bet? Is the cafeteria any good? This book will tell you all this – and much, much more.

If you're wondering what all those snazzy icons in our company entries are for, or how we developed our information, read on. Here's a guide to the information you'll find in each entry of our book.

THE METERS

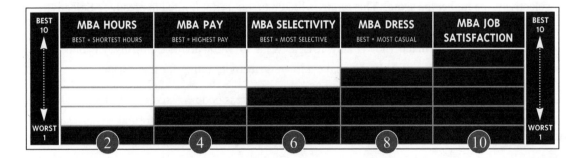

BEST 10 ⬆ WORST 1	MBA HOURS	MBA PAY	MBA SELECTIVITY	MBA DRESS	MBA JOB SATISFACTION	BEST 10 ⬆ WORST 1
	BEST = SHORTEST HOURS	BEST = HIGHEST PAY	BEST = MOST SELECTIVE	BEST = MOST CASUAL		

The Vault Reports Meters are scored on a 1-10 scale, with 10 being the highest. The scores are based upon how a particular firm compares to the average MBA employer. A firm with a score of "5" in pay signifies that the firm has an average salary for an MBA employer (though the firm might be well above average for companies in general, and might pay its non-business degreed employees very low wages). In determining our ratings, we looked at both company data and our own surveys and benchmarking of companies (derived from years of research).

The meters attempt to give an at-glance look at a company. However, keep in mind that the issues they measure are complex, and a closer look at the entry is necessary for a fuller view.

MBA Pay: A company's pay score is based on home office pay, with bonuses (and likelihood of achieving them) factored in. We did not factor in cost of living or stock options.

MBA Work Hours: The shorter the workweek, the higher the score. We also factored in the pressure to bill a certain number of billable hours. We did not adjust these scores based on the company location. Working 70 hours a week may be a vacation at some New York companies, but it's still a mighty long workweek. For example, to get a 1 (the lowest score, indicating longest hours) on our meter, MBA employees must report workweeks that regularly top 90 hours.

MBA Satisfaction: Employee satisfaction is based on our extensive interviews and surveys of MBA employees at the firm.

MBA Selectivity: This score is based on how selective a firm is in hiring. The higher the selectivity, the higher the score. This rating is linked to, but is not limited to prestige. Selectivity when it comes to recruitment, is effected by simple supply (how many MBAs does the employer want to hire?) and demand (how many MBAs want to work at the company?) economics. Companies growing very quickly may have a lower selectivity rating for this reason.

MBA Dress: The higher the score, the more casual the dress code. A score of 10 means shorts and ripped T-shirts (nobody got a 10); a score of 1 means strict business formal. These scores indicate dress for positions that MBAs fill (finance, marketing, etc.). If the engineers at a company can wear sandals, it doesn't necessarily help the company's score if the strategy planners can't too.

THE BUZZ

In the survey that we used to compile our prestige rankings, we asked our respondents not only to rank firms, but also to reveal their impressions of each company listed. We've collected a sampling of their comments in "The Buzz." We did this in order to gauge the nuances of the reputation of the top MBA employers – as these subtle outsider perceptions can mean all the difference when deciding where to work. In choosing three or four quotes for each firm to include, we tried to include quotes representative of the common perception of the firms, even if the quotes, in our opinion (based on interviews with insider at that company), did not accurately describe the firm. Some of the comments are fair, some rather nasty, a few hilarious. It was interesting to note how many of our top firms were dubbed both "aggressive" and "nerdy."

THE GRAPHS

The information given in the graphs for each company are drawn from a variety of sources. Much of the basic financial and employment data (net income, number of employees, etc.) for public companies comes from business information provider Hoover's Online. For some of the private companies, we relied on information compiled by other organizations, (such as Kennedy Information, which follows management consulting firms). Finally, in many cases, the companies and firms themselves supplied data.

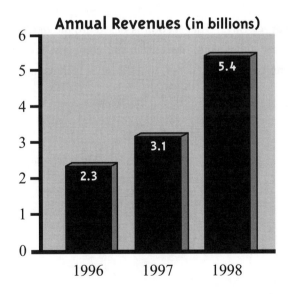

Annual Revenues (in billions)

Year	Revenue
1996	2.3
1997	3.1
1998	5.4

MBA Job Seekers: Receive free e-mailed job postings matching your interests & qualifications! Register at www.VaultReports.com

VAULT REPORTS™

www.vaultreports.com

5

THE ENTRIES

Each of our entries is broken into three sections: The Scoop, Getting Hired, and Our Survey Says.

The Scoop: This section includes information about the company's history, strategy and organization, recent business performance, and other points of interest.

Getting Hired: This section includes information about the company's hiring process for MBAs, concentrating on on-campus recruiting, summer associate programs and functional.

Our Survey Says: This section is based around quotes and comments from MBAs and other employees from the company, and covers topics such as company culture, pay, perks, social life, as well as many others.

Overview

At Harvard University's annual commencement exercises a few years ago, President Neil Rudenstine gave his customary words of congratulations and advice to the graduate schools affiliated with the school. The medical school students would go forth and heal, the business school students would grow the economy and create jobs while bound by the "wise restraints" imposed on them by the law school students, etc. In the middle of his address, the boisterous soon-to-be MBAs began chanting: "MBA... MBA... MBA."

"I said 'wise restraints,'" Rudenstine admonished the grads-to-be.

It's no wonder MBAs are feeling their oats. In the past few years, unemployment has approached its lowest point in 25 years, and the demand for B-school graduates has grown considerably. The consulting business, a major employer of MBAs, has been exploding since the late 1980s. The booming stock market has financial companies scrambling for qualified individuals to staff mergers and acquisitions and IPO deals. And high-tech firms are looking for people with a specific combination of management skills and technical expertise. Even the latest hiccups in the stock market and the collapse of financial markets in Asia, Russia, and other emerging markets are unlikely to reverse the growth of business in the globalizing economy.

THE PRICE OF THE MBA

It's no wonder that many are heading back to get their graduate business degrees. Getting an MBA is still the surest route to accelerating career growth or easily changing careers. Many companies still possess an unwritten rule that you can only go so far in a company without an MBA; and after the ruthless downsizing of the early 1990s, people realize that loyalty to one company is a thing of the past. An MBA makes anyone more marketable and mobile.

The costs, both financial and personal, involved in attaining an MBA are high. While the classic MBA student spends two years as a full-time student, attending school in this manner is necessarily an expensive and time-consuming proposition. Some employers offer tuition reimbursement for employees who want to return to school. But for those who can't attend full-time MBA programs, whether on their own nickel or the employer's tab, part-time and express MBA programs are taking on increased importance.

THE PART-TIME, ONLINE OPTION

Part-time MBAs still bear a slight stigma, no doubt stemming from the days when prestigious business schools declined to offer part-time or shorter-term MBA programs, or else gave them short shrift. Some programs even offered a different degree to part-time students. Those days are dwindling. Many schools now actively cater to the part-timer, expanding their evening and weekend course schedules, building satellite campuses, and creating industry-specific programs for part-timers in areas like health and high-tech. Prestigious schools like Carnegie Mellon and Johns Hopkins now bestow an identical degree upon full-time and part-time students. Even more innovative are programs like the University of Pittsburgh's "flex-MBA" program, which is offered via satellite to students around the country.

Increasingly trendy is the so-called Executive MBA, geared towards busy mid-career executives. During these 18- to 24-month courses, student/professionals enjoy 'executive' conveniences, and spend two weeks studying in Europe, Asia or Latin America, in order to gain a 'global perspective.' Tuition usually includes a laptop loaded with the necessary software, all books and study guides (delivered to their desks so they don't waste time in bookstores; and catered meals and snacks before and after class. The newest versions of the executive MBA programs hold most classes online – perfect for execs with unpredictable schedules, or those who travel a great deal.

Most of these programs combine Internet studies with residential (traditional classroom) sessions. Students study using interactive technology – including web-based audio and video lectures, chat sessions, and e-mail. Weekly assignments are taken from the home page, and students break into groups to divide up project work. They communicate with each other online using chat rooms, bulletin boards and e-mail, and consult with professors via e-mail and phone. The most convenient aspect of these programs is 24-hour access to class materials and information – though it requires participants to be disciplined and organized enough to set aside time for study. Now that schools like Purdue University and Duke's Fuqua School of Business are offering them, online MBA programs are commanding more respect in the business world. Tuition for these programs ranges from $6800 a year at the University of Phoenix to $85,800 for Duke's 19-month program.

There is debate about the true value of the online MBA. Students miss out on traditional classroom discussions, and the related feedback from professors. They are also less likely to develop the relationships with peers that lead to innovation. Some maintain, however, that what is lost in classroom discussion is made up for by the diverse makeup of the virtual classroom – it gives students exposure to people with a wider variety of perspectives. Students also gain experience in communicating, doing research and preparing presentations online, and leave their programs with a fuller understanding of how new technologies can be used to manage global organizations.

Despite the advent of the part-time option, it still makes economic sense to take the time for a full-time degree, especially at the most prestigious schools. Harvard Business School, for example, has a 99 percent placement rate, and its 1997 graduates made a median starting salary of $82,000. By comparison, the median base starting salary for MBAs from the University of South Carolina at Aiken was about $50,000. Instead of staying with their previous employers (like most part-timers), full-time MBAs look forward to being wooed by employers waving around signing bonuses, tuition reimbursements, and interest-free loans.

ENTREPRENEURIAL MBAS

Increasingly, business school students attend not to get a job in a company, but to learn how to start their own. Business schools have taken note. About 120 of the country's 300 accredited business schools offer entrepreneurial studies as a major, and more will surely follow. Along with basics like accounting and finance, students concentrating in this area learn about angel investors, how to pick funding, and the painful realities of starting a business, like financial ruin and other forms of failure. Students learn the ropes by setting up mock ventures and participating in business plan competitions where students present their ideas to venture capitalists, and the winners actually set up their own companies.

MBA Job Seekers: Receive free e-mailed job postings matching
your interests & qualifications! Register at www.VaultReports.com

VAULT
REPORTS™   9
www.vaultreports.com

TECHNOLOGY R US

Another popular addition to the business school smorgasbord is the technology MBA. Now that most companies have the technical basics in place, they are looking for people who know how to make technology work for their businesses – from information management to electronic commerce. With hardware and software evolving at a rapid rate, companies need people who can assess their needs and determine when they should invest in new technologies. The technology MBA is increasingly considered superior to the garden variety MBA.

BIG BUCKS

After several years of record economic growth, competition for qualified MBAs has intensified. Companies are extending offers within 24 hours, and top students often have to withdraw themselves from consideration in order to narrow down their options. Recruiters are aggresssively courting top candidates; some have gone so far as sending fruit baskets and other gifts (General Mills, for example, will send samples of its own products) to soften up prospective hires.

The growth of the three-day West Coast MBA Consortium held each winter in Irvine, California is a good indicator of the strength of the MBA job market. When it started in the early 1990s, about 15 employers attended the event and many business school students who attended left empty-handed. At the 1998 event, however more than 60 companies had rushed to sign up by September, and most MBA candidates came away with multiple interviews.

As companies strive to lure their desired candidates, the salary bar keeps rising. At UC Irvine, business school officials reported a $5,000 jump in the median MBA salary in 1997. In 1997, Goldman Sachs raised its average offers to business school graduates – they now range between $65,000 and $85,000 – and rival firms had no choice but to follow suit. According to *Fortune*, top students earning degrees at the country's most prestigious schools can expect starting salaries that average somewhere between $75,000 to $150,000. But that's not all – the standard compensation package for MBAs now includes a hefty bonus. In a 1997 study of close to 400 employers by the Virginia-based Society for Human Resource Management, more than 150 companies said they had used signing bonuses to attract candidates. Of those who had used bonuses, 43 percent had only begun offering bonuses in the past year. Typical signing bonuses range from $10,000 to $20,000, and some companies even reimburse recent graduates all or part of their tuition. Accelerating salaries and bonuses aren't only benefiting graduates of the most elite schools – at the Goizueta Business School at Emory, the average bonus reported in 1997 was $10,000, and more than half the school's 150 graduates received bonuses, the highest percentage in the history of the school.

QUALITY OF LIFE

At the same time, today's MBA graduates are more likely than their predecessors to prioritize quality of life issues. Some have families to consider, but even those who don't still want time to do their own laundry. Also important is how the job will affect their subsequent prospects. They want training, good management and mentoring and a name that will get them far. Job options for MBAs have also expanded now that more companies from different industries are pursuing them. You want to be a product manager but don't want to work for a conservative consumer goods company? Consider high tech. You like planning strategy but don't want to work long consultant hours? Find a company with an internal consulting arm. The best candidates feel free to simply flat-out demand perks such as flex-time and specific job locations. "I told them when I interviewed, I said 'No Kansas City,'" says a recent MBA graduate who landed at a major corporation headquartered in the nation's heartland. "And they said 'OK.'"

MBA Job Seekers: Receive free e-mailed job postings matching your interests & qualifications! Register at www.VaultReports.com

VAULT REPORTS™
www.vaultreports.com

11

Major Industries

MBAs are generally welcome in any industry, but they tend to gravitate toward certain ones, either because the pay is high (consulting, investment banking), or the potential upside is enormous (high tech). Here's a look at the industries that most MBAs currently prefer.

VAULT REPORTS™
www.vaultreports.com

13

Management Consulting

The consulting industry was born in 1886, when Arthur Dehon Little, an MIT professor, set up shop in Massachusetts to offer his technical expertise to companies in the throes of the Industrial Revolution. The field of management consulting began to truly take shape in the 1920s, when industry leader McKinsey was founded by a University of Chicago management professor. Many major firms, such as Bain and BCG, were created as recently as the 1960s and 1970s, when the consulting industry became an indispensable part of the business world.

Basically, consultants are hired by a company (or sometimes, a government entity, university, or a nonprofit organization) to assess its problems, plan its future or take its temperature. These companies believe that consultants are neutral outsiders with more overall industry experience that the client itself. Teams of consultants then work on projects – usually called "engagements" – for the client that can last anywhere from a couple of weeks to several years.

Because consultants are always moving to new engagements and learning new information about their clients and their industries, consulting – whether strategy, operations or information technology in nature – is a unique career that offers the chance to work within many industries and companies, rub shoulders with CEOs, and travel throughout the country and the world. Consulting firms sell knowledge, and the skill and expertise of their employees. Expect to work long hours, don't make any firm weekend plans, and share your workdays with some of the brightest and most ambitious people you've ever met.

UPPERS

- Plenty of frequent flyer miles
- Novelty of new engagements
- Intellectual fulfillment
- Camaraderie and teamwork with co-workers

DOWNERS

- Constant travel
- Little chance to see plans translated into action
- Many firms have strict "up-or-out" policies
- Long and capricious hours

VAULT REPORTS™
www.vaultreports.com

OUR SURVEY SAYS

The consulting industry is offering business school graduates generous salaries these days. "Associates usually start here at $95,000 plus bonus," explains one MBA at a top-level consulting firm, adding that "the signing bonus for first-year MBA grads places the total pay package easily into the six figures." At another consulting firm, where MBAs are hired into the company as associates with an overall salary of $120,000-$130,000, an insider says the company pays "industry average for management consulting – which is to say, it's awesome." But with MBAs working harder than ever, overall pay may not mean great pay per hour: "The pay is fine, but with the hours I work, I could probably do better on an hourly basis as an assistant manager at the Gap," says one consultant.

While jobs may be plentiful, getting promoted once you've found work won't be quite as easy. In some cases, employees are given a very specific timetable to advance, and are told to find employment elsewhere if they don't measure up. This practice, often called an "up-or-out policy," is common among consulting firms but is practiced in other industries, too. Even if an employer's promotion policy isn't so formal, subtle up-or-out pressure is often applied. "It takes from two to four years to get promoted from one level to the next," says one MBA in consulting. "Basically, if you are not being promoted, you should get the message and look elsewhere." And even at one newly-established consulting firm without a well-defined career path, one associate tells us: "After a while, if you're not promoted, you will have to move on to something else."

Frankly, our contacts in the industry say it's "best for those who are unattached," because "you're rarely home." Consulting is notorious for exorbitant travel requirements and extremely long hours (they get what they pay for, after all). For some people, "15 hours a day, six days a week, is not uncommon; plus half a day on Sunday," says one insider at a fast-growing management consulting firm. Another contact says the hours "never go below 60 and the high end can be 90 to 100 hours a week." "Then there is all the damn airplane time," complains another source, who notes that he is "required to be available for travel 100 percent of the time." Some consider all the traveling a perk, however – especially considering all the frequent flyer miles they earn. One former consultant boasts that consulting afforded him "unbelievable opportunities to travel around the world and enjoy myself in style."

MBA Job Seekers: Receive free e-mailed job postings matching your interests & qualifications! Register at www.VaultReports.com

VAULT REPORTS™
www.vaultreports.com

15

Socially, consulting firms tend to be especially cliquey. Says one consultant: "It depends on the team you're working with, but a lot of off-the-job interaction is encouraged by the firm. I mean, we go out almost every night for dinner together when we're on the road, which is most days. And besides that we have a social dinner once a week, we play golf together on a weekly basis, and we have a lot of events scheduled for us on the weekends, which you have the option to go to or not." Another consultant describes his firm as "very social, very fun. At the end of the day, at 9 or 10, someone will send an e-mail around asking if anyone wants to go out for dinner or drinks. There are intramural teams, and every weekend there's usually some kind of volunteer activity people can participate in." "I like the people here a lot more than I thought I would," adds another recent MBA grad. "In fact, people here hang out all the time."

MAJOR MANAGEMENT CONSULTING EMPLOYERS INCLUDE:

- ◆ Bain & Co.

- ◆ Booz-Allen & Hamilton

- ◆ Boston Consulting Group

- ◆ McKinsey & Co.

- ◆ Monitor Company

For more information on careers in management consulting, read the Vault Reports Guide to Management Consulting Firms.

For more information on management consulting interviews including actual case interview, guesstimates and brainteasers, read the Vault Reports Guide to the Case Interview.

VAULT REPORTS™

www.vaultreports.com

Orit without the hard hat

After dating a Harvard Business School student during a leave of absence from the intelligence wing of the Israeli army Orit Gadiesh decided to apply to the distinguished school herself. Despite her shaky English, Gadiesh was accepted at Harvard and proceeded to distinguish herself, becoming a Baker Scholar (an honor reserved for the top 5 percent of the class). She also won the Brown prize as the class's most outstanding marketing student. Her nickname was "Machine Gun Orit," for her rapid speech and no-nonsense stance; it was rumored she'd driven a tank in Israel. These days, Gadiesh heads Bain & Company, one of the world's most prestigious consulting firms.

Orit Gadiesh, to say the very least, isn't your typical white-shoe consulting firm CEO. Possessing two X chromosomes would be enough to differentiate the Israel-born Gadiesh from other firm leaders; her aubergine-hued halo of hair and glitzy costume jewelry set her firmly outside the mainstream of consulting fashion. Her background is also exceptional. The daughter of an Israeli general, Gadiesh served in the intelligence wing of the Israeli army before teaching psychology at Hebrew University.

Gadiesh intended to head for New York or London after her graduation from business school in 1977, but a conversation with Bain founder William Bain during her interview at her firm persuaded her to sign on. She was taken by the firm's aggressive stance toward implementation, very unusual for consulting firms at that time. When Bain was rocked by falling revenues, scandal and wrenching change in the late 1980s and early 1990s – including the decision of founding father William Bain to leave his firm – Bain & Co. needed a fresh start. In 1993, the firm turned to the marketing genius with the purple hair. Under Gadiesh's leadership, Bain has turned around and now enjoys growth of over 30 percent annually. While Gadiesh spends nearly 100 hours a week at work at Bain, more than two-thirds of it with clients, she also takes time out to read and attend the theater.

Investment Banking

Tom Wolfe called them "Masters of the Universe" in *The Bonfire of the Vanities*; Michael Lewis called them a few unprintable things in *Liar's Poker*. Who are they? Investment bankers, traders, and salespeople. Of course, investment banks aren't like your local branch office with ubiquitous ATMs (those are "commercial banks," like Chase Manhattan or BankAmerica Corp.); instead, investment banks work with corporations, governments, institutional investors and extraordinarily wealthy individuals to raise capital and provide investment advice.

However, the legal barrier between commercial and investment banks has been rapidly disintegrating since the 1980s, and this decade has witnessed the arrival of huge commercial banks entering the investment banking market. Firms like Germany's Deutsche Bank have been spending enormous amounts of money to establish their own investment banking arms (Deutsche Bank Securities), while other commercial banks have been acquiring small and medium-sized investment banks at a rapid rate. Baltimore-based Alex. Brown, the oldest investment bank in the nation, was recently acquired by Bankers Trust, Montgomery Securities was purchased by NationsBank, and Robertson Stephens & Co. was acquired by Bank of America – and then sold to BankBoston. Mergers between investment banks and other financial firms are another trend – witness the recent conjoinings of Morgan Stanley and Dean Witter, and Salomon Brothers and Smith Barney (now called Salomon Smith Barney). These combinations and mergers mean big changes and big opportunities in the investment banking industry – and indeed, positions in these temples of lucre are more highly sought after than ever.

What do investment bankers do with their 80 to 100 working hours a week? Investment banks serve clients who wish to raise capital, and clients who want to invest capital. Investment bankers help huge clients, such as corporations, conglomerates and major world governments raise capital, go public, divest or acquire businesses and business assets, and assist clients with their financial strategies. Investment banks also help those who want to invest money, both high net worth individuals (i.e., rich people) and corporations or other institutional investors. Supporting these operations are a cadre of skilled researchers and analysts who follow companies and industries, some so savvy and influential that their recommendations affect the value of the stocks and companies they follow.

MBA Job Seekers: Receive free e-mailed job postings matching your interests & qualifications! Register at www.VaultReports.com

VAULT REPORTS™

www.vaultreports.com

19

UPPERS	DOWNERS
• Generous pay	• High stress
• Breathtaking bonuses	• Very long hours
• Power	• Inflated egos
• Free dinners	• Layoffs common during economic slumps

OUR SURVEY SAYS

At prestigious I-banks, starting salaries are unparalleled. At the high end, starting associates just out of business school receive a package that's "close to $150,000 a year." While these packages are surely impressive, they are also in many cases important when it comes to future earnings. "Future increases in pay are based on the previous year's pay, so you basically have to push for a large first-year package to make the biggest bucks later on," says one MBA.

I-banks are notoriously "aggressive, sink-or-swim environments" where workweeks are always onerous and largely unpredictable. "Most last only until they're about 35," one source remarks, "then go off and do something else." "Sales and trading works about 60 to 65 hours a week," explains one associate trader on Wall Street. "There is usually at least one 15- to 16-hour day each week, but the nice thing is that your weekends are usually your own." In both corporate finance and M&A, associates say simply "the number and variability of hours can ultimately make this job undoable." Across the board, Wall Streeters say that work "just gets to be too much at times." Most banks make it clear from the beginning that "the firm comes first, second and last." One veteran guarantees that "you'll come close to cracking." But the fact is, the employees that "are willing to work the skin off their butts are invariably rewarded with better pay and promotions."

Furthermore, "if you have a particular interest," advises one MBA, "it is up to you to let people know, to get your name in the game." Mentors seem to be a key to advancement in many firms. At one top investment bank, an insider says: "You find out who is moving up in the company, and you make sure you're their boy." This is not to say that advancement is always political. One recent MBA hire at a major investment bank notes: "One thing I find significant about [my bank] is that people are taken at face value here." Says another associate at that bank: "When you first meet someone of any rank, if you come off as competent, they will treat you as competent. If you make a mistake, you'll have a long time living it down."

Though most bankers complain that they can hardly find time to get to the gym, most firms sponsor a slew of events and activities – ostensibly to give employees a chance to de-stress. One MBA at a top investment bank says the company's athletic leagues "can get frighteningly popular at times – it makes the office more interesting." Another Wall Street firm tries "to organize a lot of social events with people's families as opposed to outings for just firm members." "Most of us like this policy because it encourages familial friendships," says one insider.

MAJOR INVESTMENT BANKING EMPLOYERS INCLUDE:

- ◆ Goldman Sachs
- ◆ Morgan Stanley Dean Witter
- ◆ J.P. Morgan

- ◆ Merrill Lynch
- ◆ Donaldson, Lufkin & Jenrette

For more information on careers in investment banking, read the Vault Reports Guide to Investment Banking Firms.

For more information on investment banking interviews including actual finance interview, guesstimates and brainteasers, read the Vault Reports Guide to Finance Interviews.

MBA Job Seekers: Receive free e-mailed job postings matching your interests & qualifications! Register at www.VaultReports.com

VAULT REPORTS™

www.vaultreports.com

21

Consumer Products/ Brand Management

Are you fascinated by the endless variety of products you pass on your trips down supermarket aisles? Do you like to scrutinize particularly eye-catching cereal boxes or shampoo bottles? Do you watch TV advertisements and think about what type of consumers they are targeting, and how well they are accomplishing their goals? Do you see those endless spin-offs of existing products, and think you can come up with better versions? If so, brand management may be your calling.

With an overflow of advertising emanating from ever-forming genres of mass media, and with a surplus economy that allows the masses to increasingly indulge in status symbols, we all essentially live in a branded world. But there are MBAs who make handsome livings for thinking in terms of brand, or more precisely, for manipulating the branded world. They are called brand managers. These are the people who devise new products, decide how to package them, how to price them, and most importantly, how to market them. And while Wall Street may control our purse strings, and Hollywood may control our dreams and imaginations, it is the brand managers whose guiding hands shape everything we eat and wear, and in fact, shape the way we think about these things.

In many leading consumer goods companies, such as General Mills and Procter & Gamble, brand management is the track to upper (general) management. Insiders in the industry describe brand management as running one's own business – utilizing operations, marketing, and finance knowledge and ability. Brand management does not require as intense a lifestyle as consulting or investment banking – hours are reasonable, and travel is minimal. On the other hand, don't expect the excitement of Wall Street: many of the top consumer products companies are located in nondescript, relatively homogeneous cities kindly described as "nice places to raise a family."

VAULT REPORTS™
www.vaultreports.com

UPPERS

- Reasonable hours

- Numerous free products

- Minimal travel

- Independent work

DOWNERS

- Headquarters often in poky towns

- Pay lower than other MBA careers

- Bureaucracy rampant

OUR SURVEY SAYS

Off Wall Street, and outside the travel-intensive career of consulting, hours can be kinder for MBAs. One MBA in brand management says his weeks typically range from 50 to 75 hours, and remarks that "some weeks aren't even that long." An associate with a top MBA employer in the Midwest reports working "10 to 12 hours a day and an occasional weekend." One recent MBA hire tells Vault Reports this about his Southern employer: "I never work weekends. People here are not so unreasonable as to not understand the need for a life." Hours do get heavy, however, during the budget-planning season. And because many of these companies are expanding abroad, time-consuming international assignments may also arise.

As for money: "you'll never be rich," notes an insider at a leading brand company, "but you'll be very comfortable." Salaries for MBAs in marketing management are in the $60,000 to $80,000 range – not as high as those for consultants and bankers, but more than sufficient considering that many of these companies are located in low cost-of-living areas. What top brand companies do offer are potentially lucrative pension plans and profit-sharing bonuses.

Many brand managers say the most frustrating part of their job is the excessive bureaucracy. "It's very difficult to get things done," says a former assistant brand manager from a leading consumer goods company. That insider describes what happens when a new idea is presented:

MBA Job Seekers: Receive free e-mailed job postings matching your interests & qualifications! Register at www.VaultReports.com

VAULT REPORTS™

www.vaultreports.com

23

it is sent by memo to a superior, and then 'niggled' – sent back with comments in the margin. The memo is then rewritten and sent to the next higher level, where it's 'niggled' again. And so on.

If that doesn't stress out young employees enough, the up-or-out policies instituted at major brand companies certainly will. "Either you make your numbers on a fairly consistent basis," said one source from the industry, "or you should start looking for employment elsewhere." At one leading consumer goods company, if an employee is not promoted within an established timeframe, they are placed on "special assignment," one former employee reports. "This means two months in an office with just a phone and a desk to find another job."

Overall, brand management is known as a family-friendly industry, and employers commonly encourage socializing between employees. They sponsor sports teams, community service activities, and various outings. However, your social life is largely dependent on location and lifestyle – if you're single and your employer is located in a remote area, "there's not a whole lot to choose from." But some companies recruit actively at B-schools, so if you're lucky you'll end up working with other recent grads. One assistant marketing manager says their employer hires "30 new MBAs every year from all over the country, many single." One employee at a major food company says he met his wife at work. "They have a lot of husbands and wives working here," reports a marketing insider from a top brand company, "they think this helps keep you [in the area]."

Because these companies rely on marketing to different demographic groups, a diverse employee makeup is a highly valued asset. Employees at some big firms, however, say their companies still have "a long way to go." The industry has historically been pretty open women, and especially accommodating to working mothers. Says one marketing insider at a consumer goods company: "You are free to leave and take care of matters when you have to." One contact at a leading apparel company says advancement opportunities for women "depend on your department." Says a marketer at a major auto manufacturer: "Within the marketing area, I would say [a woman's] chances are pretty good. However in the finance area, there are very few women in management positions, and I would say that [her] chances are not as good." Another industry contact agrees: "In the areas of marketing, merchandising and product development, there is a good representation of both women and minorities in senior management."

VAULT REPORTS™
www.vaultreports.com

MAJOR CONSUMER PRODUCTS EMPLOYERS INCLUDE:

- Procter & Gamble

- General Mills

- Nike

- Coca-Cola

- Kraft

- Johnson & Johnson

For more information on careers in consumer products and brand management, including actual case interview questions, read the Vault Reports Guide to Marketing and Brand Management.

MBA Job Seekers: Receive free e-mailed job postings matching your interests & qualifications! Register at www.VaultReports.com

VAULT REPORTS™

25

www.vaultreports.com

High Tech

While the high-tech industry has historically been run by engineers and other techno-types, at some companies, such as industry giants like Sun Microsystems and 3Com, MBAs are increasingly calling the shots. Sun's CEO Scott McNealy has an MBA and an undergraduate degree in economics. Says one insider at 3Com: "MBAs have done very well at 3Com. The only obstacle in an MBA's career path is likely to be another MBA." This is not to say that technical knowledge can be completely ignored. One contact at 3Com tells us the company "really likes engineers with MBAs. Know your technical stuff before interviewing."

Working at a tech company involves some unique challenges. Due to the rapid rate of technological change, the industry is much more fluid than other industries – the group an MBA is assigned to may not exist in its present form in a year. In the tech industry, it's not necessarily the best product that wins out, but the one most in use (it has "mindshare"). That means that high-tech firms must constantly search for new applications for their products, and create new ones that need to be sold. This makes the duties of MBA product managers more essential than ever. At some firms, marketers in the field identify product openings and direct research and development efforts. And marketing no longer targets merely the converted who think in code and have their own domain names – the average consumer is the new source of growth for many tech companies. Witness Intel, which was one of the first hardware computer firms to "brand" its image to the mass market, a strategy that has led to enormous growth this decade. Others, like Cisco Systems, have followed suit. MBAs entering the high-tech industry should also be aware that, unlike their counterparts going into investment banking and consulting, they are entering a less structured industry that rewards initiative. Don't expect any hand-holding.

UPPERS

- Cutting-edge work

- Potentially lucrative stock options

- Casual dress the norm

- Minimal hierarchy

DOWNERS

- Small cubicles

- High stress

- Companies have high rate of failure

OUR SURVEY SAYS

High-tech firms tend to be team-oriented and "very social." "The culture here is focused around doing great work," says one industry contact, "but it is also a very fun place to be." Many companies have an "open door" policy, which "loosens things up quite a bit." "We work together in small teams," explains an employee at a technology firm, "so even though this is a large company, you always feel like an important part of a team." One insider reports that "a good chunk of my day is spent in other people's offices… discussing how to accomplish some task or the latest industry news." This cooperative attitude is the reason why stock options are so common in high-tech firms. The concept of 'everyone owning the company' is extremely popular. One insider at a large telecom reports "less hierarchy and structure than one would expect of a 50,000 employee company."

There may be a lot of support and communication between co-workers, but few high-tech companies offer formal training for MBAs. There's "no executive training programs where you are eased into the culture," reveals one insider, adding "I love it, because you have the freedom to take risks and make things happen, but many people find it a difficult environment." They eventually adjust, however – these firms pride themselves in only hiring the cream of the crop – usually from the top schools. Employees at these firms invariably remark that they are "impressed with the quality of people" they work with. An employee at one of the country's most prestigious high-tech firms says "there are literally millions of people

MBA Job Seekers: Receive free e-mailed job postings matching your interests & qualifications! Register at www.VaultReports.com

VAULT REPORTS™

www.vaultreports.com

27

who'd like to work here. Few of them get to." No wonder one insider from a major telecom remarks that MBA grads at her company "are contacted by headhunters all the time."

Our sources in the industry agree that promotion timetables in the high-tech world are often less structured than at other big MBA-employers. MBAs at one major employer say promotions come when higher-ups think associates can handle the pressure. If that's a year and a half into the program, so be it. At the same time, "there have been a few cases where the three years have been up and they say 'We think you're not ready to be a director,' and the person has left," reports one associate. Conversely, one industry bigwig reputedly has a process where "employees are ranked up against each other by their managers. This means your immediate supervisor can basically ruin your life," acknowledges one insider.

If you're really serious about working in high-tech, you should definitely apply for a summer internship in the industry. "It's the perfect way to get your foot in the door," advises one contact. And if you don't get one at Microsoft, don't balk at opportunities to work for smaller companies. You'll still gain valuable experience, and prove that you're dedicated to the industry.

MAJOR HIGH-TECH EMPLOYERS INCLUDE:

- Microsoft

- Dell Computer

- Intel

- Cisco Systems

- Hewlett-Packard

For more information on careers in the high tech industry, including brainteasers and other interview questions, read the Vault Reports Guide to High Tech.

Scott McNealy, CEO: Sun Microsystems

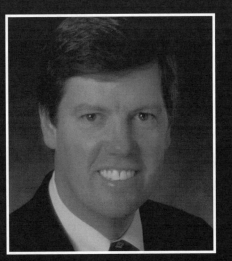

Here come's the Sun (CEO)

The son of a former vice chairman of American Motors Corp., McNealy's first exposure to the corporate world came on the golf courses where his father played against Detroit executives like Chrysler Chairman Lee Iacocca. After graduating from Harvard with a degree in economics, he took a job as foreman of Rockwell International Corp.'s truck hood plant in Ohio. He had been rejected for MBA programs at Harvard and Stanford, and would collect several more rejections before finally enrolling at Stanford, where he met the men with whom he would eventually co-found Sun Microsystems.

After graduating from business school, McNealy did a brief stint as director of operations at the now-defunct computer-maker Onyx. In 1982, he collaborated with three friends to build and market hardware and software for workstations – powerful computers that make PCs look like manual typewriters. McNealy began as VP of Manufacturing, and was named CEO in 1984 when one of his co-founders retired. The company, called Sun Microsystems, went public in 1986, and reached $1 billion in revenues two years later. The company has only seen one losing quarter (the summer of 1989), as a result of inventory problems and unchecked growth. But McNealy nipped those babies in the bud right away. This positive performance has not gone unnoticed – in 1995, *Industry Week* named the company one of the world's 100 best managed companies, and *Business Week* named McNealy one of the nation's top 25 managers.

An early example of the growing trend of high-tech companies tapping MBAs to lead them, McNealy is known around company HQ as fun loving, but with a "severe" work ethic. He considers his position to be "a 24-hour-a-day job," though he does make time for his family and is often the willing recipient of Suns' much-publicized April Fool's pranks. One year, he was "kidnapped" and taken to play hockey (his favorite hobby) with the San Jose Sharks. Not surprisingly, the hard-charging businessman is also known for his extremely competitive nature – he's been fighting an extended (and rather vicious) battle of egos and industry vision with Bill Gates for years. Largely through his criticism of Gates, McNealy has become a media darling with headline-grabbing witticisms. Positing himself as the champion of the consumer's freedom to choose, McNealy has made it his aim to break the Wintel duopoly in the name of free markets and better products.

Investment Management

Asset managers fall into three basic categories: hedge funds and proprietary trading desks, mutual funds and asset managers, and 'other' – which includes, insurance companies, municipal governments, etc. If you've read *Liar's Poker*, a seminal book about high-stakes finance, asset managers are the "customers," or "buy side." On the "sell side" are the traders and salespeople – the Citibanks, Deutsche Banks and Nomuras of the world. (Investment bankers are a whole other ball of wax – they create stocks and bonds through underwriting, or change companies through M&A.) The title is pretty much self-explanatory: a client gives money to an asset manager, who then invests it to meet the client's objectives. The people on the sell side provide information to the buy side (research, ideas, meetings with officials), and try to get the asset managers to trade through them (the sell side makes a commission for every trade it facilitates). These days, many banks are looking to grow their asset management businesses because they are largely protected against the volatility of the market. Asset managers are generally paid a percentage of the entire amount they handle, whether they make or lose money for the client. Because their salaries are based on the amount of money they manage, asset managers make less money than investment bankers (unless they work for hedge funds). They don't necessarily make big bonuses, but on the upside, they know what they're getting paid whether they make or lose money for the client. Be advised, however, that asset managers typically have contract terms of three years or less – AMs can't keep clients if they underperform.

As the bull market fueled the popularity of mutual funds over the last few years, lots of freshly minted MBAs were able to score high paying investment analyst and portfolio management positions. This is a relatively new trend, as investment management is an industry that values experience (read: age – the older the better). Investment management is one of the few places where people refuse to reveal their real ages because they're a bit too young. According to Morningstar, a research company, only 30 of the approximately 1088 U.S. diversified equity funds are managed by people 35 or younger. Wealthy individuals and institutions are often wary about handing their money over to young people. For this reason, you're not going to find neophytes at the head of a big fund, they're treated more like understudies. Now that we're on the cusp of a downturn, there is much worry that these youngsters will be unable to handle the

MBA Job Seekers: Receive free e-mailed job postings matching your interests & qualifications! Register at www.VaultReports.com

VAULT REPORTS™

31

www.vaultreports.com

pressure. At the same time, young people are highly valued when it comes to investing in industries like high tech – which are dominated by young people. Mutual fund firms including Putnam, Fidelity and T. Rowe Price aggressively recruit fresh MBAs, and put a great deal into training and developing them for analyst and portfolio management positions. Other firms do hire a fair amount of recent B-school grads, but usually only from a few top schools.

UPPERS	DOWNERS
• Great hours	• Pay is lower than that for I-banking
• Free dinners and tickets to events from sell-side firms	• High stress at hedge funds
• More stable than the rest of the financial world	• Fusty co-workers

OUR SURVEY SAYS

Asset managers say they enjoy "great work hours" – an average of 60 hours a week – and in some cases, "the summer is a bit lighter." They gloat that, unlike traders and others on the sell side, "there is a fair amount of stability." "Work is generally confined to the week," so they can "have outside lives, thank God!" Throughout the industry, there is a "get your work done and leave" attitude. "Unfortunately," one source remarks, "the only people leaving at 5 work for old-line insurance companies." After work, "there is minimal out of office interaction," as "the investment management crowd tends to be older and live in the suburbs." "Quality of life and work duties are very, very good," beams one fixed-income research analyst. "You have to get comfortable with paying your dues for a lot longer than in other financial service industries," notes another. "It's not as exciting a lifestyle," but "it can be home for those who don't want the 'excitement' of lousy hours and working on the weekends." For some, there is even travel involved: "If you're lucky enough to work with international stocks or bonds," says one portfolio manager in emerging markets, "you may be sent on reconnaissance missions – though not really at the junior level." Those who deal with domestic markets (including junior people) do get to travel to road shows, conferences, company tours and off-site meetings.

Many point out that salaries are is "significantly lower than on the sell side," "especially at lower levels." One contact emphasizes the fact as "a significant disincentive for many cash-strapped MBAs. It is humbling to have graduated from a school where the median first-year compensation is $125k, when my first-year total compensation was $95,000." Both of those figures include signing bonuses, and that source goes on to add that "now that I am no longer getting a signing bonus, my salary has dropped significantly and will be in the five-digit range for at least a few years." Considering the oppressive tax rate in a place like New York, student loan payments, and sky-high rents, post-MBA life may not be all it promised to be if you choose to go into investment management. "People who do buy side research should really love their work," another source explains, "because the money doesn't come for a while." If you just want to pay off your loans, "the rise in pay is much quicker on the sell side." According to Buck Consultants, the average senior stock fund manager was paid about $158,900 in 1998, down from $176,100 in 1997.

Though the buy side is not as turbulent as the sell side, our contacts report that asset managers are under "a good deal of pressure to perform well." However, it is rare to find the cutthroat competition in asset management that is bred in other areas – a contact tells Vault Reports that "the motivation is to do good research." As one source explains: "At the junior level, assignments that are done well are stepping stones to more responsibility and an eventual promotion. Later on, at the portfolio manager position, everyone wants to get credit for their good performance, avoid blame for mistakes, and at the end of the year have their ego rewarded with a big bonus (twice your base or more)." However, "you are a lot lower profile unless you work at a place that has a 'star' system like Fidelity." One source notes that "most other places don't like their employees to be too chatty with the press." "At Fidelity or T. Rowe Price these guys have high profiles, they're in magazines" reports one industry insider, who says that the big names in the business thrive on the media attention and "switch firms like major league ballplayers." The pressure to perform is compounded by the fact that asset management is a business often fraught with frustration. "you have to get used to being wrong

MBA Job Seekers: Receive free e-mailed job postings matching your interests & qualifications! Register at www.VaultReports.com

www.vaultreports.com

VAULT REPORTS™

33

a lot of the time." Sometimes the market will move against your predictions, for reasons you could never have anticipated. This is not a career for the sensitive – you can lose lots of money – usually much faster than you can make it. Says one portfolio manager: "I heard one guy at a hedge fund lost a billion and had a nervous breakdown."

As they are on the "buy side", asset managers often receive perks from the traders and salespeople who want their business. According to our sources, sometimes "the traders just get the salespeople to fuck over the customers as much as possible, making tons of money or getting rid of positions they don't want. But because there are so many sell side firms to choose from, they try not to screw a customer too much." Usually, they try to butter up investment managers by providing them with "all their resources, which besides research also includes steak dinners and Knicks tickets." One contact also alluded to talk around the office regarding "the occasional night out with a client to Atlantic City or Flashdancers," courtesy of some generous salesperson. An insider from the IM side of a major investment bank says "I have been to Yankees games, Knick games, the U.S. Open, a rock concert, and eaten at over a dozen of the city's finest expensive restaurants. It's good to be the client." At the same time, a source from a major firm remarks that "it's important to be somewhat conservative. No firm wants to have it known that their guys have a lavish lifestyle and are out partying all night long; it might make it hard to convince the Carpenter's Union that you will do the best job possible managing their money."

MAJOR INVESTMENT MANAGEMENT EMPLOYERS INCLUDE:

- ◆ Fidelity Investments

- ◆ T. Rowe Price

- ◆ Vanguard Group

- ◆ Zurich Kemper Scudder

VAULT
REPORTS™
www.vaultreports.com

Media & Entertainment

The word of the day for aspirants to the media and entertainment industry is "proactive." Unlike most other MBA employers, media companies don't really recruit. They don't have to – everyone wants to be a part of the glamour. Some major companies (Disney, Paramount) do recruit for finance positions, and others (Fox, Warner Brothers) advertise job openings on their web sites and in industry magazines like *Billboard* and *Variety*. But in the end, media is a who-you-know business – you have to network. Do your research, contact alums from your undergraduate and business schools, identify companies and departments you'd like to work for, and start making contacts. Don't be afraid to be aggressive, no one's going to do you a favor or give you a lead because you didn't call. In addition, just about every top school has a media & entertainment club. In addition to the networking opportunities, clubs like these usually bring in speakers and offer important information for the job search.

The most common jobs for MBAs in media and entertainment are on the corporate side, in fields like finance, marketing, strategic planning, and business development. (One reminder: you're going to make less on the corporate side of the entertainment biz than you would doing the same job in another industry, so be sure you're doing it for love.) Some corporate jobs are slightly more glamorous – positions in talent agencies (film), or artists & repertoire departments (music). When it comes to getting creative positions, MBAs are not much better off than anybody else – you have to start at the bottom no matter how educated you are. Many get jobs as assistants to higher-ups, others start off on the corporate side and somehow make the switch.

UPPERS

- Do what you love

- Relatively short hours

- See all movies for free

DOWNERS

- Internecine strife between "suits" and "creatives"

- Often must cater to high-strung talent

- May have to start at the bottom

MBA Job Seekers: Receive free e-mailed job postings matching your interests & qualifications! Register at www.VaultReports.com

VAULT REPORTS™

www.vaultreports.com

35

OUR SURVEY SAYS

Some insiders note that media companies, perhaps more so than other major industries that MBAs enter, are keen on finding candidates who really want to work for them. "They used to recruit on campus. Now they kind of wait for people to come to them," says one insider at a major conglomerate. Companies that do recruit "only go to a few top schools." Another source adds: "They don't go on to campus to hire MBAs because they don't think it's efficient. For example, one division really likes MBAs, and hires them a lot. Although they don't go onto campuses, but they really appreciate the business school education." That contact explains his hiring process: "I just met with as many people as possible. They were very open to talking to me – it was a very collegial, informal hiring process." Sometimes getting a position comes down to having the right combination of skills, or being in the right place at the right time. "If you have a media background, you're in good shape. If you don't it's still doable," says an insider from a major media power. "You just have to sell them on your passion." "Some companies look for people with a consulting background," explains a contact in the finance division of an entertainment corporation, "and sometimes they are looking specifically for someone with an MBA in finance."

Being an MBA in media and entertainment is quite removed from the surrounded-by-suits feeling of I-banks or consulting firms. "You have to be able to work with the creative types," explains one MBA with experience at a couple of media companies. "You're not going go be successful if they don't think you are going to be able to talk to a director or a musician or an author." An MBA is sometimes like a scarlet letter in the entertainment biz. Creatives tend to peg MBAs as 'suits' and give them little respect. Another source tells Vault Reports that "there is this constant creative-vs-corporate animosity, which can be very trying." An MBA at a top magazine publisher notes that "there's creative types at the top," and "there's always a danger that you'll be viewed as a suit." "If you have an education that has anything with numbers," gripes one contact, "they consider you 'support staff.'" That source adds that "you can make it as a creative without a higher degree, and often people on the business side encounter people who just do not respect your education. Some act like 'suits' could never understand the business." Another downer – the politics are relatively unfettered in media. "Someone who likes you can help you 'cross over' to the creative side," explains a source, "but if you make enemies, they can just as easily prevent that."

Our contacts say corporate people in the entertainment industry "live a very un-Hollywood lifestyle." "The pay is about 60 percent of what you would make as a consultant or I-banker," and "the hours are pretty regular." Says one contact in finance at a major media conglomerate, "I have the weekends off to do my own thing." "I guess the biggest advantage to me is that the hours are so civilized," notes a B-school student, "I worked from 9:30 to 5, and some of my friends who were in I-banking barely slept, and this was a summer internship."

MAJOR MEDIA AND ENTERTAINMENT EMPLOYERS INCLUDE:

- ◆ Walt Disney
- ◆ Time Warner
- ◆ Sony
- ◆ Viacom

For more information on careers in the media and entertainment, including actual interview questions, read the Vault Reports Guide to Media and Entertainment.

MBA Job Seekers: Receive free e-mailed job postings matching
your interests & qualifications! Register at www.VaultReports.com

VAULT
REPORTS™   37
www.vaultreports.com

Venture Capital

While an investment bank likes to play with "other people's money," the venture capital firm is dedicated to investing its own capital in companies in return for a hefty share of stock – and future profits. The "father of venture capital," Georges Doriot, co-founded the first modern VC firm – American Research and Development – in 1946; but VC did not become really popular until the 1970s. Historically, the people who have gotten into the business have been seasoned executives looking for a career change, or MBAs with several years of experience and a deep knowledge of a specific industry.

But in the past five years, MBA grads have had the chance to kick off their post-degree career in venture capital. Established venture capital funds have been looking for younger talent to fill their ranks and learn the business from the inside. Their goal is to groom choice B-school grads and form a new generation of leadership that is still young enough to schmooze the clients effectively. Younger employees are also reputedly more energetic, and more likely to actively seek out deals and do extra legwork to follow them through. And young people are drawn to the industry because of the diversity of the work – venture capitalists evaluate companies and business plans, create strategies, make deals, and recruit the executives to head their businesses. They also sit on boards and advise the companies they fund. They live and die by their Rolodexes – and really learn how to work a network. Venture capital is admittedly sexier than brand management or consulting. Who wants to market lunchbox snacks or advise steel workers in Boise when they could be building the next Netscape, Microsoft or Yahoo?

Venture capital depends a great deal on networking, charisma and luck – and the same holds true for getting hired in the industry. The most important step in getting hired is to "network, network, network," say industry insiders, who also urge aspirants to do their research in order to discern which types of candidates each firm prefers. This task is made more difficult by the fact that most firms keep an extremely low profile. Even Harvard professors advise their MBA students not to count on getting a job in VC right away. Most firms look for people with operating experience (a startup); or internship experience. Aspirants have more chance of getting hired if they secure an internship with a VC firm during the summer between semesters. Harvard, the source of the most comprehensive research on the industry, is a veritable VC recruiting farm. An estimated 70 percent of all venture capitalists possess Harvard MBAs.

According to the *Boston Business Journal*, a qualified Harvard MBA has a 50 to 1 chance of getting a job in VC straight out of school. In 1995, less than 20 HBS grads landed VC jobs; close to 40 were hired in 1996. In Boston, the number of jobs at VC firms has been increasing by about 8 percent each year, while the number of resumes they receive has been increasing by about 25 percent. Potential venture capitalists should also consider companies like Intel, which already have VC divisions; and large corporations that are launching small VC arms to support companies that fit their strategic direction.

Investors in computer and information technology are eager to lay out huge sums of money to fund start-up businesses – with hopes of attaining annual returns of 30 percent or more. In fact, heated competition among investors has resulted in serious inflation of the cost of investing in start-ups. But these high returns are proving harder to get, as some established firms have been taking a step back – especially in light of the recent fall in the market. Some sources say the industry is due for a shakeout, after three years of tremendous growth, but others think it can sustain itself for the time being. Insiders say the established firms – like Kleiner Perkins and Hummer Winblad – will weather any storm, but smaller firms have something to worry about. Is there a venture capital fund for venture capital firms?

UPPERS

- Play with money all day

- Lots of schmoozing

- Very lucrative

DOWNERS

- Long hours

- Few available jobs in the industry

- More firms chasing fewer high-growth companies

MBA Job Seekers: Receive free e-mailed job postings matching
your interests & qualifications! Register at www.VaultReports.com

VAULT REPORTS™

www.vaultreports.com

39

OUR SURVEY SAYS

It's a tired cliché but it's true – venture capital is to today's B-schoolers what Wall Street was to the MBAs of the Big 80s. "Everyone wants to do VC," groans one HBS student. "It's a freakin' nightmare." The sad fact of the matter is that there's not enough space on the bandwagon for all the wannabes. Basically the only way to get a job in the business is through contacts. An estimated 70 percent of all venture capitalists are HBS grads, "and almost all the rest are from Stanford," remarks one industry insider. "If you're not from one of those schools, you've got to have some concrete experience – preferably in a startup. Failing that, you better be very good at seeing market trends."

One contact tells Vault Reports that there are three important things to consider when investing in a company: the people involved, the technology or product being made, and the market. "You are investing in people," he explains, "so you need good character judgement; you're investing in a technology, so you have to understand it; and you have to understand the market trends." He says "you learn all the basics in business school, but nothing can replace actual operating experience."

As a venture capitalist, "you're constantly calling tons of people." "You have to network, build your Rolodex, and cold call companies." Personal skills are priority here – as one source put it, "you have to be a good communicator – pleasant but probing, and you've got to be really smart." Now that startups are all the rage, "you're not going to find a good investment at a trade show anymore," declares a contact from a young VC firm, "you have to get them much earlier than that."

Those concerned about wobbles in the industry should remember that "the good guys always make money," according to one insider. "Companies would rather take a bad deal with Kleiner Perkins than a good deal with one of the new little VC firms – they have no clue. The old guys are not going anywhere."

MAJOR VENTURE CAPITAL EMPLOYERS INCLUDE:

- American Research and Development

- Draper Fischer Associates

- Hummer Winblad

- Kleiner Perkins

- OneLiberty Ventures

MBA Functions

Some business school directories index people by their "functions," as if employees were so many interchangeable cogs. What can you do? In any case, one of the hottest buzzwords among MBAs and employers these days is "cross-functional" – or movement between functions like finance, marketing and operations. Not only do cross-functional employees have the chance to check out different functions that might interest them, but the broad experience benefits those with their eyes on top (general) management levels. Many top MBA employers, such as Ford and Sprint, offer rotational programs for MBAs that allow marketers to peer into the finance world, and vice versa. "One of our marketing people actually did a rotation in manufacturing on the operations side," says an insider in Ford's Marketing Leadership Program.

Here's a look at some of the different functions MBAs can serve:

FINANCE

Money makes the world go round. Consequently, financial specialists fast with the spreadsheets do a lot of the spinning. The most common industries for finance MBAs to join are, of course, investment banking and investment management, but finance officials are needed at all companies interested in making money (that is, all of them). With a virtual infinity of options to choose from, finance MBAs must take care to understand just what role their function plays in the companies they are considering. In some cases, such as Procter & Gamble, the finance department takes a back seat to the marketers of Ivory and Jif; in others, such as Ford Motor Company and American Airlines, finance assumes a leading role. Differences in functional hierarchies may occur between very similar companies. Says one finance official who left one packaged food company for another: "I looked ahead and saw that all the big decisions at my former employer were being made by marketing people."

The finance function, of course, isn't just limited to financial analysis. Other options: trading, risk management, bond structuring, and a host of other roles. And these functions are no longer confined to banks or securities firms. Witness GE Capital, the financial services arm of General Electric, which makes 40 percent of its parent GE's incomes. Or Enron, which, while exploring foreign lands for gas fields and building pipelines, spends much of its energy developing and hawking energy risk management products like derivatives.

MARKETING

You can cut costs and project revenues all you want, but if you don't sell your product, you won't make any money. That's where marketers come in. Marketing is most important where the difference between products is virtually negligible, and brand image and customer loyalty determine most sales. Why have sales of Sprite zoomed ahead of 7Up in recent years? Not because of a sudden shift in how much people like the taste of either lemon-limey beverage, but because of Sprite's hip "Image is Nothing" TV ad campaign. In more technology-led industries, like high tech or the automotive industry, marketers are less influential. Of course, this doesn't mean marketing has no place in such companies. High-tech firms are beginning to pour money into brand-building exercises – 3Com, for example, paid millions to get San Francisco's Candlestick Park named 3Com Park for several years. 3Com clearly believes that as high-tech products, like modems, become more mass market, having a recognizable name will translate into billions in sales.

Marketers don't base their decisions merely on "gut feelings" – they need numbers and research to back them up. Huge amounts of market research is used to gauge customer response to everything about a product, from its package design, to its price, to its fragrance or color. Most companies have market research departments or hire outside agencies to perform studies for them. Marketing MBAs direct the research in several ways. They decide what facets of a product to test market. They decide on the process by which research is carried out: focus groups or free samples with questionnaires or geographic test trials, etc. Finally, MBAs decide what all that research means. And that's why the color of your shampoo bottle changes now and again.

OPERATIONS

Those in the operations function are chiefly concerned with the day-to-day running of a business – ensuring that production deadlines are met and that distribution networks are running smoothly. As such, they are often much more visible to the bulk of company employees than are managers in other functions. Sometimes, operations managers take the meaning "hands on" to its logical extreme: hard-charging former Silicon Graphics COO Tom Jermoluk often jumped into frenzied manufacturing runs, taping boxes and soldering wires onto computer boards. MBAs starting out in the operations functions should expect to take a hands-on role to start: Many companies, such as Cargill, groom their MBA employees with year-long stints at manufacturing plants.

Operations management and strategy formulation are often viewed as two sides of the same coin: Chief Operating Officers often also carry the title of President and work closely with the Chairman and CEO. At many corporations, COOs are considered the heirs apparent to the CEO position.

INFORMATION SYSTEMS MANAGEMENT

As online business and interconnectivity increase for companies large and small, information systems management has been thrust into the spotlight. Many MBAs with technical prowess choose to work for consulting firms with practices in technology management, such as American Management Systems, Electronic Data Systems, and the "Big Five" professional services firms. High-tech companies such as Oracle and Unisys also have technology consulting arms to help their clients implement their products and operating systems. Other MBAs join corporations as managers of the company's own systems, hoping to rise to Chief Information Officer or Chief Technology Officer. Many IS managers receive engineering or computer science degrees in college, work in IS for a few years, and then get their MBAs. Companies will often pay for promising IS employees to get MBAs.

MBA Job Seekers: Receive free e-mailed job postings matching
your interests & qualifications! Register at www.VaultReports.com

VAULT REPORTS™

www.vaultreports.com

45

GENERAL MANAGEMENT/STRATEGY

A role in general management and strategy is a goal of many ambitious MBAs. Companies train their employees for general management in different ways. Many consumer products companies use brand management as proving grounds. Some companies, such as Sprint and Cargill, use rotating associate programs. Still others, like Coke and Ford, have no set path of promotion. MBAs in these firms must decide for themselves what experience is necessary to advance (hint: finding a mentor helps).

For those who would prefer to go straight into plotting strategy, there's management consulting. In fact, experienced management consultants are sometimes tapped by clients to run divisions – or even entire companies – because they are considered to have a strong background in strategy and a grasp of the "big picture." Other companies try to grow their own strategists. Many companies are now creating internal consulting departments, in part to diminish reliance on pricey consulting services. For example, American Express spent $290 million on outside consultants from 1990 to 1993. In 1996, the company created its Strategic Planning and Business Development Group, which focuses on strategy and new business development. The group currently handles less than 10 percent of Amex's consulting, but the company wants to push that figure up to 50 percent.

VAULT
REPORTS™
www.vaultreports.com

The Vault Reports

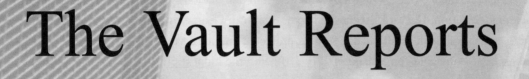

MBA Employer Rankings

THE RANKINGS METHODOLOGY

To determine America's top 50 MBA employers, we first compiled a list of top employers which we asked MBAs to rank. To compile this list, we consulted publications such as *Fortune,* which have compiled lists of the companies MBAs have indicated they would most like to work for. We also conducted our own surveys and interviews of MBAs. Our final list, when compiled, consisted of over 70 companies.

We then contacted over 1,000 MBA alumni from the nation's leading business schools (including Wharton, Harvard Business School, Stanford, Georgetown, Anderson/UCLA, and others) and asked them to fill out a password-protected online survey. The survey asked grads to rank these companies on a scale of 1-10 (10 being the highest prestige, and 1 the lowest). 256 MBAs responded completed surveys.

Vault Reports then tabulated all 256 completed surveys and averaged the score for each firm (excluding the top and bottom 10 rankings for each firm). The firms were then ranked in order, starting with the highest average prestige score as #1 (Goldman Sachs) on down to #50, to determine the Vault Reports MBA 50. (In this book, we have also included profiles of those companies on the survey that did not make our top 50.)

Most of our respondents were enthusiastic about our prestige survey, and volunteered their rankings and opinions with great aplomb. We understand that there are problems inherent in any prestige ranking. Different companies have strengths in different industries or market segments, there are geographic biases, and there is the risk that a few vindictive graduates might try to wreak sabotage on their competitors. However, we found that the rankings typically paralleled conventional wisdom – with a few exceptions. Please remember that these rankings are not based on the opinions of Vault Reports, but are based on our exclusive surveys of MBAs.

VAULT REPORTS™
www.vaultreports.com

VAULTMATCH™

A free service from Vault Reports!

Job Seekers: VaultMatch from Vault Reports is free, convenient way to help you in your job search. We will e-mail you job openings which match your criteria and qualifications. Here's how it works:

1. You, the job seeker, visit www.vaultreports.com and fill out a simple online questionnaire, indicating your qualifications and the types of positions you want.

2. Top companies contact Vault Reports with job openings.

3. Vault Reports sends you an e-mail about each position which matches your qualifications and interests.

4. For each position you are interested in, simply reply to the e-mail and attach your resume.

5. Vault Reports laser prints your resume on top-quality resume paper and sends it to the company's hiring manager within 5 days!

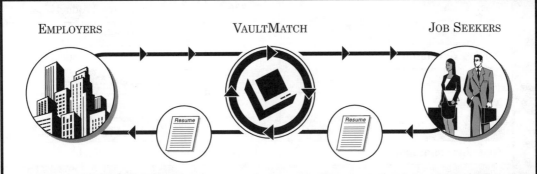

To find out more about using VaultMatch from Vault Reports, visit www.VaultReports.com

The 50 most prestigious MBA employers

RANK	FIRM	PRESTIGE SCORE	INDUSTRY
1	Goldman Sachs & Co.	9.039	Investment Banking
2	McKinsey & Co.	8.884	Management Consulting
3	Boston Consulting Group	8.449	Management Consulting
4	Bain & Co.	8.016	Management Consulting
5	Microsoft	7.975	High Tech
6	Morgan Stanley Dean Witter	7.808	Investment Banking
7	Dell Computer	7.513	High Tech
8	Intel	7.383	High Tech
9	JP Morgan	7.353	Investment Banking
10	Merrill Lynch	7.221	Investment Banking
11	Walt Disney	7.211	Media and Entertainment
12	Donaldson, Lufkin & Jenrette	7.167	Investment Banking
13	Cisco Systems	7.107	High Tech
14	GE Capital	7.025	Financial Services
15	Coca-Cola	6.876	Consumer Products
16	Hewlett-Packard	6.712	High Tech
17	Procter & Gamble	6.711	Consumer Products
18	Fidelity	6.684	Investment Management
19	Merck	6.658	Pharmaceuticals
20	Lucent Technologies	6.653	Investment Banking
21	Netscape Communications	6.496	High Tech
22	Enron	6.373	Energy
23	Monitor Company	6.348	Management Consulting
24	Booz · Allen & Hamilton	6.328	Management Consulting
25	Mercer Management Consulting	6.327	Management Consulting

RANK	FIRM	PRESTIGE SCORE	INDUSTRY
26	**Salomon Smith Barney**	6.302	Investment Banking
27	**Sun Microsystems**	6.301	High Tech
28	**Johnson & Johnson**	6.297	Consumer Products
29	**Nike**	6.287	Consumer Products
30	**Credit Suisse First Boston**	6.248	Investment Banking
31	**Motorola**	6.000	High Tech
32	**IBM**	5.949	High Tech
33	**BancBoston Robertson Stephens**	5.874	Investment Banking
34	**PepsiCo**	5.860	Consumer Products
35	**Time Warner**	5.823	Media and Entertainment
36	**3Com**	5.775	High Tech
37	**Lehman Brothers**	5.760	Investment Banking
38	**Oracle**	5.750	High Tech
39	**Silicon Graphics**	5.748	High Tech
40	**Citibank/Citigroup**	5.700	Commercial Banking
41	**American Express**	5.675	Financial Services
42	**Bankers Trust**	5.656	Investment Banking
43	**Colgate-Palmolive**	5.638	Consumer Products
44	**Levi Strauss**	5.628	Consumer Products
45	**NationsBanc Montgomery Securities**	5.496	Investment Banking
46	**Nestle**	5.491	Consumer Products
47	**Andersen Consulting**	5.469	Management Consulting
48	**Kraft Foods**	5.444	Consumer Products
49	**3M**	5.442	Consumer Products
50	**General Mills**	5.372	Consumer Products

Source: Vault Reports MBA Survey 1998

VAULT REPORTS™

MBA Prestige Rankings by Industry

Management Consulting

RANK	FIRM	PRESTIGE SCORE
1	McKinsey & Co.	8.884
2	Boston Consulting Group	8.449
3	Bain & Co.	8.016
4	Monitor Company	6.348
5	Mercer Management Consulting	6.328
6	Andersen Consulting	5.469
7	A.T. Kearney	5.148
8	Deloitte Consulting	5.090
9	KPMG Consulting	5.077
10	PricewaterhouseCoopers	4.888

Media and Entertainment

RANK	FIRM	PRESTIGE SCORE
1	Walt Disney	7.211
2	Time Warner	5.823

Source: Vault Reports MBA Survey 1998

VAULT REPORTS™
www.vaultreports.com

Investment Banking

RANK	FIRM	PRESTIGE SCORE
1	Goldman Sachs & Co.	9.039
2	Morgan Stanley Dean Witter	7.808
3	JP Morgan	7.535
4	Merrill Lynch	7.221
5	Donaldson, Lufkin & Jenrette	7.167
6	Salomon Smith Barney	6.302
7	Credit Suisse First Boston	6.248
8	BancBoston Robertson Stephens	5.874
9	Lehman Brothers	5.760
10	Bankers Trust	5.656

Commercial Banking

RANK	FIRM	PRESTIGE SCORE
1	Citibank/Citigroup	5.700
2	Chase Manhattan	5.261
3	BankAmerica	4.812

Source: Vault Reports MBA Survey 1998

MBA Job Seekers: Receive free e-mailed job postings matching
your interests & qualifications! Register at www.VaultReports.com

VAULT REPORTS™
www.vaultreports.com

53

High Tech

RANK	FIRM	PRESTIGE SCORE
1	Microsoft	7.975
2	Dell Computer	7.513
3	Intel	7.383
4	Cisco Systems	7.107
5	Hewlett-Packard	6.712
6	Lucent Technologies	6.653
7	Netscape Communications	6.496
8	Sun Microsystems	6.301
9	Motorola	6.000
10	IBM	5.949

Telecommunications

RANK	FIRM	PRESTIGE SCORE
1	Sprint	5.239
2	Nortel Networks	4.867
3	AT&T	4.715

Source: Vault Reports MBA Survey 1998

VAULT REPORTS™
www.vaultreports.com

Consumer Products

RANK	FIRM	PRESTIGE SCORE
1	Coca-Cola	6.876
2	Procter & Gamble	6.711
3	Johnson & Johnson	6.297
4	Nike	6.287
5	PepsiCo	5.860
6	Colgate-Palmolive	5.638
7	Levi Strauss	5.628
8	Nestle	5.491
9	Kraft Foods	5.444
10	3M	5.442

Energy

RANK	FIRM	PRESTIGE SCORE
1	Enron	6.373
2	Atlantic Richfield (ARCO)	3.764

Source: Vault Reports MBA Survey 1998

MBA Job Seekers: Receive free e-mailed job postings matching
your interests & qualifications! Register at www.VaultReports.com

VAULT REPORTS™

55

www.vaultreports.com

The Vault Reports

MBA 50

Goldman Sachs & Co.

Investment Banking

85 Broad Street
New York, NY 10004
(212) 902-1000
www.goldmansachs.com

Goldman Sachs

LOCATIONS

New York, NY (HQ)
Boston, MA • Chicago, IL • Dallas, TX • Houston, TX • Los Angeles, CA • Memphis, TN • Miami, FL • Philadelphia, PA • San Francisco, CA • Washington, D.C.

Bangkok, Thailand • Beijing, China • Cayman Islands • Frankfurt, Germany • Hong Kong • London, England • Madrid, Spain • Mexico City, Mexico • Milan, Italy • Montreal, Canada • Osaka, Japan • Paris, France • Sao Paulo, Brazil • Seoul, South Korea • Shanghai, China • Singapore • Sydney, Australia • Tokyo, Japan • Toronto, Canada • Vancouver, British Columbia • Zurich, Switzerland

DEPARTMENTS

Asset Management • Controllers • Credit • Equities • Fixed-Income • General Services • Investment Banking • Principal Investments • Global Investment Research • Global Operations and Technology • Information Technology • J. Aron Currency and Commodity • Management Controls • Personnel • Training and Development • Treasury

THE STATS

Annual Revenues: $17.2 billion (1997)
No. of Employees: 12,500 (worldwide)
No. of Offices: 39 (worldwide), 13 (U.S.)
A privately-owned company
Co-Chairmen and Co-CEOs:
Jon S. Corzine and Henry M. Paulson Jr.

KEY COMPETITORS

- J.P. Morgan
- Merrill Lynch
- Morgan Stanley Dean Witter
- Salomon Smith Barney

THE BUZZ
What MBAs are saying
about Goldman Sachs

- "Cream of the Street"
- "Cult-like"
- "Greed is good"
- "Prestigious, but stiff and arrogant"

Goldman Sachs & Co.

UPPERS

- High pay and prestige
- Dinner allowance
- Free car service after 8 p.m.

DOWNERS

- Marathon workdays
- Uneven treatment by superiors
- Little job training

EMPLOYMENT CONTACT

Goldman Sachs
Recruiting Department
85 Broad Street
22nd Floor
New York, NY 10004
(212) 902-1000

Pretax Profits (in millions)

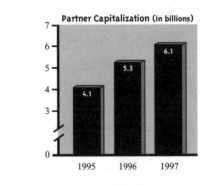

Partner Capitalization (in billions)

Employees

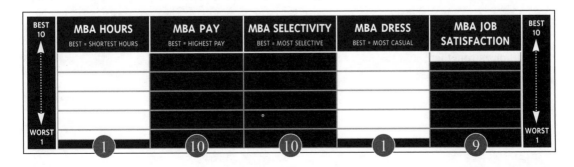

	MBA HOURS BEST = SHORTEST HOURS	MBA PAY BEST = HIGHEST PAY	MBA SELECTIVITY BEST = MOST SELECTIVE	MBA DRESS BEST = MOST CASUAL	MBA JOB SATISFACTION	
	1	10	10	1	9	

MBA Job Seekers: Receive free e-mailed job postings matching
your interests & qualifications! Register at www.VaultReports.com

VAULT REPORTS™
www.vaultreports.com

59

THE SCOOP

Founded in 1869 by Marcus Goldman, a European immigrant, Goldman Sachs is one of the nation's oldest and most prestigious investment banking firms. The firm provides a wide array of investment banking and research services to its corporate clients. Goldman is especially renowned for its stock research department and its ability to raise money in the public capital markets by helping companies issue stocks and bonds.

The company has made an impressive comeback since 1994, when it posted one of its worst results in its entire 127 years in business. After restructuring its management and refocusing on client service, Goldman is once again posting impressive profits. Most of Goldman's clients are the nation's largest and most established corporations, such as H&R Block, Kroger supermarkets, and Times Mirror. Recently, however, Goldman has made an effort to attract businesses from more entrepreneurial companies, including Internet companies such as Yahoo! and Wired Ventures, publisher of *Wired* magazine. Goldman is also politically well connected, and is one of the nation's largest campaign contributors; former Goldman co-chairman Robert Rubin serves as U.S. Treasury secretary. In 1998, the firm's partners voted to go public. The initial offering was expected to be the largest ever for a financial services company, and was expected to value the firm at about $30 billion.

Analysts believe the decision was driven by two major factors. The first was that without stock leverage, Goldman could not acquire other banking businesses, and would eventually not be able to keep pace with competitors like Merrill Lynch and Morgan Stanley Dean Witter which boast large retail brokerage capabilities (and thus can more easily sell the securities they underwrite to individual investors). The second was that Goldman's partners sensed that the market was at its peak, and wanted to cash in their chips. However, with world financial markets in turmoil in the late summer and fall of 1998, Goldman execs decided to shelve the IPO indefinitely, although they report that they intend to proceed with an offering when market conditions strengthen.

GETTING HIRED

Goldman's interviewing process is notorious for its grueling intensity. Candidates go through at least three rounds of interviews. The first and second rounds usually consist of two half-hour sessions, where the applicant interviews with two Goldman professionals, typically one associate and a Vice President. The third round is the most rigorous; it consists of five or six two-on-one interviews, each of which is 45 minutes long and involves one or more of the firm's partners. There is no clear delineation of personal and professional questions during the three rounds; candidates must be prepared to answer any question at any time. Candidates who have claimed on their resume or cover letter to have a strong financial background should be prepared to receive several detailed and probing questions on business and finance issues. All candidates are questioned on their willingness and ability to work hard as team players in an intense and demanding work environment. Interviewers say that they look for "people with smart personalities who aren't afraid to work hard. We especially don't want big egos around the place, so we try and find out how you will be able to work with someone you don't like too much personally." Recent interviewees remark that they were surprised by the number of "detailed questions" that interviewers asked them about their grades at college and graduate school, even where school policy prohibited such questions.

When hiring MBAs as associates, Goldman Sachs departments expect work experience that demonstrates an interest in the financial markets. Goldman is unusual among investment banks in that it also recruits at several law schools (Harvard, Yale, NYU, and University of Pennsylvania) for both associate and summer associate positions. Several Goldman recruiters acknowledge that getting an offer at Goldman is easier for law students than for MBAs because the applicant pool is far smaller.

MBA Job Seekers: Receive free e-mailed job postings matching your interests & qualifications! Register at www.VaultReports.com

VAULT REPORTS™

www.vaultreports.com

61

OUR SURVEY SAYS

Goldman Sachs' work place is legendary for its "intense, goal-driven" ethic, where "success is taken for granted." While the rest of the world may exalt Goldman employees as the "Masters of the Universe," employees themselves note that the firm "cuts their egos down to size." Goldman Sachs makes it clear from the beginning that "individual personalities are insignificant," and that "the firm comes first, second, and last." New hires take some time to get used to the careful scrutiny to which they are subjected, and they sometimes feel that they "are under constant surveillance." Analysts and associates praise their fellow employees for being "intelligent and perceptive" while also being "prepared to make the sacrifices that have to be made for the team to succeed." However, working as part of a team of Goldman Sachs employees "can also be challenging, because you have to hold up your end, and there's always pressure to measure up to your co-workers' high standards." Some employees also feel that Goldman's emphasis on teamwork comes at a cost – "individuality and creativity usually are considered much less important than being a good team player." Even the most successful Goldman employees confess that "occasionally the stress of work can get to be too much, and you come close to cracking."

Goldman Sachs employees work "extremely long hours," but that should come as no surprise to them. After all, one of the most commonly asked questions in a Goldman interview is, "How will you cope with working 90-hour weeks, or longer, for three years?" For the first few years, analysts usually work between 80 and 110 hours a week, and generally come in to the office "at least six days a week, though you're usually there every day of the week." Working until 10 at night is virtually an everyday affair, and "all-nighters are pretty frequent" as project deadlines draw near. Even those employees who say that they love working for Goldman concede that the hours "just get a bit too much at times." One trader notes exasperatedly that "sometimes I don't have enough time to take lunch – or even to go to the bathroom." New hires, however, should take heart from the fact that "the hours loosen up as you get promoted." Vice presidents rarely work all day on weekends; they usually "just drop in for a couple of hours on Saturday mornings, tell the analysts and associates what to do, and then leave."

Goldman's support staff wins high marks from employees for being "thoroughly efficient and professional." According to Vault Reports surveys, Goldman bankers enjoy better support services than anywhere else on the Street. Even analysts have secretaries to answer their calls, although they have to share secretaries – usually one secretary is assigned to four or five analysts or associates. Goldman's support staff infrastructure ensures that back-up secretaries are always available to fill in any gaps caused by illness or absence among the regular support staff. The highly-paid support staff (like other Goldman employees, support staff receive year-end bonuses) not only perform standard administrative and clerical duties such as faxing and filing, but also help associates and analysts with making graphs, setting up databases, and creating charts and tables. Every floor at Goldman's New York headquarters has a word processing room staffed with "friendly, knowledgeable" people. Goldman's Data Resources and Library staff are also "superb" but tend to "grumble about last-minute requests." Overall, Goldman employees remark that their top-notch support staff plays an "integral" role in ensuring the smooth execution of pitch books and presentations.

To order a 50- to 70-page Vault Reports Employer Profile on Goldman Sachs & Co. call 1-888-JOB-VAULT or visit www.VaultReports.com

The full Employer Profile includes detailed information on Goldman's departments, recent developments and transactions, hiring and interview process, plus what employees really think about culture, pay, work hours and more.

MBA Job Seekers: Receive free e-mailed job postings matching your interests & qualifications! Register at www.VaultReports.com

VAULT REPORTS™

www.vaultreports.com

63

McKinsey & Company

Management Consulting

55 East 52nd Street
New York, NY 10022
(800) 221-1026
Fax: (212) 446-7200
www.mckinsey.com

McKinsey & Company

LOCATIONS

New York, NY (HQ)

Atlanta, GA • Boston, MA • Chicago, IL •
Cleveland, OH • Dallas, TX • Los Angeles,
CA • Minneapolis, MN • Pittsburgh, PA • San
Francisco, CA • Washington, D.C.

Barcelona • Berlin • Buenos Aires • Dublin •
Hong Kong • Mexico City • Paris • Tokyo •
Toronto • Vienna • Other offices worldwide

DEPARTMENTS

Consulting
Information Technology

THE STATS

Annual Revenues: $2.2 billion (1997)
No. of Consultants: 4,500 (worldwide)
No. of Partners: 600
No. of Offices: 75 (worldwide)
A privately-held company
Managing Director: Rajat Gupta

KEY COMPETITORS

◆ Andersen Consulting
◆ A.T. Kearney
◆ Bain
◆ Booz•Allen & Hamilton
◆ Boston Consulting Group
◆ Mercer Management Consulting
◆ Monitor Company

 THE BUZZ
What MBAs are saying
about McKinsey & Co.

◆ "Need to fit the mold to enjoy it"
◆ "The dream"
◆ "Pompous, powerful, prestigious"
◆ "Big picture work"

UPPERS

- High pay
- Extensive job training
- Worldwide prestige

DOWNERS

- Frequent travel
- Somewhat square and snobbish consultants
- "Up-or-out" stress

EMPLOYMENT CONTACT

Karen Kidder
McKinsey & Co.
55 East 52nd Street
New York, NY 10022
(800) 221-1026
Fax: (212) 446-7200

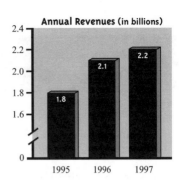

Annual Revenues (in billions)

- 1995: 1.8
- 1996: 2.1
- 1997: 2.2

Employees

- 1995: 3,650
- 1996: 3,944
- 1997: 4,500

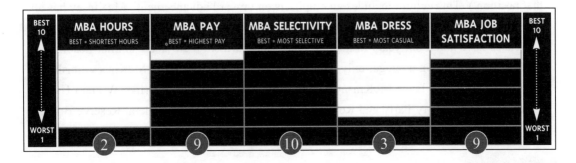

	MBA HOURS	MBA PAY	MBA SELECTIVITY	MBA DRESS	MBA JOB SATISFACTION	
BEST 10 ... WORST 1	BEST = SHORTEST HOURS	BEST = HIGHEST PAY	BEST = MOST SELECTIVE	BEST = MOST CASUAL		BEST 10 ... WORST 1
	2	9	10	3	9	

MBA Job Seekers: Receive free e-mailed job postings matching
your interests & qualifications! Register at www.VaultReports.com

VAULT REPORTS™

www.vaultreports.com

65

THE SCOOP

In an industry with a handful of leaders, McKinsey & Company has come to be regarded as the most influential consulting firm in the world. Founded by James O. McKinsey in 1926, McKinsey earns more money per consultant than any other consulting firm. Now with 75 offices in 38 countries and more than 4000 professional employees, McKinsey shows no signs of slowing its dramatic growth. Among its employees and clients, McKinsey is known simply as "The Firm" (predating John Grisham). McKinsey dominates its industry. When rival consulting firms want to give themselves a boost, they say they're second only to McKinsey. McKinsey consultants profit from this aura of prestige – per head, consultants are said to bring in $450,000 annually. Clients are the bluest of the blue chips and include AT&T, Pepsi, IBM, GE and General Motors. A consultant at competitor Bain sums up: "The hardest part about competing with McKinsey is that they have these deep relationships with senior management that lead companies to return to McKinsey unquestioned." Besides serving huge global companies, wealthy commercial banks, and vast technology firms, McKinsey also prides itself on offering pro bono assistance to educational, social, environmental, and cultural organizations. The firm is also increasingly serving emerging market companies and family-owned ventures. The bulk of the firm's work is in the private sector, but McKinsey also advises public sector organizations.

McKinsey consultants become part of a global network and a truly international firm. Despite its far-flung empire, McKinsey adopts a "one firm" approach and makes an effort to maintain a consistent "McKinsey culture" in each of its offices worldwide. (At present, a non-American majority controls the governing committee, 60 percent of revenues come from overseas, and the firm's managing director, Calcutta native Rajat Gupta, is the non-Western person to hold that position.) This culture includes an emphasis on upward advancement. McKinsey has an "up-or-out" policy, and consultants must either earn promotion or leave the company. New associates have about six years to make partner, and partners then face a similar deadline to become a director. On average, only one in 11 consultants who start at McKinsey finish this journey. Those who leave McKinsey may find themselves in politics (like William Hague, leader of Britain's Tory Party and Roger Ferguson, Governor of the Federal Reserve Board), best-selling authors (the authors of the enormously successful business guide *In Search of Excellence* were former McKinsey employees), or may even start up rival consultancies (as Tom Steiner did with Mitchell Madison). And of course, many McKinsey consultants wind up with top spots with corporations: the CEOs of IBM, Federal Express and Levi Strauss are all alums of The Firm.

GETTING HIRED

McKinsey hires only 1 percent of the approximately 75,000 candidates who apply to the firm each year. Successful candidates usually have excellent academic records and degrees from top universities. Although McKinsey was recently slapped with a gender discrimination lawsuit by a former employee, the firm is well known for actively recruiting talented women, minorities, gay men and lesbians.

Although MBAs are hired into McKinsey as associates, 40 percent of the firm's associates don't have business degrees – the firm also recruits law students, PhDs and MDs for associate positions. The firm's interview process typically two rounds on campus, and then a third, final round in the office at which the candidate wants to work. McKinsey will fly final-round candidates cross-country (or cross-ocean), if need be. The final round is normally half a day of inteviews, plus a meal (either lunch or dinner). Most final-round interviews are case interviews. It is McKinsey's intention that all candidates visit the office where they want to work before they get an offer. While clearly some offices are larger than others, McKinsey is flexible about placement, believing there is always room for talent.

At business schools, each recruiting team decides which case(s) they want to use in the interviews. The morning of the interview session, school team members normally present their cases to the team leader (a partner) who approves their cases or suggests new ones. These cases are usually based on the interviewer's own recent projects or assignments. The interviewers are told to use the same case all day, so they can gauge how well the candidates perform. "The downside, of course," admits one interviewer, "is that word gets out about the

MBA Job Seekers: Receive free e-mailed job postings matching your interests & qualifications! Register at www.VaultReports.com

VAULT REPORTS™

www.vaultreports.com

67

case." McKinsey "doesn't like brainteasers," but will give guesstimates if there is reason to believe that the candidate has a quantitative deficiency. McKinseys interviewers have high expectations of MBAs in the case interview, anticipating that they will answer in a highly strucutred way using MBA-level frameworks.

On many campuses, McKinsey evaulates candidates through a "town hall" process, during which salient information about the candidate is flashed up on a screen, including the candidate's resume, what McKinsey events he or she attended, and other intelligence on the person, including opinions from former business analysts who attend classes with the individual. Normally a consensus quickly develops ("90 percent of the time"), otherwise, the firm will try to break the tie through one more interview or more extensive questioning of McKinsey alums who know the candidate.

OUR SURVEY SAYS

McKinsey's high turnover rate is not due to employee dissatisfaction. Though McKinsey consultants are "universally elated" with their "challenging," "rewarding" assignments, they leave because they are actively recruited by corporate America to serve as executives; many McKinsey consultants are hired away by their clients. McKinsey employees appreciate the "thorough" training they receive as well as the camaraderie of their colleagues, who are "bright, interesting, and fun to be around." However, one consultant opines that "a lot of the people here are pretty square." Some consider the culture to be "on the snobbish side," perhaps because consultants are the most highly paid in the industry: McKinsey consultants with a few years' experience receive more than $200,000 a year. Still, says one consultant: "Most people are down to earth. Some are very elitist, but those people usually find that in the long run they don't survive. When you visit a client you can't come off as uppity." Unlike most companies, moving up the corporate ladder at McKinsey means loosening, or even losing the ties, insiders say, although beginning consultants stay buttoned up.

McKinsey is "vigilant about pushing out those who don't meet its exacting standards." An integral part of this process is the firm's performance review procedure, insiders tell us. "About 50 percent of your promotional chances depend on your feedback," which involves "page upon page of blunt criticism." If you want to work at McKinsey, you should expect to work long hours. "Hours never go below 60 and at the high end can be 90 to 100 hours a week." While the firm is "proactive" about recruiting minorities and women, the numbers are "hard to find" at the higher levels. All in all, say consultants, they have "a lot of respect" for McKinsey. The firm "offers great promotional prospects," and "when you're ready to move on to another firm or industry, McKinsey gives you a tremendous variety of career prospects."

"There is definitely a move toward greater industry specialization going on at McKinsey," discloses one insider. "The number of generalists is still high, but we are hiring more and more industry experts. In my department, we've recently taken in a healthcare expert and a market research expert." How does McKinsey decide who qualifies as an "expert" in a particular field? "Our experts are usually PhDs," confirms another insider, "or those with a great deal of experience in a desired industry – especially on the strategic side." What factors account for this change? "I think there are two reasons," replies one thoughtful insider. "First, industry-specific firms like Greenwich Associates are giving us a lot of competition. And second, the other large strategy consulting firms like Bain and Andersen are gaining industry-specific expertise that they didn't have five or ten years ago. To compete, we've needed to become sharper, more focused."

To order a 50- to 70-page Vault Reports Employer Profile on McKinsey & Company call 1-888-JOB-VAULT or visit www.VaultReports.com

The full Employer Profile includes detailed information on McKinsey's departments, recent developments and transactions, hiring and interview process, plus what employees really think about culture, pay, work hours and more.

MBA Job Seekers: Receive free e-mailed job postings matching your interests & qualifications! Register at www.VaultReports.com

VAULT REPORTS™
www.vaultreports.com

69

BOOM! WHEN YOUR JOB OFFER IS RIGGED TO EXPLODE

Not all job offers are created equal. Some are "exploding" – that is, set to expire after a certain length of time, ranging anywhere from 24 hours to three months. Other companies will reduce a signing bonus for candidates who fail to sign up within a certain time period... that's expensive indecision!

For instance, one management consultant tells Vault Reports that his firm made him the following proposition – sign within two weeks of receiving the job offer, and receive a $7000 signing bonus. For every day past the deadline, that bonus would go down by $1000. One week after the job offer, the signing bonus would disappear entirely. Three weeks after the job offer, the offer of employment itself would expire. (The ploy worked – the consultant accepted his offer before the first 24-hour deadline was up.)

Are exploding offers for real? If a company really wants you, are they willing to lose you just because you want an extra week to decide? The answer, according to our research: it depends. One insider reports: "I let my investment banking offer explode after three days. When I later decided I wanted the offer after all, I was told to check back with the firm in March, after it had completed its hiring." Another MBA insider says he "knows several people who received exploding offers, but successfully negotiated with the firm for more time to decide." In this sense, an exploding offer may be just an elaborate game of chicken. Other companies resort to more drastic measures to entice candidates to accept their exploding offers. A management consultant tells Vault Reports the tale of how he dithered when given an exploding offer by a leading consulting firm. One of the senior partners called him in, and pulled out his wallet, extracting five one-thousand-dollar bills. "You can have your signing bonus in cash, right now, if you join," the candidate was told. He demurred and took a job at another firm.

Because of the nature of summer internship recruiting, summer positions often have very short-term exploding offers. For example, at Wharton and Harvard, where first-year MBA students interview for summer positions at most top firms in a single weekend, some firms cram in their final rounds before competing firms can have theirs, and then give offers designed to explode before their competitors' final round takes place. One MBA reports getting a call fromone top Wall Street firm on a Saturday and being told to "come out to dinner and accept our offer tonight." The MBA was to undergo Goldman's final round on Monday. "If I didn't go," he says, "the recruiter made it clear that I had until midnight Sunday to accept the offer, otherwise it would be rescinded." Avoiding the phone call won't work – "they'll just leave the message on your answering machine." Because summer interviews transpire in such a short period, "it's really not possible to call up other firms and try to wedge in your interviews before an offer explodes," though one MBA says: "I turned down an exploding offer in order to go to another firm's final round, which was the following day. I made sure I mentioned that fact in the interview, and I'm sure it helped me get the offer."

Why do firms give exploding offers? Company reps Vault Reports talked to say it's because they like to plan their hiring needs quickly and need to determine how many more people to recruit, although one recruitment veteran terms this explanation "a load of crap." "These firms can usually make offers to as many good people as they find," says one recruiter at a firm which does not give exploding offers. "The firm is just trying to pressure people into taking its offers without exploring all their other options." Are candidates cowed by the pressure? "Some are, if they're just nervous by nature, or if they think they might not get another chance, while others who are more confident basically don't give a damn and just decide on their own time."

So should you accept an exploding offer? Most of the people surveyed who accepted such offers said that they had been inclined to take the offer anyway. An exploding offer does "clarify the mind," admits one consultant, who used the exploding offer to pressure other firms of interest to hurry up their decision. Nothing concentrates the mind like a deadline.

A final word of advice – if you're starting your job search, ask around. Try to find out which firms hand out exploding offers. Knowing that a firm is prone to give exploding offers, you might want to start the application process at that firm a bit later. "Basically," says one insider, "I might have ended up at my firm anyway, but the exploding offer forced me to cut the job interviewing process short by nearly a month."

MBA Job Seekers: Receive free e-mailed job postings matching your interests & qualifications! Register at www.VaultReports.com

VAULT REPORTS™
www.vaultreports.com

71

The Boston Consulting Group

Exchange Place, 31st Floor
Boston, MA 02109
(617) 973-1200
Fax: (617) 973-1339
www.bcg.com

Management Consulting

THE BOSTON CONSULTING GROUP

LOCATIONS

Atlanta, GA
Boston, MA
Chicago, IL
Dallas, TX
Los Angeles, CA
New York, NY
San Francisco, CA
Washington, DC
38 other offices around the world

DEPARTMENTS

Strategic Consulting

THE STATS

Annual Revenues: $660 million (1997 est.)
No. of Employees: 1,720
No. of Offices: 46 (worldwide)
A privately-held company
CEO: Carl Stern

KEY COMPETITORS

- Andersen Consulting
- Bain & Co.
- McKinsey & Co.
- Mercer Management Consulting
- Monitor Company

THE BUZZ

What MBAs are saying
about BCG

- "Cerebral, white-collar, intellectual"
- "Smart but know it"
- "Tops in theory"
- "Great work/life balance"

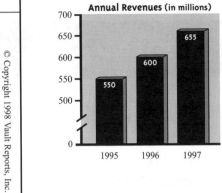

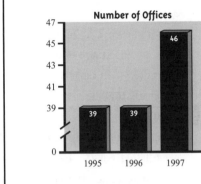

UPPERS

- Opportunity to be creative in devising client solutions
- Flat organizational structure
- Emphasis on work/life balance
- Better hours than other top consulting firms

DOWNERS

- Can be initially scary because of lack of reliance frameworks
- Extensive travel
- Overimpressed with flashy work

EMPLOYMENT CONTACT

Roxane Cullinan
The Boston Consulting Group
200 South Wacker Drive
27th Floor
Chicago, IL 60606
(312) 993-3300
Fax: (312) 876-0771

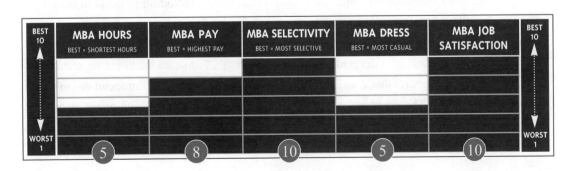

MBA Job Seekers: Receive free e-mailed job postings matching
your interests & qualifications! Register at www.VaultReports.com

VAULT
REPORTS™

www.vaultreports.com

73

THE SCOOP

While BCG has lagged ever so slightly behind industry leader McKinsey in terms of prestige, BCG has nevertheless over the years been responsible for a number of major management consulting innovations, such as "time-based competition" and "capability-driven competitive strategies." One of BCG's best-known innovations is the renowned "BCG Matrix" which explains the relationship between a company's profitability and its market share. (However, that framework is "not really used any more," according to one consultant. "It's based in a time when there were large industrial conglomerates, and there aren't many of those anymore.") In fact, BCG, and its late founder Bruce Henderson are credited with "being the father of strategic consulting, in every sense of the word," according to a BCG alum, Thomas Doorley. Doorley told the *Boston Herald:* "Historically, the policy decisions were made by a bunch of folk sitting around a table thinking big thoughts. It was [Henderson's] view that it wasn't that easy." Henderson also "had faith in the abilities of young men and women to contribute to solving complex problems," and to marry quantitative data to seat-of-the-pants strategizing. Today, close to 2000 consultants in 46 offices around the globe work at the company Henderson founded.

BCG organizes its work into industry practices. While BCG serves clients from a wide variety of industries, the firm focuses on clients in the energy, telecommunications, automobiles, financial services, pharmaceuticals, and consumer goods sectors. Consultants can work at the firm for six years (including time as an associate) before electing a specialty.

In recent years, BCG has expanded its presence in the international market and has a number of major overseas clients, including the Russian government. BCG has been active in Eastern Europe since 1985, advising on acquisitions and restructuring, including projects in banking. The firm has played a major role in preparing companies for deregulation and privatization in the new post-Cold War Europe, by predicting the cost structures and service levels that would be necessary for success in a deregulated environment. BCG has an excellent reputation in Europe; one survey reports that it is one of the top five firms for which European consultants would like to work. The company gets half of its revenues from consulting engagements in Europe, and a third from the Americas (the rest comes from its Asian offices).

VAULT REPORTS™
www.vaultreports.com

GETTING HIRED

BCG's interview format for MBAs consists of two rounds of interviews. The first round is comprised of two interviews, each of which is 45 minutes long; this round consists entirely of case interviews. In the second round, interviewees go through two more case interviews, this time with managers at BCG. In addition, at this second round, each candidate is subject to three one-on-one interviews with vice presidents at the firm, during which the candidate is tested primarily for interpersonal qualities and fit for the firm.

Each round consists of about ten minutes of conversation (meant to suss out personal qualities desirable to consultants), half an hour of case, and five minutes of time in which the candidate may ask questions.

"The cases tend to be very conceptual," says one insider. They do look to see that you can understand basic concepts about an industry. They do test quantitative skills. There aren't any guesstimates per se, but you do have them within cases – I was asked a few times to estimate the market size for a particular product." Several insiders say the firm "rarely, if ever, asks brainteasers, because that's just not applicable to what we do."

Some candidates report having all case interviews, though experiences vary by office. "In my second round," reports one consultant, "I met with a partner (called officers at BCG) and a manager and had lunch with two associates. One of my interviews was a case interview and the other was completely personal, a chat session. We talked a lot about my summer experience. They want to see if you are a people person, and maturity is a big thing for them." One person who interviewed with both McKinsey and BCG said that while McKinsey's interviews were straightforward – "along the lines of 'How many customers would you need to have this restaurant turn a profit?' There is a definite answer they want." – BCG's questions, according to this insider, were more creative and open-ended, "so theirs would be more like 'Tell me all the reasons this restaurant might be losing customers.'" Classmates who have compared notes after first-round interviews often note that they all get the same case interviews at BCG (usually based on a business problem at the firm). "There are no handouts," notes one interviewee, "so you need to ask questions."

MBA Job Seekers: Receive free e-mailed job postings matching your interests & qualifications! Register at www.VaultReports.com

VAULT REPORTS™

www.vaultreports.com

75

OUR SURVEY SAYS

Boston Consulting Group employees think highly of each other and their firm. The "lean organization" places little emphasis on seniority. Entry-level employees, therefore, receive "golden opportunities" to contribute their ideas and implement them. The "grueling" hours and "extensive" travel are "taxing," but the firm's prestige and pay scale offer "just rewards." With the pleasure of intellectual activity comes more work. "We tend not to have specific types of analyses done already, so in some sense, we have to reinvent the wheel each time. This is definitely more creative, and gives better solutions to the client, but it also means much more work for us," says one employee. Some recent hires comment that they were at first surprised by the "heavily theoretical" nature of their consulting assignments, but they also comment that they are finding the challenges "even more rewarding" than they expected.

Hours "aren't horrible, but not a piece of cake." They are "on average, about 55 hours a week," but "it's hard to define work hours. Generally, weekends are free, but not always." BCG sponsors "around one activity every four or five weeks," with "summertime and fall really big activity times." The pay at BCG is "very competitive. You won't go hungry, even in New York. The pay in itself is good, but the bonus – which can be substantial, up to 20 percent on top of base pay – makes things even better. A good and bad thing about BCG's pay is that it's based on performance, so how much you get depends on your own self," says one consultant. An associate in the New York office remarks that the "401(k) is good, and the performance bonuses are really substantial." (Actually, the firm has a profit-sharing retirement fund rather than a 401(k); the fund, unlike a 401(k), does not require the employee to make any contributions.)

Employees unanimously confirm BCG's reputation as a pleasant place to work. "BCG is the best firm in the business for quality of life issues," insiders say, although dress in some offices is business formal with casual Fridays. Half of the firm's offices are business casual all week, and the firm plans to move to daily business casual in every office by 2000. "The partners are very fun and very relaxed, and they don't treat you badly. There's a real emphasis on lifestyle versus just doing the work," says one consultant. However, the creativity and emphasis on individuality may mean that management tends to value "smart work way above hard work, which means that those who have a flashier style of working do better than diligent workers." Also remember that job satisfaction is "relative to [consulting], which doesn't have too many [satisfied] people on the whole." Despite these caveats, most BCG consultants are happy with the "excellent opportunities for minorities" and "outstanding" treatment of women. As an extra perk, there is a "constant flow of free, good dinners" while entertaining clients and recruits.

BCG consultants claim that their work affords them "a lot of creativity. It's not like associates are drones that are told to fill in the templates and get the answers." Even the lowliest of the associates say that their work "involves a lot of creativity and strategic thinking. You have a section of a case, what we call a module. You ultimately learn to run it and structure your own way, and make your own presentations." This sort of independence is one reason why BCG "wants people who can work alone and make their own decisions. That is scary for some people and there is always a time in which you are floundering around a bit at first. But the [case leader] will give you help, and frameworks, if you need them." While some adore this flexiblity – for instance – "if you want to work at home for a while, that is rarely a problem," it means that BCG is "not the best place for someone who likes structure. That's nothing to be ashamed of. Many people function very well with some structure. But BCG favors those who can think in the white space [undoubtedly a trendy new term for 'out of the box'] and who can be self-starters."

To order a 50- to 70-page Vault Reports Employer Profile on The Boston Consulting Group call 1-888-JOB-VAULT or visit www.VaultReports.com

The full Employer Profile includes detailed information on BCG's departments, recent developments and transactions, hiring and interview process, plus what employees really think about culture, pay, work hours and more.

MBA Job Seekers: Receive free e-mailed job postings matching your interests & qualifications! Register at www.VaultReports.com

VAULT REPORTS™

www.vaultreports.com

77

Bain & Company

Management Consulting

Two Copley Place
Boston MA 02116
(617) 572-2000
www.bain.com

BAIN & COMPANY

LOCATIONS

Boston, MA (HQ)
Atlanta, GA
Chicago, IL
Dallas, TX
Los Angeles, CA
San Francisco, CA
19 international offices

DEPARTMENTS

Strategy Consulting

THE STATS

Annual Revenues: $480 million (1997 est.)
No. of Employees: 2000 (worldwide)
Number of Professionals:
1500 (worldwide)
No. of Offices: 25 (worldwide), 6 (U.S)
A privately-held company
Chairman: Orit Gadiesh
Worldwide Managing Director:
Thomas Tierney

KEY COMPETITORS

* Andersen Consulting
* Booz·Allen & Hamilton
* Boston Consulting Group
* McKinsey
* Monitor Company

THE BUZZ
What MBAs are saying
about Bain & Co.

* "Cliquey, fraternity-like, snooty"
* "Entrepreneurial, best of consulting class"
* "Aggressive, very low ethics"
* "Fun, young, too many MBAs"

UPPERS

- Not as much travel as other consulting firms
- "TLC" in training
- Flex-time, parental leave and sabbaticals
- Convivial culture

DOWNERS

- Up-or-out culture
- Very long hours
- Lack of industry specialization

EMPLOYMENT CONTACT

Crisolita Alvez-Pontes
Two Copley Place
Boston MA 02116
Recruiting fax: (617) 572-2427

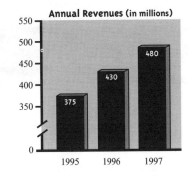

Annual Revenues (in millions)

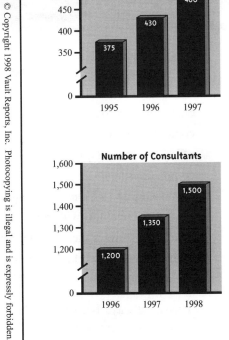

Number of Consultants

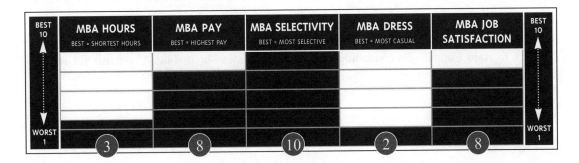

	MBA HOURS	MBA PAY	MBA SELECTIVITY	MBA DRESS	MBA JOB SATISFACTION	
BEST 10 / WORST 1	BEST = SHORTEST HOURS	BEST = HIGHEST PAY	BEST = MOST SELECTIVE	BEST = MOST CASUAL		BEST 10 / WORST 1
	3	8	10	2	8	

MBA Job Seekers: Receive free e-mailed job postings matching
your interests & qualifications! Register at www.VaultReports.com

VAULT REPORTS™
www.vaultreports.com

79

THE SCOOP

Bain & Company is among the world leaders in international strategy consulting. Founded in 1973 with a handful of employees, Bain now boasts a consulting staff of 1500 and has served clients in over 80 countries on five continents. The firm has 25 offices in 18 countries, though, compared to its main competitors McKinsey and the Boston Consulting Group, many of its offices are still relatively young. Its client base consists primarily of diversified, international corporations in all sectors of business and industry, among them financial services, health care, manufacturing, and a new leveraged buyout practice (developed in San Francisco in 1994, and expanded into a firm-wide practice in 1998). Unlike many of its consulting competitors, which are moving toward increased industry specialization, Bain remains a pure generalist, strategy shop. It must be working -- the company projects 10-15 percent growth in revenues in 1998 and in 1999 as well.

It hasn't always been thus. The firm ran into trouble in the mid-1980s when one of its employees working for Guinness in London was implicated in a share-dealing scandal. Around the same time, a disastrous ESOP (Employee Stock Ownership Plan) overloaded the company with annual payments. Falling business forced the firm to lay off over 20 percent of its workforce, and Bain nearly went bankrupt in 1991.

Since then, Bain has not only recovered its prestige, but enjoys a high reputation for confidentiality and integrity even in England. Since a management buyout in 1991, the company's revenues have risen year after year. Bain maintains the air of an "elite secret society" with its ultra-selective screening process. While it shares its headquarters building with Bain Capital, a venture capital firm founded by William Bain in 1984, the two firms have no official connection. However, Bain Capital does exhibit a "preference" for Bain when it needs to hire a consulting firm for its due diligence work, and the two companies are said to use a similar "results-based" operative framework. Bain consultants routinely make the (short) move to Bain Capital; the consulting firm even circulates "help wanted" e-mails for its VC cousin.

Bain is a very close-knit firm. Its consultants are affectionately called "Bainies," and the firm has what some call a collegiate and close-knit culture. "What are you going to do Monday morning at 8 a.m?" is a catchphrase at this consultancy, which concentrates on producing immediately implementable and valuable results for its clients. Orit Gadiesh (or "OG"), the brilliant, flamboyant (and purple-haired) chair of Bain & Company, insists that it's better to have an 80 percent solution that is immediately implementable than a perfect, 100 percent solution that is purely theoretical.

GETTING HIRED

Bain & Company makes a concerted effort to recruit the best and most qualified MBAs. The company hired approximately 200 MBAs in 1998, and plans to hire about 200 more MBAs for the class of 1999. The MBA hiring process starts with a first round that transpires on campus or at a local hotel. The first round consists of two separate interivews, one a "fit" interview "that's meant to tell if you are a dynamic, friendly, hyper-smart person who would fit well into the Bain culture, but is mainly going over your resume" the other a case interview. These preliminary interviews are short – twenty or thirty minutes each.

The candidates Bain deems worthy of a second interview are interviewed either on campus or at a nearby Bain office. This second round consists of three 40-minute interviews. One of these interviews is a more intense non-case "fit" interview, while the other two are case interviews.

Bain caters to its most-desired MBAs. At some of its larger core schools – such as Harvard, Wharton, Kellogg, Stanford and Chicago – Bain will make a campus rep available to answer questions. A consultant is available to fly in and answer any questions recruits have about the firm.

Bain & Company gives all of its employees – including recent hires – "as much responsibility as they can handle." The "intense," "upbeat" corporate culture emphasizes teamwork "constantly," employees say, comparing the firm to "an elite fraternity or sorority – Beta Alpha Iota Nu." Even chairman Orit Gadiesh spends about 70 percent of her time on client work.

MBA Job Seekers: Receive free e-mailed job postings matching your interests & qualifications! Register at www.VaultReports.com

VAULT REPORTS™
www.vaultreports.com

81

OUR SURVEY SAYS

Consultants say that the firm makes a "good faith" effort to put them on assignments in which they are interested and also offers them the flexibility they need to balance their work schedules with the demands of their personal lives. Insiders say that "the level of the assignments is top-notch." "Excellent researchers" on case teams also help solve client problems. We hear that "the hours fluctuate a lot, from 50 to 80 hours a week, and sometimes strange hours." However, say consultants, "we don't travel as much as other consultants, maybe one day a week." Plenty of applicants want to join in the fun. The firm "has been known to get 100 resumes a day."

Employees interact "frequently" with senior employees, especially at Bain's numerous social events. A special perk at Bain is the "Bain Band," a semiprofessional musical ensemble composed of Bain employees that plays at special events. "Suits are required" at this prestigious firm, "except for Fridays. For a few years, people violated the dress code regularly, until the company cracked down." As for diversity, the firm's record is fairly clean. "Although the breakdown of men to women is about 70/30, I felt women were well-accepted in the organization," says a female former employee. "And of course, the chairman is a woman, Orit Gadiesh." While minorities are "treated as equals," "at the end of the day, there were few minorities in the company." At the present time, Bain has no office in New York. Some insiders claim the reasons for this are twofold. "First of all, Bain thinks it's more efficient to have fewer and larger offices, and second, most of the partners with families don't want to move to New York," we are told. The firm, however, says it is now actively evaluating the possibility of opening a New York office – not because Bain has any difficulty serving its New York clientele from Boston, but because many potential recruits have expressed a desire to live and work in the city.

The amount of travel seems to vary from consultant to consultant and from office to office. One insider remarks, "I worked for Bain for a year and a half. I never traveled internationally and my domestic travel was maybe once a month." Another insider has a different tale to tell: "I traveled constantly. At least three days per week." Another remarks, "I worked on a Japanese case for six months, but spent only six weeks in the country. The same with the

France project. I worked almost entirely out of the domestic office; it was only the last two and a half weeks of the project that I flew to Paris." Generally, the firm is "good about transferring its personnel from one office to another, especially if it truly wants you. For example, if Bain needed a healthcare expert in Sydney, it would set you up with a really nice housing situation. On the other hand, [when changing offices] financial gradation depends on how badly you want it versus how badly the client needs you." According to insiders, Bain's more popular offices include San Francisco, London ("you can be abroad, but still speak English"), Paris ("because, well, it's Paris"), Sydney, and Johannesburg ("it's an exciting time to be in South Africa"). Foreign language proficiency, although not a requirement of the company, "is common among Bainies. Many people have studied or lived abroad."

Bain offices aree well-equipped, insiders say. "There are some secretaries and a lot of research staff. You can do your own research or sometimes you give your requirements to the support staff," says one. "They'll either give you the stuff the next day or that evening, depending on how much of a rush it is. You can get hundreds of pages sometimes." Responds another insider, "every team has a team assistant, who handles the administrative details. There's also a word processing bay, where you drop stuff off after you write it out. The library is very modern; it has laserdiscs and CD-ROMS, the whole bit."

To order a 50- to 70-page Vault Reports Employer Profile on Bain & Company call 1-888-JOB-VAULT or visit www.VaultReports.com

The full Employer Profile includes detailed information on Bain's departments, recent developments and transactions, hiring and interview process, plus what employees really think about culture, pay, work hours and more.

MBA Job Seekers: Receive free e-mailed job postings matching your interests & qualifications! Register at www.VaultReports.com

VAULT REPORTS™
www.vaultreports.com

83

High Tech

One Microsoft Way, STE 303
Redmond, WA 98052-8303
www.microsoft.com

Microsoft®

LOCATIONS

Redmond, WA (HQ)
Houston, TX
Numerous plants and software development centers throughout the world

DEPARTMENTS

Operations
Research & Development
Sales & Support

THE STATS

Annual Revenues: $11.4 billion (1997)
No. of Employees: 22,232 (worldwide)
No. of Offices: 60+ (worldwide)
Stock Symbol: MSFT (Nasdaq)
CEO: William H. Gates
Average age of employee: 34.3 years

KEY COMPETITORS

- Adobe
- America Online
- Apple Computer
- AT&T
- Computer Associates
- Hewlett-Packard
- IBM
- Netscape
- Oracle
- Sun Microsystems

THE BUZZ
What MBAs are saying about Microsoft

- "Hated but the establishment"
- "Aggressive, demanding"
- "Killer"
- "Cutting edge, market leader"

UPPERS

- ◆ Stock options
- ◆ Company bonuses
- ◆ Company gym
- ◆ Flexible scheduling
- ◆ Little bureaucracy
- ◆ Tuition assistance

DOWNERS

- ◆ Reputation as Evil Empire
- ◆ Little training

EMPLOYMENT CONTACT

Recruiting
Microsoft Corporation
One Microsoft Way, STE 303
Redmond, WA 98052-8303
resume@microsoft.com

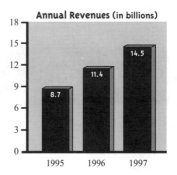

Annual Revenues (in billions)

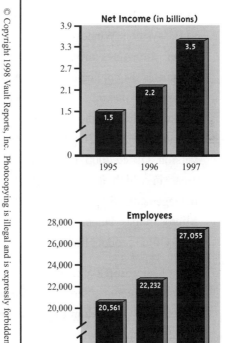

Net Income (in billions)

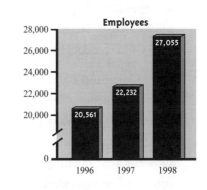

Employees

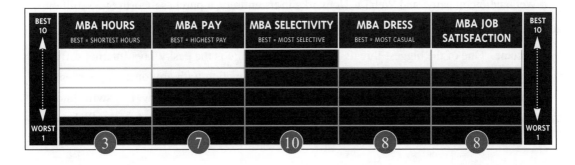

	MBA HOURS	MBA PAY	MBA SELECTIVITY	MBA DRESS	MBA JOB SATISFACTION	
BEST 10	BEST = SHORTEST HOURS	BEST = HIGHEST PAY	BEST = MOST SELECTIVE	BEST = MOST CASUAL		BEST 10
WORST 1	3	7	10	8	8	WORST 1

MBA Job Seekers: Receive free e-mailed job postings matching
your interests & qualifications! Register at www.VaultReports.com

VAULT REPORTS™

www.vaultreports.com

85

THE SCOOP

Microsoft is undeniably the world's number one software company. The company has a wide array of products, from operating systems for personal computers to interactive media programs. It is unlikely that a single modern office in the world functions without Microsoft products. Over 80 percent of the world's PCs run on Microsoft operating systems. In addition to PC systems Windows 95 and Windows 98, systems like Windows NT run the networks of larger companies around the globe. From spreadsheets to word processing, Microsoft dominates the applications market as well. Microsoft was the first software company to bundle its applications into a single suite, taking Microsoft Word, Excel, and PowerPoint, and marketing them in the package deal known as Microsoft Office. Not a bad idea – Office now accounts for about 30 percent of the company's revenues. Microsoft plans to release the next version, Office 2000, during the first half of 1999. The company is also branching out into areas in which it traditionally has not had a strong market presence, such as database management. Stepping up its efforts to compete with industry leaders Oracle and Informix, Microsoft has launched the SQL Server 7.0 to boost the already growing success of its BackOffice product line.

One of Microsoft's greatest assets is, well, its assets. With nearly $14 billion in cash and short-term investments at the end of fiscal 1998, and over $22 billion in total assets, Microsoft has a great deal of freedom to pursue new business interests. CEO Bill Gates is now flexing his monetary muscles with an amazing acquisition spree that has spanned the past few years and shows no sign of letting up. Since 1995, Microsoft has bought an 11.5 percent interest in cable company Comcast, worth $1 billion; a 15 percent stake in UUNet, an Internet service provider; a 5 percent stake in VDONet, an Internet video company; 10 percent of Progressive Networks, a Web-audio company; and WebTV Networks in its entirety, a purchase worth $425 million.

Such impressive figures do not mean, however, that Microsoft has no difficulties yet to overcome. One of the biggest threats to Microsoft's future is the pesky Java Internet software language created by Sun Microsystems. Designed to function with any operating system (or "platform"), Java breaks programs up into small "applets" that allow for swift Internet transmission. This would allow centralized servers to do much of the work currently handled by installed software (a.k.a. Microsoft's bread and butter). At the same time, new applications software is being programmed for Java because it is multi-platform. Gates may live to rue the day in 1995 when he announced that Microsoft would be Java-compatible, in order to fight the relatively small threat of Netscape, the same way that IBM probably regrets allowing MS-DOS to be licensable to PC-clone producers. Now Sun is suing Microsoft over the company's use of Java in its 4.0 version of Internet Explorer, claiming that Microsoft's program fails its compatibility tests.

To Gates and laissez-faire capitalists everywhere, a far more insidious challenge is coming from the United States government. In May 1998, the Department of Justice and a coalition of 20 state attorneys general charged Microsoft with engaging in monopoly business practices in violation of antitrust laws. By integrating any new technological innovation into Windows, contends the DOJ, Microsoft unfairly limits competition. The suit claims that by incorporating its Office suite into the operating system, and then making it financially impractical for PC manufacturers to include a rival product, Microsoft did just that. And even more important to the future of computing, Microsoft bundled its Internet Explorer with Windows software, thereby damaging rival Netscape Communications Corp. Microsoft argues that the browser is integrated into Windows 98, and that removing it will cause damage to the operating system. To bolster its case, the DOJ has incorporated evidence intended to establish that Microsoft had engaged in a pattern of anticompetitive practices dating back to well before the Netscape controversy began. Now that the two sides are finally seeing the inside of a courtroom, the eventual outcome (whatever it is) will be sure to send shockwaves throughout the software industry.

GETTING HIRED

For MBA students, Microsoft "conducts on-campus interviews at the top 15 schools and posts openings at a half-dozen more, but encourages students from all other schools to apply. Microsoft conducts "early recruiting in November." Applicants go through "an on-campus interview first with two people. If you pass that, they fly you to Redmond." For the second

MBA Job Seekers: Receive free e-mailed job postings matching
your interests & qualifications! Register at www.VaultReports.com

VAULT REPORTS™

www.vaultreports.com

87

round, candidates "interview with four to six people in one day." Interviewers include three peers, one to two people in the lead position, and, finally, one group manager. Each meeting lasts for about an hour, and applicants may interview with members of two different groups. The process is "very intense," but somewhat disorganized. The interviewers do not agree ahead of time on which areas each will cover. As a result, the session entails "a lot of overlapping questions." Most of these are "questions about software. They are not too lofty. They are [just] looking for enthusiasm for software." The occasional real-world case question rears it head. The other warning insiders give is that "the interviewers e-mail each other" to find out the candidate's strengths and weaknesses while the session is going on. While the meetings are "very much improvised," those conducting the later interviews may try to tailor them according to the information they have gleaned from their colleagues.

Candidates do not have to wait very long to find out their fate. The "decision is made at the end of the day based on the feedback of the recruiter and all the people who met with [the candidate]. There's no mulling it over, though it may take a couple of days" before the lucky phone call comes. This year, Microsoft "plans on hiring 30 to 60 full-time MBAs and the same number of interns."

Microsoft is well aware of its advantageous bargaining position. "Traditionally, they give a flat offer, and the offer's the offer," says one source. "I spent weeks negotiating, and got an extremely tiny change" in the original salary offer. Besides being so set-in-stone, initial salaries can be "20 percent lower than other software companies." Microsoft is, however, "really good in [offering] stock. They give a lot more than other companies. It is designed to be a bigger component" of the compensation package than is the case at other software companies. New MBA hires are also given "a moving and start-up bonus" which are "not extravagant." The latter is usually "the difference between your old salary and your new salary." The company also pays expenses for a home buying trip, including airfare and a tour of the area. In sum, recruiters say, Microsoft's "goal is to lead the market in terms of total compensation." While in practice this may not necessarily be the case, there is a major up side to this process. "The only place where there's a lot of room for negotiation is in picking your job," says one employee. "You can interview with one group, and it doesn't [necessarily] matter. The strategy is just to get an offer. Don't worry about the position."

OUR SURVEY SAYS

"The culture here is focused around doing great work, but it is also a very fun place to be," says one insider. The atmosphere is far from stuffy, leaning if anything toward sophomoric: "We have a basketball hoop in our hall, which is a great way to blow off steam in the evenings or the middle of the day." While average citizens probably would like to write off software programmers as lonely and uncommunicative, Microsoft employees usually disagree. One designer says: "The atmosphere is very social – a good-sized chunk of my day is spent in other people's offices or with other people in my office discussing how to accomplish some task or the latest industry news." And while the company has swiftly grown to a $14.5 billion monster, insiders say they "don't feel lost." "We work together in small feature teams, so even though this is a large company, you always feel like an important part of a team," says another MBA.

If there's one thing surveyed Microsoft employees universally applaud, it's the "free sodas, all the soda you can drink!" Another popular perk are the "cheap eats" at the subsidized Microsoft cafeteria where, "the food is good and for the price is great." Other employees are a bit more serious-minded. One cites the "package with salary, stock options, 401(k) matching, employee stock purchase plan, and more." Location can be a plus since "living in Seattle is a perk alone. If you're not affected by gray skies, it's a beautiful place." The Microsoft campus itself sports "lots of lawns, and basketball and volleyball courts." If a more structured exercise environment floats your boat, don't worry, Microsoft pays for employees' gym memberships. MBAs whose stock options haven't yet vested will appreciate the "10 to 20 percent discounts on products and services" at businesses around Seattle.

According to Microsoft employees, the dress code is "non-existent." High-tech companies are not known for their suavely-clad employees. "If you're a hot-shot programmer, no one's going to stop and say, 'But he's wearing sandals!' Get real." In fact, the company insists on its web page that it doesn't even matter what you wear to your job interview. Take this, however, with a grain of salt. Dress is still context-specific: "We wear whatever we want to work (shorts, jeans, T-shirts are most common), but this varies according to what job you do. Marketing people and lawyers dress up more than software developers."

MBA Job Seekers: Receive free e-mailed job postings matching your interests & qualifications! Register at www.VaultReports.com

VAULT REPORTS™
www.vaultreports.com

89

On the whole, Microsoft's track record with women and minorities is good, probably because "people are valued based upon their contribution to the company rather than some superficial quality. Sex and race are not a factor at all." Employee groups, including Blacks at Microsoft (BAM) are visible on campus, hosting career days for students of color. Nonetheless, minority representation is skewed toward "Indians and East Asians. Most of the blacks are not American but are from the Caribbean, South America, or Africa." In what is a fairly progressive move, the company has included sexual orientation in its non-discrimination policy. While the company is responsive to women on the whole, there may be something of a glass ceiling. Of the top 15 executives, not a single one is female. Only three of the 36 top executives are women as well, but female employees, "don't feel uncomfortable around the office." For a company founded in 1975 (with no holdover executives and partners from the days of fewer opportunities), this is still a surprisingly weak showing. One female respondent insists that it depends a lot on which department one is in: "I'm in marketing and I work with about 80 percent women."

To order a 50- to 70-page Vault Reports Employer Profile on Microsoft call 1-888-JOB-VAULT or visit www.VaultReports.com

The full Employer Profile includes detailed information on Microsoft's departments, recent developments and transactions, hiring and interview process, plus what employees really think about culture, pay, work hours and more.

Most Selective MBA Employers

FIRM	SELECTIVITY (on a 1-10 scale)
Bain & Co.	10
Boston Consulting Group	10
Goldman Sachs & Co.	10
McKinsey & Co.	10
Microsoft	10
Morgan Stanley Dean Witter	10
Coca-Cola	9
Donaldson, Lufkin & Jenrette	9
GE Capital	9
Intel	9
JP Morgan	9
Merrill Lynch	9
Monitor Company	9
Nike	9
Procter & Gamble	9
Salomon Smith Barney	9
Walt Disney	9

Source: Vault Reports MBA Survey 1998

RANKING
6

Morgan Stanley Dean Witter

Investment Banking

1585 Broadway
New York, NY 10036
(212) 761-4000
www.msdw.com

MORGAN STANLEY DEAN WITTER

LOCATIONS

New York, NY (HQ)
Atlanta • Austin • Boston • Chicago • Denver • Houston • Los Angeles • Menlo Park • Orlando • San Francisco • Amsterdam • Bangkok • Beijing • Frankfurt • Geneva • Hong Kong • Johannesburg • London • Luxembourg • Marid • Melbourne • Mexico City • Milan • Montreal • Moscow • Mumbai • Paris • Sao Paolo • Seoul • Shanghai • Sydney • Taipei • Tokyo • Toronto • Zurich

DEPARTMENTS

Corporate Financial Management • Corporate Treasury • Credit • Fixed Income Sales & Trading • Information Technology • Investment Banking • Private Client Services • Public Finance • Reengineering Services

THE STATS

Annual Revenues: $27.1 billion (1997)
No. of Employees: 47,277 (worldwide)
No. of Offices: 435
Stock Symbol: MWD (NYSE)
CEO: Philip J. Purcell

KEY COMPETITORS

- Credit Suisse First Boston
- Goldman Sachs
- J.P. Morgan
- Merrill Lynch
- Salomon Smith Barney

THE BUZZ
What MBAs are saying about Morgan Stanley

- "White shoe, first class"
- "Almost as sexy as Goldman"
- "Prestigious, demanding"
- "Powerhouse"

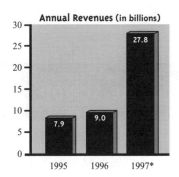

Annual Revenues (in billions)

UPPERS

- Top prestige
- Evaluation process permits vengeance
- Extensive exposure to upper management

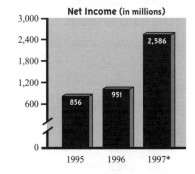

Net Income (in millions)

DOWNERS

- Long workdays
- Beepers

EMPLOYMENT CONTACT

Recruiting Manager
1585 Broadway
29th Floor
New York, NY 10036
(212) 761-0053

Employees

*Reflects merger of Morgan Stanley and Dean Witter

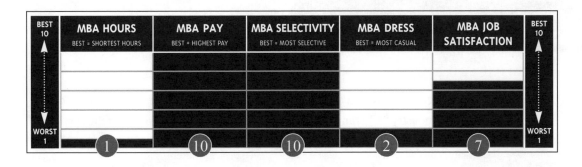

	MBA HOURS	MBA PAY	MBA SELECTIVITY	MBA DRESS	MBA JOB SATISFACTION	
BEST 10 ↑ ... WORST 1	BEST = SHORTEST HOURS	BEST = HIGHEST PAY	BEST = MOST SELECTIVE	BEST = MOST CASUAL		BEST 10 ↑ ... WORST 1
	1	10	10	2	7	

MBA Job Seekers: Receive free e-mailed job postings matching
your interests & qualifications! Register at www.VaultReports.com

VAULT REPORTS™

www.vaultreports.com

93

THE SCOOP

In 1997, Morgan Stanley, long considered one of Wall Street's most prestigious investment banking firms, completed its multi-billion dollar merger with the retail brokerage firm of Dean Witter, Discover. The union resulted in Morgan Stanley Dean Witter the world's largest securities firm in terms of assets managed and revenues. Even before the merger, both companies were near the top of their respective fields. As an investment banking house, Morgan Stanley leads investment banks in M&A and debt and equity underwriting; Dean Witter, Discover has established itself as the nation's third-largest retail brokerage house (after Merrill Lynch and Smith Barney) and as the third-largest issuer of consumer credit. The marriage is one of misfits, culturally. Morgan Stanley has a reputation as blue-blooded as the Morgan name suggests; Dean Witter was, until 1993, owned by Sears. As economic historian Ron Chernow said about the merger: "This is as shocking as the duchess suddenly announcing that she's marrying the footman."

Thus far, the marriage has been an unconventional fairy tale. Cognizant of cultural clashes that often result from mergers between investment banks and retail brokerage houses-usually because high-flying investment brokers bristle at the more austere culture of commercial banks – Morgan Stanley and Dean Witter have decided to consummate their brokered marriage slowly, promising autonomy for both companies. Although Morgan Stanley and Dean Witter have remained separate entities, culturally and legally, their businesses have complemented each other well. As of June 1998, the firm's stock had doubled, and new accounts and mutual-fund sales were up 40 percent since the merger.

GETTING HIRED

Morgan Stanley's interviews are, according to current employees, "quite formal, even for the investment banking industry." Technical questions are common; one business school student interviewing for a trading job reports that for his final round he was asked to sit in a chair while a senior director peppered him with macroeconomic questions. "All he did was pace around and throw questions at me - if I was wrong he'd correct me, and then just go to the next one… I remember thinking, 'God, I'm glad I know some of this stuff.' It was a lot of macroeconomics: inflation, interest rates, currencies." Says that contact: "They had me interview with pretty senior people, the head of all Treasury trading, the second in charge of all fixed income." Some recent associate-level hires report undergoing more than one call-back round when going through the B-school recruiting process. "I had three more rounds, all in New York (after the on-campus round)," reports one.

OUR SURVEY SAYS

As one of Wall Street's preeminent "white-shoe" firms, Morgan Stanley cultivates an "extremely professional environment" geared toward the "bright, motivated individuals that fill the halls." Employees say that "everyone seems to have an MBA from a top business school" and that "no other firm matches Morgan Stanley in terms of education and attitude." Not everyone appreciates this atmosphere, however. One former employee calls "the people at Morgan Stanley" his "biggest disappointment." He explains, "They are boorish, aggressive, and elitist – even more so than the rest of Wall Street." Another who left the firm recalls that he found his supervisors to be "shallow, uninspiring and heartless."

One of the famed aspects of Morgan Stanley's culture is that bankers are required to wear beepers, which some other banks enjoy pointing out as a flaw when competing for top recruits. "Depending on how you think about that, there's a good side or bad side," says one MBA insider. "The bad thing is, everyone's got access to your number. But the good side is that if you ever want to take a two-hour lunch, you can, because they can page you. If anyone ever complains that you weren't in the office, you can just say 'Why didn't you page me?'" Continues that contact: "And at night, it becomes a terrific social resource. People start paging people, next thing you know, you've got 50 people there."

MBA Job Seekers: Receive free e-mailed job postings matching your interests & qualifications! Register at www.VaultReports.com

VAULT REPORTS™
www.vaultreports.com

95

Morgan Stanley is also famed for its innovative evaluation system. "You get evaluated every six months and it leads directly into your compensation. You have a 360-degree performance evaluation," explains one insider. "So everyone you work with you put on your list, and that list goes to HR department. The HR department sends an evaluation form to everyone you work with. They take this very seriously, everyone you work with will give you a formal evaluation."

"All the evaluations are collected, and a VP or Principal who's in your group is assigned to collate all the information and pull together what the overall evaluation should be. This happens once in winter, and summer." Although the firm works on a three-tier evaluation system, "there's infinite room in all the tiers, it's not like a forced curve." Morgan Stanley awards its bonuses in July; each tier is awarded a bonus that represents a different portion of base salary.

"You not only get feedback from people above you, but you give them evaluations. The downward evaluations are named, upward are anonymous," says one former analyst. "So if your associate is being a total pain in the ass, you slam them in the reviews. They take very seriously the opinions of the junior people when evaluating for bonuses – so associates go out of the way to be helpful." "I'd say that is a very unique thing about Morgan," says that contact, who points out that the Morgan Stanley evaluation model was actually a case study at his business school.

To order a 50- to 70-page Vault Reports Employer Profile on Morgan Stanley Dean Witter call 1-888-JOB-VAULT or visit www.VaultReports.com

The full Employer Profile includes detailed information on Morgan Stanley's departments, recent developments and transactions, hiring and interview process, plus what employees really think about culture, pay, work hours and more.

Best MBA Employers for Pay

FIRM	PAY (on a 1-10 scale)
Donaldson, Lufkin & Jenrette	10
Goldman Sachs & Co.	10
Morgan Stanley Dean Witter	10
Andersen Consulting	9
BancBoston Robertson Stephens	9
Bankers Trust	9
Credit Suisse First Boston	9
JP Morgan	9
Lehman Brothers	9
McKinsey & Co.	9
Merill Lynch	9
NationsBanc Montgomery Securities	9
Salomon Smith Barney	9

Source: Vault Reports MBA Survey 1998

RANKING
7

Dell Computer

High Tech

One Dell Way
Round Rock, TX 78613
(512) 338-4400
Fax: (800) 224-3355
www.dell.com

LOCATIONS

Round Rock, TX (HQ)
Austin, TX
Bracknell, UK
Hong Kong
Kawasaki, Japan

DEPARTMENTS

Administration
Human Resources
Information Systems
Manufacturing Operations
Product Development
Product Support
Project Management
Sales and Marketing

THE STATS

Annual Revenues: $15.2 billion (1998)
No. of Employees: 16,000 (worldwide)
No. of Offices: 32 (worldwide)
Stock Symbol: DELL
Stock Exchange: NASDAQ
CEO: Michael S. Dell

KEY COMPETITORS

- Compaq
- Gateway
- Hewlett-Packard
- IBM
- Micron Electronics

THE BUZZ

What MBAs are saying
about Dell Computer

- "Masters of made to order"
- "Ground breakers, young"
- "Get options!"
- "Hot hot hot"

Dell Computer

UPPERS

- Powerhouse stock options
- Employee discounts on computers
- "Dell Discounts" on shopping and dining
- Company gym
- Extensive social events

DOWNERS

- Frequent shifts in company organization

EMPLOYMENT CONTACT

One Dell Way
Round Rock, TX 78613
Fax: (512) 728-9628
E-mail: careers@us.dell.com
http://dellapp.us.dell.com/careers/resume/.asp

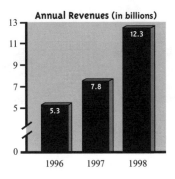

Annual Revenues (in billions)

1996	1997	1998
5.3	7.8	12.3

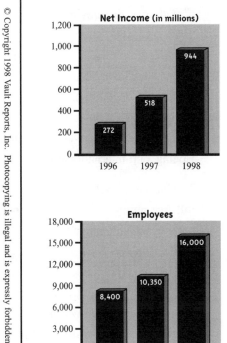

Net Income (in millions)

1996	1997	1998
272	518	944

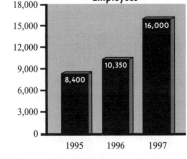

Employees

1995	1996	1997
8,400	10,350	16,000

	MBA HOURS BEST = SHORTEST HOURS	MBA PAY BEST = HIGHEST PAY	MBA SELECTIVITY BEST = MOST SELECTIVE	MBA DRESS BEST = MOST CASUAL	MBA JOB SATISFACTION	
BEST 10 / WORST 1	4	7	8	9	10	BEST 10 / WORST 1

VAULT REPORTS™
www.vaultreports.com

THE SCOOP

Dell's success is amazing by any measure – even more so when you consider the company is less than 15 years old. Based in Austin, Texas, Dell is now the leading direct-seller of computers in the world. In 1997, Dell's sales totaled over $7.7 billion, with 46.5 percent growth over the previous year. As recently as 1992, sales were under $1 billion annually. In 1998, revenues should exceed $8 billion. Dell started out making desktops and now manufactures a line of desktop computers, notebooks, workstations and servers. Desktops still account for 78 percent of this rapidly growing company's business. Dell sells primarily to small and medium-sized businesses and government agencies, though increasingly the company is targeting the consumer market. Dell still sells more than 90 percent of its products to businesses and government entities. Corporate customers include Ford Motor Company, Boeing, and international giant Deutsche Bank.

The business is relatively simple. Roughly 50,000 calls, most of them orders, come into Dell's toll-free numbers each day. Though Dell assembles a computer specifically for each order, making and shipping a PC usually only takes Dell 36 hours. Dell builds all of these computers at plants in Austin, Texas; Limerick, Ireland; and Penang, Malaysia. In the early 1990s, Dell entered the retail market by striking deals with retail chains to sell its computers at mail-order prices. Though many were skeptical when Dell began selling computers online, the company now sells $6 million worth of equipment on the Web daily. Dell prides itself on its customer-service. Custom-building computers according to each order means Dell can respond rapidly to the changing needs of the marketplace. Dell was the first PC maker to offer direct, toll-free technical phone support and next-day, on-site service.

Michael Dell, the founder of this self-named company, is the richest man in Texas. It's no wonder – the company's stock is going gangbusters. A hundred dollars of Dell stock purchased in 1990 would have been worth over $20,000 by September 1997. A $10,000 stake at the initial public offering in 1988 would by that time have been worth over $1 million. In the past three years, Dell's stock has risen faster than Coca-Cola's, Intel's, or Microsoft's. While Dell's stock began to fluctuate through the autumn of 1997, it did so not because of serious negative indicators but because analysts couldn't imagine that the stock could keep

VAULT REPORTS™

www.vaultreports.com

rising. However, Dell continues to grow: In the first two quarters of 1998, the company posted its 15th & 16th consecutive quarters of record sales. The company is also hiring like gangbusters: From 1995 to 1997, the company nearly doubled its workforce.

Recently, Dell has been increasing its presence outside the U.S., particularly in Latin America and Asia. Dell's international expansion is all the more remarkable given the current global financial crisis. While major U.S. high-tech companies have been scaling back their investments in these two volatile regions, Dell has been aggressively pushing forward. In 1998, the company began a new mail-order service in Hong Kong, Japan, and Singapore, a new Asia/Pacific Customer Center in Malaysia, and direct-sales operations in South Korea and Taiwan. Dell also began production in 1998 at a new factory in Xiamen, China. Company officials announced plans to expand Dell's Latin American market share (a region where it lags far behind IBM, Hewlett-Packard, and Compaq) by opening a new plant in Brazil.

GETTING HIRED

According to insiders, most positions at Dell require three interview sessions. The first session serves "mainly to see if you are the right kind of person and have the relevant experience to perform the position." This interview will be with a human resources recruiter. The following interviews will be with managers or subject experts (depending on the field). Remember that they are looking for "the right people technically as well as socially." "The biggest function of the interview is to try to determine if you would fit in to the culture," says one insider. "With the fast pace and multitasking required, we need team players that are also self-starters."

While Dell reportedly does not use brainteaser questions like Microsoft, you should be familiar with the Dell Direct Business Model. The Dell model means low inventory, just-in-time manufacturing, built to order products, and direct customer relationship with manufacturer. There are many benefits to this system. By cutting out the middleman, Dell can afford to sell its products well below retail. Since Dell builds a computer only when it gets an order, it keeps very low inventories, allowing the company to switch to the latest technologies faster than

MBA Job Seekers: Receive free e-mailed job postings matching your interests & qualifications! Register at www.VaultReports.com

VAULT REPORTS™

www.vaultreports.com

101

firms with pre-built stocks in warehouses. Understand this model. In an industry that is essentially a commodity business, this model explains Dell's success where so many others have failed.

OUR SURVEY SAYS

Dell prides itself on a "flat" corporate structure that encourages each worker to contribute "innovative" ideas, and its employees say they appreciate this "openness" and "absence of hierarchy." This "unstructured," "decentralized" environment allows Dell's "young," "energetic" employees to "gain responsibilities quickly and get a chance to prove yourself." "Managers that respect you" establish good relations. "There is much less corporate politics than in many other environments, which is a refreshing change," says one MBA intern. Dell is not a company for those who like to take things slowly, because "everything moves quickly." "Working at Dell is like jumping out of an airplane with your hair on fire," says one employee. "Everything about Dell is fast. We call it velocity," explains another.

Combined with Dell's "explosive" growth, the "meritocratic" promotion policy enables "talented management" to "rise rapidly." "There are some tremendous opportunities if you want to work hard and think 'out of the box,'" says one insider. Employees say they are generally satisfied with their compensation packages, adding "the pay is fair, swell perks (401(k)/employee stock purchase plan) are great." A profit-sharing plan "comes out to about an extra eight percent of your base pay per year," according to one insider. Other perks employees mention include discounts on computers and various establishments in Austin (including rent in some apartment complexes).

Employees also like the casual, "family-like" atmosphere, which includes a "lax" dress code. While dress codes differ by department, some employees can come to work in shorts and sandals while others go with "business casual dress." "There are even a couple of people with purple hair," says one. Insiders say there are "many minority employees, especially Asians and Asian-Americans." One technical support worker in Austin says "women are given opportunities that I did not see at my former employer." All agreed that "performance" and "not gender or skin color" moved employees up the career ladder. "For what it's worth, I'm gay, and I felt relatively comfortable interacting with the folks at Dell," says one employee. "The EEOC could take lessons from Dell," says another.

The overall level of employee satisfaction is astonishing. Numerous MBAs say exactly the same thing: "Dell is the best job I've ever had." Most had "absolutely no complaints," but obviously no company is perfect. As one technician says, "The only bad thing is that there are some 'Dell ways' of doing things. Since a lot of areas are new, when you hit those new areas, things can slow down." Minor criticisms aside, when employees say things like, "I have found the place I intend to retire from. The only way I'll leave is kicking and scratching," it must be a pretty good place to work.

To order a 10- to 20-page Vault Reports Employer Profile on Dell Computer call 1-888-JOB-VAULT or visit www.VaultReports.com

The full Employer Profile includes detailed information on Dell's departments, recent developments and transactions, hiring and interview process, plus what employees really think about culture, pay, work hours and more.

MBA Job Seekers: Receive free e-mailed job postings matching your interests & qualifications! Register at www.VaultReports.com

VAULT REPORTS™   103
www.vaultreports.com

Intel

High Tech

P.O. Box 1141
Folsom, CA 95763
(408) 765-8080
www.intel.com

LOCATIONS

Santa Clara, CA (HQ)
Albuquerque, NM • Folsom, CA • Fort Worth,
TX • Phoenix, AZ • Portland, OR • Sacramento,
CA • Salt Lake City, UT • Seattle-Tacoma, WA
• Munich, Germany • Shanghai, China •
Swindon, England

DEPARTMENTS

Finance • Human Resources • Information
Technology • Integrated Circuit Engineering •
Integrated Circuit Manufacturing • Marketing
• Materials and Planning • Operations • Sales
• Software Engineering • Systems Hardware
Engineering and Manufacturing

THE STATS

Annual Revenues: $25.1 billion (1997)
No. of Employees: 63,700
No. of Offices:
Stock Symbol: INTC (Nasdaq)
CEO: Craig R. Barrett
% Minority: 28
%Male/%Female: 68/32

KEY COMPETITORS

- Advanced Micro Devices
- Cyrix
- LSI Logic
- NEC

THE BUZZ
What MBAs are saying
about Intel

- "Big, but nimble"
- "Will never die"
- "Leader, too big to be exciting"
- "Great company, army-like"

UPPERS

- Bonuses
- Stock options
- Tuition reimbursement
- Paid sabbaticals
- Fitness facility

DOWNERS

- Paranoia can be contagious
- Massive bureaucracy
- Increasing threat from competitors

EMPLOYMENT CONTACT

Staffing Department
705-2 East Bidwell Street
Suite 246
Folsom, CA 95630
jobs2@intel.com

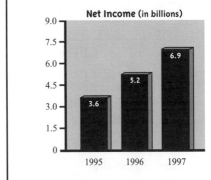

Annual Revenues (in billions)

1995: 16.2
1996: 20.8
1997: 25.1

Net Income (in billions)

1995: 3.6
1996: 5.2
1997: 6.9

Employees

1995: 41,600
1996: 48,500
1997: 63,700

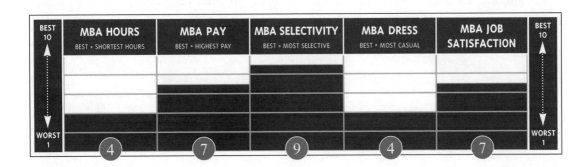

	MBA HOURS BEST = SHORTEST HOURS	MBA PAY BEST = HIGHEST PAY	MBA SELECTIVITY BEST = MOST SELECTIVE	MBA DRESS BEST = MOST CASUAL	MBA JOB SATISFACTION	
BEST 10 → WORST 1	4	7	9	4	7	BEST 10 → WORST 1

THE SCOOP

Nostalgic for the salad days of 19th century monopolies? Look no further than the Silicon Valley juggernaut Intel. Its microprocessors – also known as chips – power an estimated 89 percent of personal computers worldwide. The firm is just as dependent on its microprocessors as computers around the world are on its products; Intel garners 80 percent of annual revenues from chip sales. As consumers clamor for more computing might and sharp programmers (like those at Microsoft) concoct increasingly intricate software, Intel supplies the chips that will make computers run those new-fangled programs (and the old ones, too) faster and better.

Intel's products have become increasingly complex and widespread. The firm now earns 60 percent of its revenues from outside America, with new chips like the Pentium II and the Pentium II Xeon chip. Coming up – something called "multilevel memory," which permits Intel engineers to fit even more transistors onto microprocessors (making them more powerful) and the Hewlett Packard-Intel collaborative effort called the Merced, a chip that should be three times more powerful than the speediest Pentium II to date. Can anything shake this microprocessor powerhouse? Nothing's impossible – but in the meantime, Intel's one of the most valuable companies in America. PC makers may grouse about the lack of choice in the microchip market, but their lack of choice is Intel's boon.

Nonetheless, nothing lasts forever. Fierce competition has cut into Intel's profits forcing the company to slash its prices in order to compete with the cheaper microchips that are powering the under $1000 computers that are flooding the market. In June 1998, Intel announced that commercial distribution of its highly touted Merced chip will be delayed until the middle of year 2000. The Federal Trade Commission has also filed an anti-trust suit against Intel, charging the company with using its near-monopoly to stifle competition by withholding technical information from its rivals.

GETTING HIRED

Most positions in marketing and finance are the province of MBA grads at Intel. Intel recruits extensively at campuses and at job fairs; its internship program is also a sort of meta-recruitment endeavor. "Don't get stressed out [about the interview]," says one Intel insider. "All the interviewees are placed in little cubicles. There are about 40 other people being interviewed at the same time and the managers just keep going from person to person." After your interview, you'll be ranked on criteria like technical ability, analytical ability, communicative skills, and personal qualities. The last question on every interviewer ranking form: "Would you want to work with this person?" So remember: smile! If you're offered a job at Intel, you'll get a call anywhere from 24 to 72 hours after your interview.

While MBAs applying for financial analyst positions do not necessarily need technical knowledge, it will assuredly come in handy and enhance the application. Intel encourages rotations in both its marketing and finance functions. MBAs at Intel sometimes land in the materials and corporate services (MCS) department. Financial analysts are usually promoted to managerial positions within two to three years; those in marketing usually start as managers.

OUR SURVEY SAYS

Intel has a very particular culture – on the one hand emphasizing egalitarianism and meritocracy, on the other hand bestowing upon its insiders featureless cubicles and a healthy dose of paranoia. Insiders say "Intel is a flexible meritocracy. They increase responsibilities of people who show they can do the work and want to do more. Raises and promotions are also based on meritocracy." Don't expect to relax at this firm. "Intel is a little more uptight compared to other big Silicon Valley companies. There is more discipline and more of a business-oriented focus. That is one reason why the company is so successful." And don't expect a lot of hand-holding, either. "There is no executive training programs where you are

MBA Job Seekers: Receive free e-mailed job postings matching your interests & qualifications! Register at www.VaultReports.com

VAULT REPORTS™

107

www.vaultreports.com

eased into the culture. I loved it, because you have the freedom to take risks and make things happen, but many people found it a difficult environment." The upshot of all this independence and discipline is that "Intel expects you to speak your mind and express your viewpoint. But once a decision is made, you must back it 100 percent and do what you can to make your project a success. Office politics and project sabotage is not tolerated at Intel." Fortunately, says a former Intel insider, you should be able to get your point across. "Intel culture is something I miss very much. Your success depends on how well you can convince people of your point and your ability to communicate. There is not as much of a problem with stagnant 'old boy networks' as at other firms."

Intel's meritocracy and discipline has its downsides – paranoia and bureaucracy. Intel insiders want to give you a tip: "Word of advice – meetings suck. They are just an excuse for the managers to justify their stock options. Avoid." One employee in a forward-looking division reports, "Intel is so paranoid that your bag will be searched on the way out." An engineer assesses the firm through its motto output. "Intel has a couple of company slogans. One of them is 'A great place to work,' which is also one of our values, and another is from (former CEO) Andy Grove, 'Only the paranoid survive.' Yes, we are number one, but there is always someone who wants to take us down. So put those two together and maybe you can get an idea of what Intel is like."

Though Intel is a king in its market, don't expect posh digs at Intel offices. "Everyone sits in a cubicle, except in the labs and the conference rooms. In fact, there are very few doors. That makes it easier to have our 'Open Door' policy." "The offices at Intel are cubicles. No one has an office, not even Andy Grove the chairman. This promotes a very open environment. I like it, but I know that not having an office drives some people crazy," says one manager. Don't even count on keeping a stable cubicle. One employee reports "My office in Folsom is growing so fast that our cubicle size was reduced, from 9 x 9 to 6 x 9. This is called compression. It's a little cramped." Another Intel insider mentions "By walking through the offices, you would have a hard time figuring out where one departments ends and another one starts." One employee tells us "We all sit in rows and columns. I call it the Cube Farm." As for other office attributes, say insiders, "there is a fitness facility on-site, which is handy because I don't have time to go anywhere else." Another Intel employee says "some people like the locations of the offices, but I am in Chandler, Arizona and I can't wait to move. It's a big desert full of scorpions, including my manager."

VAULT REPORTS™
www.vaultreports.com

Intel doesn't shun sociability. "Each quarter the department has a quarterly event off-site. Each summer the division has a company picnic. Each winter the division (and sometimes the site) has a formal ball. When on a cross-functional team, the division sponsors team-building events, like cross country skiing." There is such thing as a free lunch at Intel – we hear that "some meals are provided when there are meetings during lunchtime, or late. Every Friday, during the 8 a.m. meeting, continental breakfast is served. One employee loves the free "fitness facility on site." Hard-working Intel employees can earn some time off – "every seven years, employees earn a sabbatical of eight paid weeks off in addition to regular vacation time." As for health and retirement benefits, "there's the full medical coverage (free), dental plan (free), vision care (free), life insurance (free), the 401(k). One employee thinks "the greatest, absolute best perk Intel gives me is stock options and the ESOP [employee stock option plan – open to all Intel employees]. That means cash, and sending my kids to college."

Employees are thrilled by their total compensation, but are well aware that salaries alone are "competitive, but on the low end of competitive." One Intel insider lists various bonuses available at Intel. "Individuals can be recognized by other individuals for outstanding work with bonuses up to $100. Each division honors people with bonuses each quarter for outstanding contributions. All employees receive semi-annual profit-sharing bonuses." Intel also offers annual employee bonues based on corporate and division performance. One employee says "because of its powerhouse status, Intel doesn't use base salary to attract top talent. It only pays at industry average. That's been a source of gripes for me and my colleagues. But over time, the complaints taper off as we watch the stock climb." A happy Intel employee reports: "Intel is not the highest paying company out there, as far as salary goes. But the whole package, or 'total compensation,' as they call it, is quite substantial. We got four bonuses this year. One was a $1000 'thank you' bonus, one was for 15 days of pay, one for 17 days of pay, and the last was for about five percent of yearly salary. Can't beat that." In bonus and profit, Intel paid over $900 million to employees in 1997.

MBA Job Seekers: Receive free e-mailed job postings matching your interests & qualifications! Register at www.VaultReports.com

VAULT REPORTS™

109

www.vaultreports.com

To order a 50- to 70-page Vault Reports Employer Profile on Intel call 1-888-JOB-VAULT or visit www.VaultReports.com

The full Employer Profile includes detailed information on Intel's departments, recent developments and transactions, hiring and interview process, plus what employees really think about culture, pay, work hours and more.

Best MBA Employers
for Job Satisfaction

FIRM	JOB SATISFACTION (on a 1-10 scale)
Boston Consulting Group	10
Dell Computer	10
Atlantic Richfield (ARCO)	9
BancBoston Robertson Stephens	9
Cisco Systems	9
Deloitte Consulting	9
Goldman Sachs & Co.	9
Hewlett-Packard	9
Lucent Technologies	9
McKinsey & Co.	9
Monitor Company	9
Sun Microsystems	9

Source: Vault Reports MBA Survey 1998

JP Morgan

Investment Banking

60 Wall Street
New York, NY 10260
(212) 483-2323
www.jpmorgan.com

JPMorgan

LOCATIONS

New York City, NY (HQ)

Boston, MA • Chicago, IL • Dallas, TX•
Houston, TX • Los Angeles, CA • Newark,
DE • Palm Beach, FL • Philadelphia, PA • San
Francisco, CA • Washington, DC

Numerous international locations including
ones in Buenos Aires • Brussels • London •
Paris • Singapore • Tokyo

BUSINESS LINES

Investment Banking • Equities • Fixed
Income• Emerging Markets • Foreign
Exchange • Commodities • Private Client
Group • Investment Management

THE STATS

Annual Revenues: $7.22 billion (1997)
No. of Employees: 16,000 (worldwide)
No. of Offices: 50 (worldwide), 11 (U.S.)
Stock Symbol: JPM (NYSE)
CEO: Douglas ("Sandy") A. Warner III

KEY COMPETITORS

- Credit Suisse First Boston
- Lehman Brothers
- Goldman Sachs
- Merrill Lynch
- Morgan Stanley Dean Witter
- Salomon Smith Barney

THE BUZZ
What MBAs are saying
about JP Morgan

- "White-shoe, intellectual"
- "Trying hard but not doing it"
- "Take care of their employees"
- "Great name but always second rate"

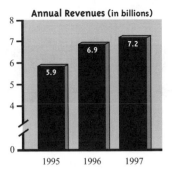

Annual Revenues (in billions)

UPPERS

- Emphasis on job training
- Subsidized gym memberships
- Generous vacation policies
- Great diversity for Wall Street

DOWNERS

- Struggling firm
- No more free lunch
- Somewhat stuffy

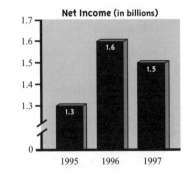

Net Income (in billions)

EMPLOYMENT CONTACT

JP Morgan
60 Wall Street
New York, NY 10260

Check out the web site at
www.jpmorgan.com for addresses
of MBA recruiting in principal locations.

Employees

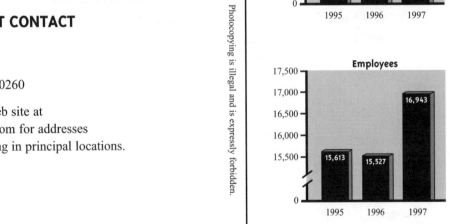

	MBA HOURS BEST = SHORTEST HOURS	MBA PAY BEST = HIGHEST PAY	MBA SELECTIVITY BEST = MOST SELECTIVE	MBA DRESS BEST = MOST CASUAL	MBA JOB SATISFACTION	
BEST 10 → ... WORST 1	2	9	9	1	8	BEST 10 ↑ ... WORST 1

MBA Job Seekers: Receive free e-mailed job postings matching
your interests & qualifications! Register at www.VaultReports.com

VAULT REPORTS™
www.vaultreports.com

113

THE SCOOP

The financiers of household names such as U.S. Steel, General Electric, and AT&T, not to mention most of America's railroad network, J.P. Morgan is more than an investment bank – it's an American institution. The firm's founders, father Junius Spencer Morgan and son J. Pierpont, rose to fame as a powerful banking team in the second half of the 19th century. Working on both sides of the Atlantic, the Morgans were responsible for bringing from Europe to the U.S. the capital that was crucial to the nation's growth. After Junius died in 1890, J. Pierpont consolidated the family businesses as J.P. Morgan and Company and reigned as a symbol of Wall Street's power.

Despite its hallowed name, J.P. Morgan still hasn't made it into the coveted investment banking elite. The firm has for years attempted to transform itself from a commercial bank into an investment bank. Unlike other large commercial banks, such as NationsBank and Deutsche Bank, which have built its I-banking practices by acquiring firms, traditional Morgan has decided to grow its business from within.

Firm officials and Wall Street analysts cite Morgan's ability thus far to transform itself – the firm ranks respectably in league tables – as an astounding story of successful restructuring. In 1980, about 50 percent of the bank's revenue came from traditional commercial banking businesses such as corporate lending; in recent years, 75 percent has come from investment banking businesses such as trading and underwriting. Industry observers point to the firm's folding its lending operation into its fixed-income trading business in December 1997 as symbolic of this change.

But while Morgan has been successful in its transformation, the bank hasn't been utterly triumphant. In comparison to already established investment banks like Goldman Sachs and Merrill Lynch, the firm's actual performance is much less impressive than its stellar name. In 1997, the firm's 13.4 percent return on equity fell behind the 17.5 percent average of money-center banks and the 21 percent average of investment banks. The firm's strategy to grow its investment banking business organically has revolved around building off its corporate lending relationships. This has worked well in fields such as M&A and bond underwriting, but not as well in areas such as stock underwriting, since many of Mogan's prime customers – blue-chip, established companies – have little need for stock offerings.

J.P. Morgan has taken huge financial hits recently, especially in the fourth quarter of 1997 and the first quarter of 1998, when its earnings fell 35 and 48 percent, respectively. Part of the reason for the faltering profits is that Morgan had invested heavily in Asia, where a financial crisis hurt many banks. In response, the firm has looked for ways to cut spending. It announced a 5 percent cut in staff in February 1998, and also began to trim fat elsewhere, most notably by axing the firm's free-lunch policy. In May 1998, the firm announced that it planned to slash between $300 to $500 million in costs annually.

GETTING HIRED

J.P. Morgan has formal recruiting programs at 15 business schools. At chosen business schools, there is typically one big presentation. After that initial presentation, Morgan's individual business lines often go back to the campus to make focused presentations. These are generally club sponsored; the firm's asset management division, for example, will be sponsored by a school's investment management club.

Morgan also hosts dinners at the major business schools. "The goal is to get to know you," explains one recruiter. These dinners are usually held one to two months before interviewing begins. Candidates applying to Morgan through the firm's on-campus recruiting efforts go through the process of a lengthy on-campus interview and then a full day of callbacks at the firm's New York headquarters (for summer hires, the second round is held locally). The firm's investment banking department does a "Super Saturday," when many candidates are brought to the headquarters to run the gantlet of interviewing. A candidate usually interviews with five to eight people during the second round.

The investment banking, markets, private client group and investment management departments all hire MBAs as associates, who have the opportunity to work in several different areas during their careers at J.P. Morgan, sometimes in international assignments. Says one recent MBA hire: "I received more responsibility than peers at other firms. It's been a terrific learning experience. I rotated through two departments, which has broadened my perspective."

MBA Job Seekers: Receive free e-mailed job postings matching your interests & qualifications! Register at www.VaultReports.com

VAULT REPORTS™
www.vaultreports.com

115

OUR SURVEY SAYS

Employees refer to J.P. Morgan as "all of Wall Street without the attitude." They say that J.P. Morgan's "positive" and "open" corporate culture "promotes cooperation" among employees and the different departments within the firm. J.P. Morgan's "challenging" training programs win the praise of those who have started with the firm recently, as does the "extensive exposure to senior bankers." The company "focuses on teamwork and professionalism" and promotes an "energetic" atmosphere. Employees "love finance" but also say that they thrive on "the client contact, action, and verbal communication" that distinguish J.P. Morgan from its rivals.

Life at J.P. Morgan is notably perkful. Benefits include a "generous year-end performance bonus" based on firm and employee performance, a month of vacation and annual profit sharing. Insiders also receive "tickets to the best plays" and a "great subsidized gym membership program." Some employees even list "the opportunity to interact with extraordinarily bright people" as a "top perk." However, the firm's recent emphasis on cost-cutting caused it to end its much-loved free lunch program as of October 1998. The free lunch is now a "subsidized lunch." Associates still get generous vacation time – four weeks worth.

Despite the firm's recent troubles, employees still bask in their firm's peerless reputation. "Feeling prestigious is a given at J.P. Morgan," says one employee – a sentiment echoed by her peers. J.P Morgan "views the employees as the cause of success," says one, "and the firm makes us feel every bit a part of it all." Employees call J.P. Morgan "an utterly amazing company – in about 10 years, they have built an investment banking capability that puts them into the bulge bracket." "This is a difficult industry to break into in the first place," a recent hire states. "Making it in J.P. Morgan is like taking the crown."

You'll be spending a lot of time at J.P. Morgan. "You're basically looking at 10-12 hour days," one MBA reports, "plus the occasional weekend." "But the hours can be flexible," another comments, "you just have to expect some peaks." As one contact summed up: "Just be sure that you're willing to put in 90 hours a week at any given time" and "don't expect much notice, either." Still, according to one veteran, "You'd be hard-pressed to find a dissatisfied employee."

The opportunities for both women and other minorities at Morgan is "surprisingly good for this business," employees say, emphasizing J.P. Morgan's "excellent gender diversity." Reports one I-banking insider: "I work in a very diverse group – several different races and good representation of women." Another insider comments that "there certainly are more women here than at any other Wall Street firm – Morgan puts a big effort forward in this area, and it's definitely paying off for them." Reports one supervisor: "I supervise a group of all women." Says an associate in investment banking: "The head of my group is a woman and almost half of all junior personnel are women." But Morgan is still on Wall Street, and some women believe their opportunities could be improved. One woman associate says that while receptivity to women is "very good," "it becomes increasingly difficult to rise to the 'next level' with each promotion. While this is true of men, too, I think it is more pronounced for women."

As for ethnic and other minorities, "J.P. Morgan's diversity efforts are known by all employees," says one vice president. Every business area is overseen by the 'Diversity Steering Committee,' a group of senior managers brought together to discuss diversity issues affecting the firm on a global basis. Regarding Morgan's minority recruitment efforts, one employee reports: "If you're black or Hispanic, Morgan definitely wants to hire you. Another employee says: "If you're a minority and you want to leave the job, they'll sit you down for an interview to try to find out what it was that made you want to leave this place." Two of Morgan's three vice chairmen are foreign born. In August 1997, Morgan announced same-sex domestic partner benefits, the first Wall Street firm to do so. One insider puts it simply: "Morgan has a huge diversity initiative."

To order a 50- to 70-page Vault Reports Employer Profile on JP Morgan call 1-888-JOB-VAULT or visit www.VaultReports.com

The full Employer Profile includes detailed information on JP Morgan's departments, recent developments and transactions, hiring and interview process, plus what employees really think about culture, pay, work hours and more.

MBA Job Seekers: Receive free e-mailed job postings matching your interests & qualifications! Register at www.VaultReports.com

VAULT REPORTS™

www.vaultreports.com

117

Merrill Lynch

World Financial Center
North Tower
250 Vesey Street
New York, NY 10281
(212) 449-1000
www.ml.com

Investment Banking

Merrill Lynch

LOCATIONS

New York, NY (HQ)
Atlanta, GA
Los Angeles, CA
Louisville, KY
New Orleans, LA
Princeton, NJ
San Francisco, CA
Washington, DC
Tokyo, Japan
Toronto, Canada
London, United Kingdom
As well as locations around the nation and
worldwide

No. of Offices: 550+ (worldwide)
Stock Symbol: MER (NYSE)
CEO: David H. Komansky

KEY COMPETITORS

- Charles Schwab
- E*Trade
- Goldman Sachs
- J.P. Morgan
- Morgan Stanley Dean Witter
- PaineWebber
- Salomon Smith Barney

DEPARTMENTS

Capital Management
Corporate Finance
Investment Banking
Mergers & Acquisitions
Private Client Services
Sales & Trading

THE BUZZ

What MBAs are saying
about Merrill Lynch

- "Huge, solid firm"
- "Sausage factory, faceless"
- "Incredible training"
- "Revolving door"

THE STATS

Annual Revenues: $31.7 billion (1997)
No. of Employees: 56,600 (worldwide)

UPPERS

- Good social life
- Not as stuffy as some other investment banks

DOWNERS

- No company gym
- Can be extremely bureaucratic and political

EMPLOYMENT CONTACT

Roslyn Dickerson
Vice President
Merrill Lynch
World Financial Center
North Tower
250 Vesey Street
New York, NY 10281

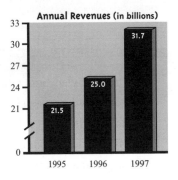

Annual Revenues (in billions)

1995: 21.5
1996: 25.0
1997: 31.7

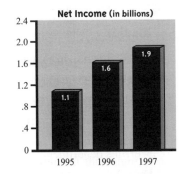

Net Income (in billions)

1995: 1.1
1996: 1.6
1997: 1.9

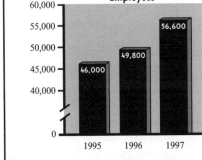

Employees

1995: 46,000
1996: 49,800
1997: 56,600

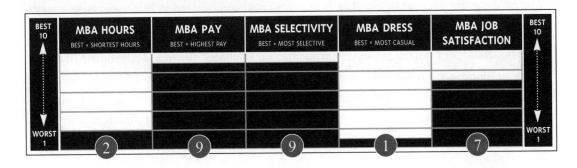

BEST 10 ↑ WORST 1	MBA HOURS BEST = SHORTEST HOURS	MBA PAY BEST = HIGHEST PAY	MBA SELECTIVITY BEST = MOST SELECTIVE	MBA DRESS BEST = MOST CASUAL	MBA JOB SATISFACTION	BEST 10 ↑ WORST 1
	2	9	9	1	7	

THE SCOOP

Founded in 1914 as an underwriting firm by Charles Merrill and his friend Edmund Lynch, Merrill Lynch survived the Great Depression by cutting loose its retail customers and limiting itself to investment banking services. Through a 1940 merger with Wall Street firm E.A. Pierce, Merrill Lynch reacquired its retail business, and in 1971 the company became the first Big Board member to have its shares listed on the New York Stock Exchange.

For years, Merrill Lynch was unique among major Wall Street firms. Unlike most investment banks, which specialize in serving institutional clients like corporations, governments and big investors, or retail brokerages, which sell stocks, bonds, and mutual funds to the general public, Merrill Lynch caters to both markets.

Merrill's departments are at the top of their respective league tables (the rankings of investment banks) – or, at the very least, hover somewhere in the top five. In 1997, the firm ranked No. 1 in underwriting common stock, No. 1 in investment grade debt, No.1 in high-yield debt (including issues whose ratings were split between investment grade and high-yield), and No. 1 in asset-backed securities. Merrill ranked No. 2 in worldwide convertibles and IPOs, and No. 3 in worldwide M&A advising. In recent years, Merrill has been at the forefront of a number of major deals in the American market, including the $8.8 billion acquisition of U.S. Healthcare by Aetna and Bell Atlantic's $33 billion merger with Nynex Corporation. In 1998, the firm advised NationsBank in its $61 billion merger with BankAmerica.

Not only does Merrill have leading I-banking capabilities, it also has a massive brokerage army eager to distribute the stocks and bonds the firm helps underwrite. The firm's retail brokerage unit, which has more than 13,000 financial consultants and serves more than 7 million accounts worldwide, is the world's largest. The firm's retail business is based in Princeton, New Jersey, and is comprised of more than 600 offices. Merrill's mutual funds and other asset management businesses (such as managing pension funds for institutional clients) are also wildly popular – the firm has $1.3 trillion of assets under management, more than double its $557 billion mark in 1993.

Because of its historical willingness to cater to retail investors, Merrill has the reputation of a "down-market" firm, at least when compared to blue-blooded competitors like Goldman Sachs and Morgan Stanley. But now, many of Merrill's competitors are following in the giant's money-making footsteps. In 1997, Morgan Stanley merged with retail brokerage Dean Witter (which until recently hawked its wares from Sears department stores). That year, famed Wall Street bank Salomon Brothers merged with retail-heavy Smith Barney. And when in 1998, the crème de la crème of investment banks, privately-owned Goldman Sachs, announced that it would make an initial public offering, industry observers speculated that the firm was attempting to free up capital in order to finance acquisitions.

But Mr. Dow had something to say about all these grandiose banking plans. Goldman shelved its IPO indefinitely in summer 1998 as global market conditions tightened, hurt by the collapse of emerging markets in Asia and Russia. Merrill took major trading losses and announced its first quarterly loss since 1989 for the third quarter of 1998. The firm announced that it would lay off 3400 employees in its hardest-hit departments in October 1998.

GETTING HIRED

Merrill Lynch accepts resumes by regular mail, fax, and e-mail. Resumes should be accompanied by a cover letter detailing the applicant's interests, abilities, and geographical preferences. Applicants can consult Merrill Lynch's employment Web page, located at www.ml.com/careers, in order to find out about job openings and contact information for the various groups within the company. Most associate positions require an MBA.

Resumes submitted to Merrill via either mail or through their school are sorted out by Merrill's recruiting personnel, and qualified applicants are invited for an interview. The first round of interviews is held on the applicant's campus, and those applicants who make the cut are invited to further rounds at the New York office. Merrill Lynch, like many other firms, gives preference to those MBAs who worked as summer associates when hiring for full-time positions. However, one Merrill employee confesses that "in recent years, Merrill has

MBA Job Seekers: Receive free e-mailed job postings matching your interests & qualifications! Register at www.VaultReports.com

VAULT REPORTS™
www.vaultreports.com

121

overhired for its summer programs, with the result that only 50 percent of the summer class have received offers to work at the company." Insiders also report that Merrill's interviews, even the initial on-campus screening interview "can last a lot longer than the typical half-hour interviews that other firms conduct." Summer associates who are made an offer of employment are generally required to respond within 30 days.

OUR SURVEY SAYS

Merrill's culture is "different from department to department." The investment banking division, according to one analyst, "is more laid back than most bulge-bracket investment banks, primarily because investment banking at Merrill is relatively new. Historically, you must remember, Merrill was a 'huge lumbering elephant' because that was the culture in the dominant retail side of business. However, things are changing as Merrill becomes one of the top three investment banks, and we're becoming more like Goldman or Morgan Stanley day by day. But we're still different from those places. The people are nicer and there's a much lower asshole factor than at other banks." The contact says, however, that "as with any big company, there will be people who are nasty for no particular reason. There will be assholes in any place. But there are fewer at Merrill." A former trader at Merrill says that Merrill gave him the chance "to work with very talented people with whom you'll keep in touch for the rest of your life." "No one breathes down your neck here," says one.

Most insiders feel that the best aspect of working with Merrill is "gaining exposure to the very best firms as your clients, and seeing how they run." "I worked on one fancy project for a large sports company," reports one associate. "The project was great because I was involved with it from start to finish, and I learned a lot about the company and also got a feel for how management at a large, professionally managed company operates. The work environment at Merrill provides a top learning experience."

The major drawback of working for Merrill, most agree, is the "horrendous" bureaucracy, which "can sometimes combine with office politics to make life miserable and incomprehensible. Sometimes, for no apparent reason, you get blamed for things you didn't do, and get assignments you're not supposed to have, and there's no one to complain to – life becomes like a page from a Kafka novel." According to one financial consultant, "while I'm in the world outside, I'm proud to be working for Merrill. But on the inside, I know that bureaucracy and politics can make life pretty miserable." Perhaps the booze-enhanced social life is a compensation. One insider raves that "every Friday, there's a happy hour where everyone goes. It's a great meat market. Everyone's looking to pick someone up. Secretaries are looking for investment bankers to marry, and investment bankers are looking for secretaries for the weekend. It's fantastic."

Merrill Lynch's headquarter offices are "impressive and large." While "they're not furnished in a particularly lavish fashion, they're always tastefully decorated." Employees at the New York office state that "the most impressive feature of Merrill's offices is that they're located in the World Financial Center – Merrill has an entire building to itself. The views from that office are spectacular. The analysts are actually housed in a bullpen and you have a corner view of the Statue of Liberty in that office." Another employee says, "The World Financial Center neighborhood has great bars and shops – though everything is priced exorbitantly." Unfortunately, reports one insider, Merrill's environment isn't the best for staying in shape: "I worked so many hours at the office that I gained a substantial amount of weight. I got fat, to avoid euphemisms. The problem is, you spend so much time sitting at your desk, with no time to exercise, and you're always eating a lot at meetings at night or ordering food from different restaurants." Alas, that associate laments, "there's no company gym for easy, during-the-day access to weights or jogging."

To order a 50- to 70-page Vault Reports Employer Profile on Merrill Lynch call 1-888-JOB-VAULT or visit www.VaultReports.com

The full Employer Profile includes detailed information on Merrill's departments, recent developments and transactions, hiring and interview process, plus what employees really think about culture, pay, work hours and more.

Walt Disney

Media and Entertainment

500 S. Buena Vista St.
Burbank, CA 91521
(818) 560-1000
www.disney.com

LOCATIONS

Burbank, CA (HQ)
Anaheim, CA
Glendale, CA
New York, NY
Orlando, FL
Paris, France
Tokyo, Japan

DEPARTMENTS

Architecture and Engineering
Creative Development
Design and Production
Finance and Administration
Human Resources
Information Systems
Project Management
Real Estate Development

THE STATS

Annual Revenues: $22.5 billion (1997)
No. of Employees: 62,000 (worldwide)
No. of Offices: 7 (worldwide), 5 (U.S)
Stock Symbol: DIS (NYSE)
CEO: Michael D. Eisner

KEY COMPETITORS

- Bertelsmann AG
- Dreamswork SKG
- Seagram
- Sony
- Time Warner
- Viacom
- Yahoo!

THE BUZZ
What MBAs are saying
about Walt Disney

- "Crappy pay, political"
- "Depends, strat planning is cool"
- "Entertainment king, great leadership"
- "Slave-driving, worse than I-bank"

UPPERS

- ◆ Free admission to theme parks
- ◆ Merchandise discounts
- ◆ Social events
- ◆ Everybody loves your company
- ◆ Job training

DOWNERS

- ◆ Political work environment
- ◆ "Sweatshop" hours
- ◆ Unrelenting corporate cheerfulness

EMPLOYMENT CONTACT

Walt Disney
500 S. Buena Vista St.
Burbank, CA 91521
(818) 560-1000
(818) 558-2222 (job hotline)
Fax: (818) 560-1930

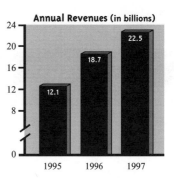

Annual Revenues (in billions)

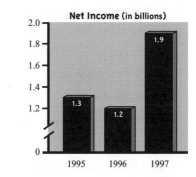

Net Income (in billions)

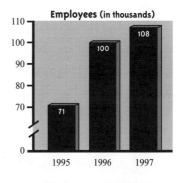

Employees (in thousands)

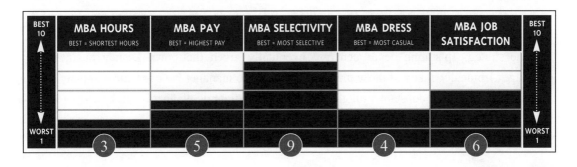

	BEST 10 — WORST 1	MBA HOURS BEST = SHORTEST HOURS	MBA PAY BEST = HIGHEST PAY	MBA SELECTIVITY BEST = MOST SELECTIVE	MBA DRESS BEST = MOST CASUAL	MBA JOB SATISFACTION	BEST 10 — WORST 1
		3	5	9	4	6	

MBA Job Seekers: Receive free e-mailed job postings matching
your interests & qualifications! Register at www.VaultReports.com

VAULT REPORTS™

125

www.vaultreports.com

THE SCOOP

Disney's history reads like one of its own movie scripts. Walt and Roy Disney started their film studio in 1923, and Walt directed the first Mickey Mouse cartoon five years later. Feature films like *Snow White*, *Fantasia*, and *Pinocchio* established Disney as a major Hollywood force, and the opening of Disneyland in Anaheim, California in 1955 and Disney World in Orlando in 1971 made the company a staple of family vacations for generation after generation. Now, Disneyland Paris has become France's biggest tourist attraction and its production studios, including Buena Vista, Miramax, and Touchstone, are turning out bigger and more successful movies each year.

In addition to its world-renowned theme parks and motion picture studios, Disney's empire includes a booming retail business, several publication companies, its own cable television network, a majority share in popular sports network ESPN, and a professional hockey team. And Disney continues looking for new ways to market its name. After contracting for Premier's Cruise Line's "Big Red Boat," Disney decided in 1998 to launch its own passenger ship, the Disney Magic, with a second ship, the Disney Wonder, to follow in 1999. In June 1998, Disney bought 43 percent of popular Internet search engine Infoseek for $860 million, and plans to launch a new portal site, the Go Network, at the end of 1998.

Despite the warm and fuzzy material it produces, at its core Disney is still a corporate bureaucracy. At the top of the Disney organizational pyramid, decisions about new business developments and financial operations are made through an unusual process first instituted by late president Frank Wells and former chief financial officer Gary Wilson. In addition to a manager, a member of the "strategic planning department" oversees each division. The head of that department reports to CEO Michael Eisner independent of the division managers, thus acting as a check on their power. This method invites constant tension between managers and planners, which Disney believes results in optimum efficiency and creativity. Many members of the strategic planning department are eventually given their own Disney business to manage. Ironically, many of those planners promoted to manager have left the company after growing weary of the constant struggle with their own strategic planners.

GETTING HIRED

For MBAs, Disney prefers "entertainment experience or corporate finance experience," although "they don't penalize you if you don't have an entertainment background." Either way, in inimitable Disney fashion, "they want happy, happy, happy people. The more you smile, the better off you are."

Disney "comes on campus very early for corporate America." The 25-minute first-round interview with business school students is "conducted by a functional line manager or a finance manager" and is "more of a behavioral assessment. They are not probing deep." There is also one other gatekeeper, the "greeter from human resources you meet first. She is supposed to be there just to answer questions, but is really judging you just as much as the interviewer. They are looking for enthusiasm, your interest in the company, and if you show passion."

After the first round, Disney will "discard the mean people, and put the remaining resumes in a big pile." These are then sent out to different departments to try to find an appropriate match. "Just because you 'make it through' the first round, you're not guaranteed a second-round interview," warns one former interviewee. Among the lucky ones, "at the top 15 business schools, they take the top candidates and fly them in around mid-November." Second-round candidates are then subjected to "a full day of interviews, usually on a Friday." Interviews are about "50 minutes each" and the day entails meeting "seven people in seven hours" from different areas. Fortunately, these generally are "easy interviews, with not a lot of detailed questions." Remarks one cast member who went through the process, "Disney is a pretty easy place to interview. You have a lot of amateurs [conducting interviews], so you've got to take control to have a great one." In the course of the seven meetings, candidates can expect "one case study question." Further extending the process, the winners "find out about a month a half later."

Candidates with MBAs tend to get hired into either Strategic Planning, Consumer Products, or Operations Planning. Most MBAs work in finance positions, such as Operations Finance in one of the theme parks, or in Marketing and Sales Finance. Some go into Financial Reporting (basically an accounting group), although in that field, "most come from regional MBA programs, like Rollins." A lucky few are drafted into Imagineering, or the real estate groups.

MBA Job Seekers: Receive free e-mailed job postings matching your interests & qualifications! Register at www.VaultReports.com

VAULT REPORTS™

127

www.vaultreports.com

OUR SURVEY SAYS

Insiders say that the image of the Happiest Place on Earth is a bit of a façade. "Disney is a big company, and it comes replete with the problems of a big bureaucracy. It has all those problems plaguing massive companies that you hear about," says one MBA. Disney is "a big company and they act like one. The culture is very bureaucratic and straitlaced, and they make very few decisions on the fly." Most sources simply advise prospective employees to understand that there is more to the company than just cuddly characters and exciting attractions. Says one insider, "it's important not to lose sight of the fact that Disney is a huge company which is in business for the sake of our stockholders – owners who want to make money by growing the company's value. Often times new cast members are disillusioned because they envision The Walt Disney Company as a Magic Kingdom kind of place which is a fairytale land devoid of bureaucracy, politics, and other unsavory things like financial analysis. No such place exists and often new cast members who come to us with unrealistic expectations leave unhappy."

The Disney pay scale, unfortunately, "doesn't match the high sheen of the Disney name." What with "the exorbitant executive salaries," employees on the lower end often feel as though they are "constantly coming out on the short end." Disney has "a hard time attracting MBAs because of the pay scale," according to insiders. Among those who are hired, "they expect that people will leave, [which creates a further] sense of alienation."

In recruiting, "Disney is not very open to negotiations. They just pitch a package to you," which the prospective cast member can either accept or decline. "Disney is an 800-pound gorilla in the marketplace," says one Disneyite. "They know it and aren't afraid to use it, which can be frustrating." Insiders advise candidates to keep each other apprised of their negotiations, and let Disney know that they are aware of what others have been offered. Once "you accept, they make everything smooth," such as relocation and other issues. The pay scale is said to be "10 to 15 percent below the market" for comparable work elsewhere. Raises come in "a slow progression." Corporate employees get a "shitty four percent raise per year, [although] year-end bonuses can be 10 percent." When performance and tenure-based raises are given, they are usually in the 10 to 15 percent range. People in "strategic planning come in at $85,000, but it's more selective and they work much more – about 65 hours a week." Employees in other groups find that "there are people that have been here five years making the same as people right out of MBA programs going into consulting jobs."

Some employees feel, however, that "in a way, you're paid just with the Disney name." This works to Disney's advantage, but can be a trap. Warns one insider, "once the pixie dust wears off, if the only [other] thing keeping you here is money, it won't work."

"At the same time, there is no other job I'd rather have at this point in my life," a longtime employee comments, and many at Disney would agree with such a sentiment. "My job has exceeded all expectations," another comments, adding that "there's a lot of responsibility to go around, and you get exposure to upper management – which is always ready for dialogue and feedback." Another employee states, "So far it's been like a five-year vacation for me. I've gained experience that I never could have earned somewhere else." A number of caveats must be heeded before taking a job, however. According to one employee, "[you get] a lot of satisfaction from what you do, but you must put up with the bureaucracy to get there." Some MBAs and others with similar credentials may find that "you don't have the exposure to use you skills." Overall, advises one Disney veteran, "you have to come here for the right reasons. Having Disney on a resume and spending time in this sector will go a long, long way. [You should] look at it as a building block."

To order a 50- to 70-page Vault Reports Employer Profile on Walt Disney call 1-888-JOB-VAULT or visit www.VaultReports.com

The full Employer Profile includes detailed information on Disney's departments, recent developments and transactions, hiring and interview process, plus what employees really think about culture, pay, work hours and more.

MBA Job Seekers: Receive free e-mailed job postings matching your interests & qualifications! Register at www.VaultReports.com

VAULT REPORTS™
www.vaultreports.com

129

Donaldson, Lufkin & Jenrette

277 Park Avenue
New York, NY 10172
(212) 892-3000
www.dlj.com

Investment Banking

Donaldson, Lufkin & Jenrette

LOCATIONS

New York, NY (HQ)

Atlanta, GA • Bala Cynwyd, PA • Boston, MA • Dallas, TX • Houston, TX • Menlo Park, NJ • Miami, FL • San Francisco, CA • Los Angeles, CA • Bangalore, India • Buenos Aires, Argentina • Geneva, Switzerland • Hong Kong • London, England • Lugano, Switzerland • Mexico City, Mexico • Paris, France • Sao Paulo, Brazil • Tokyo, Japan

DEPARTMENTS

Investment Banking
Institutional Equity Research
Institutional Equity Sales
Investment Services Group
Taxable Fixed Income

THE STATS

Annual Revenues: $4.6 billion (1997)
No. of Employees: 7,000
No. of Offices: 22
Stock Symbol: DLJ (NYSE)
CEO: Joe L. Roby

KEY COMPETITORS

- Credit Suisse First Boston
- Merrill Lynch
- Morgan Stanley Dean Witter
- Goldman Sachs
- J.P. Morgan
- Salomon Smith Barney

THE BUZZ

What MBAs are saying about DLJ

- "Best people working 110 hours a week"
- "High powered, stressful, collegial"
- "Sweatshop, big bonuses"
- "Flash in the pan"

Donaldson, Lufkin & Jenrette

UPPERS

- Early responsibility
- Strong presence on West Coast
- Lavish offices
- Extensive exposure to upper management

DOWNERS

- Long work days, even by Wall Street standards
- Demanding workload

EMPLOYMENT CONTACT

Elizabeth Derby
Director of Recruitment, Investment Banking
Donaldson, Lufkin & Jenrette
277 Park Avenue
New York, NY 10172
(212) 892-3000
Fax: (212) 892-7272

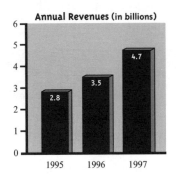

Annual Revenues (in billions)

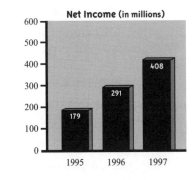

Net Income (in millions)

Employees

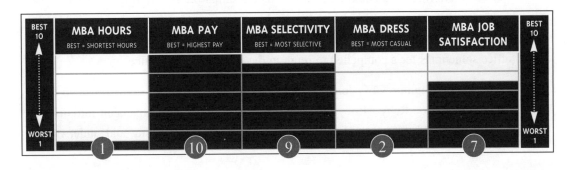

	BEST 10	MBA HOURS BEST = SHORTEST HOURS	MBA PAY BEST = HIGHEST PAY	MBA SELECTIVITY BEST = MOST SELECTIVE	MBA DRESS BEST = MOST CASUAL	MBA JOB SATISFACTION	BEST 10
	WORST 1	1	10	9	2	7	WORST 1

MBA Job Seekers: Receive free e-mailed job postings matching
your interests & qualifications! Register at www.VaultReports.com

VAULT REPORTS™
www.vaultreports.com

131

THE SCOOP

Founded in 1959 by three Harvard MBAs, Donaldson, Lufkin & Jenrette (DLJ) has grown rapidly to become one of Wall Street's most influential investment banks. When it was founded, the new firm established its reputation on Wall Street as a research firm. In 1970, DLJ created a media sensation by becoming the first New York Stock Exchange firm to go public. DLJ entered quickly into the hostile takeover market of the 1980s, advising legendary corporate raider T. Boone Pickens on some of his more audacious forays.

DLJ probably won't be offended if you call it junky – the firm has profited enormously from underwriting junk bonds (high-yield debt) at a time when other banks thought the category was dead for good. In fact, when the kingdom of junk bond czar Michael Milken, Drexel Burnham Lambert, collapsed in 1991, DLJ zoomed in and scooped up its best and the brightest employees, unlike other firms, who shied away from even the hint of scandal. Today, DLJ is the perennial leader in junk bond underwriting. DLJ showed its long-term savvy again in 1995 – while other banks cringed at the onset of the peso crisis, DLJ recognized the future potential of the region remained unchained and hired away several of Bankers Trust's Latin American analysts.

Majority-owned by the Equitable insurance company, DLJ provides a full range of investment banking services, including stock and debt offerings, equity and fixed income research, and sales and trading. In addition, the firm has an immensely successful merchant banking operation, through which the firm invests its own money in venture capital, leveraged buyouts, and other deals. DLJ tends to target small to medium-sized banks to pump up its growth. Its Los Angeles branch office commands enormous respect through the West Coast as a leader in high-yield debt offerings and entertainment and media initial public offerings. DLJ has also developed especially strong franchises in Asia and Latin America. DLJ has been aided by the high degree of autonomy the firm grants to its branches and departments – though the New York office sometimes feels compelled to reign in the risk-taking LA office.

In February 1998, longtime CEO John Chalsty stepped down to turn the firm over to then-president and COO Joe Roby. Roby has pursued several immediate expansion initiatives – opening a London office to specialize in junk bonds, as well as trading and underwriting

European securities. The firm also planned to more than double its I-banking operations in London. The firm also has been looking to boost its performance in investment-grade bond underwriting, hiring away several senior-level bankers focused on the "non-junk" bonds in the summer of 1998.

GETTING HIRED

MBAs join Donaldson, Lufkin & Jenrette as associates, usually in one of the following groups: Investment Banking, Institutional Equity Research, Institutional Equity Sales, Investment Services Group, or Taxable Fixed Income. In New York, DLJ's MBA recruits may start work either as generalists or specialists. In regional offices, hires may remain generalists for their entire career, although some locations have an office-wide focus. Houston, for example, focuses on the energy markets, while Menlo Park focuses on technology issues. The firm's New York office conducts the entire firm's recruiting. DLJ looks for candidates who can demonstrate "initiative" and "creativity" and who will fit in with DLJ's "entrepreneurial" culture. The firm conducts three, or sometimes four, rounds of interviews in a highly competitive recruiting process. Both of the first two rounds involve two-on-one interviews. (The second round is usually held at a hotel near the business school.) The third round is a "super day" held at the firm's headquarters. Expect five to six hours during this round, including a lunch with all of the candidates (the firm brings in between five and eight per day) and interviewers.

The firm also ofers summer associate positions in investment banking for business school students. The process for summer hires is condensed to two rounds. The firm reports that more than 85 percent of the firm's summer associates receive full-time offers.

MBA Job Seekers: Receive free e-mailed job postings matching your interests & qualifications! Register at www.VaultReports.com

VAULT REPORTS™
www.vaultreports.com

133

OUR SURVEY SAYS

DLJ has a "fiercely entrepreneurial" culture that is "individualistic and exciting," employees say. One insider suggests that "to understand DLJ's culture, think of DLJ and Goldman as being the two opposite poles of the world of investment banking. Goldman is solidly conservative, and extremely team-oriented. DLJ is daring and individualistic." An associate in the New York office comments that because of DLJ's aggressive attitude "people are better rewarded here for their performance than in other banks. DLJ is more of a meritocracy than other firms. If you work hard, you move through the whole spectrum of jobs really rapidly. Everything that goes on is really based on performance. So there's nothing in the way of people getting moved up more quickly or getting higher compensation if they're doing something good. DLJ keeps the politics away." Investment banking employees praise the company for being "bold enough" to permit them to invest their own money in company transactions – "something that Goldman would never agree to do." Says another insider: "The environment is collegial, aggressive and hard-working."

Despite this reputed gung-ho culture, DLJ now wears the honor of being named one of the top 100 best places to work by *Working Mother Magazine,* and offers flex-time, job sharing, a unisex three-month parental leave policy, and other family-friendly measures. DLJ states that 19 percent of its vice-presidents are women and seven percent of senior executives are female. "DLJ is more of a meritocracy than other firms," says one insider. "If you work hard, you move through the spectrum of jobs really rapidly… there's nothing in the way of people getting moved up more quickly or getting higher compensation if they're doing something good."

It's a good thing your co-workers will be nice and fair, because you'll be spending a lot of time with them. DLJ's hours "may be worse than at other investment firms": Analysts "easily work 90 or 100 hours every week," with associates putting in "80 or 90-hour weeks." Even one vice president says that while "the longer you stay, the less you work," it's still "a lot. I work 70 or 80 hours a week – at least 8 a.m. to 8 p.m. every day." Still, say employees, "people here are happier here than elsewhere," since the "sink or swim environment" leads "those who don't like the work to get out early – which is better for them and the firm." Putting in those hours and contending with the tough environment also brings pay that's "a little better" than other investment banks, and unusual benefits – like the opportunity to invest your own money in DLJ deals. Dress at DLJ is formal except for "casual Fridays in the summer in some offices." The firm's NY headquarters also has a subsidized cafeteria. The cafeteria is closed for dinner, but employees can order food – there's a $25 limit in I-banking. There's also "free flowing Starbucks coffee in investment banking."

To order a 50- to 70-page Vault Reports Employer Profile on Donaldson, Lufkin & Jenrette call 1-888-JOB-VAULT or visit www.VaultReports.com

The full Employer Profile includes detailed information on DLJ's departments, recent developments and transactions, hiring and interview process, plus what employees really think about culture, pay, work hours and more.

MBA Job Seekers: Receive free e-mailed job postings matching your interests & qualifications! Register at www.VaultReports.com

VAULT REPORTS™

135

www.vaultreports.com

WALL STREET HOURS: IT'S MIDNIGHT ALREADY?

Everyone knows that investment banking hours are long, but Vault Reports brings you the inside scoop on what the hours are really like on Wall Street, straight from the analysts and associates who work there.

Goldman Sachs asks its interviewees how they plan to cope with "working 90 hours a week, for three years or more." That's a fair question to ask yourself if you're interested in investment banking. At virtually all I-banking firms, excruciatingly long workweeks are the norm. "If you are hired for finance, expect no other life than work for the first four or five years," warns one associate. Typically, new hires in investment banking can safely expect "upwards of 80 hours a week, not including weekends," say insiders. Hours are "unpredictable," and you should be prepared to "give up your weekend plans and work 100 hours a week at a moment's notice." Project deadlines can sometimes mean back-to-back all-nighters: "Sometimes I don't have enough time to take lunch or even go to the bathroom," complains one analyst. Although investment bankers generally say that "there's no face time – if you're done with your work, you can leave at 6 or 7," they admit: "that rarely happens." Some Wall Street insiders say that the work "just gets to be too much at times," and "you come close to cracking."

Can you be a player in finance without those back-breaking hours? You're not without recourse. Bankers concur that non-hotspots like Chicago and Los Angeles are "more laid back" (with DLJ's L.A. office a notable exception!). And those in sales and trading will find their workweeks more modest and predictable. Generally, salesmen and traders work from "60 to 80 hours a week." Traders say work on weekends is "rare." A career with a smaller investment bank is another option. At one smaller investment house, bankers say they work only "70 to 80 hours a week, with one weekend day." "It's because we work smarter," claims one associate at a smaller bank. "At a larger firm, you can spend 30 percent of your time reading and filling out documents." And if you hang in there, insiders say your hours should subside somewhat. At one Wall Street investment bank, "analysts work 90 to 100 hours a week, associates work 80 to 90 hours, but vice presidents work around 70 hours a week." "Vice presidents just drop in a few hours on Saturday mornings, tell the analysts and associates what to do, then leave," say Wall Street insiders. But careerists beware – "what you gain in an additional hour or two a week of free time, you lose in all the additional pressure on you as you climb the ladder."

VAULT REPORTS™

www.vaultreports.com

For more information on careers in Investment banking, including actual finance interview questions, read the Vault Reports Guide to Investment BankingFirms.

MBA Job Seekers: Receive free e-mailed job postings matching your interests & qualifications! Register at www.VaultReports.com

VAULT REPORTS™

137

www.vaultreports.com

Cisco Systems

High Tech

170 W. Tasman Drive
San Jose, CA 95134-1706
(408) 526-4000
Fax: (800) 818-9201
www.cisco.com

LOCATIONS

San Jose, CA (HQ)
Chelmsford, MA
Irvine, CA
Research Triangle Park, NC
Santa Cruz, CA
Additional sales locations nationwide
and abroad

DEPARTMENTS

Customer Engineering
Finance and Administration
Human Resources
Manufacturing
Marketing
Sales
Software & Hardware Engineering

THE STATS

Annual Revenues: $8.4 billion (1998)
No. of Employees: 11,000 (worldwide)
No. of Offices: 5 (U.S.)
Stock Symbol: CSCO (Nasdaq)
CEO: John T. Chambers
Year Founded: 1984

KEY COMPETITORS

- 3Com
- Cabletron
- Lucent Technologies
- Nortel Networks

THE BUZZ

What MBAs are saying
about Cisco Systems

- "High growth, exciting industry"
- "Innovative, cool"
- "Killer company, getting too big"
- "Well positioned"

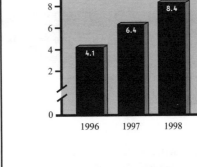

UPPERS

- Widely renowned job training
- Beautiful corporate offices
- Free T-shirts
- All-u-can-eat popcorn

DOWNERS

- Low pay relative to industry
- Competing for cubicles

EMPLOYMENT CONTACT

Cisco Systems
P.O. Box 640730
San Jose, CA 95164
Fax: (800) 818-9201
jobs@cisco.com

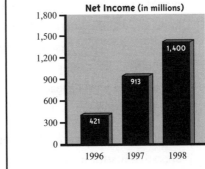

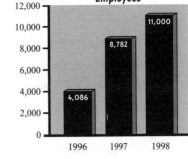

	BEST 10	MBA HOURS BEST = SHORTEST HOURS	MBA PAY BEST = HIGHEST PAY	MBA SELECTIVITY BEST = MOST SELECTIVE	MBA DRESS BEST = MOST CASUAL	MBA JOB SATISFACTION	BEST 10
	WORST 1	3	5	8	8	9	WORST 1

MBA Job Seekers: Receive free e-mailed job postings matching
your interests & qualifications! Register at www.VaultReports.com

VAULT REPORTS™

www.vaultreports.com

139

THE SCOOP

Some call Cisco Systems the third leg in the "triopoly" that also includes Microsoft and Intel. Optimistic employees already have coined a term for the synergy – "Wintelco." While Microsoft writes the software and Intel makes the powerful chips that run PCs, Cisco manufactures the routing systems and switches that help computers talk to each other via networks and the Internet. Founded in 1984 by Stanford University scientists Leonard Bosack and Sandra Lerner, Cisco has built its fortunes upon the surging demand for reliable network technology. The company sold its first router in 1986, and saw its market explode. Cisco is currently the world's leading supplier of networking products, including multiprotocol routers, bridges, workgroup systems, ethernet switches, and network management software.

Cisco's Internetworking Operating System (IOS) allows computers running from different operating platforms to work together seamlessly. The Internet explosion has translated into a booming business for Cisco, which makes more than 80 percent of the routers that serve as the Internet's backbone, as well as much of the technology that connects individual networks to the World Wide Web – routers, LAN and WAN switches, dial and other access modes, SNA-LAN integration, web site management tools, and network management software.

Cisco is prone to acquiring companies; technology expertise acquired through such acquisitions includes network management, digital subscriber line (DSL), and voice/data/video integration. Cisco Systems expects such acquisitions to play "an ongoing role in... leadership strategy." Also playing an important role: partnerships with other companies. Cisco is leery of the "go-it-alone" strategy, and has formed partnerships with Microsoft, Intel, Hewlett-Packard, GTE, Alcatel, and Dell.

Now, Cisco wants to promote its own strong brand identity, or as the company says in its own literature: "A compelling Corporate Identity that expresses our personality and leadership position in the marketplace is important to Cisco. As our growth continues, the necessity to establish a consistent global presence in this expanding industry has become even more apparent. The Cisco brand is equal in value to our products and services. It cannot be compromised. And it must be enhanced."

While a mega-merger is unlikely, partnerships appeal to Cisco. In 1998, the data networking company initiated talks with telecommunications giants Lucent Technologies and Northern Telecom (now called Nortel), but was firmly rebuffed. Both companies have plans to enter Cisco's turf and develop products that would compete directly against Cisco's. Lucent echoed its refusal a few months later, when it leveled a patent infringement lawsuit against Cisco, alleging a violation of eight data networking patents; Nortel bought Cisco competitor Bay Networks for $7.6 billion. Cisco remains the market leader, however; the firm hit $100 billion in market capitalization in July 1998.

GETTING HIRED

Cisco hires MBAs into a business 10-week development internship which allows business school students to combine financial analysis and market research. The interns end their summer by preparing a summary business plan for strategy in a particular industry or area. Marketing, finance, and business development positions available are posted at the company's web site at www.cisco.com. The company has a strong name and presence at top business schools; a list of visits for information sessions and interviewing is also posted at the company's web site.

OUR SURVEY SAYS

Cisco employees work in a "high energy" environment that stresses "productivity above all else." Recent hires praise the "incredible" training that they receive and relish the chance to work for a company where "intelligence, learning aptitude, and resourcefulness are more highly prized than the ability to kiss butt." *Wired* said of Cisco employees: "Nobody has this

MBA Job Seekers: Receive free e-mailed job postings matching
your interests & qualifications! Register at www.VaultReports.com

VAULT REPORTS™

141

www.vaultreports.com

much fun going to work. All [Cisco employees] do is smile, smile, smile." An insider adds: "If you are remotely entrepreneurial, you will work crazy hours because you want to, not because you have to." Happily, though, "there is 'extra-duty' pay for salaried employees working weekends and holidays."

Any complaints? The pay is "not up to snuff," complain some employees. One insider says: "Considering the cost of living in [San Jose], it isn't great – maybe better than many, but worse than many... the pay scales definitely need adjustment to reflect the extremely high cost of living, as well as the fact that most people in my department are recent college grads with big loans." However, as a bonus, "other companies will pay lots more – up to 60 percent more – to hire us away." Some employees are none too thrilled about Cisco's "non-territorial offices," the company's policy of not having assigned desks for most employees (except support staff, which need access to their files, and managers, with their sneaky managerial secrets) – all cubicles are first-come, first-served basis. "There can be some competition for the best spots," says one insider. "It's like always being on line for a movie, and then the doors open." Summing up the bright side of working at Cisco, one employee says "I've learned more in eight months here than in the years I spent in college. Eventually, I'll be able to take this knowledge somewhere where I don't have to worry about making the rent every month."

To order a 10- to 20-page Vault Reports Employer Profile on Cisco Systems call 1-888-JOB-VAULT or visit www.VaultReports.com

The full Employer Profile includes detailed information on Cisco's departments, recent developments and transactions, hiring and interview process, plus what employees really think about culture, pay, work hours and more.

Best MBA Employers
for Casual Dress

FIRM	PAY (on a 1-10 scale)
Dell Computer	9
Nortel Networks	9
Silicon Graphics, Inc.	9
Levi Strauss	8
Microsoft	8
Netscape Communications	8
Nike	8
Sun Microsystems	8
3Com	7
AT&T	7
Enron	7
Ford Motor	7
Monitor Company	7
Motorola	7
Oracle	7

Source: Vault Reports MBA Survey 1998

GE Capital

Financial Services

60 Long Ridge Road
Stamford, CT 06927
(203) 357-4000
www.ge.com/gecc18.htm

LOCATIONS

Stamford, CT (HQ)
Other offices across the nation and worldwide

DEPARTMENTS

Accounting
Customer Service
Finance
Information Management
Programming
Sales
Technical Support

THE STATS

Annual Revenues: $33.4 billion (1997)
No. of Employees: 65,000 (worldwide)
No. of Businesses: 27
Subsidiary of General Electric
CEO: Gary C. Wendt

KEY COMPETITORS

- Capital One
- Citigroup
- Ford Motor Credit
- Household International
- Leasing Solutions
- Trinity Industries

THE BUZZ

What MBAs are saying
about GE Capital

- "Aggressive, street-smart, practical"
- "Into themselves, yet great company"
- "Develop their people"
- "Good firm, best management, but big"

UPPERS

- Excellent training
- Good stock purchase plan
- Special "exotic" trips
- Some entrepreneurial divisions

DOWNERS

- Conservative corporate culture
- Slow-moving bureaucracy

EMPLOYMENT CONTACT

Human Resources
GE Capital
201 High Ridge Road
Stamford, CT 06927

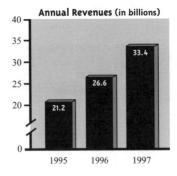

Annual Revenues (in billions)

1995: 21.2
1996: 26.6
1997: 33.4

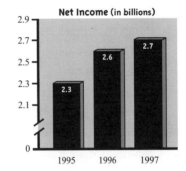

Net Income (in billions)

1995: 2.3
1996: 2.6
1997: 2.7

Employees

1995: 37,000
1996: 49,400
1997: 65,000

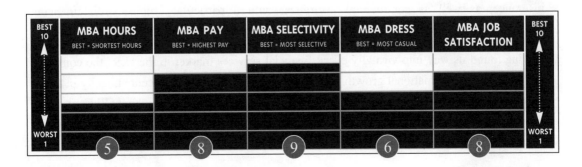

	MBA HOURS BEST = SHORTEST HOURS	MBA PAY BEST = HIGHEST PAY	MBA SELECTIVITY BEST = MOST SELECTIVE	MBA DRESS BEST = MOST CASUAL	MBA JOB SATISFACTION
	5	8	9	6	8

BEST 10 / WORST 1

MBA Job Seekers: Receive free e-mailed job postings matching your interests & qualifications! Register at www.VaultReports.com

VAULT REPORTS™

www.vaultreports.com

145

THE SCOOP

GE illuminates the world, and owns a lot of it too. Just one of the mega-corporation's many divisions, GE Capital was started in 1933 to help broke consumers buy refrigerators and other General Electric consumer products. The company grew steadily, financing everything from trucks to receivable inventory, to private credit cards and airplanes, and using its parent company's great credit to borrow more and grow faster. Since 1993, when it surpassed GMAC, GE Capital has been the largest finance arm of a major corporation. Comprised of 28 separate businesses, the company's made a tidy $3.3 billion in 1997 for its parent – a full 40 percent of GE's income. In 1997, GE Capital posted a mind-boggling 23rd consecutive increase in profit. In fact, GE Capital head Gary Wendt's shrewd moves are credited as the driving force behind its big-name parent company's recent success. Innovative risk controls, top-notch market intelligence, and a hefty appetite for growth that has led many to call GE Capital a "gorilla with a gold card," make up Wendt's finance arsenal.

The company provides a wide range of financial services to consumers, small business, and corporations. Each of the 28 businesses operates independently, and is responsible for achieving its own goals. The company's Consumer Financial Services, for example, offers MasterCard and Visa credit cards under the GE Rewards and Exxon brands. The Equity Capital Group is a venture capital fund that invests in young, growing companies seeking to raise capital. The Structured Finance Group arranges long-term equity and debt financing for major projects such as a new Chinese power plant and the privatization of Hungary's telecommunications and airport operations. While the company has emphasized the expansion of its venture capital and investments in recent years, its historic strength has been in insurance. GE Capital Insurance services includes a wholesale insurance network for individual life insurance, as well as commercial insurance, with a particular emphasis on financial institutions. Employers Reinsurance provides insurance services to small business.

Having found its way into virtually every financial services market in the U.S., the company is now targeting international growth. GE Capital hopes to grow 40 percent annually in terms of revenue and assets in Asia for the next several years. And in Europe, where GE Capital has only had a presence for a dozen years, the financial services arm already has topped $53 billion in assets; the company's profit has grown by a factor of five since 1994.

GETTING HIRED

GE Capital provides a smorgasbord of positions for MBAs – from financial analysis to venture capital to strategic planning. The company has a strong summer associate program for MBAs, with many positions available both in Connecticut and worldwide. Applicants can visit the GE Capital Web site at www.ge.com/gecc18.htm, to obtain the address of the specific company for which they want to work. Most (but not all) of the more than 25 businesses that make up GE Capital have their headquarters in Connecticut. One insider reports, "Depending upon what geographical area you're interested in, the interviewing process varies."

MBA candidates going through on-campus recruiting can expect several rounds and some technical finance questions, insiders report. Some recent hires report having panel interviews, with "four to five people interviewing you at once." Still, one GE Capital contact insists that "I don't consider the interview process grueling. However, GE can pretty much pick from the cream of the crop so you've got to stand out from the crowd." Insiders advise that qualities that help candidates stick out from the crowd at GE Capital include a global focus and the ability to develop and coach others.

OUR SURVEY SAYS

Because of its many offices and variegated businesses, GE Capital insiders stress that pinning down the company culture is difficult. For example, one consultant with GE Capital notes, "My office allows jeans and casual dresses, but some offices insist on business casual, and at others, like the corporate headquarters in Stamford, Connecticut, it is strictly formal." In general, though, the company's headquarters is described as much more formal and conservative than other offices. At headquarters, the business dress code is "strictly enforced and business casual dress is observed only on Fridays and in the summer months." Several contacts at the Stamford offices complain of "stifling bureaucracy." Says one: "It's very

MBA Job Seekers: Receive free e-mailed job postings matching your interests & qualifications! Register at www.VaultReports.com

VAULT REPORTS™

147

www.vaultreports.com

conservative and family-oriented." Says another: "It's a big company so there's lots of bureaucracy." And an MBA who spent a summer internship at GE Capital's headquarters reports: "GE Capital has a very strong corporate culture that may be difficult for those who have worked in smaller, more entrepreneurial environments."

However, not everybody at headquarters agrees. "The culture is stereotypical GE – no nonsense – but less bureaucratic than expected," reports one venture capital associate. Says another: "The culture is smart, friendly and fun." Several contacts note that at least GE Capital's employees, if not its corporate structure, are young and energetic. "It's a very young and social place – but you definitely know when you have to get your work done," one insider says. Says another: "The people are young, extremely bright, and highly motivated." And contacts in farther-flung offices describe a completely different GE Capital. Says one MBA in Europe: "It's very non-hierarchical, open and fluid."

Whatever their feelings about GE Capital's culture, employees agree that the company's name can light up a resume. "In its favor, GE Capital has enormous resources at its disposal and a very well respected name in the business community." Insiders also rave about the company's emphasis on training. The company sponsors "lots of internal training" and "they send new employees – entry-level management – to tons of training classes." For those thinking about working while studying toward an MBA, GE Capital provides up to $10,000 a year in tuition reimbursement. And while some insiders complain that the company is skimpy on the perks, the company provides annual exotic trips to "top performers." In 1998, the trip was a "safari in Africa." Through the company's 401(k) program, employees can buy GE stock with pretax compensation, and the company will match up to 3.5 percent of a salary with additional shares.

Most agree that women and minorities are "highly regarded" in every business of GE Capital, with "a lot of women and minorities in senior positions." One notes, "We have vast cultural diversity, we have a strict policy of non discriminatory principles, and women and minorities are encouraged by senior management to apply for opportunities as they come." Another common thread – Jack Welch's vision of "Speed, Simplicity and Self Confidence," values which one insider says "all of the 26+ businesses within GE Capital try to incorporate." That contact reports, "GE is not IBM, but it is also not a start-up, hang-loose Netscape-type either. Change is the rule around here – every business knows, in Jack Welch's own words, if your business is not No. 1 or No. 2 in its market, you won't be around for long."

To order a 10- to 20-page Vault Reports Employer Profile on GE Capital call 1-888-JOB-VAULT or visit www.VaultReports.com

The full Employer Profile includes detailed information on GE Capital's departments, recent developments and transactions, hiring and interview process, plus what employees really think about culture, pay, work hours and more.

MBA Job Seekers: Receive free e-mailed job postings matching your interests & qualifications! Register at www.VaultReports.com

VAULT REPORTS™
www.vaultreports.com

149

Coca-Cola

RANKING
15

Consumer Products

P.O. Drawer 1734
Atlanta, GA 30301
Attn: USA 635
(404) 676-2121
Fax: (404) 515-7226
www.cocacola.com

LOCATIONS

Atlanta, GA (HQ)
Houston, TX (HQ of the Minute Maid
Company)
Facilities in all 50 states and worldwide

DEPARTMENTS

Advertising
Art
Consumer Promotions
Consumer Research
Field Sales
Finance
Media
Packaging
Public Relations
Technical/Research & Development

THE STATS

Annual Revenues: $18.9 billion (1997)
No. of Employees: 29,00
Stock Symbol: KO (NYSE)
CEO: M. Douglas Ivester

KEY COMPETITORS

- Cadbury Schweppes
- Ocean Spray
- PepsiCo
- Seagram
- Triarc

THE BUZZ
What MBAs are saying
about Coca-Cola

- "Sexiest brand"
- "Ubiquitous"
- "Formal, stiff"
- "Marketing geniuses"

UPPERS

* All the Coke you can drink
* Kick-ass campus
* Unparalleled prestige
* Stock options for a historically lucrative company

DOWNERS

* Conservative atmosphere
* Can be difficult to advance
* Formal dress code
* Highly political company
* Pepsi products forbidden

EMPLOYMENT CONTACT

The Coca-Cola Company
P.O. Drawer 1734
Atlanta, GA 30301
Fax: (404) 515-8221

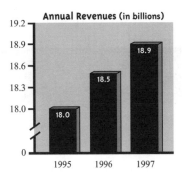

Annual Revenues (in billions)

Year	Revenue
1995	18.0
1996	18.5
1997	18.9

Net Income (in billions)

Year	Net Income
1995	3.0
1996	3.5
1997	4.1

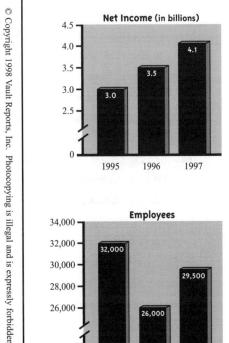

Employees

Year	Employees
1995	32,000
1996	26,000
1997	29,500

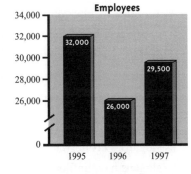
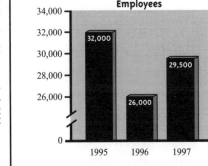

	MBA HOURS	MBA PAY	MBA SELECTIVITY	MBA DRESS	MBA JOB SATISFACTION	
	BEST = SHORTEST HOURS	BEST = HIGHEST PAY	BEST = MOST SELECTIVE	BEST = MOST CASUAL		
	6	3	9	1	7	

BEST 10 — WORST 1

MBA Job Seekers: Receive free e-mailed job postings matching your interests & qualifications! Register at www.VaultReports.com

VAULT REPORTS™
www.vaultreports.com

151

THE SCOOP

The Real Thing was invented by Atlanta pharmacist John S. Pemberton in 1886 in the basement of his house, its name devised by a bookkeeper and based on two of the main ingredients in the top-secret recipe: coca leaves and kola nuts. Four years later, pharmacist Asa Candler had taken over operations, and the soda was available nationwide by 1895. In 1899, the bottling rights were sold for $1 to Benjamin Thomas and John Whitehead, who introduced Coke in the C. J. Root Glass Company's shapely green bottle 17 years later. The company bought Minute Maid in 1960 and the following year introduced Sprite, today the world's best-selling lemon-lime soda. Coca-Cola floundered in the cola wars of the 1980s against its feisty upstart, Pepsi, prompting the launch of the infamous "New Coke." After that fiasco, Coca-Cola spun off its non-core assets – such as Columbia Pictures – and reaffirmed its status as the leader of the global soft drink market. The company has the most valuable brand name in the world (Coke) estimated to be worth $40 billion. Although the company controls a 44 percent domestic share, Coke is truly "it" overseas: 80 percent of its profit comes from outside North America. Coke controls a 48 percent (and growing) share of the world's soft drink market; rival Pepsi boasts only 13 percent. Since the death of longtime CEO Robert Goizueta in late 1997, Coca-Cola faces new leadership and a new era. and is shooting for a 50 percent domestic share by 2001. That goal is certainly within reach: the company already controls 44 percent of the domestic market.

Coke has introduced a waiting world to a litany of successful marketing campaigns and slogans. From "The Pause that Refreshes" (1929) to "It's the Real Thing" (1941), Coke's slogans have infiltrated the language, while infectious commercials – ranging from the Mean Joe Greene commercial to "I'd like to teach the world to sing" – have infused the popular consciousness. They'd better – Coke has an advertising budget of more than $1 billion a year. Along with its successful conventional advertising campaigns, the company is well known for its product-pushing through major sports and entertainment events: Coke has deals with the NFL, NASCAR and World Cup Soccer. The company has also built a longtime relationship with the Olympic Games – first promoting its drinks in the 1926 Games. (In 1996, however, many sports fans felt Coke had gone overboard with its overwhelming advertising presence at the 1996 Atlanta Games.)

Coke has been trying to move beyond its older core customer base by reaching out to younger drinkers with hip and more alternative drinks, such as Fruitopia. In 1997, the company introduced Surge, a hypercaffinated rival to Pepsi's growth brand Mountain Dew. In the meantime, the company has been busy fending off an anti-trust lawsuit brought by Pepsi. which accuses Coke of unfair business practices. Pepsi has good reason to be worried. Wendy's just recently signed an exclusive deal with Coke to sell the beverage at its 1400 restaurants. French regulators, however, in 1998 squashed Coke's pending acquisition of Orangina, fearing the beverage giant would become completely dominant in France.

GETTING HIRED

Coca-Cola is a hard (kola) nut to crack. For MBAs interested in marketing, Coke has in the past offered a limited number of summer internship programs: a Brand intern program, a Marketing Program Development program (which involves implementing Brand programs), a market research program, and positions with Presence Marketing. For each of the programs, Coke hires from "core" business schools. Applicants who forward their resumes by fax should send them to the attention of "RESUMIX" at 404-515-8221. A very few (about two each year) internships have been offered in finance, but these do not typically lead to full-time positions.

Unlike some other consumer goods companies, Coke is not led by any one particular department. Insiders say there "there is no set career path." MBAs with their eyes on general management will eventually need to get experience in finance, operations and marketing. There is something of a tradition at Coke of higher-ups "scouting" the young talent and calling them up into higher positions, insiders say, and one can move up without actively seeking advancement. Usually, however, moving up involves "finding yourself a mentor to ask questions and advice." "You have to proactively manage your career," says one insider, which "means making the right contacts within the company. Another contact states: "If you have a particular interest, it is up to you to let people know, to get your name in the game."

MBA Job Seekers: Receive free e-mailed job postings matching your interests & qualifications! Register at www.VaultReports.com

VAULT REPORTS™
www.vaultreports.com

153

Insiders tell Vault Reports that the most important thing for prospective employees to do during interviews is express that they strongly wish to work for the company. "We want to know for certain why the individual is jazzed about our company and industry." Coke is looking for employees that fit a certain mold: "The biggest thing is they're looking for long-term thinkers," says one insider. "They don't want cowboys. They want conservative people who are into adding shareholder value."

OUR SURVEY SAYS

At The Coca-Cola Company, employees are fervently attached to their employer. "Everyone is very loyal to the company," one former employee says. "They are very proud of all of the accomplishments achieved there." "It is a wonderful company," says another insider, a 15-year Coke veteran. "There is a certain amount of pride many of us take knowing that we have helped get us to this point." Indeed, Coke is the very lifeblood of the company, and its employees shun the sainted liquid at their peril: "People here are expected to drink Coke," one contact says simply.

But it's not just a matter of red-and-white pom-poms and megaphones at Coke. The "intense" loyalty meshes with what is invariably described as a "conservative" atmosphere. "Coke has a very corporate, conservative culture," says one insider. "People are very nice here, but it's definitely a reserved atmosphere." "The company's culture is aggressive but can seem slow if you don't see the big picture – steering a tanker is not like steering a 20-foot sailboat," reports one insider. Befitting its conservative atmosphere, Coke has a business formal dress code: "People are expected to wear suits or business attire every day," says an employee at corporate headquarters. "Most men wear dark suits, women are expected to wear skirt suits," says another. As one Coke insider sums up: "The dress code here is business attire. No casual days, as we are a professional organization that must always look that way. Casual day is not in the corporate dictionary." This mix of "rah-rah" cheerleading and "stuffy reserve" leads to somewhat cryptic comments from insiders like: "Coke people tend to be professional in dress and nature, and tend toward the conservative in behavior. This is not to say enthusiasm is not appreciated. In many cases, it is required."

Moreover, many insiders say that advancement at Coke, more so than other large companies, depends a lot on who you know. "Coke is a very political place," says one former employee. "You will do well if you know the right people and make the right contacts and 'suck up' to the right people. One of the reasons I am not there now is that I would not suck up to certain people." A Coke business development insider sums up: "This is a club. It is an exclusive club. And you've got to know somebody not only to get in, but to move up."

Insiders say compensation at Big Red is good, but not stellar. However, they describe the benefits as "the best around." These perks begin with Coke's Atlanta headquarters. "The complex basically has all you need right here," says one insider. "There's a cafeteria, a gift shop, a travel agency, and a medical services office all in the complex. People don't tend to leave to go out to lunch, because the cafeteria here is so big and inexpensive." The headquarters of Coca-Cola, located in downtown Atlanta, also houses a credit union office, a bank, a health club, a dry cleaning service, a gift shop, and its very own branch of the U.S. Post Office. Of the attractions at headquarters, the cafeteria seems to hold a special place in employees' hearts. "The cafeteria is the best I have ever eaten at, food and prices," says another insider. "Since drinks are free, you can eat lunch there every day under $3.00. And for that you get an entrée, two vegetables, and dessert."

Besides the benefits of the corporate campus, same employees have tuition reimbursement, a stock-purchase plan, and enjoy a 401(k) plan that has made many a Coke employee's retirement a golden one. There are also "days off at Six Flags Atlanta" (employees get off at 3 in the afternoon one day each September for a free outing at the amusement park), "Thanksgiving Dinner," and "available concert tickets in the Coca-Cola section – the front – at almost any major venue in the country" (employees can buy tickets at the company's campus). And of course, there is the "all-you-can-drink" aspect of working at Coke. The pause that refreshes is reportedly distributed through coolers, fountains, and vending machines rigged so all you have to do is push the button and the Coke comes out. "You never need pay for a soft drink again between 9 a.m. and 5 p.m," says one employee. (In fact, refreshments are available 24 hours a day at Coke's headquarters.) "You can OD on the free Cokes, Sprites, and Frescas." Perhaps the best perk at Coke are the stock options. Says one employee: "In the

MBA Job Seekers: Receive free e-mailed job postings matching your interests & qualifications! Register at www.VaultReports.com

VAULT REPORTS™

www.vaultreports.com

155

long run, total compensation is probably higher than it is elsewhere, but you need to be patient – options can have long vesting periods, and bonus only comes in at a given threshold that entry-level employees are unlikely to obtain to very soon." One finance MBA is less reserved: "They start out small and they fool you. I think people fail to realize how potentially lucrative this place is. By the time you're 55, you're sitting on $10 million, and it's growing exponentially. There are secretaries floating around here who are millionaires."

Workdays vary from department to department but are generally on the long side, although not nearly as long as consulting or investment banking hours. "People tend to arrive early and work late," says one insider at corporate headquarters. "Hours can vary from a 40-hour work week to a 60 or 70-hour week, which many of us seem to be working on a regular basis," another says. "If you are on salary, you work until the job is done, however long that takes." However, one recent MBA hire tells Vault Reports: "People here are not so unreasonable as to not understand the need for a life. I never work weekends."

If employees in Atlanta are to be believed, corporate headquarters is teaching the world to sing in perfect harmony. "One of the things I especially liked was the many languages you could hear spoken in the cafeteria and hallways of the corporate offices. It is truly an international company," says one insider. "Coke hires people of all different races, religions, and cultures. It is a very diverse company," says another. Employees tend to be less effusive when discussing the status of women at headquarters. Although no one mentions any special programs or hard-hitting recruiting efforts, female employees tell Vault Reports they are treated "fairly," with "good opportunities for advancement." "There are many women in management," says one former employee.

To order a 50- to 70-page Vault Reports Employer Profile on Coca-Cola call 1-888-JOB-VAULT or visit www.VaultReports.com

The full Employer Profile includes detailed information on Coca-Cola's departments, recent developments and transactions, hiring and interview process, plus what employees really think about culture, pay, work hours and more.

"There are secretaries floating around here who are millionaires."

– *Coke insider*

MBA Job Seekers: Receive free e-mailed job postings matching
your interests & qualifications! Register at www.VaultReports.com

VAULT
REPORTS™

157

www.vaultreports.com

High Tech

3000 Hanover St, MS 20APP
Palo Alto, CA 94304-1181
(415) 852-8473
Fax: (415) 852-8138
www.jobs.hp.com

LOCATIONS

Palo Alto, CA (HQ)

Andover, MA • Atlanta, GA • Boise, ID • Colorado Springs, CO • Corvallis, OR • Lake Stevens, WA • Rohnert Park, CA • Roseville, CA • San Diego, CA • Santa Rosa, CA • Spokane, WA • Vancouver, WA • Wilmington, DE • As well as sales offices around the country and offices worldwide

DEPARTMENTS

Finance
Factory Marketing
Learning Products
Marketing
Information Technology
Procurement
Research & Development

THE STATS

Annual Revenues: $42.9 billion (1997)
No. of Employees: 127,200
Stock Symbol: HWP (NYSE)
CEO: Lew Platt

KEY COMPETITORS

- Compaq
- Dell Computer
- Gateway
- IBM
- Packard Bell
- Sun Microsystems
- Xerox

THE BUZZ
What MBAs are saying
about Hewlett-Packard

- "Techy, friendly environment"
- "Supportive environment, solid firm"
- "Comfortable"
- "Blue-chip, staid"

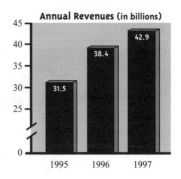

UPPERS

- Generous benefits
- Flexible scheduling options
- "Nice guy" environment

DOWNERS

- Facing increased competition
- Infrequent employee interaction

EMPLOYMENT CONTACT

Hewlett-Packard
Employment Response Center
3000 Hanover Street, MS 20APP
Palo Alto, CA 94304-1181
www.jobs.hp.com
resume@hp.com

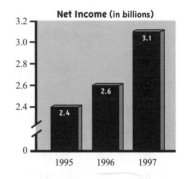

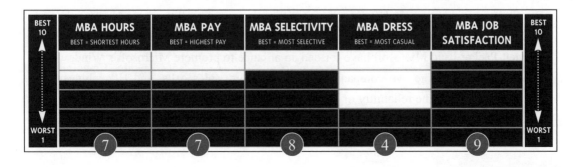

	MBA HOURS	MBA PAY	MBA SELECTIVITY	MBA DRESS	MBA JOB SATISFACTION	
BEST 10	BEST = SHORTEST HOURS	BEST = HIGHEST PAY	BEST = MOST SELECTIVE	BEST = MOST CASUAL		BEST 10
WORST 1	7	7	8	4	9	WORST 1

MBA Job Seekers: Receive free e-mailed job postings matching
your interests & qualifications! Register at www.VaultReports.com

VAULT REPORTS™
www.vaultreports.com

159

THE SCOOP

Founded by a pair of engineers in a garage in 1938 with just over $500 in capital, today Hewlett-Packard is a large and diverse company with broad interests stretching across the technological spectrum. While mainly known now as a computer company, HP still makes products in its older fields such as measurement and testing equipment and medical electronics. Products from these older divisions include everything from stethoscopes to atomic clocks. But the computer industry is clearly the company's bread and butter now, accounting for $35.5 billion of its $42.9 billion in annual revenues. Hewlett-Packard ranks as one of the top five providers of personal computers, servers, printers, and both systems integration and contract programming services. The company's newfound success as a PC producer is probably its most impressive recent achievement. HP has gone from the 11th-largest vendor of PCs in 1993 to the third-largest worldwide, with 5.5 percent of the world market share in 1997. PC sales in 1998 continued to be strong, with HP grabbing 21.8 percent of the domestic market during the first quarter of the year.

Competitive pressures spurred HP's jump into the PC market. Though PCs had never been a big part of Hewlett-Packard's sales, company executives feared that HP would quickly be marginalized without a solid market position. The sad fact is that companies that do not sell personal computers are unlikely to score contracts for integration and support services. IT consulting happens to be a highly profitable area and one in which HP enjoys an exceptional reputation. Although the recent jump into the top three is certainly a good sign for Hewlett-Packard's future in the industry, the picture is not entirely rosy. The company's laptop sales, for example, have been extremely sluggish; HP sells more high-priced servers than laptops annually, even though the market for laptops is much larger overall.

Despite its recent successes, HP executives aren't stopping to smell the roses. Instead they are pushing forward, planning joint ventures with fellow technology titans Microsoft and Intel. Hewlett-Packard and Microsoft have formed an alliance to promote Microsoft's Windows NT operating system. The two companies are making joint sales calls, and HP engineers are working to improve the reliability of Microsoft's system so it meets the rigorous standard for installation in Hewlett-Packard machines. HP and Intel's alliance, though it centers on a tiny chip, is also causing a huge buzz. The companies are collaborating on a new microprocessor called the Merced that will reportedly run 10 times faster than the Pentium. When the Merced is ready – it's projected to be on the market in 2000 – Hewlett Packard's computers will be the first to contain the souped-up microprocessor. The firm hopes HP computers equipped with glitch-free Microsoft operating systems and ultra-speedy Merceds will sell like hotcakes.

The company is also looking to develop Internet software that will enhance electronic commerce. In May 1997, HP introduced "Domain Commerce" for businesses to identify and differentiate Internet users who visit their Web sites. The firm's "OpenPix Image Igniter" will allow Internet users to see the products that retailers and catalog companies place in their electronic showrooms in greater quality and detail. HP is also working with a Canadian bank to create an "electronic bank of the future" where financial transactions and services are performed online.

While Hewlett-Packard is known for reliable hardware, HP's Software & Services Group is perhaps most responsible for the company's sterling reputation and rabid customer loyalty. In professional and support services, HP invariably scores high marks for customer satisfaction in both consulting and technical. As Hewlett-Packard moves into mass-market computer product lines and faces cutthroat competition from the likes of IBM, Compaq, and Dell, the firm must rely on its good name to stand out in this crowded field and attract inexperienced new buyers.

GETTING HIRED

With more than 120,000 employees, Hewlett-Packard is always in need of young, talented people to replenish its ranks. HP recruits at major business schools twice a year, once in the fall and once in the spring. HP also interviews at seven diversity conferences. The majority of MBAs go into either the marketing or finance function. There is also "a small contingent in an IT consulting function" and a few in human resources. MBAs begin at the company as product managers in marketing, or finance analysts in the finance department. Once in the

MBA Job Seekers: Receive free e-mailed job postings matching your interests & qualifications! Register at www.VaultReports.com

VAULT REPORTS™

www.vaultreports.com

161

door, the possibilities are numerous. "HP develops you," says a source. "They are open if you want to move from R&D to marketing or marketing to finance." The company is happy to let employees get acquainted with different areas. Agrees another, "HP is worldwide – that's one of the huge advantages of working for HP. If you play your cards well, you can create your own opportunities and move around the company." Insiders say HP is different from many companies in that it "always promotes managers from within." MBAs should also consider the companies 10-week summer Student Employment and Education Development (SEED) program.

For MBAs, "the [interview] questions are easy to answer and the interviews are fairly casual." Recalls one, "They asked about my background and resume. They asked questions like 'Why HP?' 'Why marketing?' 'Why do you feel you're the best candidate?'" The MBA interview may also involve "some hypotheticals. They are like soft case interviews, very much based on what they're doing. They are not oddball questions like 'How many phone booths are there?'" The company "also typically sends candidates to a non-interview lunch with someone from the team to give the candidate a chance to ask questions in a more relaxed atmosphere."

OUR SURVEY SAYS

All of HP's company literature emphasizes the importance of teamwork at Hewlett-Packard. When you recall that two friends working side-by-side in a garage founded the corporation, it isn't hard to understand why. Potential employees should find out if this is their ideal work environment. Says one engineer, "the key is to find out if you fit into HP's low-key, nice-guy and team-oriented work environment." One employee insists "the key word is informal." With all of the emphasis on teamwork and the "HP Way," one could get the idea that conformity is the rule, but as a longtime manager at the company puts it, "it's a good environment for people with all types of skills and backgrounds."

Expect to make some cash if you score a job at Hewlett-Packard. This Silicon Valley firm is known for compensating its employees out of its huge profits. While the range varies, employees say HP's pay ranks it "among the leaders in the industry."

In terms of workplace environments, you're not going to get the big corner office. No one has an office at Hewlett-Packard. As one employee describes the situation, "even the CEO has a cubicle. He's got a real big one, though." While gopher-holing isn't everyone's idea of a good time (one employee repeatedly mentioned how much "cubes suck"), there is a rationale: "It encourages the open door policy." Obviously, where there is no door, it is difficult to close one. Other employees say the cubicle-heavy offices have a "minimalist, modern feel."

Hewlett-Packard employees have nothing but praise for their co-workers, saying that they "are the best, but not in an arrogant way." Another employee insists, "I don't see office politics at the lower levels that I hear of at other places." Indeed, "behaving in an overtly ambitious manner is not supported." One insider remarks, "I have never seen individual engineers trying to grab the glory." As pleased as HP employees are with the quality and integrity of their co-workers, they say "the office atmosphere deters interaction between them." In fact, at a company where job satisfaction is extremely high, the lack of social contact between workers is one of the biggest complaints.

To order a 50- to 70-page Vault Reports Employer Profile on Hewlett-Packard call 1-888-JOB-VAULT or visit www.VaultReports.com

The full Employer Profile includes detailed information on H-P's departments, recent developments and transactions, hiring and interview process, plus what employees really think about culture, pay, work hours and more.

MBA Job Seekers: Receive free e-mailed job postings matching your interests & qualifications! Register at www.VaultReports.com

VAULT REPORTS™
www.vaultreports.com

163

Procter & Gamble

RANKING 17

Consumer Products

P.O. Box 599, TN-4
Department WWW
Cincinnati, OH 45201-0599
(513) 983-1100
www.pg.com

Procter&Gamble

LOCATIONS

Cincinnati, OH (HQ)
Approx. 50 sales offices and plants in AL •
AZ • CA • CO • FL • GA • IL • IN • IA • KS
• KY • LA • MD • MA • MI • MN • MO • NJ
• NY • NC • OH • PA • SC • TN • TX • WI

DEPARTMENTS

Administration
Brand Management
Customer Services/Logistics-Product Supply
Engineering
Financial/Accounting Management
Market Research
Research & Development
Sales Management

THE STATS

Annual Revenues: $37.2 billion (1997)
No. of Employees: 110,000 (worldwide)
No. of Offices: 52 (U.S.)
Stock Symbol: PG
Stock Exchange: NYSE
CEO: John E. Pepper

KEY COMPETITORS

- Avon
- Body Shop
- Clorox
- Colgate-Palmolive
- Estee Lauder
- Gillette
- Johnson & Johnson
- Kimberly-Clark
- Unilever

THE BUZZ
What MBAs are saying about P&G

- "Extremely anal"
- "Powerful business model"
- "Marketing school"
- "Premier brands, stodgy, stiff"

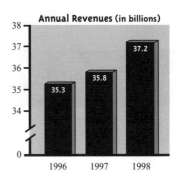

Annual Revenues (in billions)

UPPERS

- Stock purchase plan
- Great pProfit sharing plan
- Extensive training at "P&G College"
- Tuition reimbursement program
- Relocation assistance program

DOWNERS

- Excessive bureaucracy
- Up-or-out policy in Brand Management

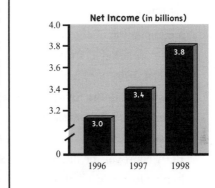

Net Income (in billions)

EMPLOYMENT CONTACT

Recruiting Services Center
Procter & Gamble
P.O. Box 599, TN-4
Department WWW
Cincinnati, OH 45201-0599

Cover letters and resumes can
be e-mailed to careers@pg.com

Employees (in thousands)

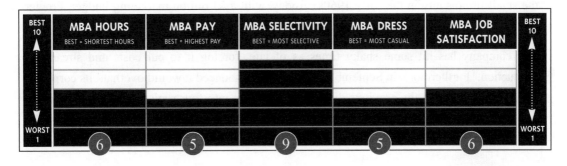

	MBA HOURS	MBA PAY	MBA SELECTIVITY	MBA DRESS	MBA JOB SATISFACTION	
BEST 10 / WORST 1	BEST = SHORTEST HOURS	BEST = HIGHEST PAY	BEST = MOST SELECTIVE	BEST = MOST CASUAL		BEST 10 / WORST 1
	6	5	9	5	6	

MBA Job Seekers: Receive free e-mailed job postings matching
your interests & qualifications! Register at www.VaultReports.com

VAULT REPORTS™
www.vaultreports.com

165

THE SCOOP

Irish immigrants William Procter and James Gamble met when they married sisters. Procter, a candle maker, and Gamble, a soap maker, formed their company with about $3500 a piece in 1837. After growing steadily and reaching $1 million in sales in 1859, the company hit it big with Ivory soap in 1879. The 20th century at Procter & Gamble sounds like a commercial for a compilation of consumer goods' greatest hits. The company's research centers have churned out a remarkable string of successful innovations: Crisco, the first all-vegetable shortening (1911); Tide, the "washing miracle" that was the nation's first synthetic laundry detergent (1946); Crest, the first toothpaste with fluoride clinically proven to fight cavities (1955); and Pampers, the first mass-produced disposable diaper (1961). More recently, the company has introduced Pantene Pro-V (1992), the world's leading shampoo, and in 1996, received U.S. FDA approval for the use of Olestra, a calorie-free fat replacement. In 1998, the company, hoping to create a "fabric refresher" product category, introduced spray cleaner "Fabreze," and "Dryel," a home dry cleaning kit. Procter & Gamble remains the world's largest manufacturer and marketer of household products. The company currently reaches across a spectrum of more than 300 products that it markets in 140 countries worldwide.

As much a pioneer in marketing and advertising as in product innovation, Procter & Gamble has also produced some of the most famous campaigns in advertising history. The famous 99 4/10ths percent pure Ivory soap campaign was one of the first to directly target the P&G consumer. In 1923, Crisco sponsored cooking shows on the radio; in 1932, P&G began sponsoring daytime radio dramas. The company aired its first TV commercial during the first televised major league baseball game in 1939. And long before Peoria became popular among politicians gauging the pulse of America, P&G played there – Pampers were test-marketed in the small Illinois city in the early 1960s. Today, with a $3 billion marketing budget, Procter and Gamble is the world's biggest advertiser.

The company has hit some shaky times as of late, forcing it to cut costs and streamline production. Furthermore, in September 1998, P&G announced it would overhaul its corporate structure, eliminating the previous division of business into four regional categories. In the future, seven executives will manage units charged with marketing products on a global scale.

Also, Durk Jager will take the helm of the company when CEO John Pepper retires in September 1999. The restructuring is designed to boost sales and keep P&G on track to meet its rather ambitious goal of doubling sales by 2006.

GETTING HIRED

Procter & Gamble recruits for its management-track jobs at most prestigious business schools and undergraduate colleges. It also prefers to hire through its internships rather than directly into full-time positions at the company. Internships last about 12 weeks in the summer. The company asks that applications be submitted by January for the internships, as they try to fill them by March. Recruiting schedules, and in some instances, P&G contacts for certain schools, are posted on the company's career center web pages. The screening process is very selective. It usually involves several rounds of interviews and always includes a company-designed multiple-choice test designed to test critical thinking skills (formerly called the P&GMAT, and now officially called the "Problem Solving Test"). Procter & Gamble is equally concerned with the personal traits of its hires, and also gives applicants a questionnaire designed to probe characteristics the company believes will predict job success. The basis of Procter & Gamble's recruitment and evaluation for managers are what it calls the 'What Counts Factors.' The most important of these, insiders say, are leadership, initiative and follow through (execution), innovation, and critical thinking.

Procter & Gamble's summer internship programs are the best way to get started at the company. Says one MBA intern who planned to accept a company offer: "Summer internships almost always result in job offers. This summer, interns received their offers before they left P&G. During this past summer, the CEO stated that one of his long-term goals was to recruit brand people only from the intern pool." Another MBA intern says she knew of no one in the program who did not receive an offer.

MBA Job Seekers: Receive free e-mailed job postings matching your interests & qualifications! Register at www.VaultReports.com

VAULT REPORTS™

167

www.vaultreports.com

OUR SURVEY SAYS

As would be expected of a company whose logo contains a reference to the original thirteen colonies, Procter & Gamble is not the hippest of work environments. Still, the winds of change waft through even Cincinnati. One employee describes the company as "very conservative." "To fit," he says, "you should be a typical yuppy, drive a Saab." However, most other employees say the atmosphere is shifting. "The culture here is a bit on the conservative side, though it seems that the younger generation is changing that," according to one insider. "I am finding an emerging diversity of thought and dress. More and more men are finding it 'OK' to keep their hair long or have an earring," says another. "Obviously we're still a somewhat conservative company. But there is more openness and acceptance of those who don't fit the 'traditional, conservative' look or views.'"

Accounts of how P&G operates run the gamut from "surprisingly nimble and non-bureaucratic," to "extremely structured and hierarchical," but enough insiders complain about its being overly bureaucratic to suggest that the description, while perhaps not unilateral, is far from a fluke. "What I did not like was that the company was large and sometimes very bureaucratic, which meant that change sometimes happened very slowly and that entrepreneurship was sometimes stifled," says one former international brand manager.

Within brand management, teamwork and communication is stressed – 50 percent of a brand manager's evaluation is based on the development of employees in the brand. Most employees speak glowingly about their treatment by superiors, saying their bosses take real interest in their development, and treated their opinions with real respect. But bureaucracy can rear its ugly head when it comes to interdepartmental movement. "Many of the functions (outside of Brand and Finance) do not have the performance incentives we have. As a result, they can be bureaucratic and will use Brand's failure to follow procedure or guidelines as an excuse," says another employee. But within Brand, the company can also be overly stiff. "It's definitely bureaucratic, it's very difficult to get things done at P&G," says a former assistant brand manager. "Things just move at a very slow pace." That former employee says that when a new idea is presented, it is sent by memo to a superior, and then 'niggled' – sent back with comments in the margin. The memo is rewritten and sent to the next higher level, and then 'niggled' again. And so on. "It's a pretty stifling place," he says.

In the summer in Cincinnati, the company rents out an amusement park for employees and their families to enjoy for free. In the winter, it does the same for events such as David Copperfield, Harlem Globetrotters or ice-skating shows. Sales reps get a company car and keep their frequent flyer miles. There's also a company gym, holiday gift packs, and coupons for P&G products. Says one employee: "I haven't bought detergent or soap for nine years!" And the perks aren't confined to the P&G campuses. "All kinds of perks all over town," a contact brags. "P&G owns Cincinnati."

P&G also was one of the first companies to offer "FlexComp," which gives employees a wide range of healthcare and other insurance choices. And P&G also gives 2 to 4 percent of an employee's salary (above base pay), which workers can use to pay for their benefits.

But by far the most impressive perk P&G offers is its company profit-sharing retirement plan. Initiated in 1887 to address labor unrest, the program is the longest-running profit-sharing plan in the United States. Under the plan, the company automatically kicks in stock worth from 5 percent to 25 percent of a participants annual base pay, with the maximum company contribution coming after 20 years of service. The plan is considered a real gem because, unlike the pension programs at many companies, it's not a matching program: P&G makes the contributions above base salary regardless of what the employee does. "It's automatic, you don't even have to think about it," according to one employee. "I've had job offers with higher salaries but have never been able to make the long-term math pay out over what I can reasonably expect here," another employee says.

To order a 50- to 70-page Vault Reports Employer Profile on Procter & Gamble call 1-888-JOB-VAULT or visit www.VaultReports.com

The full Employer Profile includes detailed information on P&G's departments, recent developments and transactions, hiring and interview process, plus what employees really think about culture, pay, work hours and more.

MBA Job Seekers: Receive free e-mailed job postings matching your interests & qualifications! Register at www.VaultReports.com

VAULT REPORTS™
www.vaultreports.com

169

RESEARCHING EMPLOYERS:
DON'T FORGET TO DO YOUR HOMEWORK

Doing your homework doesn't apply just to class. Some job seekers do more research picking out their next CD player than getting the inside scoop on their future employer or career. It's always a wise idea to learn everything possible about potential future employers before you even send in that resume, and certainly before you walk into an interview

How can you stay ahead of the game? The first obvious place to go is the company web site. Most large companies will have a web site full of information on recent engagements, products and services, job openings, and other vital information. Some larger companies have sections of their web site that are specifically targeted toward college and MBA students. Any company will expect you to have read this information before applying or interviewing.

Through work or school, you may have access to Nexis/Lexis, the online database of newspaper and magazine articles. Nexis is a superb resource for finding tidbits about companies that you might not have otherwise known – or deciding that perhaps you don't want to work at this company, after all.

Whether you're in school or an alum, your alumni network is an excellent resource. One of the best ways to learn about the joys and pitfalls of an individual company is to talk to someone who works there (or used to).

Of course, Vault Reports can also save you significant research time. We've already scoured every publicly available resource on more than 1000 companies and firms, talked to thousands of insiders, and accessed information not available elsewhere.

What should you look for when researching potential employers?

- How big is this company?

- How fast is it growing?

- Where is it based?

Don't forget to do your homework, cont'd

- What opportunities will I have for travel/overseas assignments?

- Will I get stock options?

- Is this a company I could spend the next year at, or my entire career?

- What qualifications do successful candidates have?

MBA Job Seekers: Receive free e-mailed job postings matching
your interests & qualifications! Register at www.VaultReports.com

VAULT
REPORTS™

www.vaultreports.com

171

Fidelity

Asset Management

82 Devonshire Street, 22K
Boston, MA 02109-3614
(617) 563-7000
Fax: (617) 563-3677
www.fidelity.com

LOCATIONS

Boston, MA (HQ)
Cincinnati, OH • Dallas, TX • Marlborough, MA • Merrimack, NH • New York, NY • Salt Lake City, UT • Smithfield, RI • London, England • Hong Kong • Tokyo, Japan
Over 80 retail offices across the U.S.

DEPARTMENTS

Brokerage
Corporate Administration
Customer Service
Finance/Accounting
Human Resources
Investment Management and Research
Marketing/Communications
Operations
Sales
Technology
Venture Capital

THE STATS

Annual Revenues: $5.9 billion (1997)
No. of Employees: 25,000 (worldwide)

No. of Offices: 15
Private Company
CEO: Edward C. Johnson III

KEY COMPETITORS

- Citigroup
- Merrill Lynch
- Morgan Stanley Dean Witter
- T. Rowe Price
- Vanguard Group
- Zurich Kemper Scuder

 THE BUZZ
What MBAs are saying
about Fidelity

- "Very clubby"
- "Peaked"
- "The biggest and one of the best"
- "Large but sharp"

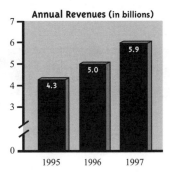

UPPERS

- Profit sharing
- Tuition reimbursement
- Good firm for women
- Numerous and flexible maternity
  leave options

DOWNERS

- Lack of teamwork in Equity division
- Little at-work (or after-work)
  socialization

EMPLOYMENT CONTACT

Human Resources
Fidelity Investments
82 Devonshire Street, 22K
Boston, MA 02109-3614
Fax: (617) 563-3677
E-mail: resumes@fidelity.com (text only)

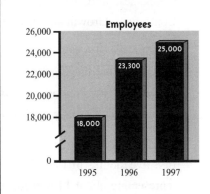

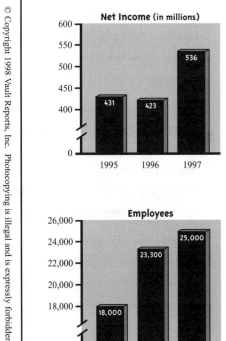

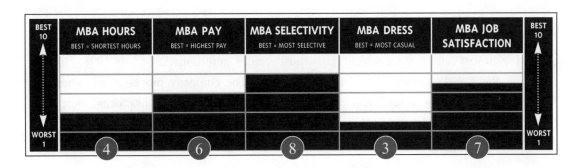

THE SCOOP

Edward Crosby Johnson II started Fidelity Investments in 1946 to manage the Fidelity mutual fund, which was started in 1930. Under his management, the fund's assets grew from under $3 million to over $3 billion. During the 1970s, Fidelity began to make funds directly accessible to individual investors and set an industry standard by eliminating mutual fund sales charges. An early leader in discount brokerage, Fidelity was the first to see that the future of financial services depended on empowering individual investors to take advantage of investment opportunities.

To describe Fidelity is to make use of superlatives. With $645.4 billion in mutual fund assets under management and 14 million customers, the company is the largest privately-held financial services company in the nation, the second-largest discount brokerage firm in the nation, the leading provider of company-sponsored 401(k) retirement plans to the Fortune 500 companies, and the largest mutual fund company in the world. Notable funds include Contrafund, Growth and Income, and Magellan, the largest mutual fund on the market.

Fidelity Investments is the trade name for Fidelity Management and Research Company (FMR), the holding company through which CEO Edward "Ned" Johnson controls the empire of financial institutions that his father established. Fidelity Investments breaks down into seven principal groups, each with their respective sub-groups.

Fidelity's power was notably demonstrated by the company's investment in Yahoo!. In the first five months of 1997, Fidelity snapped up 2.5 million shares of the search engine's stock, representing about 14 percent of stock not held by insiders, according to *SmartMoney*. The move helped Yahoo's stock price rise form $65 to $120 during those months.

In the mid-1990s, poor product performance and management problems led many to wonder if Fidelity had finally lost its edge. The company seems, however, to be rebounding after working on cost cutting, management restructuring, and vigorous marketing. In 1998, Fidelity remains the world's largest mutual fund company. The company processes an estimated 72,000 trades a day for its retail and institutional clients, and its phone sites process more than half a million incoming calls daily.

Despite economic turmoil abroad, Fidelity continues to pursue vigorous international expansion. One of its international branches, Fidelity Investments Ltd., saw its assets in Europe grow by nearly 50 percent in 1997. The company has also grown in Asia. In Japan, Fidelity has recently introduced six new funds for Japanese investors, and struck agreements to market its products at dozens of branches of Asahi Bank.

GETTING HIRED

While Fidelity does not specify educational requirements, it does look for entrepreneurial candidates who can succeed in a fast-paced environment. Most new hires have some financial or business background, but there are also opportunities for those with technology and computer expertise. Fidelity's employment Web page, located at www.fidelity.com/employment, discusses the different departments within the company and the skills that they require. The Web page also allows applicants to search a job database, build their resumes on-line, and submit resumes via e-mail.

Fidelity prefers MBAs for positions that include Quantitative Equity Analysts, Regional Service Representatives, Product/Service Consultants, Investment Managers, Quantitative Analysts, and Performance Analysts. For MBAs applying for analyst positions, having a love for the stock market seems to be the most important qualification. If you are sending in your resume, insiders recommend attaching a stock report. "They love that," says one insider. "It will definitely increase your chances of getting an interview."

MBA Job Seekers: Receive free e-mailed job postings matching
your interests & qualifications! Register at www.VaultReports.com

VAULT
REPORTS™
www.vaultreports.com

175

OUR SURVEY SAYS

Fidelity's corporate culture wins high marks from employees for being "enlightened" – because of its "high degree of tolerance in dealing with its people." According to one recent summer associate, "Fidelity understands that workers can't always be perfect. They don't have a problem with people being grouchy." Unlike many other companies in the industry, Fidelity "assigns a great deal of autonomy, both personally and professionally" to its employees.

Recent hires say that one of the "striking" characteristics of working for Fidelity is that "Fidelity's workplace has a major dichotomy between the fixed income and equity divisions. The culture at fixed income is completely different from the culture in the equity division." Employees in the fixed income division praise their "team-oriented work place" and feel that "the best of working for this company is your co-workers, the best in the game." However, an associate in the equity departments laments his department's "individualistic, even 'dog-eat-dog' environment." "Equity," he notes, "is not very social at all." He goes on to add: "It's not for someone who really likes a team effort environment. Not that it's not friendly, but although you interact with other people, you work a lot on your own. It's also stressful, so if you can't handle up and down stressful times, you should look elsewhere." Another equity employee says that "Fidelity and its culture are more solitary than at other companies. In general, your job's going to be solitary if you work in buy-side mutual environment. But Fidelity's even more solitary than usual absolutely no after-work social life. It's stressful during the day but then people go their separate ways after work. It's not a place for someone who wants work to be the center of their lives."

It's "impossible to talk of Fidelity without mentioning Ned Johnson somewhere," insiders assert. "Ultimately, this place is an autocracy, and one man is ruler – Ned Johnson," one longtime employee comments, adding ruefully, "Ned Johnson has the power to make decisions with no checks on that power. He's a smart guy, but occasionally he makes a very non-optimal decision. And we have to bear the consequences of his occasional wackiness." Another agrees: "This is Ned's candy store. He was given this firm by his father. He'll come up with the quirkiest, strangest idea in the middle of the night, and everyone has to deal with it. It's very frustrating."

A recent female summer intern in the fixed income division states that "Fidelity is very anxious for women to work for it. My immediate superior was a woman and was very candid with me when soliciting my assistance in identifying good female candidates." One contact notes: "one of the most powerful people around the company is a woman – Abigail Johnson, who'll probably run this company very soon. And that will be a great day for women." Another, when asked about the effect of Abigail Johnson on the workplace, replies: "I don't think it matters. There were a few other women where I worked. I felt like we were treated fine. They don't treat women any different, there are just fewer of them. In a lot of ways that can be an advantage – there are more opportunities."

Employees are particularly appreciative of Fidelity's many family-friendly programs, which, according to one female employee, ensure that "Fidelity's a good place for working women and families." Another contact agrees, noting that "there are a ton of people here on maternity leave." Fidelity's family programs include Adoption Assistance, Child Care assistance, Vacation Programs for School-Age Children, College Planning and Scholarship Information Service, Elder Care Resource & Referral, Employee Assistance Program and Mortgage Service. Other perks that draw praise include Fidelity's comprehensive training opportunities and an "excellent" retirement benefits consisting of a 401(k) package with a matching contribution by Fidelity.

To order a 50- to 70-page Vault Reports Employer Profile on Fidelity call 1-888-JOB-VAULT or visit www.VaultReports.com

The full Employer Profile includes detailed information on Fidelity's departments, recent developments and transactions, hiring and interview process, plus what employees really think about culture, pay, work hours and more.

MBA Job Seekers: Receive free e-mailed job postings matching your interests & qualifications! Register at www.VaultReports.com

VAULT REPORTS™

177

www.vaultreports.com

RANKING
19

Merck

Pharmaceuticals

One Merck Drive
P.O. Box 100 WS 1F-55
Whitehouse Station, NJ 08889
(908) 423-1000
Fax: (908) 423-2592
www.merck.com

MERCK
Human Health

LOCATIONS

Whitehouse Station, NJ (HQ)
Albany, GA • Atlanta, GA • Blue Bell, PA • Chicago, IL • Columbus, OH • Danville, PA • Dallas, TX • Elkton, VA • Iselin, NJ • Kansas City, KS • Los Angeles, CA • Rahway, NJ • Somerset, NJ • West Point, PA • Wilson, NC • Kirkland, Canada • Madrid, Spain • Pomezia, Italy • Riom, France • Terlings Park, United Kingdom • Tsukuba, Japan • and several other locations in Latin America, Europe, Australia, and Asia

DEPARTMENTS

Accounting & Finance
Engineering
Manufacturing
Product Marketing
Research & Development
Services Marketing
Systems Operations

THE STATS

Annual Revenues: $23.6 billion (1997)
Income: $4.6 billion (1997)
No. of Employees: 53,800 (worldwide)

No. of Offices: 50 (worldwide)
Stock Symbol: MRK
Stock Exchange: NYSE
CEO: Raymond V. Gilmartin

KEY COMPETITORS

- Bristol-Myers Squibb
- Eli Lilly
- Glaxo Wellcome
- Pfizer
- Schering Plough
- Warner-Lambert

THE BUZZ
What MBAs are saying about Merck

- "Great at what they do"
- "Good product and mission"
- "A nice firm"
- "The establishment"

UPPERS

♦ On-site fitness facilities with personal trainers
♦ On-site daycare and summer camp programs
♦ Stable, progressive workplace

DOWNERS

♦ Bureaucratic administration
♦ Mainstay products facing increased competition

EMPLOYMENT CONTACT

Merck & Co.
One Merck Drive
P.O. Box 100 WS 1F-55
Whitehouse Station, NJ 08889
Fax: (908) 423-2592
E-mail: Resumes@Merck.com

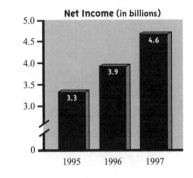

Annual Revenues (in billions)

Net Income (in billions)

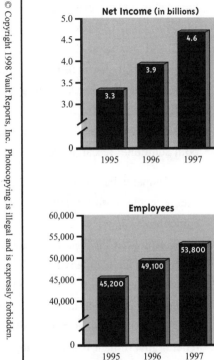

Employees

	MBA HOURS BEST = SHORTEST HOURS	MBA PAY BEST = HIGHEST PAY	MBA SELECTIVITY BEST = MOST SELECTIVE	MBA DRESS BEST = MOST CASUAL	MBA JOB SATISFACTION	
	7	7	6	4	8	

MBA Job Seekers: Receive free e-mailed job postings matching your interests & qualifications! Register at www.VaultReports.com

VAULT REPORTS™
www.vaultreports.com

179

THE SCOOP

Merck, the largest drug manufacturer in the United States, was founded when Theodore Weicker came to the States in 1887 to establish an American branch of E. Merck AG, a German chemical company. The American branch at first served as an importer for the German parent company; and it was only in 1904 that Merck opened its first American factory, in Rahway, NJ. Merck's first research lab, opened in 1933, isolated and manufactured vitamin B-12 and produced the first steroid, cortisone. During WWII, George Merck, CEO and grandson of the German founder, gave 80 percent of Merck's German-held stock to the U.S. Government, keeping the other 20 percent for himself. After the war, the Government holdings went public. Merck researchers earned five Nobel prizes in the 1940s and 1950s, and a 1953 merger with sales powerhouse Sharp & Dome helped the drug conglomerate achieve both additional research prestige and a formidable market share.

The company has in recent years tried to move outside its core pharmaceutical business. Merck made a foray into the managed-care market with its 1993 purchase of Medco Containment Services, a pharmacy-benefits manager. In August 1998, the company reached a settlement with the Federal Trade Commission to end the agency's long standing antitrust inquiry into the company's purchase of Medco, now called MerckMedco Managed Care LLC. Under the agreement, Merck pledged unrestricted access to prescription drugs for its health plan customers and to keep confidential market information from being leaked from company officials to its benefits management subsidiary. The settlement comes at a time when the federal government is scrutinizing the relationships between the pharmaceutical industry and company-owned prescription benefit managers. Merck is expanding in other areas, as well. The 1997 merger of Merck's animal health divisions with the French company Rhone-Poulenc ensured Merck's dominance in the veterinary market.

However, the company's main emphasis remains pioneering pharmaceutical research. Merck's extensive product line includes Recombivax HB, the first recombinant vaccine for Hepatitis B, Pepcid gastronomical medicine (as well as the over the counter Pepcid AC), Cozaar (anti-hypertension), MMR II (measles, mumps, & rubella vaccine), and Varivax (a chicken pox vaccine), among many others. After ten years of struggle to create an effective treatment of

HIV, Crixivan, a protease inhibitor used for the treatment of HIV in adults, was introduced to much fanfare in 1996. The revolutionary drug was so desperately needed that the typically stringent FDA released it for use after only 42 days of trials. In the months that followed, Crixivan proved to reduce AIDS-related deaths by 60 percent and, when used in combination with two other HIV drugs, cut the spread of HIV infection by 90 percent within an 18-month period. Crixivan is now the most widely used protease-inhibitor. What makes Merck distinctive from other drug manufacturers is its commitment to in-house research, as opposed to buying up ideas and research from young biotech firms or contracting freelance specialist organization. Only 5 percent of Merck's research spending is distributed outside of the corporation, compared to rival pharmaceutical firms, who outsource up to 80 percent of the research. Though this tactic has brought mixed reactions from the pharmaceutical industry, Merck has repeatedly proven the viability of their strategy with a steady stream of successful innovations, most notably with Crixivan.

In the meantime, Merck gets top ratings as a workplace. *Fortune* magazine ranked the firm ninth in its 1998 survey "The 100 Best Companies to Work For." Merck is proud of its diversity record. More than half (52 percent) of its United States employees are women, and more than 24 percent are ethnic minorities. These solid numbers hold up on the managerial level, where 32 percent of managers are women and 16 percent members of minority groups. Working-parent friendly Merck allows alternative work arrangements such as flex-time, job-sharing and telecommuting. Merck sponsors a Black Employees Network to provide both personal and professional support to workers at all levels. The former president of Spelman College, Dr. Johnnetta Cole, is one of two African-Americans on Merck's twelve-member Board of Directors.

The company's progressive employment policies haven't prevented it from taking some lumps as of late. In July 1998, the company announced that it would not meet annual profit projections after disappointing second quarter earnings. Merck's dissapointing numbers panicked investors – its stock had slid more than 9 percent in two days following the announcement, costing the company more than $11 billion in market capitalization. Analysts say Merck's weak performance is due to increased competition in markets the company usually dominates: AIDS and cholesterol. Sales of Crixivan, once Merck's cash cow, are being impacted by Agouron Pharmaceuticals' Viracept, a protease inhibitor that is easier to take. The

MBA Job Seekers: Receive free e-mailed job postings matching your interests & qualifications! Register at www.VaultReports.com

VAULT REPORTS™

181

www.vaultreports.com

company's cholesterol-lowering Zocor is also being whipped soundly – by Warner-Lambert's Lipitor, a more potent drug in the category.

GETTING HIRED

Merck is known among MBAs as a top-of-the-line employer in the healthcare industry, and has a strong presence at many business school campuses. MBAs are hired primarily into finance and marketing; the company offers summer internships in both functions. Reports one former intern in financial analysis: "I was assigned an independent project to present to the CFO. Throughout the summer, I was exposed to very senior management at Merck." Another insider reports that "marketing is where all the action is and the best place to advance. Most of the MBA-types are there." Information about MBA positions can be found at www.merck.com.

A PhD is a huge plus in certain lofty positions. "In research… the management positions are all held by PhDs," reports one contact. "In manufacturing and sales, with only an MBA, you could theoretically advance to president of the division." Because of Merck's emphasis on international growth, the company likes marketing and sales applicants with foreign language proficiency and a yen for overseas work.

OUR SURVEY SAYS

Merck employees frequently work as many as 60 hours a week in a fun, "team-centered environment." Insiders say "Merck is a family-friendly company" and point to "generous family leave policies" and to on-site child care programs. Merck even extends its tuition reimbursement policy to employees' families. Bilingual candidates will find abundant international business opportunities because of Merck's "aggressive expansion, especially in

Latin America." Insiders also report that especially in sales and marketing, "women and minorities are very well represented and hold management positions. These numbers have only been getting better in the past few years."

Contacts say "Merck takes care of its employees very well, both in terms of financial compensation and benefits." To decide the salaries of its employees, Merck reportedly "targets 75 percent of the highest compensation in the industry," in other words employees are paid "75 percent of the industry maximum for positions." There is also a bonus plan based on "company performance, division performance, department performance as well as personal performance." The food's not bad either – "the cafeterias are not the cheapest way to get a meal, but they are excellent and convenient." In manufacturing plants, the cafeterias are a bit nicer looking than a university cafeteria, but those at corporate sites reportedly resemble fairly nice restaurants.

MBA Job Seekers: Receive free e-mailed job postings matching your interests & qualifications! Register at www.VaultReports.com

VAULT REPORTS™
www.vaultreports.com

183

Lucent Technologies

High Tech

600 Mountain Avenue
Murray Hill, NJ 07974
(908) 582-8500
www.lucent.com

Lucent Technologies
Bell Labs Innovations

LOCATIONS

Murray Hill, NJ (HQ)
Warren, NJ
As well as 70 offices across New Jersey
and others in 90 countries

DEPARTMENTS

Engineering
Finance
Marketing
Sales
Software Development

KEY COMPETITORS

- 3Com
- Cisco Systems
- Nortel
- Siemens

THE STATS

Annual Revenues: $30.1 billion (1998)
No. of Employees: 136,000 (worldwide)
No. of Offices: 90+ (worldwide)
Stock Symbol: LU (NYSE)
CEO: Richard McGinn

THE BUZZ
What MBAs are saying
about Lucent

- "Geeky but great company"
- "Cutting edge high tech"
- "Big but going places"
- "Hot sector"

UPPERS

- Flexible scheduling options
- Company culture becoming looser
- Paid-for network access from home
- Recently has become MBA-happy

DOWNERS

- Slow promotion process
- Unpleasant New Jersey locale

EMPLOYMENT CONTACT

Lucent Technology
600 Mountain Avenue
Murray Hill, NJ 07974
www.lucent/com/work/work.html

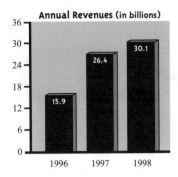

Annual Revenues (in billions)

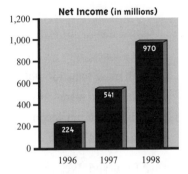

Net Income (in millions)

Employees (in thousands)

	MBA HOURS BEST = SHORTEST HOURS	MBA PAY BEST = HIGHEST PAY	MBA SELECTIVITY BEST = MOST SELECTIVE	MBA DRESS BEST = MOST CASUAL	MBA JOB SATISFACTION
	5	6	7	5	9

BEST 10 / WORST 1

MBA Job Seekers: Receive free e-mailed job postings matching
your interests & qualifications! Register at www.VaultReports.com

VAULT REPORTS™
www.vaultreports.com

185

THE SCOOP

Lucent may be little more than a couple of years old, but this is one toddler that already knows how to run. Lucent Technologies is one of the world's leading designers, developers, and manufacturers of telecommunications systems and software. Until 1996, Lucent was part of AT&T; now it is already the nation's leading manufacturer of both the hardware and the software of global communications networks – business communications technology, telephones, wireless networks, and switching equipment. Lucent is now its very own firm, with more than 136,000 employees in 90 countries worldwide. (Twenty-five percent of Lucent employees work outside the United States.) Revenues in 1998 were a very healthy $30.1 billion, and net income reached $2.3 billion. By spring 1998, Lucent's market value actually exceeded AT&T's.

AT&T and Western Electric founded Bell Laboratories in 1925 to conduct research and development. Soon after WWII the company developed the transistor, for which its scientists won a Nobel Prize. The transistor's "switching" ability makes possible the zillions of super-fast calculations needed to run your average computer. That was merely the first in a string of inventions that include the communications satellite, the solar cell, and the UNIX computer operating system. During the 1984 break-up of AT&T, the corporate giant was allowed to keep its research and manufacturing facilities, which came under the name of AT&T Technologies. However, AT&T later decided to spin off Lucent in what was the largest initial public stock offering in U.S. history at the time. The new company consolidated its operations and sold off its non-core business to become even more competitive in this quickly changing industry.

By separating from AT&T in September 1996, Lucent has become free to do business with other telecommunications companies without conflicts of interest. As part of its efforts to boost its core businesses, Lucent acquired the smaller company Agile Networks in October 1996. Agile provides advanced intelligent switching products useful for the Ethernet, as well as asynchronous transfer mode (ATM) tech. In September 1997, Lucent nabbed Octel, which provides voice, fax and electronic messaging technologies that should dovetail nicely with those already offered by Lucent. The company agreed in October 1997 to acquire Livingston Enterprises, a global provider of Internet equipment. To top off the shopping spree, Lucent bought Optimay, a German firm that makes software for cellular phones, for $65 million. The company has also won some high profile contracts, including a three-year $700 million pact with Sprint PCS, a $280 million agreement with AT&T owned Telecorps, and a $100 million deal with Venezuelan carrier Telecel.

To create quicker market response and enhanced customer focus, Lucent has recently reorganized to form smaller customer units. These units, not including Bell Labs, which remains its own discrete unit, are: Microelectronics; Data Networking Systems; Wireless Networks; Business Communications Systems; Optical Networking; Switching and Access Systems; Network Products; Communications Software; New Ventures; and Intellectual Property.

Despite Lucent's success so far, the company is feeling the heat of competition. In June 1998, Lucent sued Cisco, the top networking equipment company that has begun encroaching into Lucent's turf, alleging infringement of eight data-networking technology patents. Earlier that month, the company reached a new contract with 43,000 workers affiliated with the International Brotherhood of Electric Workers and the Communication Workers of America, ending a brief strike that would have crippled Lucent's operations.

GETTING HIRED

Lucent has become a hot MBA employer in recent years and maintains an employment Web page named "work@lucent" that can be reached at www.lucent.com/work/work.html. The Web page provides access to current job listings, college recruiting information, and an on-line application program. After applicants complete their resumes on-line, Lucent keeps them in its "electronic files" and matches them with new job opportunities that arise. Lucent has a Financial Leadership Development Program, a 24- to 30-month intensive program for those with degrees in accounting, finance, or other business-related fields. Lucent also offers internships and co-ops year round for interested students. Those who are looking for a position in a specific field, take note of an insiders explanation that "by sending a resume to HR, you

MBA Job Seekers: Receive free e-mailed job postings matching your interests & qualifications! Register at www.VaultReports.com

VAULT REPORTS™
www.vaultreports.com

187

trigger a process where your resume is scanned and sent through an optical character recognition system. Key words are pulled out, and anyone within the company seeking a matching keyword is sent the resume. For example: ATM, software, object technology, DSP."

OUR SURVEY SAYS

Relative newborn Lucent is still making the transition from a "tradition, technocentric view of the world" to a more "customer-focused and entrepreneurial climate." Employees say Lucent's company culture is "undergoing rapid change. In Bell Labs, the culture is moving from 'academic' to being high-relevance and having a big impact on Lucent's business." Not only is this shift "creating new opportunities every day," it has also helped make the company more "exciting" and "dynamic." Employees say that morale at Lucent is currently "higher than ever before" and that they feel "empowered" to tackle the "thorny challenges" that are part of their work, thanks in part to their "universal access" to the "best in current technology." Individual empowerment at Lucent, however, does not mean working alone. Employees praise the "extensive exposure to executives and other upper management officers," the continuous feedback, and the way in which they are treated as "essential team players" from the first day on the job.

One longtime Lucent employee reports that "staff comes from all over the world. There is a particularly large segment of our staff of Asian background, led by China, India, Bangladesh and Korea. Europeans, Canadians, African-Americans, Middle Easterners and Hispanics are also heavily represented." However, another insider says Lucent is "above average for large technical corporations for minority and female representation at most levels, but there are still few that have advanced to senior level positions. There are 10 Group Presidents, and of those only one is a woman." "Lucent is a very large company," so the culture varies quite a bit. "Bell Labs is the most relaxed area, very much like a university environment. There are lots of jeans, T-shirts and sandals in the summer, without a necktie or pantsuit in sight. But there are other areas of the company, especially sales, marketing and business areas, with direct contact with customers, where suit and tie for men and dresses for women are expected." The physical ambience "ranges from fair to pretty darn good, depending on whether you are at a 30-year-old building or a new one. Nowhere are we shabby."

Support for employees at Lucent varies somewhat. While department-level managers have secretaries "some male, some female," most employees "type their own reports." However, "everyone has a PC or terminal with shared printers nearby. Office supplies are usually available in a stockroom. We all have access to voice mail on our phone lines. Most have company-owned PCs at home and Lucent will pick up the cost of an extra phone line or long distance charges for network access from home." A Lucent manager tells Vault Reports that "in a recent survey of employees, the question 'Would you recommend Lucent as a good place to work?' got more than a 90 percent 'yes' response. That's very high for any company."

MBA Job Seekers: Receive free e-mailed job postings matching
your interests & qualifications! Register at www.VaultReports.com

VAULT
REPORTS™   189
www.vaultreports.com

Netscape Communications

High Tech

501 E. Middlefield Road
Mountain View, CA 94043
(650) 254-1900
Fax: (650) 528-4124
home.netscape.com

NETSCAPE

LOCATIONS

Mountain View, CA (HQ)
Offices in every major U.S. city and seven international cities.

DEPARTMENTS

Finance & Accounting
Information Systems
Legal
People Department
Marketing
Product Development
Sales & Technical Support

THE STATS

Annual Revenues: $533.9 million (1997)
No. of Employees: 2,385 (U.S.)
No. of Offices: 1 (U.S.)
Stock Symbol: NSCP (Nasdaq)
CEO: James L. Barksdale

KEY COMPETITORS

- America Online
- Arriba
- Excite
- Lycos
- Microsoft
- Yahoo!

THE BUZZ

What MBAs are saying about Netscape

- "Cool, fighting"
- "Good company going down"
- "Daring but losing"
- "Young, unfocused"

UPPERS

- Casual office atmosphere
- Exciting industry
- Social environment

DOWNERS

- Long work days
- Company suffering heavy losses
- Tough competitor in Microsoft

EMPLOYMENT CONTACT

Allyn Edmonds
College Recruiting Representative
501 E. Middlefield Road
Mountain View, CA 94043
(650) 937-4984
Fax: (650) 528-4135

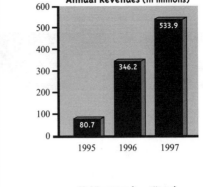

Annual Revenues (in millions)

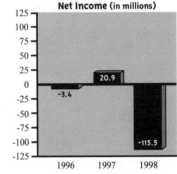

Net Income (in millions)

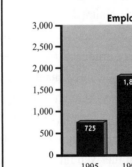

Employees

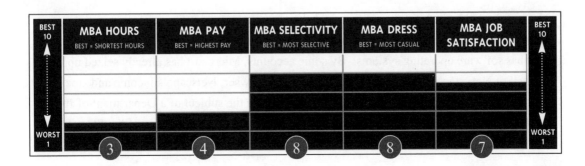

	MBA HOURS BEST = SHORTEST HOURS	MBA PAY BEST = HIGHEST PAY	MBA SELECTIVITY BEST = MOST SELECTIVE	MBA DRESS BEST = MOST CASUAL	MBA JOB SATISFACTION	
BEST 10 ... WORST 1	3	4	8	8	7	BEST 10 ... WORST 1

MBA Job Seekers: Receive free e-mailed job postings matching
your interests & qualifications! Register at www.VaultReports.com

VAULT REPORTS™
www.vaultreports.com

191

THE SCOOP

By distributing its World Wide Web browser, Navigator, free of charge over the Internet, Netscape has become a paramount feature of the Web. In addition to its browser and portal site, the company makes related software products that enable companies to use the Web for commercial purposes, as well as software that integrates Web browsing with other applications. Netscape has also been successful with server software for corporate intranets – networks that connect computers within an individual company. Netscape clients have included Chrysler, Lockheed Martin, and Prudential Securities. The company also has a contract with five regional Bell companies to make the default browser for their new Internet services.

Netscape's meteoric rise in the technology world began when Marc Andreessen played a key role in developing Mosaic, an Internet software program, at the University of Illinois-Champaign. Andreessen co-founded Mosaic Communications in 1994, but when the University claimed the right to the software's license, Andreessen changed the company's name to Netscape. After a few years of uncontested industry dominance by Netscape, Microsoft introduced its own free internet browser, Explorer. Netscape has done battle with Microsoft ever since, managing, however, to keep an edge in the area of Internet software. The company has entered into agreements with other technology companies, such as Sun Microsystems, Oracle, and IBM, to integrate its software into other packages and servers. One of the hottest companies of the 1990s, Netscape is currently developing new software that will transform the Web into an even more exciting – and profitable – medium, and is busy adding features to its own web site on the Internet, transforming it into an Internet "portal" that Web users will keep as their own homepage.

Netscape's major foe? Microsoft – which has bundled a competing web browser, Internet Explorer, with its operating systems software in order to gain control of the Internet market just as it has software operating systems. By some accounts, Microsoft has already seized up to 50 percent of Netscape's share by giving away its web browser; Netscape's income and stock has plummeted. However, Microsoft's strategy has become the subject of a Department of Justice antitrust suit, which charges that Microsoft is unfairly using its dominance of the PC software market to attempt to dominate a new market. Gates and Microsoft contend that Internet Explorer is an integral part of its Windows software, though Netscape offers uninstalling software on its own web site, saying that getting rid of Explorer has no effect on Windows.

Whether the allegations are true or not, one thing remains clear: Microsoft has clearly taken a huge bite out of Netscape's browser dominance. Netscape, which once controlled 90 percent of the market, has seen its 1997 share drop to 50.5 percent, down from 54.6 percent in 1996. In contrast, Microsoft's Internet Explorer rose from 16.4 to 22.8 percent in the same period. In 1998, Netscape was forced to admit defeat, and began to give away its browser for free. The browser had previously represented Netscape's biggest source of revenue.

As a result, Netscape is now shifting gears and focusing on selling software to businesses and beefing up its booming Netcenter Web Site. In 1998, Netscape recently announced a partnership with Excite to create a search service on Netcenter, which acts as a "portal," the first site consumers see when they access the Web. The company hopes to leverage its 70 million software users into "the world's biggest media network." Netscape also inked a $15-20 million deal with Citibank to build the financial corporation's electronic commerce infrastructure. Such promising developments led Netscape in August 1998 to report a small profit for the second quarter, surprising many analysts who had watched the company post repeated quarterly losses, including a total loss of $44.7 million in 1997.

GETTING HIRED

Netscape's recruitment site, located at home.netscape.com/jobs, describes current openings, including their responsibilities and requirements. Each position lists a job reference number, which applicants should include with their resumes. Each department has a separate e-mail address for applicants to use when e-mailing their resumes; Netscape accepts faxed resumes as well. The employment web page also describes the company's college recruitment schedule. For marketing and product marketing jobs, Netscape prefers MBAs with some computer or technical experience. For product development jobs, Netscape prefers applicants with

MBA Job Seekers: Receive free e-mailed job postings matching your interests & qualifications! Register at www.VaultReports.com

VAULT REPORTS™
www.vaultreports.com

193

bachelors, masters or doctorate degrees in computer science. In addition to technical savvy, Netscape looks for lots of personality in its new hires: the official title of the head of recruiting is "Director of Bringing in the Cool People." The company's interview process usually begins with a screening conversation by phone, insiders say. After that, Netscape conducts two or more rounds of face-to-face interviews. Although the interviewers normally dress very informally, the interviewees often (and should) wear suits. Says one insider, "We don't hire experience as much as we value smart people looking for a challenge."

OUR SURVEY SAYS

Netscape employees work "unending days," and let their "work take over their lives," but some "love every minute of it." Employees enjoy the "excitement" of a company "on the constant cusp of technological innovation" and like the "underdog cachet" of working for "David in the shadow of Microsoft's Goliath." As one employee says: "This is a fascinating company. Netscape deals with unprecedented challenges in a furiously changing industry." Recently hired employees at this "awesome company" comment that they have been encouraged to "dive in immediately" and "quickly acquire significant responsibilities." "The company is driving, demanding, exhausting, but it is also rewarding, nurturing and fulfilling," says one insider. "It's a company of extremes," agreed another. Because of Netscape's recent difficulties, however, all is not rosy in Mountain View: Goliath casts a cold shadow. "The current atmosphere is subdued but optimistic. Otherwise, Netscape has been the best company I have worked at." "Frankly, if there were no Microsoft in the world, this would undoubtedly be the most popular place of employment for anyone beginning in the software field," says another glum Netscaper. "But there is a Microsoft."

Many contacts characterize Netscape as "busy," "stressful," and a "a very fast-paced company, a very demanding place – no excuses." And, as layoffs in recent years indicate, because of competitive pressures, Netscape "is definitely assuming some of the characteristics of larger companies." Still, a key component of what employees call a "team" atmosphere at Netscape is a "casual, informal" corporate culture that encourages collegiality. "It feels like being a graduate student," one Netscape insider says, pointing to the games of ping-pong, table hockey, and football that he plays near his cubicle. Another has a slightly different take: "Walking around Netscape is like bar-hopping in the city."

To order a 10- to 20-page Vault Reports Employer Profile on Netscape Communications call 1-888-JOB-VAULT or visit www.VaultReports.com

The full Employer Profile includes detailed information on Netscape's departments, recent developments and transactions, hiring and interview process, plus what employees really think about culture, pay, work hours and more.

MBA Job Seekers: Receive free e-mailed job postings matching your interests & qualifications! Register at www.VaultReports.com

VAULT REPORTS™
www.vaultreports.com

195

Enron

Energy

1400 Smith Street
Houston, TX 77002-7369
(713) 853-6161
www.enron.com

LOCATIONS

Houston, TX (HQ)
Denver, CO • Dublin, OH • Omaha, NE •
Portland, OR • San Francisco, CA •
Washington, DC • Calgary, Canada • London,
U.K. • Sao Palo, Brazil • Mumbai and New
Dehli, India

BUSINESSES

Administration
Finance
Risk Management
Sales and Trading
Energy Services
International

THE STATS

Annual Revenues: $20.3 billion (1997)
No. of Employees: 20,000 (worldwide)
Stock Symbol: ENE (NYSE)
CEO: Kenneth L. Lay

KEY COMPETITORS

- AES
- Duke
- Dynegy
- El Paso Energy
- Houston Industries
- Southern Company
- The Williams Companies

THE BUZZ

What MBAs are saying
about Enron

- "Exciting firm in boring industry "
- "Smart mothers"
- "Sharks, but good ones"
- "Male dominant"

UPPERS

- Casual dress
- Fluid, flexible management structure
- Cheap rent in Houston
- International travel opportunities

DOWNERS

- Offices makes it difficult to interact with co-workers from other business units
- Occasional long workdays
- Intense work atmosphere, often stressful

EMPLOYMENT CONTACT

Cindy Shiffler
Recruiting Coordinator
Enron
1400 Smith Street
Houston, TX 77002-7369
Fax: (713) 646-3595
(800) 742-7768 (job hotline)

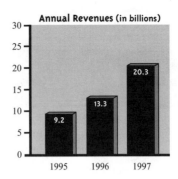

Annual Revenues (in billions)

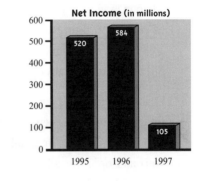

Net Income (in millions)

Employees

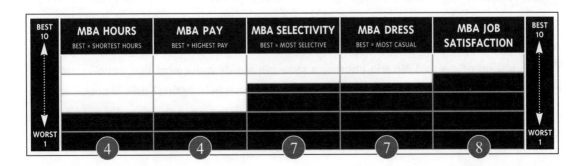

	MBA HOURS BEST = SHORTEST HOURS	MBA PAY BEST = HIGHEST PAY	MBA SELECTIVITY BEST = MOST SELECTIVE	MBA DRESS BEST = MOST CASUAL	MBA JOB SATISFACTION	
	4	4	7	7	8	

MBA Job Seekers: Receive free e-mailed job postings matching your interests & qualifications! Register at www.VaultReports.com

VAULT REPORTS™

www.vaultreports.com

197

THE SCOOP

Who or what is Enron? That was the question the Houston-based power company asked around the country before embarking on a massive public recognition campaign in 1997. The responses received from the polling expedition? A senator, a brand of golf balls, a Star Trek weapon, and hiking shoes. Okay, you may not know who Enron is yet, but in the next couple of years, you'll probably learn to curse their name, as they begin to target you with an intense advertising campaign. Or you may learn to love them, as you examine your electricity or gas bill and find it has dropped 20 percent.

Enron is intent on becoming the company that powers the world. The company envisions a future of one-stop energy shopping that it calls "integrated energy solutions." For the retail customer – families or small business owners – this means calling Enron (or having them call you) and ordering all your energy from them. For the wholesale customer – such as large industrials and municipalities – Enron delivers energy commodities and offers related services such as financing, risk management and long-term contracting. The company is the largest wholesale marketer of gas in North America.

Enron's primary businesses include exploration and production, transportation and distribution, wholesale energy operations and retail energy services. The company has nearly $30 billion in assets and $20 billion in projects under development. Enron has aggressively moved forward with international projects in recent years, including a massive $2.5 billion Dabhol power plant in India, which will be one of the largest gas-fired power facilities in the world. Enron is also a partner in the $2.5 billion, 1864-mile Bolivia-to-Brazil natural gas pipeline, the largest project ever undertaken in South America. Much of their emphasis has been on emerging markets. Other Enron-developed power projects include the 357-mile Centragas natural gas pipeline in Colombia, and a $1.2 billion power project in the U.K.

But Enron hopes to make its biggest splash in what it views as an energy revolution: the deregulation of gas and electric utilities, a slow but steady movement that, state-by-state, is opening up utilities to competition. Many industry analysts believe that Enron is poised to take the lead in the North American electricity industry, which the company estimates to be a $300 billion business – 24 times the size of the computer industry. Having moved its first electron in June 1994, Enron is now the largest seller of electricity in North America.

In 1998, the company also moved into water world – the $300 billion global water market. The company bought the British company, Wessex Water for $2.2 billion in July 1998, and in September, announced that it was setting up a water subsidiary called Azurix. Azurix is working with outside investors to pursue strategic water opportunities, particularly in the Americas and Europe.

GETTING HIRED

Enron hires MBAs as associates; the majority of Enron hires come through the company's extensive recruiting at top business schools. Recruiting schedules are posted at Enron's helpful employment web page, located at www.enron.com. The web site also includes a listing of job openings and descriptions.

Enron holds first-round interviews either on school campuses, or at a location nearby, such as a hotel. The company then has its "Super Saturdays" in December and January, interviewing marathons during which interviewees contend with up to six or seven interviews in a day. The interviewers usually sit down the next Monday, put all the names up on a board, and "rank them from first to last," one analyst who serves as a recruiter says. Offers usually come within a week of that round, often on Tuesday. About 50 percent of those brought in for the final round make it, a recruiter says, although because "the company has gone through such growth, that they'll hire people if they think they're qualified" – they don't have target numbers for a recruiting class.

Enron also offers internships to business school students, primarily in Houston but also overseas. The programs run 10 weeks, and are described by former interns as fluid and unstructured, allowing interns the chance to mold their responsibilities as they see fit, and explore different parts of the company.

MBA Job Seekers: Receive free e-mailed job postings matching your interests & qualifications! Register at www.VaultReports.com

VAULT REPORTS™
www.vaultreports.com

199

OUR SURVEY SAYS

"I've probably had the best time of my life," says one Enron associate. "It's the best company to work for if you're interested in Corporate America. There's no other place like it," reports one employee. "Due to inherent excitement and relevance of the industry, and Enron's role in building energy infrastructure worldwide, job satisfaction is high," says a former MBA summer associate. "Enron is a great place to work. I can't say enough good things about the company," says another associate. "I work with some of the brightest people I've ever met," says one associate who went to one of the country's top business schools and finds Enron employees to compare favorably to his former classmates. According to one insider: "I never wake up in the morning and don't want to go to work."

Employees describe Enron as flexible when it comes to its internal structure. "Enron is not too wrapped up in titles," says one overseas associate. "It is not hierarchical at all," says one employee at headquarters. "There's a very lean management structure," according to one insider. In a 'deal-making team' there's usually an analyst, an associate, a junior director/manager, a vice president/director, and a president. "So there's direct access, and a very collegial relationship with superiors." This is not to say that it's all hugs and kisses. "There is still politicking, even with the very lean management structure," another contact reports. But "the bosses do not manage in any sense of the word," another insider says, meaning they leave those in their charge to do their work without "telling you what kind of person you should be."

This general fluidity extends to everything from group assignments to daily activities to the company's organizational structure: "My day is generally rather unstructured and I have a great deal of control over my time," says one associate. The associate program, although described by Enron as being comprised of rotating programs, in practice can be quite different. One associate reports that because he likes where he is, and his supervisor believes he's doing a good job, they have decided that he will stay. One former analyst says he stayed a year and a half at one rotation, and then moved through other functions fairly quickly. "We have a free market system in that one can have as much work and any type of assignment one wants," another analyst says. "The company gives the employee the freedom to choose which team he or she will work with." That employee wasn't the only one to characterize Enron as a "free market." "Internally, Enron is like a free market," says an associate. "You can do what interests you." An indication of the company's flexibility is its willingness to discard organizational structure. "Enron will create groups and destroy groups within days depending on the market."

Employees describe the atmosphere at Enron as relaxed but extremely focused. "We're always throwing footballs at each other, or doing what we need to, to keep the atmosphere loose," says one associate at corporate headquarters. Despite the somewhat loose atmosphere, he says, "we are expected to work intensely. My mental inbox is always full. There's always something to do. There's no half hours spent at the water cooler." Says another associate, "The environment is more intense than even an investment bank. There you might work 9:30 to midnight, but there's a lot of downtime. At Enron, you might not even get a chance to get lunch."

To order a 50- to 70-page Vault Reports Employer Profile on Enron call 1-888-JOB-VAULT or visit www.VaultReports.com

The full Employer Profile includes detailed information on Enron's departments, recent developments and transactions, hiring and interview process, plus what employees really think about culture, pay, work hours and more.

MBA Job Seekers: Receive free e-mailed job postings matching your interests & qualifications! Register at www.VaultReports.com

VAULT REPORTS™
www.vaultreports.com

201

Monitor Company

Management Consulting

25 First Street
Cambridge, MA 02141
(617) 252-2000
www.monitor.com

MONITOR COMPANY

LOCATIONS

Cambridge, MA (HQ)
Los Angeles, CA
New York, NY
Athens, Greece
Istanbul, Turkey
Manila, Phillipines
Moscow, Russia
Munich, Germany
New Delhi, India
Sao Paulo, Brazil
Singapore
Stockholm, Sweden
Tel Aviv, Israel
Zurich, Switzerland

DEPARTMENTS

Consulting

THE STATS

Annual Revenues: $186 million (1997)
No. of Employees: 1,200 (worldwide)
No. of Offices: 25 (worldwide)
A privately held company
CEO: Mark J. Fuller

KEY COMPETITORS

- Bain
- Booz • Allen & Hamilton
- Boston Consulting Group
- McKinsey
- Mercer Management Consulting

THE BUZZ

What MBAs are saying
about Monitor

- "Exciting work but weird culture"
- "Entrepreneurial, nerdy"
- "Niche consultant"
- "Too small, too snooty"

UPPERS

- Good social scene
- Loose organizational structure
- Low turnover

DOWNERS

- Lack of support staff
- Long workdays

EMPLOYMENT CONTACT

Monitor Company
25 First Street
Cambridge, MA 02141
employment@monitor.com

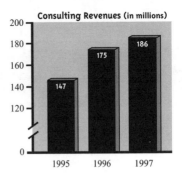

Consulting Revenues (in millions)

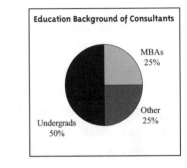

Education Background of Consultants

MBAs 25%
Other 25%
Undergrads 50%

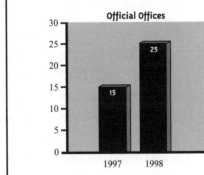

Official Offices

	MBA HOURS	MBA PAY	MBA SELECTIVITY	MBA DRESS	MBA JOB SATISFACTION	
BEST 10 → WORST 1	BEST = SHORTEST HOURS	BEST = HIGHEST PAY	BEST = MOST SELECTIVE	BEST = MOST CASUAL		BEST 10 → WORST 1
	3	8	9	7	9	

MBA Job Seekers: Receive free e-mailed job postings matching
your interests & qualifications! Register at www.VaultReports.com

VAULT REPORTS™
www.vaultreports.com

203

THE SCOOP

Monitor opened its first office in 1983 and has opened at least one new office every year since. Through 25 offices spread across the globe, the firm offers strategic management consulting services to Fortune 500 companies, international firms, government agencies, and major nonprofit organizations. Unlike some other management consulting firms, the Monitor Company does not group and divide its consultants by industry. Instead, it fully integrates its practices. The firm does, however, have "affiliate" organizations that provide support in particular areas such as market research and software support. One of Monitor's key strategies is a "horizontal" web of networked expertise and experience rather than what it views to be the vertical monolithic structure of most consulting firms. Monitor has been a leader in places like South Africa, where it was the first global management consulting company to make a long-term commitment, and the former Soviet Union, where Monitor has been active since the dawn of perestroika. Wherever it operates, the firm emphasizes profit reinvestment to provide its consultants with state-of-the-art resources.

Though he's reportedly rarely seen around the firm, and was never the CEO of the firm, Monitor is pervaded by the spirit of founding principal and Harvard Business School professor Michael Porter. Porter's book *Competitive Strategy* and successive business-oriented tomes have inspired and led generations of Monitor consultants. The books are guides to the interaction between industry structure and competitive strategy and the logic of the variables affecting a company's competitive situation. Monitor still draws inspiration from Porter, but some consultants say "we don't use his stuff as much as we used to." Monitor retains the academic slant of its founding, encouraging a university-like atmosphere, casual dress, and rafts of theories, including "Productive Reasoning," an intervention technique for handling client executives who are reluctant to hand the future of their company over to outsiders (i.e., Monitor consultants). Monitor also encourages pro bono work through its nonprofit Monitor Institute, and in January 1998 started a venture capital fund, much like competitor Bain's Bain Capital.

VAULT REPORTS™
www.vaultreports.com

GETTING HIRED

Monitor hires consultants at both the college graduate and MBA level, and also considers graduates from other advanced degree programs. While the title is the same, the starting pay and responsibility differs based on the new hire's level of schooling. On average, Monitor hires over 50 new MBAs each year.

Monitor recruits on certain business school campuses during the months of October and November. For those going through on-campus recruiting, the first two interview rounds are held on-campus, at a local hotel, or at a nearby office. The second interview will be a case interview, with a twist, insiders tell us. In a typical case interview at other firms, the case interviewer will spring a short case question upon the applicant, who then must quickly come up with pertinent questions and observations. But at Monitor, you'll be given a fairly detailed written case to read (about four or five pages, including exhibits). The final round is at the desired Monitor office – and is even odder involving a "group case" where candidates must collaborate with other applicants. Job offers are typically made the same day as the last interview or no more than 24 hours afterwards by phone. Monitor welcomes hiring inquiries from persons not attending school or at schools not directly targeted by Monitor.

Monitor courts not only MBA students but PhD and other advanced degree candidates for its summer consultant program. The program is designed to approximate the work experience of a full-time consultant as closely as possible. Monitor provides training, feedback and mentoring, and places summer consultants on case teams. The summer internship lasts ten weeks, but may start at any time that is convenient for the summer consultant.

OUR SURVEY SAYS

Monitor stresses that its organizational structure – a "deep and wide pyramid" – differs from that of other firms in the industry. Its employees report that this organizational structure

MBA Job Seekers: Receive free e-mailed job postings matching your interests & qualifications! Register at www.VaultReports.com

VAULT REPORTS™

205

www.vaultreports.com

enables new hires to receive significant responsibilities quickly. Employees enjoy an "unusual degree of independence" and "continuous, on-the-job learning." They say that Monitor has "no titles or structure" and that consultants "can move at their own pace – either rapidly or slowly." In this "meritocratic" atmosphere, consultants often have the opportunity to travel overseas or to work closely with the CEOs of major corporations. Insiders also say that "Monitor has a very low turnover rate in the ranks because we use a much more thorough screening process."

Employees work the "grueling hours" typical of management consulting; one insider reports hearing of a consultant work back-to-back 120-hour weeks. However, they appreciate both the "casual," "friendly," "non-bureaucratic" atmosphere of the firm, and their co-workers, who they describe as "friendly and young." In fact, one consultant estimates that "about 10 percent of the consultants at Monitor are dating each other." The dress code is casual except for client meetings – so casual, that one employee at the company's headquarters comments that the Cambridge office "tends to be a tad more formal – khakis instead of jeans." Monitor consultants also like the company's generous bonus system: year-end bonuses typically run up to 60 percent of base salary – larger than those given by most industry rivals – and can be as high as 100 percent of base salary. In keeping with the academic slant of the firm, consultants aren't afforded their own assistants. In fact, Monitor "recently downsized its research staff, on the theory that consultants should be able to do their own research more efficiently. We kept one guy to take care of the copy machines and stuff like that." But Monitor consultants aren't eager to graduate. "I thoroughly enjoy the work," says one consultant, "and find that I continue to learn on a daily basis."

To order a 50- to 70-page Vault Reports Employer Profile on Monitor Company call 1-888-JOB-VAULT or visit www.VaultReports.com

The full Employer Profile includes detailed information on Monitor's departments, recent developments and transactions, hiring and interview process, plus what employees really think about culture, pay, work hours and more.

Best MBA Employers for Reasonable Hours

FIRM	HOURS RATING (on a 1-10 scale)
3M	8
American Airlines	8
Atlantic Richfield (ARCO)	8
Cargill	8
Nortel Networks	8
3Com	7
American Express	7
Ford Motor	7
General Mills	7
Hewlett-Packard	7
Levi Strauss	7
Merck	7
Nike	7
Sprint	7
United Airlines	7

Source: Vault Reports MBA Survey 1998

Booz · Allen & Hamilton

Management Consulting

101 Park Avenue
New York, NY 10178
(212) 697-1900
www.bah.com

BOOZ·ALLEN & HAMILTON

LOCATIONS

Atlanta, GA • Bethesda, MD • Chicago, IL • Cleveland, OH • Dallas, TX • Houston, TX • Los Angeles, CA • McLean, VA • Monterrey, CA • New York, NY • San Francisco, CA and offices in 31 foreign countries.

KEY COMPETITORS

- Andersen Consulting
- A.T. Kearney
- Bain & Co.
- Boston Consulting Group
- McKinsey & Co.
- Mercer Management Consulting
- Monitor Company

DEPARTMENTS

Communications, Media & Technology
Consumer & Engineered Products
Energy & Chemicals
Financial & Health Services
Information Technology
Operations

THE STATS

Annual Revenues: $1.3 billion (1997)
No. of Employees: 8500
No. of Offices: 90 (worldwide)
A privately-held company
Chairman: William F. Stasior

THE BUZZ
What MBAs are saying
about Booz Allen

- "Midnight oil burners"
- "Dorky but good franchise"
- "Industry focus adds value"
- "Exciting work but aggressive culture"

UPPERS

- Great Intranet
- Generous travel budget
- Individual autonomy
- "Friday in the office" policy

DOWNERS

- Long work days
- Extensive travel
- Sometimes overly political

EMPLOYMENT CONTACT

Lonnie Nom
Booz • Allen & Hamilton
101 Park Avenue
New York, NY 10178

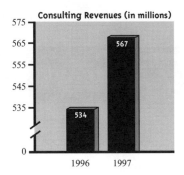

Consulting Revenues (in millions)

Distribution of Revenues

U.S. 52%
International 48%

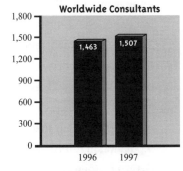

Worldwide Consultants

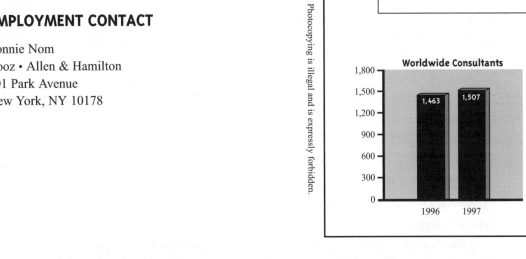

	MBA HOURS	MBA PAY	MBA SELECTIVITY	MBA DRESS	MBA JOB SATISFACTION	
BEST 10 → ... WORST 1	BEST = SHORTEST HOURS	BEST = HIGHEST PAY	BEST = MOST SELECTIVE	BEST = MOST CASUAL		BEST 10 → ... WORST 1
	2	8	8	3	6	

MBA Job Seekers: Receive free e-mailed job postings matching
your interests & qualifications! Register at www.VaultReports.com

VAULT REPORTS™   209
www.vaultreports.com

THE SCOOP

Edwin Booz founded his firm shortly after graduating from Northwestern University in 1914. From the beginning, Booz' consulting firm, one of the first such companies, worked closely with government agencies, consulting with the War Department in 1917. Booz was joined by partners Allen and Hamilton during the 1930s, and in 1940, worked with the U.S. government again in preparation for World War II. Since then, Booz Allen & Hamilton has emerged as one of the world's most prestigious management consulting firms. To this day, Booz• Allen works with government agencies, but has also expanded its reach to include manufacturing, electronics, chemicals, transportation and energy, and telecommunications. The firm is organized into industry-related practices that include communications, computing & electronics, energy & chemicals, financial services, and marketing.

With an emphasis on creating change rather than merely prescribing it, the firm reports spending about a third to a half of its time in the implementation process. Before implementation, Booz • Allen often involves the client in the consulting process and frequently integrates client management into the consulting team. In 1993, the firm adopted its "Vision 2000" plan, which reorganized the firm into its current practice areas and restated Booz's original goal of becoming "the absolute best management and technology consulting firm." As part of Vision 2000, Booz pared down the number of clients from 1200 to 300; Booz• Allen garners 80 percent of its revenues from 20 percent of its clients. Part of what the company believes will help make it the best is encouraging innovation. Here, Booz • Allen's strong reputation in information technology systems comes into play. The firm's Knowledge On-Line (KOL) is often called the best of its kind. The shared system keeps consultants from repeating each other's work, and provides info on an assortment of topics, including resumes, databases and histories of employees.

Booz • Allen is divvied into two major operations. The Worldwide Commercial Business unit (WCB), in New York, does corporate strategy, renewal, productivity improvement, growth management, acquisitions, and business restructuring, mainly for international corporations. Within the WCB, Booz • Allen is divided into Energy, Chemicals & Pharmaceuticals, Consumer and Engineered Products, Financial and Health Services, and Communications,

Media, and Technology WCB also includes three functional groups: Operations Management, Information Technology, and Strategic Leadership

The Worldwide Technology Business, based in DC suburb McLean, VA, caters to government clients in the nation's capital and in other nation-states, consulting on defense, national security, environment and energy, transportation and space, telecommunications, civil programs, international projects, and management sciences. MBAs are normally not hired for the WTB; its consultants are normally engineers who work on a different pay scale and hiring schedule.

KOL is now used widely by Booz • Allen consultants in both the Worldwide Commercial Business and Worldwide Technology Business branches. The first estimates that about 62 percent of WCB staff members access KOL monthly or more (security concerns prevent WTB consultants, who typically work with government agencies, from accessing KOL on assignments). The database is set up to promote sharing of information, and consultants often spend a considerable amount of time entering their findings into KOL. Booz• Allen achieves this informational exchange partially through an appeal to ego: consultants who contribute the database have their names prominently displayed, their entries are linked to their resumes, and it's simple to search for any given consultants contributions to the database. In addition, the firm encourages contributions through its feedback process, where a third of the evaluation is based in part on contributions such as those to KOL.

GETTING HIRED

Booz • Allen is somewhat unusual among consulting firms in that it is divided up into distinct industry practice and functional groups. The interview process consists of two rounds, the first on campus, the second at Booz offices. MBA interviewees must know which industry practice or functional group is of interest to them, as the second round of interview is exclusively with senior associates (MBA-level employees at Booz are called associates; above them are senior associates), principals (the next level after senior associate) and partners in the industry group

MBA Job Seekers: Receive free e-mailed job postings matching your interests & qualifications! Register at www.VaultReports.com

VAULT REPORTS™
www.vaultreports.com

211

of interest. Insiders say that the industry or operational group selection should be "pretty straightforward." "Don't try to psych out the interviewers," suggests one consultant. "It's a bad idea to choose one group thinking it will be easier to get in, and then try to switch to another. Be straightforward." While experience in a particular industry is a "boon," it's not necessary. "We hire people who are simply smart as well." If you have your heart set on a particular office, beware – not all practices reside at all offices. Hiring for the Worldwide Technology Business arm, which works largely with government contractors, is handled separately and does not target MBAs.

OUR SURVEY SAYS

Booz Allen's culture encourages "fiercely independent" thinking without "hand-holding" or a "rah-rah team atmosphere." Employees say that this "sink or swim" environment forces them to learn on the job and to test their "mettle" against "a series of increasingly difficult challenges." Some employees object that Booz's flexibility means there is no career management. Insiders also say that Booz • Allen's policy of integrating its consultants into with the client's management into teams at the client's headquarters results in "constant travel" that can take its toll on consultants' lifestyles. We hear that the workplace can "be very political" and that a "sponsor" in upper management is crucial for advancement. This tough attitude impacts on women and minorities. The culture at the firm is "notoriously macho and male," which female employees have found "quite repulsive," though some women say the firm has made a "genuine effort" to improve matters.

This is not to say that Booz • Allen is a completely grim, dog-eat-dog sort of workplace. For one, working at Booz is "great for anyone who has a social conscience." The firm permits some pro bono work, and employees say that "unlike most management consulting places, Booz can understand employees who have a conscience and want to help people." The pay is "awesome," with MBAs earning upwards of $120,000 annually (not including bonuses). The best perk of working for Booz • Allen, according to employees, is "the unbelievable opportunities to travel around the world and enjoy yourself in style." One consultant says: "Things I did because of my job there: flew the Concord, went to Lillehammer for the winter Olympics, took a cruise from Miami to the Bahamas, gambled in Monte Carlo, opera at Covent Garden, dinner in the Eiffel Tower, a summer afternoon at a topless beach in Nice, and the list goes on."

Toward the end of the summer, Booz • Allen takes all the summer MBA interns (as well as the five to 10 undergrad interns) and sends them on the renowned "Booz Cruise," a fabulous perk. The American interns in 1998 went to the Bahamas for four days, and the European interns went to the Costa del Sol in Spain. Asian interns visited the resort of Cebu in the Philippines. But that boat, for example, had only 500 places. Who gets to go? There's a "five-step ranking process" that prospective vacationers endure. A general e-mail goes out, and interested consultants put their hats in the ring. Then the heads of each industry department nominate people. Other considerations are who's involved in recruiting, and factors like seniority, performance, and diversity by gender and race." There are "about 30 partners on the boat, with their families." One consultant says "I served on the recruiting committee, but I didn't get chosen for the Booz Cruise. It was just as well, because it turned out I couldn't have gone anyway because of travel."

To order a 50- to 70-page Vault Reports Employer Profile on Booz • Allen & Hamilton call 1-888-JOB-VAULT or visit www.VaultReports.com

The full Employer Profile includes detailed information on Booz • Allen's departments, recent developments and transactions, hiring and interview process, plus what employees really think about culture, pay, work hours and more.

MBA Job Seekers: Receive free e-mailed job postings matching your interests & qualifications! Register at www.VaultReports.com

VAULT REPORTS™

213

www.vaultreports.com

Mercer Management Consulting

Management Consulting

1166 Avenue of the Americas
New York, NY 10036
(212) 345-8000
www.mercermc.com

MERCER
Management Consulting

LOCATIONS

New York, NY (HQ)

Boston, MA • Chicago, IL • Cleveland, OH • Pittsburgh, PA • San Francisco, CA • Washington, DC • Buenos Aires, Argentina • Hong Kong • Lisbon, Portugal • London, United Kingdom • Madrid, Spain • Montreal, Canada • Munich, Germany • Paris, France • Toronto, Canada • Zurich, Switzerland

DEPARTMENTS

Central Resource Group

THE STATS

Annual Revenues: $1.3 billion (1997)
No. of Employees: 1,200
No. of Offices: 17 (worldwide)
A subsidiary of Marsh & McLennan
CEO: Peter Coster

KEY COMPETITORS

◆ A.T. Kearney
◆ Bain
◆ Boston Consulting Group
◆ Booz • Allen & Hamilton
◆ McKinsey
◆ Monitor Company

THE BUZZ
What MBAs are saying
about Mercer

◆ "Data-driven, fresh thinking"
◆ "Up and coming"
◆ "All show"
◆ "Reasonable approach"

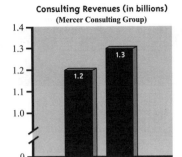

Consulting Revenues (in billions)
(Mercer Consulting Group)

UPPERS

- Extensive vacation
- Great insurance benefits
- Stock options
- Two-way feedback system
- Good support staff

DOWNERS

- Long hours
- Demanding assignments

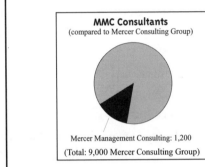

MMC Consultants
(compared to Mercer Consulting Group)

Mercer Management Consulting: 1,200
(Total: 9,000 Mercer Consulting Group)

EMPLOYMENT CONTACT

Dana Grube
Mercer Management Consulting
2300 N Street, N.W.
Suite 800
Washington, DC 20037
(202) 778-7560

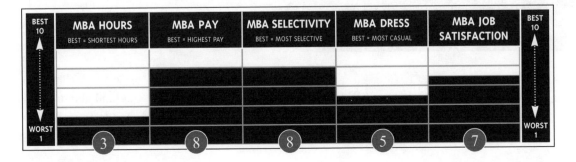

	MBA HOURS	MBA PAY	MBA SELECTIVITY	MBA DRESS	MBA JOB SATISFACTION	
BEST 10 ↑ ... WORST 1	BEST = SHORTEST HOURS	BEST = HIGHEST PAY	BEST = MOST SELECTIVE	BEST = MOST CASUAL		BEST 10 ↑ ... WORST 1
	3	8	8	5	7	

MBA Job Seekers: Receive free e-mailed job postings matching
your interests & qualifications! Register at www.VaultReports.com

VAULT REPORTS™
www.vaultreports.com

215

THE SCOOP

Mercer Management Consulting is the sparkling consulting subsidiary of insurance titan Marsh McLennan, which also owns William Mercer (an employee benefits consultancy), the National Economic Research Association (microeconomic consulting) and Lippincott & Margulies (identity strategy). Mercer Management Consulting, which focuses on strategy management advice, was formed in 1990 through the merger of Temple, Barker & Sloane and Strategic Planning Associates. Since its founding, the firm has been growing aggressively. Recent additions to Mercer Management include new offices in Europe, the Pacific Rim and Canada, and the respected 120-consultant firm Corporate Decisions, Inc. (CDI), which was snapped up by Mercer in September 1997. "Emphasis on customer-driven strategy will become even stronger through our merger with CDI," says Mercer vice chairman (co-CEO) James Down. Mercer Management Consulting now has 1200 consultants; the firm earned $300 million in revenues in 1997.

Although Mercer consults with a wide range of companies, the firm has developed special industry expertise in four specific areas: financial services, transportation, communications/information/entertainment (CIE), and a fourth catchall group that includes energy and utilities, manufacturing, and oil and gas. A member of the Mercer Consulting Group – the worldwide consulting organization of Marsh McLennan – Mercer Management is able to supplement its own expertise with the skills of the group's other firms. Mercer Management operates through a "borderless organization" that assembles consulting teams from a variety of geographical locations and industry specialties.

GETTING HIRED

Mercer hires 30 to 40 summer MBA interns each year (about 30 in the U.S. and about 12 in Europe), and hires only at its core business schools: Harvard, Kellogg, Tuck, Sloan, Stanford,

Wharton, INSEAD and IESE. "Go through the normal recruiting process," advise successful summer consultants. "Mercer doesn't have many back doors."

Mercer puts its applicants through five or six interviews in either two or three rounds. In each round, there will be one personality interview. The remainder will be case interviews. "Success on the case interviews is absolutely critical," insiders advise. Mercer may also use group exercises, which are conducted with other potential Mercer employees, and even ask experienced applicants to prepare a presentation (with plenty of lead time). Mercer urges interviewees daunted by the prospect of the case interview to relax – the firm is "not looking for a specific answer," but is "trying to gain some insight into your thought processes."

Associates join Mercer as part of the Central Resource Group, which gives them the opportunity to work on a variety of issues, functional areas and industries across any or all Mercer practices.

OUR SURVEY SAYS

Employees say that Mercer "believes in developing each and every employee." Consultants say that Mercer is "a total meritocracy." However, one employee says that while Mercer "has a history of not being very bureaucratic, that may change now that the firm is growing." As part of the firm's commitment to professional development, Mercer uses a two-way feedback system in which both junior and senior employees evaluate each other. Recent hires also benefit from "extensive contact" with more experienced consultants. A firm that is looking for its consultants to have longer tenures than those at many of its competitors, Mercer "does not equate personal sacrifice with good consulting" and works to minimize the time its consultants spend away from home. Mercer consultants also benefit from parent Marsh MacLennan. "The insurance package is very impressive – Mercer is owned by Marsh MacLennan, which is in insurance," one employee smartly notices. Other impressive perks include free sports tickets, subsidies at gyms, a "very lucrative" stock option plan; pay, however, is only average for Mercer's prestige class.

MBA Job Seekers: Receive free e-mailed job postings matching your interests & qualifications! Register at www.VaultReports.com

VAULT REPORTS™
www.vaultreports.com

217

Mercer consultants can relax their dress, as "there's no fixed dress code" at the firm – it's normally "khakis and sweaters or open collars." Despite the minimization of time away from home, hours, however, are less blissful. Consultants say that "burnout is a serious problem." To lighten the load, "there is always a secretary to help you." Case teams also have people "called case team assistants, who are basically college graduates from less prestigious schools than most Mercer consultants. They do the research coordination and data entry, basically scut work. Sometimes they get promoted to research analyst, but not very often."

Insiders rave about Mercer's social life. "Rocking!" says one consultant. "Every Friday there's a TGIF, and there are frequent weekend parties." One consultant happily reports that "a bunch of people from the office get a ski house together every winter," while another describes her co-workers as "very congenial." Mercer insiders says that the level of social activity differs from office to office. "Actually, some offices are a little more social than others," says one Mercer employee. "On the research analyst level, everyone is always social, but in some offices, like DC, even partners will come out and party." Still, "on case teams, we always got together one night a week. We would rent a room in a sports bar, or maybe have a nice dinner together."

To order a 50- to 70-page Vault Reports Employer Profile on Mercer Management Consulting call 1-888-JOB-VAULT or visit www.VaultReports.com

The full Employer Profile includes detailed information on Mercer's departments, recent developments and transactions, hiring and interview process, plus what employees really think about culture, pay, work hours and more.

CASE INTERVIEWS: WHY THE CASE?

Your impressive resume may get you an interview with a consulting firm, but it won't get you the job. Consultants know that a resume, at its very best, is only a two-dimensional representation of a multi-faceted, dynamic person.

And because consulting firms depend on employing those multi-faceted, dynamic people, the firms rely heavily on the case interview to screen candidates. The interview process is especially pertinent in the consulting industry, since consulting professionals spend the lion's share of their business day interacting with clients and colleagues, and must themselves constantly interview client employees and executives.

Furthermore, consultants must have a select set of personality and leadership traits in order to be successful. A consultant's work environment is extremely turbulent... there are nonstop engagement team changes, hostile client environments, countless political influences, and virtually 100 percent travel. These factors dictate that an individual be cool under pressure, be influential but not condescending, be highly analytical, have the ability to understand the granular aspects of a problem while simultaneously aggregating them up to see the big picture – and have the ability to self-police a balance between personal and professional lifestyle.

Consultants are often staffed in small groups in farflung areas. As a result, the individual must be able to function, and function well, without many of the traditional workplace standards: a permanent working space, the ability to return home each night, easily accessed services such as administrative assistance, faxing, and photocopying, and the camaraderie that develops among co-workers assigned to the same business unit.

All these factors necessitate a unique interview structure focused on assessing a candidate's ability to manage these particular circumstances with professionalism and excellence. The case interview has evolved as a method for evaluating just such sets of characteristics.

For more information on preparing for case interviews, including actual case interview questions with model answers, read the Vault Reports Guide to Case Interviews.

Salomon Smith Barney

Investment Banking

388 Greenwich Street
New York, NY 10013
(212) 783-7000
Fax: (212) 940-4299
www.salomonsmithbarney.com

SALOMON SMITH BARNEY

LOCATIONS

New York, NY (HQ)
As well as offices in CA • CT • DC • FL • GA
• IL • MA • NJ • PA • TX • International
offices worldwide

DEPARTMENTS

Compliance • Credit Review • Domestic
Corporate Finance • Equity • Fixed Income •
Investment Banking • Legal • Sales & Trading
• Asset Management • Capital Markets •
Finance and Administration • Information
Systems • Investment Banking • Public Finance
• Research • Sales

KEY COMPETITORS

- Goldman Sachs
- J.P. Morgan
- Lehman Brothers
- Merrill Lynch
- Morgan Stanley Dean Witter

THE STATS

Annual Revenues: NA
No. of Employees: 36,250 (worldwide),
5,000 (U.S.)
No. of Offices: 541 (worldwide)
A subsidiary of the Travelers Group
Chairmen and CEO: Deryck C. Maughan
Assets: $115+ billion

THE BUZZ
What MBAs are saying
about SSB

- "Merger creates formidable presence"
- "Wannabe, buying market share"
- "No more big bets"
- "Solid"

UPPERS

◆ High pay
◆ Company gym
◆ Free bank account
◆ Free late night dinners

DOWNERS

◆ Culture clash
◆ High pressure
◆ Merger uncertainty

EMPLOYMENT CONTACT

Lisa Burke, MBA Recruiting Manager
Salomon Smith Barney
388 Greenwich Street
New York, NY 10013

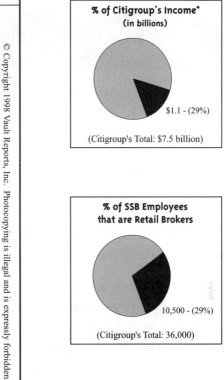

% of Citigroup's Income*
(in billions)

$1.1 - (29%)

(Citigroup's Total: $7.5 billion)

% of SSB Employees
that are Retail Brokers

10,500 - (29%)

(Citigroup's Total: 36,000)

* Citigroup's 1997 pro forma figures

	BEST 10	MBA HOURS BEST = SHORTEST HOURS	MBA PAY BEST = HIGHEST PAY	MBA SELECTIVITY BEST = MOST SELECTIVE	MBA DRESS BEST = MOST CASUAL	MBA JOB SATISFACTION	BEST 10
	WORST 1	2	9	9	2	4	WORST 1

MBA Job Seekers: Receive free e-mailed job postings matching
your interests & qualifications! Register at www.VaultReports.com

VAULT REPORTS™

THE SCOOP

When word hit Wall Street that Travelers Group chairman Sanford Weill was looking for an investment bank to add to his insurance giant, Salomon Brothers didn't wait for Weill to come a'courtin. Instead, the famed investment bank, immortalized in Michael Lewis' Liar's Poker, took the initiative to call Weill. In December 1997, Travelers bought Salomon for more than $9 billion. Salomon was merged with Travelers' brokerage arm, Smith Barney, to create Salomon Smith Barney. But Weill wasn't finished. In the spring of 1998, Travelers announced plans to merge with commercial banking giant Citicorp, a move that has created a financial services behemoth called Citigroup in a $70 billion merger.

So where does this leave Salomon Smith Barney? At the grown-up table, seated next to big boys like Morgan Stanley Dean Witter (also the product of a mega-merger), Merrill Lynch, and Goldman Sachs. Despite a somewhat rocky beginning because of restructuring costs, the merger has proved thus far to be a success. Despite initial concerns about overlapping business and clashing cultures, the merger has allowed Salomon Smith Barney to reach a "critical mass" in certain industries (the combination of clients in the energy industry, for example, has enabled the firm to become a player in that field), and strengthening its position across the board. And with the addition of Citicorp's international presence, the firm expects to have increased leverage internationally. However, the Citigroup merger has gotten off to a shaky start as far as Salomon Smith Barney is concerned. In November 1998, Jamie Dimon, the then-CEO of Salomon Smith Barney and Weill's longtime right-hand man, resigned after disagreements about the future autonomy of Salomon Smith Barney

GETTING HIRED

The 1998 recruiting season is the first in which Salomon and Smith Barney will integrate their hiring. In the past, both firms have interviewed applicants over several rounds. Since most new associates are recent B-school grads, a campus interview usually starts off the process.

Says one recent hire: "I had a first round in the morning, a second round in the evening, and then the final round in New York." Several insiders report receiving two-on-one interviews in the on-campus interviews.

The second round, for those who are invited to participate, usually involves a full day of interviews at the firm's headquarters. "It was a few hours, six interviews," reports one recent interviewee. Most applicants participate in a Saturday session referred to as a "Super Saturday." Says one contact: "The interviews start out rather informal and the final round is usually five or more interviews on a Saturday." The firm provides a recruiting calendar for business school students on its web site, at www.salomonsmithbarney.com.

OUR SURVEY SAYS

In January 1998, the Salomon Brothers and Smith Barney operations merged, during a staggered two-week moving period. Some operations consolidated at Smith Barney's Greenwich Avenue headquarters, others consolidated in Salomon Brothers' World Trade Center headquarters. "Industrial groups, transportation, environmental all moved to Salomon," explains one Salomon Smith Barney insider. "It was pretty much a power thing. The healthcare group, for example, stayed at the Greenwich Avenue location. Telecom stayed at the Salomon side. The energy group moved to Smith Barney location. You moved to where the biggest practice was." The firm's capital markets groups also were organized around power centers: "High-yield moved to Solly, bond trading moved to Solly, equities moved to Smith Barney." "All of a sudden, there was a new group of people," says one I-banking insider from the Salomon side. "We had had some sort of social session beforehand. And now, we're all integrated."

That the Salomon and Smith Barney cultures contrast is not in dispute. "Salomon is much more aggressive, much more individualistic, somewhat Neanderthal-like," explains one insider from the Salomon side. Says one who was hired initially by Smith Barney: "On the investment banking side, you could see it in terms of team players. The Solly people came out more as

MBA Job Seekers: Receive free e-mailed job postings matching your interests & qualifications! Register at www.VaultReports.com

VAULT REPORTS™
www.vaultreports.com

223

individual – the 'I don't give a shit what you need to do, I need to get my work done' thing. You get a lot of that in banking, but more so at Solly, it's a little more ruthless, Smith Barney people bent a little over backward to help you." Continues that contact: "You've got to realize that these were two very different cultures – on the Smith Barney side you had a younger bank, younger MDs, who were more gung ho about making money, less concerned about big ticket items. Salomon would go for big names, the Smith Barney guys were concerned about making money, if it's a high-yield company that is kind of on the edge, but will pay more, hey, we'll do it. The Solly guys won't even touch it."

Says one I-banking insider about the merger: "I think it's gone pretty smoothly, I was impressed with how quickly things got rolling, and we sort of became one firm, it's a tough environment to do it in, because things move really fast. I was impressed." Perhaps that assessment stems from the fact that that analyst was originally hired by Salomon Brothers. As one Smith Barney I-banker puts it: "We bought Solly, but invariably Salomon took over the investment banking operations." Insiders, however, say that the culture of the firm is driven by the firm that had the more powerful group – Smith Barney for health care, Salomon for M&A, etc.

As might be expected of a large merger with conflicting cultures, the Salomon Smith Barney combination has left behind some disgruntled employees – although many of the disgruntled have since left. While the departures of high-profile Salomon execs have been chronicled in the press, the exodus of bankers isn't confined to the top levels, insiders say. "When I left the group, they were down to four or five associates, from maybe 16. A lot of them left. Mostly associates from the Salomon side left, I think because a lot of people were drawn initially by the Salomon Brothers, Neanderthal-like atmosphere." But Salomon employees aren't the only ones who have left. Says one associate from the Smith Barney side: "In M&A, in the past three months, 17 Smith Barney employees walked out the door – they're a dying breed. In the energy group, there was a mass exodus."

Because of these changes, insiders expect that the firm's culture will begin to even out between Salomon and Smith Barney, especially because of the pending merger with Citigroup. "I would guess that it's going to come up somewhere in the middle," says one insider. "Although the Salomon culture is still stronger, a lot of people left. Especially when you get a commercial bank in there, things are bound to change."

To order a 50- to 70-page Vault Reports Employer Profile on Salomon Smith Barney call 1-888-JOB-VAULT or visit www.VaultReports.com

The full Employer Profile includes detailed information on SSB's departments, recent developments and transactions, hiring and interview process, plus what employees really think about culture, pay, work hours and more.

MBA Job Seekers: Receive free e-mailed job postings matching your interests & qualifications! Register at www.VaultReports.com

VAULT REPORTS™

225

www.vaultreports.com

Sun Microsystems

High Tech

901 San Antonio Road
Palo Alto, CA 94303
(650) 960-1300
www.sun.com

LOCATIONS

Palo Alto, CA (HQ)
Additional offices in CO • IL • MA • NY •
TX • and worldwide

DEPARTMENTS

Customer Service
Engineering
Finance
Hardware Engineering
Information Systems
Network Solutions Consulting
Operations
Software Development
Systems Engineering
Technical Phone Support
Technical Pre-Sales Support

THE STATS

Annual Revenues: $10.0 billion (1997)
No. of Employees: 26,000 (worldwide)
No. of Offices: 160+ (worldwide)
Stock Symbol: SUNW (Nasdaq)
CEO: Scott G. McNealy

KEY COMPETITORS

- ◆ Dell Computer
- ◆ Hewlett-Packard
- ◆ IBM
- ◆ Intel
- ◆ Microsoft
- ◆ National Semiconductor
- ◆ Silicon Graphics
- ◆ Tandem Computers
- ◆ Unisys

THE BUZZ

What MBAs are saying
about Sun Microsystems

- ◆ "Whiners"
- ◆ "Determined, demanding"
- ◆ "Cool culture, but low upside"
- ◆ "Looking up at Microsoft"

UPPERS

- Flexible hours
- Creative atmosphere
- Excellent job training

DOWNERS

- Long workweek
- Hectic work schedules, especially near project deadlines

EMPLOYMENT CONTACT

901 San Antonio Road
Palo Alto, CA 94303
(650) 960-1300
Fax: (650) 336-3701
college-jobs@sun.com

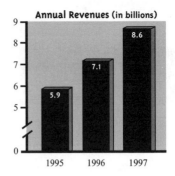

Annual Revenues (in billions)

1995: 5.9
1996: 7.1
1997: 8.6

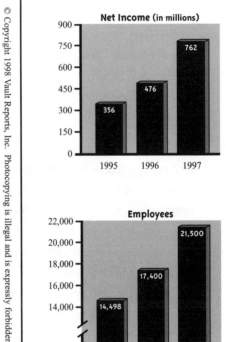

Net Income (in millions)

1995: 356
1996: 476
1997: 762

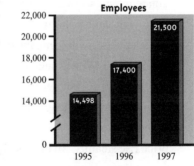

Employees

1995: 14,498
1996: 17,400
1997: 21,500

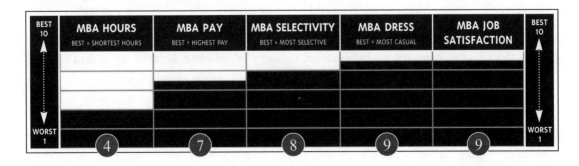

	MBA HOURS BEST = SHORTEST HOURS	MBA PAY BEST = HIGHEST PAY	MBA SELECTIVITY BEST = MOST SELECTIVE	MBA DRESS BEST = MOST CASUAL	MBA JOB SATISFACTION	
BEST 10 ... WORST 1	4	7	8	9	9	BEST 10 ... WORST 1

THE SCOOP

Originally a computer workstation builder, Sun was founded in 1982 by four 27-year-olds. Five years later it was a $500 million company, having gone public in 1986. Sun succeeded almost immediately by developing operating systems for big-name clients such as AT&T. The company has been a leader in the development of "intranet" networking systems, and Sun's current joint ventures with Oracle, IBM, and Netscape have further solidified its position as an industry leader. Just another Silicon Valley success story, you say? Maybe, but while many similar stories are now tales of sputtering organizations caught a step behind emerging technologies, Sun Microsystems has introduced a new technology with the potential to revolutionize computing technology, and has even King Bill of Microsoft worried.

Sun introduced a computer language called Java in May 1995 as a way to animate features on web pages. But in the summer of 1995, industry observers began suggesting that if Java the concept were to prove viable, there would no longer be a need for the operating systems and concomitant software with which Microsoft captivates the computing world. The years following Java's anointing as the Next Big Thing have been heady ones for Sun and its shareholders, with rampant talk of "revolution" and "paradigm shift." Meanwhile, Sun has shunned the Wintel hegemony continuing to produce its own microprocessors (it is the only major computer builder that does not use Intel chips) and developing software for UNIX-based (non Windows NT) systems. Although Windows NT is becoming increasingly popular, Sun is doing well with its sale of Unix servers and workstations, and has seen its earnings and stock price rise steadily. In late 1997, Sun filed suit against Microsoft relating to the software giant's use of Sun's Java language.

It's not as if Sun only has enemies in the high-tech world – opponents of Wintel are cheering on Sun's pugnacious stance. In 1998, Sun and IBM announced a partnership to create an operating system using Java. In June of that year, the two companies initiated a joint effort with the Chinese Ministry of Information Industry to promote Java in the world's most populous country. The Java-based system was released a couple months later.

GETTING HIRED

Sun recruits at many business schools and career fairs; a schedule is posted at the company's website, located at www.sun.com. Also at the web site is a page with which job seekers can search for open positions by function or geographic area. Sun offers summer internships for B-school students. The summer program offers an annual event with CEO Scott McNealy. For new hires going into sales and systems engineering, there is a one-year rotational "Best of the Best" program. The sales positions are for MBAs – about 10 to 12 are hired each year.

Interviews reportedly range from "half-day to full-day schedules" and will include some technical questions, but are less intense and freaky than at other high tech companies. "My experience is that they are less brainteaser oriented, and are more to find out what you know about what you say you know," reports one insider.

OUR SURVEY SAYS

Sun Microsystems pushes its employees to keep the company on the cutting edge. In this "aggressive" and "innovative" corporate culture, everyone is "expected to take the initiative, make decisions, and be creative in solving problems," employees say. There is "no hand-holding" at Sun, and "the flat hierarchy makes it easy to access people throughout the organization." While project deadlines inflate the pressure that everyone feels, Sun employees are also fond of playing practical jokes and of "blowing off steam" at company social events. Advancement opportunities, "generous" pay, and the "top-drawer" job training contribute to an "immensely satisfied" workforce that takes pride in working for a high-tech company with such a "high level of integrity, creativity, and industry prestige."

MBA Job Seekers: Receive free e-mailed job postings matching your interests & qualifications! Register at www.VaultReports.com

VAULT REPORTS™

229

www.vaultreports.com

"Sun is a typical Silicon Valley place – very high pressure," explains one engineer. "Expect a long workweek, though not as crazy as a startup." Another insider says "the work ethic is severe, with many of the movers and shakers in the company working many hours a week." This isn't to say everyone at Sun works like a fiend: "Some people I know work 40, others 70," says one engineer. However, those with their eyes on moving up in the company note that "those that work 70 are generally recognized and rewarded for it."

Despite the long hours and hectic environment, employees say that "the culture is relaxed, very California." By this they mean low-key when it comes to policies and bureaucracy, dress code, and strict hours. "Dress code?" snorts one employee. "Shorts!" Says one researcher: "Finance and marketing look more conservative." However, "on Friday, you can't tell engineering from finance." Sums up one employee in marketing: "It's business casual for most departments, suits for some positions like sales."

"Work start time is extremely flexible. Most people don't come in until 9:30 to 10 a.m., so that they don't have to sit in traffic. Others I know come in at 7 a.m. to beat the rush and leave at 3:30 p.m.," says one engineer. "It's all up to you, but you do have to try to make sure you don't miss any meetings." "Most of the engineering campus feels a lot like college: You can come and go as you please as long as you get your work done and attend staff meetings," says another. Insiders also report that there is a "strong work-from-home program." Telecommuting is encouraged if it fits your job profile," explains one insider.

To order a 10- to 20-page Vault Reports Employer Profile on Sun Microsystems call 1-888-JOB-VAULT or visit www.VaultReports.com

The full Employer Profile includes detailed information on Sun's departments, recent developments and transactions, hiring and interview process, plus what employees really think about culture, pay, work hours and more.

"Sun is a typical Silicon Valley place – very high pressure."

– *Sun Microsystems insider*

MBA Job Seekers: Receive free e-mailed job postings matching
your interests & qualifications! Register at www.VaultReports.com

VAULT
REPORTS™

231

www.vaultreports.com

Johnson & Johnson

Consumer Products

One Johnson & Johnson Plaza
New Brunswick, NJ 08933
(908) 524-0400
Fax: (908) 524-3300
www.jnj.com

Johnson & Johnson

LOCATIONS

New Brunswick, NJ (HQ)
As well as facilities in CA • FL • MA • NJ •
NY • OH • PA • TX • Australia • Belgium •
Canada • China • Egypt • France • Germany •
Greece • Hong Kong • India • Japan • Mexico
• Panama • Puerto Rico • Russia • Scotland •
Singapore • Thailand • United Kingdom •
Zimbabwe

DEPARTMENTS

Advanced Care Products • Cardiology •
Enterprise Systems Integration • Human
Resources • Marketing • Operations/Engineering
• Pharmaceutical Research • Radiology •
Sterilization Products

THE STATS

Annual Revenues: $22.6 billion (1997)
Income: $3.3 billion (1997)
No. of Employees: 90,500 (worldwide)
No. of Offices: 260 (worldwide)
Stock Symbol: JNJ
CEO: Ralph S. Larsen
**Annual Expenditures for Research
and Development:** $2.1 billion (1997)

KEY COMPETITORS

- Bristol-Myers Squibb
- Colgate-Palmolive
- Eli Lilly
- Gillette
- Glaxo Wellcome
- Kimberly-Clark
- Merck
- Monsanto
- Pfizer
- Pharmacia & Upjohn
- Procter & Gamble
- Unilever

THE BUZZ
What MBAs are saying
about Johnson & Johnson

- "Ethical"
- "Lots of variety, intelligent people"
- "Strong yet staid and boring"
- "Good products, blue collar"

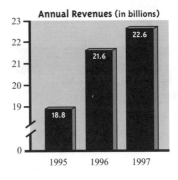

Annual Revenues (in billions)

- 1995: 18.8
- 1996: 21.6
- 1997: 22.6

UPPERS

- On-site child care centers at four locations
- Adoption assistance
- Professional child-rearing advice hotline
- Decentralized structure

DOWNERS

- Strict dress code at headquarters
- Excessive paperwork

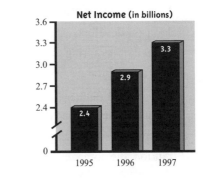

Net Income (in billions)

- 1995: 2.4
- 1996: 2.9
- 1997: 3.3

EMPLOYMENT CONTACT

Johnson & Johnson
Recruiting Services
501 George Street, Room JH215
P.O. Box 16597
New Brunswick, NJ 08906-6597

Employees

- 1995: 82,300
- 1996: 89,300
- 1997: 90,500

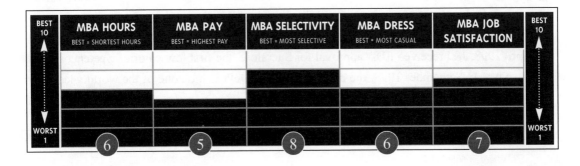

	MBA HOURS BEST = SHORTEST HOURS	MBA PAY BEST = HIGHEST PAY	MBA SELECTIVITY BEST = MOST SELECTIVE	MBA DRESS BEST = MOST CASUAL	MBA JOB SATISFACTION	
BEST 10 ↑ ↓ WORST 1	6	5	8	6	7	BEST 10 ↑ ↓ WORST 1

MBA Job Seekers: Receive free e-mailed job postings matching
your interests & qualifications! Register at www.VaultReports.com

VAULT REPORTS™
www.vaultreports.com

233

THE SCOOP

A maker of more than just its famous Band-Aids, Johnson & Johnson is the largest manufacturer of health care products in the world. Founded in 1885 by James and Edward Mead Johnson, the company's first success was the surgical dressing developed by a third Johnson brother, Robert, who joined them the following year. Early in its history, Johnson & Johnson developed its strategy of teaming up with smaller medical suppliers in partnerships instead of acquiring them outright. The strategy has paid off and enabled Johnson & Johnson to create a product line that includes artificial joints, Neutrogena skin and hair care products, and Tylenol pain killers. Although Johnson & Johnson has a proud history of high-quality products, the company confronted tragedy in 1982, when eight people died after consuming Tylenol capsules laced with cyanide. Though the product recall cost Johnson & Johnson $240 million, the company's quick and decisive action enabled it to recover rapidly.

The company splits its business up into three major segments. The Professional segment, which includes products like surgical instruments and contact lenses (including disposables Acuvue and Surevue), is the company's largest unit, accounting for $8.4 billion in sales in 1997. The company's pharmacuetical segment, maker of anemia drug Procrit and anti-psychotic drug Risperdal, accounted for $7.7 billion. The products that make up Johnson & Johnson's well-known consumer unit, offering products such as painkiller Tylenol and see-through Netrogena, brought in $6.5 billion in revenues. The company has more than 180 operating companies in 51 countries, and sells its products in more than 175 countries.

A top-tier marketing company, Johnson & Johnson spends an estimated $568 million annually on TV ads in the U.S. J&J refers to its myriad of subsidiaries as a "worldwide family of companies"; and as a parent company, Johnson & Johnson is known as very pro-family when it comes to its treatment of employees, offering on-site child care at many sites and a child care hotline. Meanwhile, the company continues to expand through new products and subsidiaries. In April 1998, J&J received FDA approval for Sucralose, the first low-calorie sweetener made from sugar. In September 1998, the company bought DePuy, Inc., one of the world's leading orthopedic products companies, for $3.5 billion.

GETTING HIRED

Since Johnson & Johnson has a decentralized structure that incorporates more than 180 subsidiaries worldwide, hiring processes are not uniform throughout the company. Applicants should consult the Johnson & Johnson recruiting Web page, located at www.jnj.com/recruit/recruit, for an extensive list of job openings, including international opportunities. Each office has different resume requirements, though nearly all accept resumes by either regular mail, e-mail, or fax.

Johnson & Johnson, which has been known as a top employer of MBAs for brand management for years, is also beginning to look at business school grads to fill finance positions. Says one financial analyst: "They're starting to hire more MBAs, shifting their work from routine tasks to analytical roles." Says one summer intern in the finance department: "J&J welcomes MBAs and is always looking for good people. Still, Johnson & Johnson remains a marketing-heavy company. Marketing MBAs enter the brand management function as assistant product directors or product directors, according to their previous experience. The company offers internships to MBAs in both brand management and finance.

OUR SURVEY SAYS

As might be expected of a company whose products are concerned with childcare and healthcare, Johnson & Johnson is described as having a "very family-friendly" culture, with a somewhat "slow pace." "It is a great company to work for," says one insider. "Good benefits, great employees perks, and a conscious responsibility to the community." Among its family friendly perks are more on-site childcare centers than any other company, $3000 reimbursement for adoption expenses, a 75 percent match of up to 6 percent of salary for its 401(k) program, and even a hotline that provides employees with childcare advice. The child care center at the company's New Jersey headquarters was designed by renowned architect

MBA Job Seekers: Receive free e-mailed job postings matching your interests & qualifications! Register at www.VaultReports.com

VAULT REPORTS™

www.vaultreports.com

235

I.M. Pei. The dress code is "strict" at J&J's headquarters in New Jersey, but more lax in some affiliate offices.

While insiders say the corporate structure "encourages individual autonomy," many employees say that the "strict rules and procedures" are "cumbersome." In addition, the "unusual level of freedom" often requires recent hires to "take initiative in seeking out feedback." Several Johnson & Johnson employees comment that the "diverse" workforce is benefiting from the company's "new emphasis" on hiring women into "more visible management positions." For those employees who join one of J&J's smaller organizations, the company's strategy of keeping subsidiaries intact pays immediate dividends. "It was a small and lean company, so there was lots of responsibility and exposure to senior management," reports one brand management summer hire.

To order a 50- to 70-page Vault Reports Employer Profile on Johnson & Johnson call 1-888-JOB-VAULT or visit www.VaultReports.com

The full Employer Profile includes detailed information on J&J's departments, recent developments and transactions, hiring and interview process, plus what employees really think about culture, pay, work hours and more.

"It is a great company to work for. Good benefits, great employees perks, and a conscious responsibility to the community."

— *J&J insider*

MBA Job Seekers: Receive free e-mailed job postings matching your interests & qualifications! Register at www.VaultReports.com

VAULT REPORTS™

237

www.vaultreports.com

Nike

RANKING 29

One Bowerman Drive
Beaverton, OR 97005-6453
(503) 671-6300
Fax: (503) 767-9855
www.nike.com

Brand Management

LOCATIONS

Beaverton, OR (HQ)
Memphis, TN
Wilsonville, OR
Other offices in Austria • Canada • Hong Kong

DEPARTMENTS

Apparel Component Sourcing & Production
Product Design & Development
Footwear Products & Components
Sales & Marketing

THE STATS

Annual Revenues: $9.5 billion (1998)
No. of Employees: 21,800 (worldwide)
No. of Offices: 9 (worldwide)
Stock Symbol: NKE (NYSE)
CEO: Philip H. Knight

KEY COMPETITORS

- Adidas-Salomon
- Converse
- Fila
- Nautica Enterprises
- New Balance
- Puma
- Reebok
- Russell Corporation
- Timberland
- Tommy Hilfiger

THE BUZZ

What MBAs are saying
about Nike

- "Sweatshop (literally)"
- "Great company, tough times"
- "No money, lots of fun"
- "All marketing, no substance"

UPPERS

- Beautiful corporate "campus"
- Company gym
- Discounts at employee store
- Sports programs
- "Thirsty Thursdays" with celebrities and special events

DOWNERS

- Hiring freeze
- Low pay
- Hell on the knees

EMPLOYMENT CONTACT

Nike
HR Service Center
One Bowerman Drive
Beaverton, OR 97005-6453
Fax: (888) 767-9855

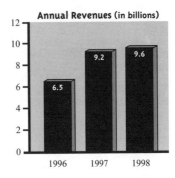

Annual Revenues (in billions)

1996	1997	1998
6.5	9.2	9.6

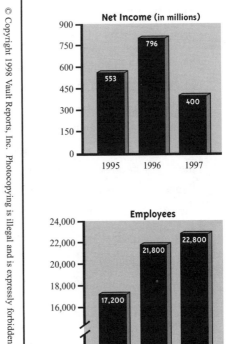

Net Income (in millions)

1995	1996	1997
553	796	400

Employees

1995	1996	1997
17,200	21,800	22,800

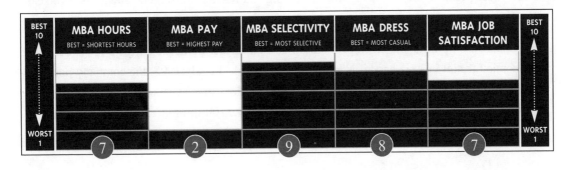

	MBA HOURS BEST = SHORTEST HOURS	MBA PAY BEST = HIGHEST PAY	MBA SELECTIVITY BEST = MOST SELECTIVE	MBA DRESS BEST = MOST CASUAL	MBA JOB SATISFACTION	
BEST 10 ... WORST 1	7	2	9	8	7	BEST 10 ... WORST 1

MBA Job Seekers: Receive free e-mailed job postings matching your interests & qualifications! Register at www.VaultReports.com

VAULT REPORTS™

239

www.vaultreports.com

THE SCOOP

The top athletic shoe maker in the U.S., Nike has become the principal myth-maker of our time. Nike's vast advertising campaigns have created a new pantheon of American heroes while fueling the dreams of playground kids and weekend warriors alike. With campaigns like "Just Do It" (borrowed from 1960s icon Jerry Rubin), the company sells more than a mere product – it sells a lifestyle.

The man behind the myth is Phil Knight, a former middle-distance runner from the University of Oregon. Knight, now among the 10 richest men in America, began the company with his track coach Bill Bowerman in 1964 as Blue Ribbon Sports. Each of them chipped in $300 to have their shoes manufactured in Japan and started selling the finished product out of the trunk of their car at track meets. Knight and Bowerman changed the company's name to Nike, after the Greek goddess of victory, in 1968 and introduced their own shoes at the Olympic trials in Oregon six years later. The fitness revolution of the late 1970s fueled Nike's early growth, and the Air Jordan basketball shoes – first introduced in 1985 – have become nearly as recognizable as Michael himself.

But even a legend can fall on rough times. Questionable employment practices at Nike plants in Vietnam, Indonesia, and China have attracted unfavorable notice in recent years. Low wages and poor working conditions at the plants attracted widespread press. The company's efforts to counter the bad publicity, which included severing ties with four factories in Indonesia in 1997, haven't wiped their image clean yet. In early 1997, documentary maker Michael Moore (creator of *Roger and Me*, a caustic filmed attack on General Motors) aimed his muckraking camera at the Nike controversy. To add injury to insult, a high-profile lawsuit was waged against the company for deceiving California consumers about its overseas employment practices.

Slumping sales, profits and stock prices have caused further domestic sorrows for Nike. The economic turmoil in Asia has hit Nike particularly hard. In July 1998, the company posted a fourth quarter loss of $67.7 million, its first quarterly loss in 13 years. In response, Nike has laid off 15 percent of its Asian workforce and slashed $100 million earmarked for celebrity sports endorsments.

GETTING HIRED

The company hires MBAs into finance, marketing and sales, and recruits on-campus and at job fairs, such as the Pacific Northwest MBA Job Fair, held in Portland in February. Insiders report that "enthusiasm, a can-do spirit, and a specific desire to work for Nike" are all pluses. Though you probably shouldn't wear running shorts to the interview, one insider reports, "being athletic is good. People who are athletic seem to advance faster." Speaking another language is also a plus since, as one contact maintains, "many developers put in a stint in one of the Asian offices (Japan, Indonesia, Korea, Taiwan, China, and Vietnam), so one of these languages would be very helpful."

One marketing insider notes that "the people who work for international are usually people who can function within the culture and language of that region." Nike offers a variety of positions at the "campus" in Oregon, as well as around the world. The company accepts resumes by mail or fax, but does not post entry-level openings nationally. Expect the competition for openings to be like the NBA playoffs: tough. Check out ww.nikebiz.com for more information about hiring. The company posts job openings, including some MBA-level jobs, such as business analyst positions.

OUR SURVEY SAYS

Nike calls its headquarters in Beaverton, OR a "campus" – and with good reason. Employees say that on any given day, one is likely to "see soccer games, runners, volleyball, and other competitive sports going on all over the place." Nike "encourages people to work out during their shift and provides sports activities for everyone throughout the day." One insider asks, "What other company lets me mix my career interests with my personal lifestyle of sports and fitness?" The "top-shelf" corporate campus includes a "world-class exercise center, an excellent cafeteria, a sports bar, a convenience store, and a hairdresser." A new northern

MBA Job Seekers: Receive free e-mailed job postings matching
your interests & qualifications! Register at www.VaultReports.com

VAULT REPORTS™
www.vaultreports.com

241

expansion of the campus will open in 1999. However, the footwear giant hasn't dodged all of the pitfalls that come with being a major player. "Nike's a small company that grew big very fast, with all that implies," one insider reports, "It's becoming more conventionally corporate all the time."

Some employees note that "the incredible atmosphere and great people are a trade off for the lower-than-average pay." One reports, "The downside of the great facilities and reputation is that we get 50,000 unsolicited resumes a year, which means Nike isn't motivated to pay high salaries to most employees. The general consensus is that we're paid somewhat below the industry average for any given position." Bonuses are based on a combination of corporate, divisional, and individual performance. Though hours vary by department, 8:30 to 5:30 days are typical. Dress code tends to be casual, one notes, "Since we get a discount on Nike shoes and apparel, you see lots of swooshes." "Jeans, sneakers, and a polo shirt," are typical office wear. That casual attitude carries over to employee relations as well, with a "culture as loose as a large corporate environment gets." "Personal issues can be dealt with without feeling guilty. For example, if you have to run an errand at lunch, there's no one who checks how long you took," one insider notes, "The unwritten rule is to not take advantage of managing yourself, which is really how the managers treat those under them."

When it comes to treatment of women and minorities, one Nike employee reports, "Don't let any bad press about Nike discourage you. Nike's taken many unfair hits from fringe groups, but if any company can be considered cutting-edge and progressive, it's Nike." "Nike was pretty much a white boy's club when I started 13 years ago," one insider notes, "but they've made a lot of progress. There are now women at nearly every level." Another reports, "As for diversity, you won't find a company more open and open-minded than Nike. You will find many women and minorities working here at all levels." Employees from various ethnicities often meet for "informal meetings." One Latino employee reports, "Our group was formerly called the Hispanic caucus, and we're in the process of realigning the caucuses. It's a fun place to meet other Latinos and network."

According to one insider, Nike has been cited by numerous groups for its progressiveness in childcare and job sharing, and is often ranked by *Oregon Business* magazine as one of the top businesses to work for in the state of Oregon. One insider reports, "There is a fantastic childcare center on campus that will care for newborns and actually includes a kindergarten (though space is limited)." Ultimately, perks such as the company gym, employee store, and the chance to rub elbows with sports and movie stars cultivate fierce employee loyalty. Nike's employees want to take care of the company because, as they put it, "the company takes care of them."

MBA Job Seekers: Receive free e-mailed job postings matching your interests & qualifications! Register at www.VaultReports.com

VAULT REPORTS™
243
www.vaultreports.com

Credit Suisse
First Boston

Investment Banking

11 Madison Avenue
New York, NY 10010
(212) 325-2000
www.csfb.com

CREDIT SUISSE | **FIRST BOSTON**

LOCATIONS

New York, NY (HQ)
Los Angeles, CA • London, UK • Zurich,
Switzerland • 50 other offices in 30 countries

DEPARTMENTS

Corporate & Investment Banking
(including Corporate Finance, Mergers
& Acquisitions and Public Finance)
Equity
Fixed Income
Derivatives
(Credit Suisse Financial Products)
Private Equity

THE STATS

Annual Revenues: $7.1 billion (1997)
No. of Employees: 13,000+
No. of Offices: 50 (worldwide)
A subsidiary of Credit Suisse Group
CEO: Allen D. Wheat

KEY COMPETITORS

- Deutsche Bank Securities
- Goldman Sachs
- Merrill Lynch
- Morgan Stanley Dean Witter
- Salomon Smith Barney
- J.P. Morgan

THE BUZZ
What MBAs are saying
about Credit Suisse

- "European, sophisticated, relaxed"
- "Almost prestigious"
- "Aggressive, gaining prestige"
- "Global, at times erratic"

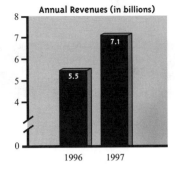

UPPERS

- Relaxed dress for Wall Street
- Friendly environment
- Great gym in New York

DOWNERS

- Recent cutbacks in perks and staff
- Bad press from Holocaust victims suit

EMPLOYMENT CONTACT

Credit Suisse First Boston
11 Madison Avenue
New York, NY 10010
wrecruit@csfb.com

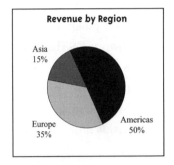

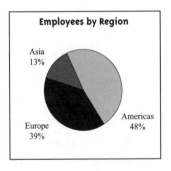

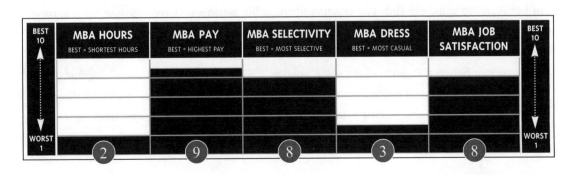

	MBA HOURS	MBA PAY	MBA SELECTIVITY	MBA DRESS	MBA JOB SATISFACTION
	BEST = SHORTEST HOURS	BEST = HIGHEST PAY	BEST = MOST SELECTIVE	BEST = MOST CASUAL	
	2	9	8	3	8

MBA Job Seekers: Receive free e-mailed job postings matching your interests & qualifications! Register at www.VaultReports.com

VAULT REPORTS™

www.vaultreports.com

245

THE SCOOP

Credit Suisse First Boston (formerly known as "CS First Boston") is one of New York's most renowned investment banks and a member of Wall Street's prestigious "bulge bracket" of top securities firms. Credit Suisse First Boston was established as the wholly-owned investment bank unit of the Credit Suisse Group, one of Europe's largest financial institutions. Credit Suisse group, one of Europe's largest financial institutions. Credit Suisse Group, formerly known as CS Holdings, intially invested in First Boston in 1988, renaming the investment bank CS First Boston. Since that infusion of Swiss cash, the firm itself has changed significantly. Credit Suisse First Boston now has a much larger capital base than First Boston ever had. CSFB's trading division is famously aggressive and profitable, and the investment banking division now has a notable global reach.

The firm is divided into five divisions. Corporate and Investment Banking (CIBD) is a leading player in M&A worldwide. The firm's Fixed Income division is one of the world's largest, trading more than $100 billion of fixed income securities each day. Other divisions include the Equity, Credit Suisse Financial Products (the derivatives division, based in London), and Private Equity.

In recent years, Credit Suisse has caught some unwanted publicity for stonewalling the descendants of Holocaust survivors who demand access to dormant accounts. Credit Suisse, along with UBS, eventually agreed in August 1998 to pay Holocaust survivors $1.25 billion over 3 ½ years. In May, CSFB also settled with Orange County in its well-publicized bankruptcy lawsuit. The $52.5 million settlement served as partial restitution for the California county's losses, but the bank denied undertaking unsubstantiated risks.

In between the suits, the firm has conducted some big business. Credit Suisse First Boston outbid competitors Goldman Sachs and Morgan Stanley in purchasing Garantia S.A., Brazil's top investment bank, for $675 million. The bank also stands to benefit as an advisor to the mega-merger between Daimler-Benz and Chrysler. CS First Boston is advising longtime client Chrysler in the largest industrial deal ever. However, the firm took major hits as the most active bank in Russia, announcing trading losses exceeding $500 million, and slashing its staff in Russia.

GETTING HIRED

MBAs enter CSFB as associates, either in the Investment Banking, Equities or Fixed Income. Sales and trading associates in Equity and Fixed Income go through a four-month formal training program. Thereafter, if successful, associates in Equity could be covering their own accounts and trading stocks within a years. One insider notes, "the trades they give you at first will be small. They definitely don't let you go balls out at first. But if you prove yourself, [CSFB] expands your responsibility quickly." Traders point to the fact that one of the most senior people in trading is only 36 years old as proof that rapid promotions are possible for talented traders. Investment banking associates go through a similar training program, after which they join a product, industry, or geographic group.

Credit Suisse First Boston looks for candidates who have outstanding academic records, come from "diverse backgrounds," and work well with others. During interviews, applicants should be prepared for finance-related questions. Several employees note that they received the question: "What stock did you most recently buy and what analysis did you perform before buying it?" The company's recruitment Web site, located at www.csfb.com, provides descriptions of entry-level positions. Applicants can submit their resumes by regular mail.

OUR SURVEY SAYS

Credit Suisse First Boston fosters a "collegial" environment in which new employees enjoy a large degree of "interaction with senior management." One former associate reports: "We would go out at least once a week. Anytime there was someone new in our group visiting from one of the other CSFB offices, it was basically their duty to take you to a bar, go out for drinks and dinner, hang out with them, so you got to drink a lot of free beer and eat free meals." CSFB emphasizes "teamwork" and says its employees must possess "quantitative and modeling skills." Support staff are "well qualified" and often "cover up for some analysts' weaknesses with using computers and high-tech equipment."

MBA Job Seekers: Receive free e-mailed job postings matching your interests & qualifications! Register at www.VaultReports.com

VAULT REPORTS™
www.vaultreports.com

247

CSFB employees "regularly" receive free tickets for sporting events and cultural events, and also the opportunity "to go out for nice dinners in nice restaurants like Lutece, Dawat, River Café, Remi, and Four Seasons." The only problem is that CSFB people spend so much time in the office that "who really has time for anything else?"

Working at CSFB has more mundane benefits. "They have lots of healthcare options, including one in which you can save money for healthcare expenses tax-free," says one insider. "So say you know that later in the year you'll have $2000 in medical expenses that won't be covered by insurance. You can save for that in a pre-tax account. So if you didn't have that account, you might have to earn $2800 to pay for the $2000 in expenses."

Professionals who stay past 7 p.m. – which is just about everyone – can have their dinners picked up by the firm. Many go to the firm's cafeteria, where "all you have to do is show your I.D." Tired bankers can also call for car service after 9 p.m. For those looking to re-energize, there's the firm's health club. The monthly fee for the club depends on one's position – "for people below VP it's $30 a month." Perhaps the biggest perk, say New York employees, is that "you get to live in Manhattan – and earn enough money to enjoy it."

Like many of its competitors, CSFB is cutting back on some of its perks because of tight times. "They sent a memo around announcing that there's only a $50 allowance per person for this year's Christmas party. Things don't look good, it's not a fat year," says one insider. "And in the health club, they used to provide free fruit, and it just went away. It's because the gym is run by another company, but the fruit was provided by CSFB."

And like most on Wall Street, CSFB's employees contend with "long," "intense" workdays and "excruciatingly tight deadlines." According to one associate: "Trading is like warfare. It can get very frantic, and then very quiet, and flare again without warning. It's long periods of silence punctuated by fear and terror. That's what makes it stressful." I-bankers are no more relaxed; one analyst says "You burn out by the time you're 30. Most people only last until they're about 35, then go off and do something else." Many employees comment that their jobs "require a high level of energy and dedication." The intensity continues with a "very business-like" dress code that stipulates "suits and ties – no sports coats at all." Since CSFB lacks the marquee name and underwriting franchise that some of its competitors enjoy, the bank maintains an "entrepreneurial" culture in which employees are "encouraged to go out and win business for the firm." Still, "having CSFB's name on your resume means much more than having any regional bank on it."

CSFB is creeping toward an ever more casual environment when it comes to dress. "Fridays are dress-downs all year, and lately, in late summer, we get one week of dress down, like the last week of August," reports one insider. Also: "dress-down is for the last day of any week, so if it's a three-day weekend you can dress down on Thursday."

And on those occasions when employees are free from the scrutiny of top management and clients, "discipline kind of breaks down. Shirts without ties, that sort of thing – you can take it a bit easier." The moment the boss or a client comes back, though, "the ties come right back on." For traders, however, the dress code is much more relaxed, and "traders in New York don't have to wear a suit during the week. We can dress business casual during the week. On Friday we can wear whatever we want, and some of us wear jeans." One New York trader recalls, "For some time we used to wear jeans even during the week, but we got remarks like, 'you really should wear something smarter.'" Employees at CSFB's foreign offices have to conform to "stricter dress codes." This is especially true in London, which is "a button-up kind of town. Everyone is formal here."

MBA Job Seekers: Receive free e-mailed job postings matching your interests & qualifications! Register at www.VaultReports.com

VAULT REPORTS™
www.vaultreports.com

249

Motorola

Telecommunications

1303 E. Algonquin Rd.
Schaumburg, IL 60196
(847) 576-5000
www.mot.com

LOCATIONS

Schaumburg, IL (HQ)
Other locations in AZ • FL • GA • NC • NM •
NY • TX • and 17 foreign countries

MARKETS

Wireless
Semi-conductors
Advanced Electrical Systems
Components and Servers, including:

- Cellular
- Two-way Radio
- Data Communications
- Personal Communication
- Automotive, Space, Defense Electronics
- Computers

THE STATS

Annual Revenues: $29.8 billion (1997)
No. of Employees: 135,000 (worldwide)
Stock Symbol: MOT (NYSE)
CEO: Christopher Galvin
%Male/%Female: 64/36

KEY COMPETITORS

- 3Com
- Ericsson
- IBM
- Intel
- Lucent
- Nokia

THE BUZZ

What MBAs are saying
about Motorola

- "Going nowhere fast"
- "Quality"
- "Progressive"
- "Past prime?"

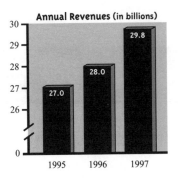

Annual Revenues (in billions)

UPPERS

- On-site child care
- Adoption assistance
- Scholarships for employees' children
- Tuition reimbursement
- Flexible scheduling
- Credit union
- Tickets to sporting events

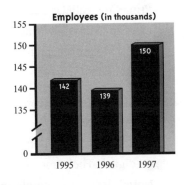

Net Income (in billions)

DOWNERS

- Recent poor performance and layoffs
- "Tenuous" attitude toward MBAs

EMPLOYMENT CONTACT

Human Resources
Motorola
1303 E. Algonquin Rd.
Schaumburg, IL 60196
www.mot.com/employment

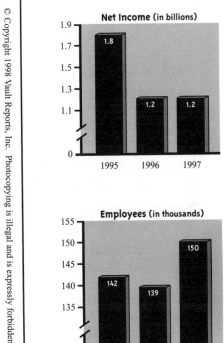

Employees (in thousands)

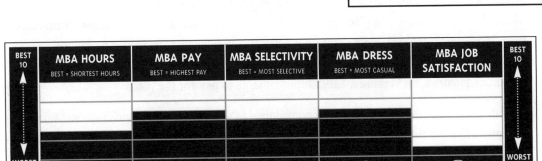

BEST 10 → WORST 1	MBA HOURS BEST = SHORTEST HOURS	MBA PAY BEST = HIGHEST PAY	MBA SELECTIVITY BEST = MOST SELECTIVE	MBA DRESS BEST = MOST CASUAL	MBA JOB SATISFACTION	BEST 10 → WORST 1
	5	7	6	7	3	

MBA Job Seekers: Receive free e-mailed job postings matching
your interests & qualifications! Register at www.VaultReports.com

VAULT REPORTS™
www.vaultreports.com

251

THE SCOOP

Motorola is the world's leading manufacturer of cellular phones, beepers, and two-way radios. Its products are so ubiquitous that its name has become synonymous with telecommunications; in China, for example, cellular phones are simply called "Motorolas." The company that would eventually become Motorola was founded by Paul Galvin in 1928. As the first manufacturer of two-way, hand-held radios, as well as a pioneering maker of semiconductors and car stereo equipment, the Galvin family's business has over the years earned 1016 patents; 403 of these were registered between 1991 and 1995. The company is one of the top three patent holders in the country.

Over the past three years, however, Motorola has not performed well. In February 1998, Prime Communications L.P, a wireless-phone service owned by Bell Atlantic, U.S. West and AirTouch Communications, cancelled a $500 million contract with Motorola after persistent failures with the company's cellular network equipment and software. In one embarrassing episode, PrimeCo's cellular network went down in Chicago as executives from both companies were meeting to discuss the network's problems. PrimeCo's action could have a significant spillover effect: Motorola supplies similar equipment and software to other large companies, including a $1.4 billion order from Spring PCS and $3.5 billion agreement with two Japanese firms.

The failed PrimeCo contract illustrates a problem that has led to Motorola's dwindling market share and profit margins: the company's technology is simply outdated. Motorola had built its market reputation on its analog cellular technology, only to see the industry and its customers go digital. The company also lacks its own switching and network software like Lucent and Nortel, leaving Motorola unable to compete for telecommunication contracts. As a result, Motorola has seen its worldwide cellular systems market share drop to 15 percent from more than 25 percent. In June 1998, Motorola officials announced a sweeping restructuring and consolidation plan, laying off 15,000 employees (10 percent of its workforce), closing numerous factories, and taking a $1.95 billion charge to pay for the plan.

Despite a weak Asian economy that has contributed to the company's financial woes, Motorola still plans to push full steam ahead in the continent it once dominated, and where it is still a major player. Construction continues on a $750 million plant in China, with several factory upgrades planned for the future. Motorola's aggressive pursuit of Asia, even as the company closes its U.S. plants, reflects CEO Christopher Galvin's gamble that the region will still be the most promising market for cellular technology and other Motorola products despite the global financial crisis.

GETTING HIRED

Motorola hires top MBAs primarily into strategy/corporate planning and marketing positions. In marketing, Motorola utilizes the traditional brand management structure, with MBAs starting as assistant marketing managers. Both internships and full-time positions at Motorola can take MBAs around the world. Incoming employees "often have the opportunity to go on rotational programs to get a feel for the different business units before choosing one to work in permanently."

Several insiders report dissatisfaction with the opportunities Motorola offers for MBAs. Says one: "The company is very engineering and product-oriented, and therefore attitudes toward marketers and MBAs are tenuous." Says one marketer who spent an MBA summer internship with the company several years ago: "There was only one MBA in my division the last time I checked." Says another insider who left the company to go to business school: "It's engineering-driven – a technical degree is a plus."

OUR SURVEY SAYS

Motorola is an "engineering and product-oriented" company that encourages "creative solutions to difficult problems." While those in finance and marketing sometimes feel that the

MBA Job Seekers: Receive free e-mailed job postings matching your interests & qualifications! Register at www.VaultReports.com

VAULT REPORTS™
253
www.vaultreports.com

technical staff keeps them "at arms length," everyone appreciates the "prestige of working for a company whose name transcends language barriers." Employees say that Motorola's decentralized organization "occasionally causes communication difficulties," but also "allows for a significant degree of departmental autonomy without excessive red tape." The dress code is described as "casual, but more professional than most high-tech firms." There are no dress codes "anywhere in engineering," but "business dress in finance and marketing."

Although one contact describes co-workers as "very cool," and the dress as "very casual," he points out that to advance in such a big company, "one needs to be very mindful of managing his or her career there. The advice to find a mentor is freely and amicably given, but there is no real process to make sure one actually finds a good mentor. Without one, many employees still do fine but find measurable career advancement often unreachable."

MBAs who have spent summer internships at the company report a variety of experiences. "It had its ups and downs," says one, who worked at the company's headquarters. "The work was interesting, but I do not believe I received adequate exposure to upper/middle management and I don't think I was given enough responsibility." Another, who worked overseas reports: "It was very unstructured, so I was able to be creative. There was lots of exposure to the CFO." Another, who worked in Asia, agrees: "It turned out to be a highly unstructured experience – a very steep learning curve and substantial exposure to upper/middle management."

"The company is very engineering and product-oriented, and therefore attitudes toward marketers and MBAs are tenuous."

– *Motorola insider*

IBM

RANKING 32

High Tech

New Orchard Road
Armonk, NY 10504
www.ibm.com
(914) 765-1900

LOCATIONS

Armonk, NY (HQ)
Offices around the world

DEPARTMENTS

Accounting
Consulting
Finance
Hardware Engineering
Information Technology
Internet
Market Research
Network Analysis
Programming
Research & Development
Software Engineering

THE STATS

Annual Revenues: $78.5 billion (1997)
No. of Employees: 269,465 (worldwide)
No. of Offices: 18+ (worldwide)
Stock Symbol: IBM (NYSE)
CEO: Louis V. Gerstner

KEY COMPETITORS

- Compaq
- Dell Computer
- Hewlett-Packard
- Hitachi
- Microsoft

THE BUZZ

What MBAs are saying
about IBM

- "Getting back on track"
- "Venerable, glacial"
- "Passe"
- "Turnaround experts"

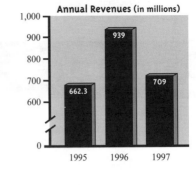

UPPERS

- Tuition reimbursement
- Stock purchase plan
- Health benefits for partners of gay and lesbian employees

DOWNERS

- Remnants of conservative culture

EMPLOYMENT CONTACT

Human Resources
IBM
New Orchard Road
Armonk, NY 10504

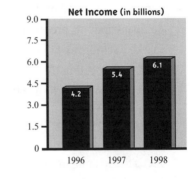

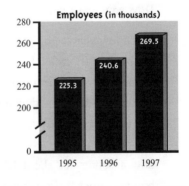

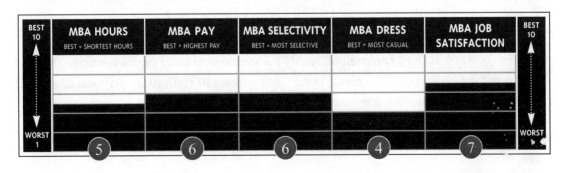

MBA HOURS BEST = SHORTEST HOURS	MBA PAY BEST = HIGHEST PAY	MBA SELECTIVITY BEST = MOST SELECTIVE	MBA DRESS BEST = MOST CASUAL	MBA JOB SATISFACTION
5	6	6	4	7

THE SCOOP

International Business Machines (IBM) began as the Computing-Tabulating-Recording Company, a floundering office machine firm rescued by National Cash Register salesman Thomas Watson in 1914. Watson turned the company around by securing government contracts during World War I; by 1920, annual revenue had tripled. Four years later, the company took its present moniker and quickly established its dominance in the office machine market, selling its tabulators, time clocks, and electric typewriters domestically and abroad. IBM introduced its first computer in 1952 and maintained control of about 80 percent of the market throughout the 1960s and 1970s.

The subsequent "PC revolution," however, found IBM unable to compete in the face of the shift to smaller, more open systems. To adapt to the new conditions, the company changed its focus to big computers, semi-conductors, software, and professional services in order to secure the top spot in the computer world. With its recent acquisitions of Lotus and Tivoli Systems, IBM now plans to extend its dominance to the business software and Internet markets.

Just a few years ago, IBM was floundering. When crafty CEO Louis Gerstner took the helm of the firm in 1993, IBM was lumbering toward a $8 billion loss. Many observers were clamoring for the firm to split up. Instead, Gerstner turned IBM's focus to meeting customer needs. Big Blue's acquisition of Lotus in 1995 and Tivoli Systems in 1996 both upped sales and allowed IBM to supply a wide variety of software, instead of just software for mainframes and other proprietary software. IBM has jumped into the software market full force. Software now accounts for about 18 percent of all IBM sales, making Big Blue, not Microsoft, the biggest software company in the world. IBM has more developers working in JAVA than Sun Microsystems, which wrote the language in the first place. The increased focus on software, including voice recognition technology, has made IBM more flexible; the firm no longer writes software solely for its own hardware. The company is also moving ahead with its encryption technology that will allow companies to verify customers purchasing products online. IBM's new mainframe, S/390 G5, is expected to run 1040 millions of instructions per second, which is 15 percent more powerful than what analysts were expecting last May.

Once-costly IBM is even delving into the sub-$1000 PC market, introducing a personal computer that sells for $999. IBM sells computers directly to customers, but, unlike its nimbler rivals Gateway and Dell, also sells computers through distributors or "middlemen" who take a slice of the profits and demand compensation when surplus inventory sits in warehouses. IBM is also looking to sell off its printer division, which analysts say could fetch up to $2 billion.

Perhaps IBM no longer needs to rely on publicity stunts to burnish its image. In 1998, IBM announced that it would no longer be a sponsor of the Olympic Games, after the company and the International Olympic Committee officials failed to ink a new contract. The Sydney 2000 Games will be the last time you will be able to see Big Blue next to the Olympic Torch.

GETTING HIRED

During a typical year, IBM hires more than 15,000 new employees in everything from accounting and data warehousing to Internet applications and software development. Applicants should consult IBM's recruitment web page, located at www.empl.ibm.com/empl/ehwrkpl.html, to find out more about opportunities within each of its various business lines. At the web site, applicants can also construct a resume on-line and send it directly to the company; IBM scans all resumes, whether electronic or paper, into a central database where they circulate for six months.

MBA Job Seekers: Receive free e-mailed job postings matching your interests & qualifications! Register at www.VaultReports.com

VAULT REPORTS™

259

www.vaultreports.com

OUR SURVEY SAYS

IBM is "trying to reengineer itself to compete in the new millennium" by shifting its emphasis to "individual empowerment and entrepreneurial thinking." Observing that even the IBM's famous "unwritten dress code" is gone, employees describe the "new IBM" as "more relaxed and informal." Many are excited about the organizational changes, but some say they "would appreciate more guidance and input" from upper management. Others worry that IBM's changes have come "at the expense of some of its longtimers." For new employees, however, the shift in IBM's corporate culture will translate into "spectacular new opportunities" at an "exciting moment in the history of one of the most storied companies in America." One insider is positive about the changes at the company: "The culture has changed from command-and-control to highly entrepreneurial. Things move fast and change often. IBM employees now have a great deal of latitude to deploy resources to opportunities while drawing upon the talents and technology of a $76 billion company. Most of the old IBM bureaucracy is gone, replaced with an environment where performance and personal contribution are what get rewarded."

Employees think their company is cutting edge indeed. "IBM is the leader in more areas and technologies than anyone else in the most important and exciting industry on the planet," concurs one insider. Changes have shaken up the traditional Big Blue, however. The dress code is business casual. Dress is selected based on what your customers expect as normal. Inside IBM, nobody much cares anymore about white shirts, dresses and all that" – this at a firm once famous for its unspoken white-shirt-dark-suit dress code. And as you'd expect from a forward-looking company, IBM has an egalitarian structure. Says one insider: "There's no differentiation between men's and women's jobs. There are several women in the executive ranks in IBM. IBM is a worldwide company, with employees in every country, so there's a lot of cultural and ethnic diversity among the employees." Perks? Yup. "Special perks include free Internet access, ThinkPad laptops, support for mobile employees, and a benefit package you would expect from a company like IBM."

Still, IBM retains a bit of the old gentility – which may not be to everyone's liking. "I have to say that, depending on who your manager is at IBM, you may or may not have a good experience," says one insider. "Generally, the newer people who don't come from a large corporate background (IBM has been hiring a lot of younger, more aggressive types) may not reflect the old IBM culture. They get frustrated with IBM's 'politeness' and eventually leave, but not before annoying a lot of people."

To order a 50- to 70-page Vault Reports Employer Profile on IBM call 1-888-JOB-VAULT or visit www.VaultReports.com

The full Employer Profile includes detailed information on IBM's departments, recent developments and transactions, hiring and interview process, plus what employees really think about culture, pay, work hours and more.

MBA Job Seekers: Receive free e-mailed job postings matching your interests & qualifications! Register at www.VaultReports.com

VAULT REPORTS™
www.vaultreports.com

261

BancBoston Robertson Stephens

RANKING
33

Investment Banking

555 California St, Suite 2600
San Francisco, CA 94104
(415) 781-9700
Fax: (415) 676-2840
www.rsco.com

LOCATIONS

San Francisco, CA (HQ)

Boston, MA • Chicago, IL • Menlo Park, NJ •
New York, NY • Palo Alto, CA • London,
England • Tel Aviv, Israel • Tokyo, Japan

PRODUCTS AND SERVICES

Corporate Finance
High-Yield Securities
Global Derivatives
Global Foreign Exchange
Institutional Brokerage
Loan Sales & Trading
Mergers & Acquisitions
Research

THE STATS

Annual Revenues: $480 million (1998,est)
No. of Employees: 900 (worldwide)
No. of Offices: 7 (worldwide), 5 (U.S)
Subsidiary of BankBoston

KEY COMPETITORS

- Credit Suisse First Boston
- Goldman Sachs
- Hambrecht & Quist
- Morgan Stanley Dean Witter
- NationsBanc Montgomery Securities
- SG Cowen

THE BUZZ

What MBAs are saying
about Robbie Stephens

- "Cutting edge in technology investments"
- "Decent, overconfident"
- "Schmoozy, unstable"
- "Stressful, gambling"

UPPERS

- Good support staff
- Entrepreneurial atmosphere
- "Lovely West Coast locale"
- Outstanding 401(k)

DOWNERS

- Long work days
- Little training
- Recently became part of bureaucratic giant BankBoston

EMPLOYMENT CONTACT

Human Resources
BancBoston Robertson Stephens
555 California St, Suite 2600
San Francisco, CA 94104

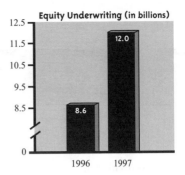

Equity Underwriting (in billions)

1996: 8.6
1997: 12.0

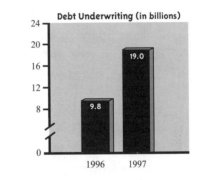

Debt Underwriting (in billions)

1996: 9.8
1997: 19.0

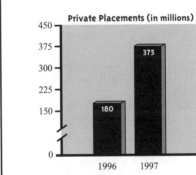

Private Placements (in millions)

1996: 180
1997: 375

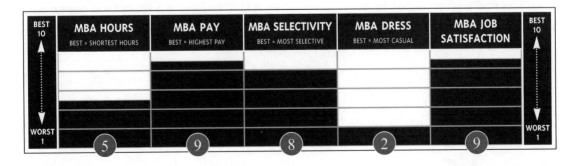

	MBA HOURS	MBA PAY	MBA SELECTIVITY	MBA DRESS	MBA JOB SATISFACTION	
BEST 10 ... WORST 1	BEST = SHORTEST HOURS	BEST = HIGHEST PAY	BEST = MOST SELECTIVE	BEST = MOST CASUAL		BEST 10 ... WORST 1
	5	9	8	2	9	

THE SCOOP

BancBoston Robertson Stephens is one of America's leading underwriters of growth companies in the technology, health care, retailing, consumer products, and real estate sectors. The firm is best known for its work in the high-tech industry. The firm was the top underwriter of technology IPOs from 1995 to 1997. BancBoston Robertson Stephens is also known as a leader in equity research, with a team of highly-rated analysts. And the firm is a player in the lucrative mergers and acquisitions business. Since its founding, Robertson Stephens has advised on 300 M&A deals, which together involved more than $70 billion.

The firm hasn't just advised on M&A activity, it's taken part in a lot of it recently. In 1997, BankAmerica the third-largest bank in the United States, agreed to acquire the formerly independent Robertson Stephens in order to take advantage of the smaller firm's expertise in stock underwriting and advising on mergers and acquisitions. The deal was sealed with a friendly handshake after months of negotiation. Clearly captivated by the strong Robertson brand, BankAmerica paid $540 million in cash for the bank, or approximately five times book value. BankAmerica's deep pockets enabled Robertson Stephens to expand its staff and to venture outside its high tech and health care IPO base. But BankAmerica put Robertson Stephens up for sale in April 1998 after it agreed to merge with NationsBank, which already had an investment banking branch – Robertson Stephens rival Montgomery Securities (now Nationsbanc Montgomery Securities). In the summer of 1998, BankBoston fronted $800 million for Robertson Stephens' equity and corporate operations (BankAmerica would retain the firm's mutual fund operation). Founder Sandy Robertson has announced plans to step down, and CEO Mike McCaffery is expected to continue overseeing operations from San Francisco. Despite Robertson's departure, the boutique bank has retained most of its senior bankers under generous purchase agreement terms, which included a $400 million employee-retention pool. When the deal closed in August 1998, bank officials said they were on track to bring in $480 million in revenue for the 1999 fiscal year.

GETTING HIRED

Every one of BancBoston Robertson Stephens's departments report growth and the need for new employees. With the exception of occasional newspaper advertisements, however, the company does not post specific job openings. Although the company recruits extensively at top schools around the country, employees still report "it's much easier to be hired if you know someone who works at the firm – many positions are filled through referrals." Applicants can mail or fax resumes to the company's headquarters, where the resumes will be kept on file for 90 days. The company's interviews are said to be "generally knowledge-based with behavioral questions." Applicants can anticipate an "informal screening interview" and then "an in-house interview with four to six different meetings." One recently-hired employee suggests that those who expect to be working in equity should "find out what stocks you might be covering if given the job and research those stocks and their industry." New hires work in Robertson Stephens' headquarters in San Francisco headquarters. MBAs can expect to pull down very tempting salaries that range from $60,000 to $100,000, not including bonus.

OUR SURVEY SAYS

BancBoston Robertson Stephens & Company – fondly known as Robbie Stephens to its employees and others in the industry – offers "little formal training" in favor of "continual on-the-job education." The company's employees enjoy being on the "cutting-edge" of the banking industry and their frequent contact with the "young, exciting" Silicon Valley companies that play a major role in Robertson Stephens' client base. One banker says "the corporate culture is strong, fun, and best of all, realistic and down to earth." Employees cite "good friendships" with co-workers that "include parties, skiing trips, and jaunts to Las Vegas." While employees say that they "regularly" work 50-60 hours a week, they add that the corporate culture is "less demanding and more fun" than that of similar firms based on the

MBA Job Seekers: Receive free e-mailed job postings matching your interests & qualifications! Register at www.VaultReports.com

VAULT REPORTS™
www.vaultreports.com

265

East coast. Then again, some people might not consider meetings at 5 in the morning fun and undemanding. "Sales, trading and research employees are all here by 5:30; investment bankers come in a bit later."

A "teamworking environment" warms the hearts of Robertson employees, and the "lack of structure" means "you can learn a lot if you are motivated." Employees are able to keep themselves hale and hearty at company expense, as they receive a discount corporate pass to gyms, and full insurance, including medical, dental and vision coverage. The 401(k) plan "is outstanding. The company puts in 13 percent of your annual salary, including overtime, whether you make any contributions or not." Most employees report that so far they "notice few changes as a result of the [BankBoston] acquisition," although many expect that eventually the corporate bureaucracy "may rear its ugly head." Most employees, however, "have seen no significant impact."

To order a 10- to 20-page Vault Reports Employer Profile on BancBoston Robertson Stephens call 1-888-JOB-VAULT or visit www.VaultReports.com

The full Employer Profile includes detailed information on Robbie Stephens' departments, recent developments and transactions, hiring and interview process, plus what employees really think about culture, pay, work hours and more.

VAULT REPORTS™
www.vaultreports.com

"The corporate culture is strong, fun, and best of all, realistic and down to earth."

– *Robertson Stephens insider*

PepsiCo

Consumer Products

700 Anderson Hill Road
Purchase, NY 10577-1444
(914) 253-2000
www.pepsico.com

PEPSI

LOCATIONS

Purchase, NY (HQ)
Bradenton, FL
Plano, TX
Somers, NY
As well as production, bottling, and
distribution facilities across the U.S.
and worldwide

DEPARTMENTS

Accounting
Distribution
Finance
Information Systems
Marketing
Operations
Sales

THE STATS

Annual Revenues: $20.9 billion (1997)
No. of Employees: 142,000 (worldwide)
Stock Symbol: PEP (NYSE)
CEO: Roger A. Enrico

KEY COMPETITORS

- Cadbury Schweppes
- Coca-Cola
- General Mills
- Nestle
- Ocean Spray
- Philip Morris (Kraft)
- RJR Nabisco
- Triarc

THE BUZZ
What MBAs are saying
about Pepsi

- "Always No. 2, still fun"
- "Snack foods only"
- "Young, hip, aggressive"
- "Underdogs"

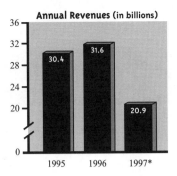

Annual Revenues (in billions)

UPPERS

- Prestigious company
- Stock options
- Tuition reimbursement
- Childcare assistance
- Company gym
- All the soda and chips you can consume

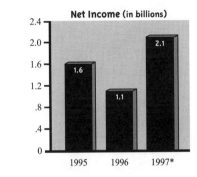

Net Income (in billions)

DOWNERS

- "Work first" culture
- Burnout problems

EMPLOYMENT CONTACT

Human Resources
PepsiCo
700 Anderson Hill Road
Purchase, NY 10577-1444

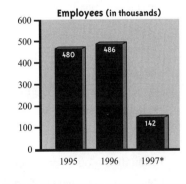

Employees (in thousands)

*Reflects restaurant spin-off

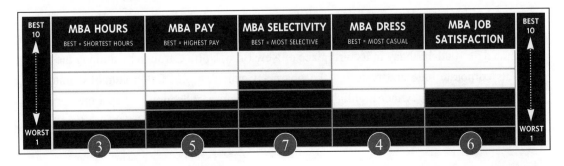

	MBA HOURS	MBA PAY	MBA SELECTIVITY	MBA DRESS	MBA JOB SATISFACTION	
BEST 10 ... WORST 1	BEST = SHORTEST HOURS	BEST = HIGHEST PAY	BEST = MOST SELECTIVE	BEST = MOST CASUAL		BEST 10 ... WORST 1
	3	5	7	4	6	

MBA Job Seekers: Receive free e-mailed job postings matching
your interests & qualifications! Register at www.VaultReports.com

VAULT REPORTS™   269
www.vaultreports.com

THE SCOOP

Pepsi-Cola was created in 1898 by Caleb Bradham, a North Carolina pharmacist who claimed the drink could cure dyspepsia. Pepsi began to produce canned soft drinks as early as 1948, and growing sales in the 1970s and 1980s ensured that its rivalry with Coca-Cola reached a fever pitch of competitiveness. While Pepsi triumphed briefly in the mid-1980s due to its "taste test challenge" – forcing Coca-Cola to revamp its hallowed formula (otherwise known as the "New Coke" debacle) – it has since fallen back into its position as the perennial No. 2 thirst-quencher.

PepsiCo may not have won the cola wars, but it still has plenty of fizz. The company has a healthy chunk of the world's cola share and its Frito-Lay division is the world's largest snack chip maker. Until 1997, the company also controlled a vast network of fast-food operations that included KFC, Pizza Hut, and Taco Bell. With 29,000 locations across the world, the restaurant group was the largest in the world. However, PepsiCo decided to spin off its restaurant business as a separate company, a restructuring deal that took close to a year to complete. The move was part of a long-term strategy to strengthen Pepsi's position in the marketplace and improve the consistency of its financial performance and shareholder returns by focusing on its beverage and snack business. Frito-Lay is keeping a new generation of couch potatoes satisfied – and even a bit less corpulent – with its new line of low-fat and fat-free products.

Pepsi hopes to improve its international cola sales by changing its packaging design and by capitalizing on its presence in high-potential markets such as China, India, and Russia – where Nikita Krushchev was first filmed downing a Pepsi in 1963. The new marketing plan: play the blues. Responding to Coke's control over the color red in its packaging and marketing, Pepsi's reaction has been to play up the color blue to give its product distinction. The new Pepsi packaging is now completely blue, except for its red, white and blue logo. In April 1998, Pepsi celebrated its 100th birthday in its birthplace of New Bern, North Carolina by draping the town with its corporate blue and restoring the pharmacy where young Caleb stumbled onto the billion-dollar product. Other highlights included the largest collection of Pepsi memorabilia ever gathered, a parade, and a dramatic performance called "The Caleb Bradham Story."

PepsiCo has enjoyed success from its other drinks, including Mountain Dew, and from its joint venture with Lipton, the country's leading maker of bottled iced tea. In October 1998, the firm launched a new one-calorie soft drink, Pepsi One, with a whopping $100 million campaign starring Cuba Gooding, Jr. as lead pitchman. Pepsi One uses a newly approved sweetener Ace-K made by NutraNova. And Pepsi claimed victory when it ousted Coke as the sole beverage distributed by the Disney-owned Edison International Field of Anaheim, home of baseball's Angels. The move enables PepsiCo to begin a relationship with fellow American icon Disney, which in the past has exclusively used Coke products in its facilities. The move marks another stride in Pepsi's plan to focus on fountain drinks, which have a higher profit margin than canned or bottled beverages.

Despite these small victories, Pepsi still looks to be losing the war, as it has watched Coca-Cola gain both domestic and worldwide market share. Although Pepsi has long pointed to Coke's fountain dominance as the primary reason for its overall market share lead, Big Red has since 1995 beaten Pepsi when it comes to retail store sales.

GETTING HIRED

Pepsi hires new MBAs primarily as strategic planners, business planners in its finance department or associate marketing managers in marketing. Those who go into strategic planning (what the company calls the Corporate Strategic Planning Group) tackle company-wide, general management issues, such as competitive analysis, identifying new markets, and M&A evaluation from the company's headquarters in Purchase, NY. After two years, strategy planners are expected to join one of Pepsi's operating divisions.

Business planners oversee operations from a financial analysis perspective at the market or business unit level. Associate marketing managers can follow the traditional brand management model, working on the marketing of a specific brand, such as Mountain Dew, or a specific distribution "channel" such as fountain drinks at convenience stores. The firm says

MBA Job Seekers: Receive free e-mailed job postings matching your interests & qualifications! Register at www.VaultReports.com

VAULT REPORTS™

www.vaultreports.com

271

it requires one year of post-MBA brand marketing experience for its associate marketing manager positions and a chance to work on some of the highest-profile marketing campaigns around.

For Pepsi "direct experience is great, but you must also must have demonstrated the ability to learn and adapt in business situations," insiders say. Pepsi wants "individuals with the potential to become senior managers." The interview process is pretty straightforward: "Just people trying to get to know you, where you're coming from, what you have to offer."

OUR SURVEY SAYS

"PepsiCo offers excellent opportunity for early responsibility and a culture that encourages initiative, risk taking and access to decision makers," says one insider. The company has a "professional but fun" corporate culture in which employees are "free to pursue their goals" without "the burden of excessive structure." The "casual" and "collegial" environment is headed by senior management "eager to hear the questions and ideas" of their more junior colleagues. Pepsi "is also a company of candor and reality."

PepsiCo is into "biological diversity – they welcome and actively recruit people of color and give them early opportunity for advancement." However, say insiders, "PepsiCo really wants one type of person, regardless of ancestry, someone who will put their job before their family or personal life." As Pepsi's "diversity is centered around birth rather than style or culture," the result for some is that PepsiCo culture is " fairly uniform: extremely competitive and very focused." However "the business units have a fair degree of autonomy" so even things such as dress code vary from office to office.

Employees praise the company's benefits program, which includes a "bountiful retirement package, a tuition reimbursement program, and even a legal assistance program." The downside of this is that "the culture is deliberately geared to churn people – the workload is extreme, your job is everything, and personal needs (family, vacation, etc.) are frowned upon."

The effect of this attitude is that "Pepsi will burn many people out very quickly." But many see Pepsi as the "ultimate corporate workplace – if you make it here you can make it anywhere." Whether the compensation is adequate is something of a debate. However, the "challenging" assignments and "accessible promotion path" aid job retention. When people do leave, they do so in a position of strength, as one employee notes, "PepsiCo experience is well thought of, and this seems to be backed up by the jobs that people hold after they leave."

The bottom line, an insider concludes, is that "Pepsi is a great place to make a name for yourself with a wide open career track, but only if you're prepared to make personal sacrifices."

MBA Job Seekers: Receive free e-mailed job postings matching your interests & qualifications! Register at www.VaultReports.com

VAULT REPORTS™

273

www.vaultreports.com

Time Warner

Media and Entertainment

75 Rockefeller Plaza
New York, NY 10019
(212) 484-7500
Fax: (212) 956-2847
www.timewarner.com

TIME WARNER

LOCATIONS

New York, NY (HQ)
Other offices include: Atlanta, GA •
Baltimore, MD • Burbank, CA • Henrietta,
NY • Indianapolis, IN • Mechanicsburg, PA •
Olyphant, PA • Ronkonkoma, NY • Terre
Haute, IN • Washington, D.C. • West
Hollywood, CA • Wilmington, DE • Brussels,
Belgium • Hamburg, Germany • London,
United Kingdom • Sydney, Australia

DEPARTMENTS

Cable Networks
Cable Systems
Entertainment
Publishing

THE STATS

Annual Revenues: $24.6 billion
No. of Employees: 70,000 (worldwide)
No. of Offices: 125 (worldwide)
Stock Symbol: TWX (NYSE)
CEO: Gerald M. Levin

KEY COMPETITORS

- ◆ Advance Publications
- ◆ Bertelsmann AG
- ◆ Sony
- ◆ Viacom
- ◆ Walt Disney
- ◆ Yahoo!

THE BUZZ
What MBAs are saying
about Time Warner

- ◆ "Monolithic"
- ◆ "Chic"
- ◆ "Always one step behind"
- ◆ "Too bureaucratic"

UPPERS

- Discounts at Warner Bros. Stores
- Gym discounts
- Tuition reimbursements
- Free admission to New York City museums
- Generous vacation policy

DOWNERS

- Unstructured hiring for MBAs
- Potential tension between MBAs and "creatives"

EMPLOYMENT CONTACT

Human Resources
Time Warner
75 Rockefeller Plaza
New York, NY 10019

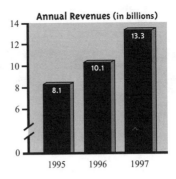

Annual Revenues (in billions)

1995: 8.1
1996: 10.1
1997: 13.3

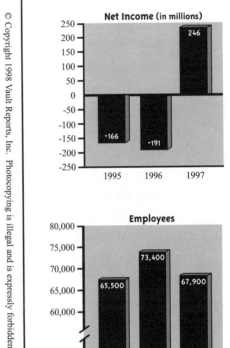

Net Income (in millions)

1995: -166
1996: -191
1997: 246

Employees

1995: 65,500
1996: 73,400
1997: 67,900

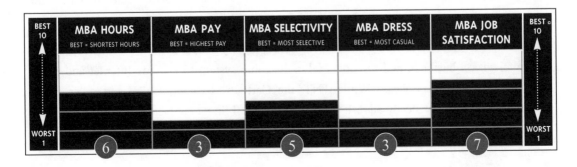

	MBA HOURS	MBA PAY	MBA SELECTIVITY	MBA DRESS	MBA JOB SATISFACTION	
	BEST = SHORTEST HOURS	BEST = HIGHEST PAY	BEST = MOST SELECTIVE	BEST = MOST CASUAL		
	6	3	5	3	7	

THE SCOOP

Formed by the 1989 merger of Time Inc. and Warner Communications, Time Warner is the largest and most prominent entertainment conglomerate in the world. Its holdings include a movie studio, music labels, cable television networks, cable television systems, and the world's largest publishing firm – not to mention Time Warner's chains of retail stores. The company's business operations are currently divided into four divisions: Entertainment, Cable Networks, Publishing and Cable Systems.

Time Warner's Entertainment division, which accounted for 43 percent of the company's revenue in 1997, includes Warner Brothers studios, maker of movies and television shows; music subsidiaries and 161 Warner Brothers retail stores. The Publishing sector includes influential Time Inc., publisher of 28 magazines; several publishing houses; and the world's largest book club, the Book-of-the-Month Club. The Cable Networks sector includes Home Box Office, the world's first and most successful premium cable television service, the Time Warner Cable television service, and the channels started by Ted Turner – CNN, TNT, and TBS – that Time Warner acquired when it bought out Turner Communications in 1996. The company's Cable Systems division boasts 12.6 million subscribers to a massive and increasingly important cable infrastructure.

When Time Inc. and Warner merged in 1989, it wasn't exactly smooth coming together. Trying to fight off a hostile takeover bid by Paramount, Time Warner was saddled with $14 billion in debt from the get-go. Ever since then, the company has been trying to keep standing and moving forward with a huge weight on its back. Consequently, no matter how well the individual units of Time Warner perform – especially its prized publishing unit – the media conglomerate has had its fair share of troubles trying to hold its own. Until recently, the company's stock price has sagged because of deep-seated financial problems.

However, the company is seeing sunny days ahead, largely because of the performance of its cable television business, and the potential of its cable system to provide Internet and other telecommunications services. While TNT, the Cartoon Network, CNN, and other cable channels have brought steady advertising cash flow, Wall Street analysts are more focused on the potential of the cables that deliver those stations. In 1997, Time Warner and US West Media Group (now called MediaOne Group), embarked on joint venture to create the nation's largest cable online business, called Road Runner. And in 1998, the company disclosed that it it was in talks with AT&T and other telecom giants about the potential use of Time Warner's cable systems for local-phone service – a market that long-distance companies have been itching to enter.

GETTING HIRED

MBAs can be hired into Time Warner's corporate umbrella structure, but should also look at the company's many divisions. "Time Warner Corporate has significant financial planning and some human resources and corporate administration, but there are only really maybe 100 employees in it," explains one insider. "In the divisions there are tens of thousands of jobs – you have to look at it almost like a holding company. An MBA should certainly target the divisions as much as Time Warner."

In part because of a decentralized corporate culture and structure, and in part because it is a media company that wants enthusiasm for the business, the company does not have a large on-campus recruiting program. "They used to do it," says one MBA. "Now they kind of wait for people to come to them. They don't go on to campus to hire MBAs because they don't think it's efficient. For example, HBO really likes MBAs, and hires them a lot. Although they don't go onto campuses, they really appreciate the business school education." That contact explains his hiring process: "I just met with as many people as possible. They were very open to talking to me – it was a very collegial, informal hiring process. They certainly hire on personality a lot. Though I don't think they'd write it down on a brochure, they'll admit as much."

Most Time Warner divisions hire MBAs as summer interns. Those hires are usually assured of full-time offers if they perform well. "They would never hire an intern that they didn't want to bring on full-time," says one insider.

MBA Job Seekers: Receive free e-mailed job postings matching your interests & qualifications! Register at www.VaultReports.com

VAULT REPORTS™

www.vaultreports.com

277

OUR SURVEY SAYS

The corporate structure at Time Warner encourages each subsidiary to operate "autonomously" and to "develop its individual corporate culture." Throughout the company, however, Time Warner "matches or improves upon" industry pay scales and also gives employees "more extensive paid vacations than any of its rivals." Nevertheless, the "daunting" size and "dizzying" pace of publishing and entertainment industries often "overwhelm" recent Time Warner hires. "Upper level managers are willing to answer any of your questions, if you can catch them!" a source says. The atmosphere at Time Warner's divisions is "busy," "exciting" – and unstructured. "You must be an independently motivated worker," a source reports. "There is little feedback along the way, but upper management respects your ideas, your analysis, and even your 'gut feeling' and expects to use the results of your work." Says one recent MBA hire, "the President (of the division) expects to see junior people at the meetings. It's not like someone above the junior person takes the information and runs with it."

Positions for MBAs in Time Warner's divisions include those in financial and strategic functions, with titles such as business manager or finance manager. "In those positions, you are in a position to suggest products. You can say, 'I have an idea, *People* should have a 'teen version,' if you could end up getting that going, they'd encourage it." MBAs should expect an experience as decentralized as the company's hiring process, with no set career path, and no "class" feeling as with I-banks or consulting firms. "There's not a sense of a class," says one MBA who spent a summer at one of Time Warner's divisions. "It's kind of too bad that way. But it's very entrepreneurial. Although you miss the organization of the program, you gain in the entrepreneurial atmosphere."

Perks for employees at Time Warner's New York locations include "free access to the museums – better than other companies. Every New York employer you can get into some museums, like the MOMA [Museum of Modern Art] or the Met, but Time Warner had really strong cultural stuff. Employees also rave about the "civilized" hours afforded for Time Warner employees. Says one MBA summer hire: "I worked from 9:30 to 5, and some of my friends who were in I-banking barely slept, and this was a summer internship."

"I worked from 9:30 to 5, and some of my friends who were in I-banking barely slept, and this was a summer internship."

– Time Warner insider

MBA Job Seekers: Receive free e-mailed job postings matching your interests & qualifications! Register at www.VaultReports.com

VAULT REPORTS™

279

www.vaultreports.com

3Com

5400 Bayfront Plaza
P.O. Box 58145
Santa Clara, CA 95052
(408) 764-5000
Fax: (408) 764-6966
www.3com.com

High Tech

LOCATIONS

Santa Clara, CA (HQ)
As well as 165 other offices located
in 42 countries around the world

DEPARTMENTS

Advanced Technology
Corporate Services
Customer Service
Diagnostics
Finance
Hardware Engineering
Manufacturing
Marketing
Software Engineering

THE STATS

Annual Revenues: $5.4 billion (1998)
No. of Employees: 12,500 (worldwide)
No. of Offices: 165 (worldwide)
Stock Symbol: COMS (Nasdaq)
CEO: Eric A. Benhamou
President and COO: Bruce Claflin

KEY COMPETITORS

- Ascend Communications
- Bay Networks
- Cabletron
- Cisco Systems
- Lucent Technologies

THE BUZZ
What MBAs are saying
about 3Com

- "Innovative home for techies"
- "Everyone loves the Palm Pilot"
- "Small-fry; interesting work"
- "Second-tier techy"

UPPERS

- ◆ Paid sabbaticals
- ◆ Flexible scheduling options
- ◆ Telecommuting
- ◆ Stock options
- ◆ Generous vacation time
- ◆ Good atmosphere for MBAs for tech company

DOWNERS

- ◆ Recent performance problems because of U.S. Robotics merger
- ◆ Lack of career support

EMPLOYMENT CONTACT

3Com Corporation
5400 Bayfront Plaza
P.O. Box 58145
Santa Clara, CA 95052
Fax: (408) 764-5001

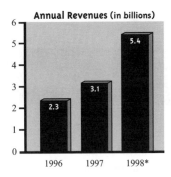

Annual Revenues (in billions)

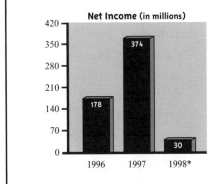

Net Income (in millions)

Employees

*Reflects merger with U.S. Robotics

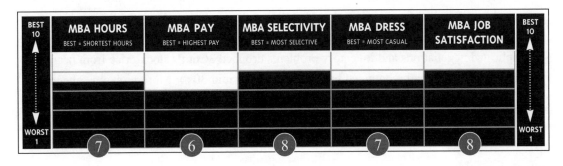

	MBA HOURS BEST = SHORTEST HOURS	MBA PAY BEST = HIGHEST PAY	MBA SELECTIVITY BEST = MOST SELECTIVE	MBA DRESS BEST = MOST CASUAL	MBA JOB SATISFACTION	
BEST 10 ... WORST 1	7	6	8	7	8	BEST 10 ... WORST 1

MBA Job Seekers: Receive free e-mailed job postings matching
your interests & qualifications! Register at www.VaultReports.com

VAULT REPORTS™
www.vaultreports.com

281

THE SCOOP

When Robert Metcalfe invented Ethernet in the famed Xerox research lab in 1979, he was a little ahead of his time. Metcalfe had developed a powerful networking tool that would, in 15 years, become the industry standard for connecting personal computers. But in 1979, few people had heard of PCs and the market for PC networking was miniscule. But when IBM came out with its first widely popular PC in 1982, the company saw sales take off. 3Com went public in 1984. Three years later, it acquired Bridge Communications, one of the first companies to sell networking equipment for PCs. The company's $8.5 billion purchase of modem maker U.S. Robotics in 1997 puts the company on the same financial scale as rival networker Cisco, though Cisco's lead in the networking business appears to some to be insurmountable.

3Com's name is simple and appropriate; it derives from three "coms" (computer, communications and compatibility) and describes what the company does. In a nutshell, 3Com helps compatible computers communicate with each other. The company's original line of business was making network cards – small circuit boards that connect computers to network wires coming out of walls. Currently, 3Com is pushing a new product, called a "telecommunications access device," which is supposed to be able to separate different types of data (high-density data that require advanced transmission techniques versus data that can easily go through phone lines, for example). One of the company's subsidiaries, Palm Computing, manufactures equipment for networking of a different kind: the PalmPilot allows techno-enthusiasts to keep track of all contacts and appointments with a computerized gizmo that fits in one's hand.

When 3Com announced its acquisition of U.S. Robotics in 1997 in a $8.5 billion deal, analysts everywhere described the move as "bold," "dramatic" and "daring." They did not, however, speak in consensus on the wisdom of the move. After the merger was announced, a series of complicated negotiations and inventory problems dropped 3Com's stock price from nearly 40 to the high 20s. (It had rebounded by late 1998 to the mid-30s.) More problems integrating U.S. Robotics led to shrinking profits and layoffs.

But in the future, U.S. Robotics' brand name may end up being extremely important to small businesses and customers looking for a familiar company to handle their networking and Internet services. With a reputation established in the traditional corporate market, 3Com is hoping its name and the U.S. Robotics moniker will be the names these new clients turn to. To help build its own brand name, 3Com even rented a baseball stadium – or at least the naming rights to the stadium: Candlestick Park in San Francisco has been 3Com Park since 1996.

GETTING HIRED

The interview process with 3Com usually involves several rounds, with interviewing by both managers and potential colleagues. Although one insider tells Vault Reports that "some managers like to use brainteasers or riddles," this practice seems uncommon. Be ready for technical questions, though, even if you're not an engineer. "As a technology company we are very concerned with having people who are technology literate even in non-technology positions, says one manager. "That does not mean that an individual needs to have a strong technical background, simply technology and possibly industry awareness." "3Com really likes engineers," says one former marketing MBA intern. "Know your technical stuff before interviewing." And, says one product manager, "learn about the product before you interview. A little knowledge goes a long way." That manager, an MBA, suggests reading the book *How Networks Work* by Frank Derfler (Ziff Davis, 1996).

Insiders also stress that when it comes to personal traits, the company values teamwork highly. "There are two aspects they look at: how you deal with yourself (motivation and enthusiasm) and your interpersonal skills (working in a group)," says one. "Be sure to have examples of each, especially the working in a group part. The big companies usually look for team players." Employees tell us that 3Com is good about making employment decisions soon – interviewees usually hear in a week or so.

MBA Job Seekers: Receive free e-mailed job postings matching your interests & qualifications! Register at www.VaultReports.com

VAULT REPORTS™

283

www.vaultreports.com

OUR SURVEY SAYS

Many employees surveyed by Vault Reports note that 3Com's company culture is difficult to define in large part because it has grown through acquisitions, not organically. "The acquired company is turned into a division and tends to keep their pre-acquisition culture," explains one employee. One thing seems certain, however – 3Com's work environment is marked by communication and teamwork. "3Com has tried to minimize the class divisions of more traditional companies. Everyone in the company, including the VPs and the CEO, have cubicles," says one employee. "They want to reinforce an open-door policy for all employees. Understandably, the executives' cubicles are larger, but still without a door." Says another, echoing the company's name origins: "Open communication is a very important part of our culture."

The absence of hierarchy which one employee describes as "fraternalistic rather than paternalistic," does have its drawbacks: "You need to fend for yourself, but you will be supported in what you are trying to do, rather than having your manager responsible for steering your career," says one employee. "It is a hard-driving place, so anyone coming here should be ready to hit the ground running, and running hard and fast," says another insider. Former U.S. Robotics employees describe much the same situation: "U.S. Robotics became big in a short time and hence the environment here is one of go-getters with less bureaucracy but that also means a bit less organized."

Still, employees seem very satisfied. Says one employee, who has stayed with 3COM for more than a decade, about his tenure, "This [length of employment] is somewhat unheard of for high tech but 3Com is a company that works hard to retain its employees." Part of the reason employees may stay is that they get to spend a lot of time away from the company. Every four years, 3Com employees get an extra one month paid "sabbatical" which employees say is "mandated." This is in addition to an already whopping 28 days of paid vacation for starting employees. Also, there is a "company wide shutdown between Christmas and New Years'." To encourage employees to take time off, 3Com "doesn't let employees accrue more than 120 hours. If you earn more you lose it because you don't take what you've got." Although many employees report working nine- to 10-hour days, and some complain about long hours, others remark that "unlike the unwritten rule at many high-tech companies who really want 50 to 60+

each week, you work hard while you're here and then go home or go play. You're expected to work 40 hours a week."

And it's not as if life at the Santa Clara 3Com campus, located next to the San Francisco Bay is particularly austere. "We have a 24-hour, 7-day-a-week, 365-days-a year on-site gym with aerobics classes, stationary and free weights, treadmills, bikes, stairmasters, and locker rooms for $20 a month," reports one health enthusiast. The gym features also include a sauna and a massage service, employees say. "There is also a café, a cafeteria, movie rentals, dry cleaners service, a Starbucks coffee shop, commuter shuttles, and a car wash service," according to another employee. As for other perks, "there is at least one free night at 3Com Park for a (San Francisco) Giants game," reports one employee. Also, "you get to purchase personal use 3Com products for a discounted price, including modems, Palm pilots, and various plug-in cards for PCs." Monetary perks include a "3reward" system that offers cash bonuses for outstanding performance, a stock purchase plan that lets employees buy company shares at a 15 percent discount (10 percent of one's gross pay can be set aside for this plan). And, all employees are offered stock options upon their hiring.

To order a 10- to 20-page Vault Reports Employer Profile on 3Com call 1-888-JOB-VAULT or visit www.VaultReports.com

The full Employer Profile includes detailed information on 3Com's departments, recent developments and transactions, hiring and interview process, plus what employees really think about culture, pay, work hours and more.

Lehman Brothers

RANKING 37

Investment Banking

3 World Financial Center
New York, NY 10285
(212) 526-7000
www.lehman.com

LEHMAN BROTHERS

Stock Symbol: LEH (NYSE)
CEO: Richard S. Fuld, Jr.

LOCATIONS

New York, NY (HQ)
Other offices in CA • DC • FL • GA • IL • MA
• NJ • PA • TX • WA • Argentina • Bahrain •
Brazil • Canada • Chile • China • Dubai • France
• Germany • Hong Kong • India • Indonesia •
Israel • Italy • Japan • Mexico • Puerto Rico •
Singapore • South Korea • Spain • Switzerland •
Taiwan • Thailand • United Kingdom • Uruguay

KEY COMPETITORS

- Bankers Trust
- Bear Stearns
- Credit Suisse First Boston
- Donaldson, Lufkin & Jenrette
- Goldman Sachs
- J.P. Morgan
- Merrill Lynch
- Morgan Stanley Dean Witter
- Salomon Smith Barney

DEPARTMENTS

Corporate Advisory
Equities
Finance
Fixed Income
Human Resources
Investment Banking
Operations
Private Client Services
Technology

THE BUZZ
What MBAs are saying
about Lehman

- "Making big bets to survive"
- "Perpetually for sale"
- "Nice guys"
- "Chip on the shoulder"

THE STATS

Annual Revenues: $16.9 billion (1997)
No. of Employees: 8,340 (worldwide)
No. of Offices: 39 (worldwide)

UPPERS

- ◆ Growing firm
- ◆ Not as stuffy as other Wall Street firms
- ◆ Excellent advancement opportunities

DOWNERS

- ◆ Sometimes fratty atmosphere
- ◆ Intense pressure

EMPLOYMENT CONTACT

Investment Banking

Dorine McManus
Lehman Brothers
3 World Financial Center
New York, NY 10285

Capital Markets

Kristin Williams
Lehman Brothers
3 World Financial Center
New York, NY 10285

Fax: (212) 526-3738

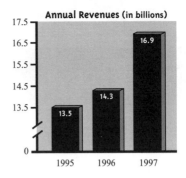

Annual Revenues (in billions)

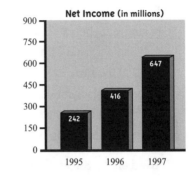

Net Income (in millions)

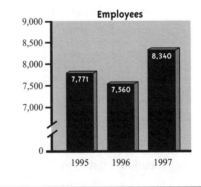

Employees

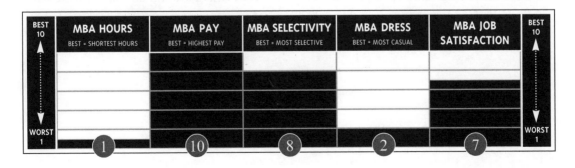

BEST 10 ← → WORST 1	MBA HOURS BEST = SHORTEST HOURS	MBA PAY BEST = HIGHEST PAY	MBA SELECTIVITY BEST = MOST SELECTIVE	MBA DRESS BEST = MOST CASUAL	MBA JOB SATISFACTION	BEST 10 ← → WORST 1
	1	10	8	2	7	

MBA Job Seekers: Receive free e-mailed job postings matching
your interests & qualifications! Register at www.VaultReports.com

VAULT REPORTS™

287

www.vaultreports.com

THE SCOOP

Founded 150 years ago as a cotton-trading business in the American South, Lehman Brothers offers a wide range of investment banking services, including fixed income and equities sales, trading and research; M&A advisory; public finance; and private client services. American Express acquired the firm in 1984; later, when American Express decided to refocus on its core business, Lehman Brothers was unceremoniously dropped. With a $1 billion parting gift, Lehman was sold off to American Express stockholders and the public in 1994. Once again a stand-alone firm, Lehman has been fighting hard to regain its position as one of Wall Street's premier investment banks. After some tough decisions, such as major layoffs and cost cutting in 1994 and 1995, the firm has boosted its revenues increased its profitability and gained market share in high-margin businesses such as equity origination, M&A, and high yield.

Word on the Street in early 1998 had Lehman coupling again, perhaps with Chase Manhattan, or Deutsche Bank. The rumors sent Lehman's stock price – and profitability – skyrocketing. In April 1998, the stock reached $84 5/8. But as the overall market began to fall midyear, Lehman fell more than most. The company's stock sank to the mid-$20 range before recovering late in the year.

But why was the firm's stock so popular before its precipitous decline? The takeover speculation was driven in part by the firm's recent strong performance. After four years as a public company, Lehman has recently been making the case that it again should be considered one of Wall Street's top investment banks. In 1996 and 1997, the trimmer Lehman began rebuilding itself; in 1997 and 1998, profits stood at record levels. As of early 1998, the firm had exceeded analyst estimates for 11 straight quarters. And recently, Lehman Brothers has built its human base back up to 8700 workers. However, Lehman is still the only firm on Wall Street with fewer employees now than it had in 1994.

Despite the turmoil in debt markets in August and September, Lehman said in September 1998 that it wasn't planning any large-scale layoffs – even as competitors such as Merrill Lynch were announcing broad staff cuts.

GETTING HIRED

First impressions are key at Lehman. After meeting students at colleges and business schools, the firm's recruiters will focus on a number of top candidates. Says one recent MBA hire: "I was targeted and was pursued hard." In fact, the firm prefers to have identified its targets by the time campus interviewing starts. The firm focuses on nine business schools (Chicago, Columbia, Wharton, Tuck, Fuqua, Stern, UCLA, Kellogg, and MIT's Sloan).

How does Lehman pick its targets? In part, through on-campus get-to-know you functions. For example, the firm's sales and trading recruiters host a "Trading Game" on campus, where they simulate three to four "pits" similar to those on the Chicago Futures exchanges. The "game" (read: tryout) lasts four to five hours. People from Lehman play one role, while students play another. The trading game allows Lehman to observe students in action, so it can identify strong candidates. Lehman also hosts cocktail parties to identify targets. Despite these ulterior motives, the firm tries to keep the events as informal and social as possible, insiders say. "The focus is on personalities."

As with many programs, Lehman's summer programs act as a feeder system for full-time hires. The firm reports that 75 percent of its incoming full-time class for the fall of 1998 were interns at Lehman. The firm also reports that 90 percent of the MBAs Lehman hires into capital markets for the summer get offers (although insiders say that the number is closer to 80 percent). Summer associates receive their offers within two weeks of the end of the program. MBAs are hired into the firm as associates. Those interested in Lehman should visit the firm's web site, located at www.lehman.com and chock full of detailed recruiting information. Most associates report an excellent recruitment process. Says one: "There was no bullshit in the recruiting process. They were honest with us."

MBA Job Seekers: Receive free e-mailed job postings matching
your interests & qualifications! Register at www.VaultReports.com

VAULT
REPORTS™
www.vaultreports.com

289

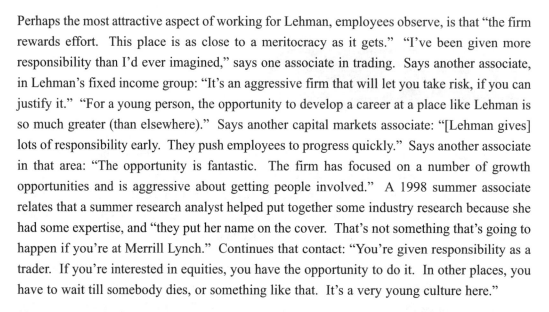

OUR SURVEY SAYS

Perhaps the most attractive aspect of working for Lehman, employees observe, is that "the firm rewards effort. This place is as close to a meritocracy as it gets." "I've been given more responsibility than I'd ever imagined," says one associate in trading. Says another associate, in Lehman's fixed income group: "It's an aggressive firm that will let you take risk, if you can justify it." "For a young person, the opportunity to develop a career at a place like Lehman is so much greater (than elsewhere)." Says another capital markets associate: "[Lehman gives] lots of responsibility early. They push employees to progress quickly." Says another associate in that area: "The opportunity is fantastic. The firm has focused on a number of growth opportunities and is aggressive about getting people involved." A 1998 summer associate relates that a summer research analyst helped put together some industry research because she had some expertise, and "they put her name on the cover. That's not something that's going to happen if you're at Merrill Lynch." Continues that contact: "You're given responsibility as a trader. If you're interested in equities, you have the opportunity to do it. In other places, you have to wait till somebody dies, or something like that. It's a very young culture here."

Lehman's culture is one of "survivors and fighters – people have been through a lot together, and they are very loyal to each other," says one recent hire. Employees speak enthusiastically about Lehman's "social" corporate offices, where "most employees are extremely nice and friendly, and very down-to-earth, unlike at some other places on the street." As one new hire says, Lehman's "culture is open," largely because of the "affable" upper management who "make an effort to be readily approachable." "Culture very much depends on which business and which desk, but overall, it is not at all stuffy," says one associate in trading. "There are fairly honest professional people."

"Lehman has more of a laid-back collegial environment than other firms that I've worked at. I've seen all the other firms, and also over the summer I visited a bunch of firms," says one associate who summered at Lehman. "It's not laid back in that people are easygoing, it just doesn't have the pretension that you might have at other places," continues that associate. "People work hard, but people also are welcoming, no one's putting on airs, that's the feeling that I got. I've been all around the firm, and I never had a situation where someone blew me off or wasn't interested in talking about him." Says one analyst in the firm's research department: "It's warm, and less intense than your typical Wall Street firm." Cozy indeed.

Although Lehman may be laid-back in the sense of not being stuffy or aristocratic, that doesn't mean the temperature doesn't rise at the firm. One ex-employee in New York notes, "There's a lot more yelling at Lehman Brothers than at my current firm." Insiders say that Lehman, like most major investment banks, has a "macho culture" and "many arrogant attitudes." Says one: "Antics are somewhat unprofessional. Many employees have something of a locker-room, fraternity culture." Says one insider: "It's meritocratic but can be easily abused by overly aggressive people."

MBA Job Seekers: Receive free e-mailed job postings matching your interests & qualifications! Register at www.VaultReports.com

VAULT REPORTS™

291

www.vaultreports.com

Oracle

RANKING 38

High Tech

500 Oracle Parkway,
Box 659202
Redwood Shores, CA 94065
(650) 506-7000
www.oracle.com

ORACLE®

LOCATIONS

Redwood Shores, CA (HQ)
Atlanta, GA • Bethesda, MD • Boston, MA • Chicago, IL • Denver, CO • Honolulu, HI • Nashville, TN • New York, NY • Richmond, VA • Seattle, WA • Beijing, China • Berlin, Germany • Buenos Aires, Argentina • Montreal, Canada • As well as locations around the U.S. and worldwide

DEPARTMENTS

Data Storage Technologies
Internet Products Group
Languages and Relational Technology Group
Oracle Server Product Management Group
Open Systems Integration and Technology
Software Engineering
Systems Management Products Group

THE STATS

Annual Revenues: $7.1 billion (1998)
Income: $814 million (1998)
No. of Employees: 36,802 (U.S.)
No. of Offices: 60 (U.S.)
Stock Symbol: ORCL

Stock Exchange: NYSE
CEO: Lawrence J. Ellison

KEY COMPETITORS

- Baan
- IBM
- Informix
- Microsoft
- Novell
- Peoplesoft
- SAP
- Sybase

THE BUZZ

What MBAs are saying about Oracle

- "Complainers"
- "Aggressive, innovative, leading"
- "Slowing growth"
- "Too sales-oriented, not enough marketing"

292
www.vaultreports.com
Vault Reports Guide to the Top 50 MBA Employers

UPPERS

- Stock purchase plan
- Tuition reimbursement
- Beautiful offices
- Excellent company gym

DOWNERS

- Heavy workload
- Occasional ass-kicking from Microsoft

EMPLOYMENT CONTACT

Human Resources
Oracle
500 Oracle Parkway
Box 659202
Redwood Shores, CA 94065
E-mail: jobs@us.oracle.com

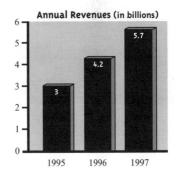

Annual Revenues (in billions)

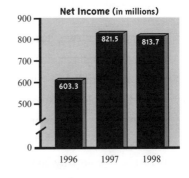

Net Income (in millions)

Employees

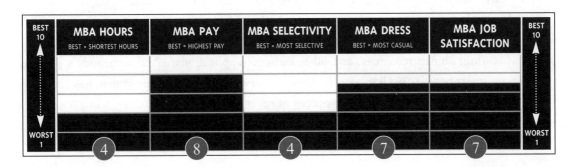

	MBA HOURS	MBA PAY	MBA SELECTIVITY	MBA DRESS	MBA JOB SATISFACTION	
BEST 10 ... WORST 1	BEST = SHORTEST HOURS	BEST = HIGHEST PAY	BEST = MOST SELECTIVE	BEST = MOST CASUAL		BEST 10 ... WORST 1
	4	8	4	7	7	

THE SCOOP

Oracle has goals that few Silicon Valley companies would have the vision or the ambition to even consider. First on the agenda is to complete its domination of the database software market. With that coming to fruition, CEO Larry Ellison and his cohorts are setting their sights on wrestling control of the world from Bill Gates.

In just over two decades, Ellison has skillfully crafted Oracle into the leading maker of database management software and a fighter capable of taking on the biggest bullies on the block. Founded in 1977 to capitalize on technology first developed – and later fumbled – by IBM, Oracle immediately experienced rapid success and growth. However, irregular accounting practices and poor product development during the early 1990s led to concerns that Oracle lacked the ability to keep up with its growth. A shareholder lawsuit forced Ellison to resign as company chairman, but the company managed to rebound. Now, with Ellison recast as a visionary developer of software ideas (his Chief Operating Officer handles the day-to-day business operations), Oracle is ready to take on the 21st century – and the evil empire of Microsoft.

As the world's second-largest software company (behind Microsoft), Oracle offers several different products, most involving either database management or network connectivity. Oracle software makes it easier for its customers, usually large businesses, to enter, store, or retrieve data like customer product orders, sales records, and personnel information. Oracle's newest program, announced in September 1998 and scheduled to ship later in the year, is Oracle 8i, a database capable of managing Internet applications over networks that thousands of corporations and individuals use every day. Oracle has also moved into new product areas to increase sales. To supplement the database software, the company, through its tools department, develops software developing tools that allow users to customize their Oracle software. Oracle applications include over 30 software items for finance and administration, manufacturing, human resources, and other business applications. And somebody's got to show customers how to use all this stuff – Oracle's service and training department has become one of the company's fastest growing sources of revenue.

GETTING HIRED

MBAs can find opportunities in Sales, Marketing, Product Management, and a number of other departments. According to insiders, "one of the hottest [areas] is enterprise resource planning systems." Oracle has recently tailored these systems to specific industries like automotive and banking, so MBAs with previous experience in such areas are particularly well suited. The company encourages employees to "marry their expertise with our software" in other areas as well. Consulting is another group hungry for MBAs, who work in "an Andersen (Consulting) – type role, helping businesses configure and implement the system." Somewhat surprisingly, "Finance is a small group, so opportunities are few and far between." For corporate and technical employees alike, Oracle suffers from poor retention. Confides one insider, "people [tend to] work three to five years, then realize they can make more money at Joe Startup down the street."

"Oracle is a very large corporation," explains an insider in understated fashion. "Because a machine as large as that requires a multitude of different parts, each performing a specialized task, to make it run, there isn't one interview process at Oracle. Each organization and department is responsible for hiring its members. There is a human resources department, but they are not primarily responsible for recruiting and hiring the company's employees. This essentially means that each department has its own approach to the hiring process." Most candidates right out of school, though, do find out about opportunities through Human Resources. That department "recruits MBAs for specific roles." Representatives go on campus to find recruits and pass on information about the various groups that are hiring. They then e-mail resumes to appropriate hiring managers. Since "its extremely hard to find someone with a technical background," the techie MBA is a hot commodity. Insiders warn that even for that rare breed though, just finding out about the better opportunities available can be difficult outside of campus recruiting. "Find someone within [the company], and start with the internal job bank," advises one. Interested candidates unable to go through these types of channels are encouraged to e-mail their resumes directly. Oracle also gets many referrals from headhunters.

MBA Job Seekers: Receive free e-mailed job postings matching your interests & qualifications! Register at www.VaultReports.com

VAULT REPORTS™
www.vaultreports.com

295

OUR SURVEY SAYS

Employees enjoy the "lively and social" atmosphere that prevails at Oracle. They say that the halls are brimming with "bright and motivated people" who have created a "young and dynamic" corporate culture. Thanks to this enthusiastic work force and to Oracle's recent performance, morale levels are "sky high throughout the company." Relations between employees are "reasonably friendly, though it's not the Midwest, so you won't get invited over for dinner by everyone."

Despite the laid-back 'tude of Silicon Valley, Oracle is still a bureaucratic organization like any other, and thus has a down side akin to corporations in other industries. Some employees complain that Oracle's "extensive" size and scope makes recognition hard to come by. "This is a huge company, and I think sometimes you have to either sink or swim. You can easily get swept up and passed over in a large corporation like Oracle." Still, most agree that "it is a very challenging environment, with great opportunities of upward mobility for those who are willing to put in the work and produce results."

Brilliant minds cannot be fettered, so for the technical staff, "as long as you dress decently, not in dirty or ripped clothes," it is acceptable to the Oracle brass. Scoffs another not-so-nattily-clad employee, "Dress code? Ha! Unless you are part of the sales force, attire is whatever you want." In general, "the dress code depends on your area of expertise. Developers are usually casual on all five days. Sales and marketing people mostly are not, while consultants are dependent on their client to make the call." Some employees feel a need to at least look presentable compared to those who are required to dress up, but this is not always the case. Jokes one insider, "My first day they told me there was one rule: don't wear a tie. That's because the project leaders don't want anyone to dress better than them."

Most employees work in that odd staple of modern corporate culture, the cubicle. Apparently, there is little rhyme or reason to how much personal space an employee gets. "Some cubicles have two people stuffed into them, some have a huge cubicle to themselves," remarks a puzzled office dweller. The company does not have "weird rules about your cubicle – you're free to do what you want." Also encouraging, Oracle had experts do "an ergonomics assessment to avoid workplace injuries. They made sure your screen was at the right height, and that no one could get carpal tunnel syndrome." When outside the cubicle, "Oracle strives to make it so you don't have to leave campus." Conveniences such as "dry cleaning, film developing, and even detailing and automotive work on your car" are all available. On campus, "every building has a cafeteria on the bottom floor with anything you could ask for." To work off that lunch, Oracle employees in the company's Redwood Shores headquarters can go to the company gym, which by all accounts "is not to be believed." It comes complete with "sand volleyball courts, basketball courts, and a heated swimming pool" as well as traditional equipment like "treadmills, stairmasters, bikes, and Sybex equipment.

To order a 50- to 70-page Vault Reports Employer Profile on Oracle call 1-888-JOB-VAULT or visit www.VaultReports.com

The full Employer Profile includes detailed information on Oracle's departments, recent developments and transactions, hiring and interview process, plus what employees really think about culture, pay, work hours and more.

MBA Job Seekers: Receive free e-mailed job postings matching your interests & qualifications! Register at www.VaultReports.com

VAULT REPORTS™   297

www.vaultreports.com

GO TECH, YOUNG MBA

Cubicles, geeks, and juicy stock options. Think you know everything about what it's like inside the booming high tech industry? Read on and see if your preconceptions meet reality.

In an industry expanding at supernova speed, you'd expect employees to move fast. And indeed, many high-tech firms are described as "not for those who like to take things slowly." "Working here is like jumping out of an airplane with your hair on fire," says one high-tech employee. "We call it velocity." Some companies appear slow-paced, though the reality is quite different. "Externally, things look relaxed: many if not most people are dressed casually, most people don't have to be in the office during specific business hours," one insider at a major software company reports. "Internally, though, it's usually quite hectic... schedules are as tight as they can possibly be." At another tech haven, employees work "unending days," let their "work take over their lives," but some "love every minute of it."

How do high tech firms get employees to run full-tilt? A casual and friendly culture helps. Teamwork is a hallmark of most high-tech firms, as products are normally developed together. One high-tech employee tells Vault Reports: "The atmosphere is very social-a good-sized chunk of my day is spent in other people's offices or with other people in my office discussing how to accomplish some task or the latest industry news." At another technology firm, an insider says: "We work together in small feature teams, so even though this is a large company, you always feel like an important part of a team." Still, most high-tech employees combine teamwork with ambition. One employee describes walking through the halls in his offices and seeing "people hanging out in small groups chatting about projects they're working on – always seeming so casual, yet there's a sort of burn in their eyes. It's hard to describe."

High-tech firms often cultivate a culture similar to that of a college dorm. "The culture here is focused around doing great work, but it is also a very fun place to be," says an insider. Many firms also feature entertainment for overstressed employees. "We have a basketball hoop in our hall, which is a great way to blow off steam in the evenings or the middle of the day," says one insider. "Those technical people – I've heard stories about them," says one financial analyst. "I've heard they have espresso machines in their offices and futons on the

Go tech, young MBA, cont'd

floor in case they have to program late into the night. I see them playing Frisbee in the halls and most wear jeans all day long." When successful, high tech firms are prone to giveaways like "free screenings of movies" and "Tag Heuer watches all around," not to mention "product discounts" and "big fat stock options," but during down times "things are very austere."

Another buzzword at most high-tech companies is "meritocracy." Companies "expect you to speak up and express your viewpoint," say insiders. "If you can get your point heard, you can make it happen." "There is no problem with stagnant old boy networks," adds one insider. "Those who do not produce do not stick around. Those who are valuable are rewarded." High-tech firms are known for their tolerance of employee diversity. "It's completely safe to be an out gay, bisexual, or lesbian," says one contact. "Black, white, brown, women, men – they will hire anyone that knows jack about computers," says one techie. Fair enough.

Yes, employees do joke about their "monitor tans" – that is, a ghostly pallor. Yes, there is a relative paucity of women – but this varies from company to company. At some companies, women may compose an appropriate 50 percent of all employees – and not just in such traditional estrogen ghettos such as human resources and secretarial services. At others, say employees, the introduction of any female is an invitation for "lots of desperate moves by deprived geeks." And as for staying up until all hours – that part of high tech is also true. "We tend to keep really weird hours," admits one programmer. "For example, I am an insomniac, and I often come to work at around 2 or 3 in the morning, then work straight for ten or twelve hours. I'm never alone when I come in, either."

For more information on careers in the high tech industry, including brainteasers and other interview questions, read the Vault Reports Guide to High Tech.

Silicon Graphics, Inc.

High Tech

2011N. Shoreline Boulevard
Mountain View, CA 94043
(650) 960-1980
www.sgi.com

LOCATIONS

Mountain View, CA (HQ)

Other major U.S. locations in:
Atlanta, GA • Boston, MA • Chicago, IL • Minneapolis, MN • Nashville, TN • New Orleans, LA • New York, NY • Portland, OR • San Diego, CA • Silver Spring, MD

Major international locations in:
Berlin, Germany • Buenos Aires, Argentina • Montreal, Canada • Tokyo, Japan

DEPARTMENTS

Administration • Engineering • Finance • Human Resources • Information Systems • Legal • Manufacturing • Marketing • Sales • Support/Service

THE STATS

Annual Revenues: $3.1 billion (1998)
No. of Employees: 9,900 (worldwide)
No. of Offices: 100 (U.S.), 134 (worldwide)
Stock Symbol: SGI (NYSE)
CEO: Richard Belluzzo

KEY COMPETITORS

- Apple Computer
- Compaq
- Dell Computer
- Hewlett-Packard
- IBM
- Sun Microsystems
- Unisys

THE BUZZ
What MBAs are saying
about SGI

- "Cool"
- "Dying"
- "Too techie, not in tune with market"
- "Nerdy, innovative, scientific"

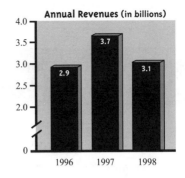

UPPERS

- Historically fun with lots of perks
- Cool company

DOWNERS

- Recent financial troubles
- Historically led by engineers

EMPLOYMENT CONTACT

Silicon Graphics, Inc.
2011N. Shoreline Boulevard
Mountain View, CA 94043
(650) 960-1980
www.sgi.com/employment

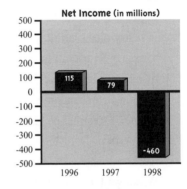

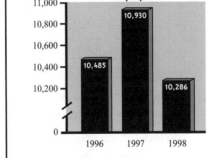

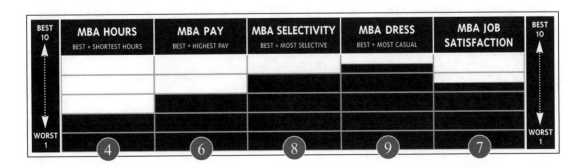

MBA Job Seekers: Receive free e-mailed job postings matching
your interests & qualifications! Register at www.VaultReports.com

VAULT REPORTS™
www.vaultreports.com

THE SCOOP

Once the darling of Wall Street and Hollywood, the company whose technology brought you *The Lost World* and *Antz* has fallen on rough times. Riding a microprocessor innovation that allowed the creation of revolutionary 3-D graphics, Silicon Graphics was one of the hottest high-tech companies in the late 1980s and the first half of the 1990s – "the next Apple," as one industry observer all too presciently described the firm. Sales leapt from $86 million in 1987 to nearly $3 billion in 1996. And unlike other high-tech concerns whose revenues were offset by absorbing losses, SGI enjoyed handsome profits nearly every year, peaking with $225 million in net income in 1995. But since 1995, the company has consistently posted poor financial results as competition in its field intensifies. SGI's powerful servers face competition from bigger companies such as IBM and Hewlett-Packard. After its expensive workstations and even its bulwark 3-D graphics unit began losing out to less expensive Windows-based PCs, the company recently began producing Windows NT/Intel workstations. Nevertheless, some analysts believe SGI still has some major assets, namely, its 3-D brand cachet and its stable of skilled employees. Now, say observers, SGI must learn to market and sell its wondrous products.

Silicon Graphics, or SGI, was founded in 1982 by former Stanford University computer science professor James Clark (who later left to help found Netscape). Clark and six students came up with new ways to build a 3-D graphics computer, and eventually, a 3-D workstation, which was first marketed in 1984 for $75,000. Their key was to create separate chips and circuits for the graphics that take the burden off a computers' central microprocessor, thus speeding the creation of 3-D models. Previous to the innovation, most workstations could only create 3-D "wireframe" models (outlines that resemble skeletons). Hollywood and advertising agencies soon caught on. Thus was born the SGI era in special effects, one that has made possible the effects in such fine films such as *Mask* and *Twister*, as well as engaging commercials starring morphing faces and dancing crackers. SGI rode its graphics-capable microprocessor to market dominance. Artists, researchers, and engineers were thrilled to bring intensely cool graphics to their desktops. In 1993, when President Bill Clinton visited the company's headquarters to witness a virtual tour of South Central L.A., he declared that the country needed more companies like SGI.

But all high-tech fairy tales, it seems, must come to an end. In the past several years, a combination of strategic mistakes and operations snafus has pushed SGI to the brink of a collapse. The company hit its lowest point (so far) in late 1997, when SGI's stock lost a third of its value in one day, after company officials warned that earnings and sales would fall far short of expectations. In 1997, then-CEO Ed McCracken, who had led the company since 1984, resigned and the company laid off nearly 10 percent of its workforce.

Since January 1998, the new CEO, Richard Belluzzo, has begun to implementing his turn-around plan, focused on a clearer market and situations focus, a redefined product plan, and a new business model. He also announced plans to work with Intel and Microsoft to produce SGI workstations based on Intel's processors and the Microsoft Windows NT operating system and spun off SGI's own chip-making unit, MIPS Technologies. But problems with SGI's Cray division, which makes supercomputers, slowed progress. By mid-1998, SGI shares had lost two-thirds of their value since 1995.

GETTING HIRED

SGI conducts an aggressive recruiting campaign on business school campuses nationwide. The company gives presentations and interviews at top schools such as Harvard, Wharton, MIT-Sloan and Kellogg, along with schools closer to its California home such as Anderson (UCLA), Stanford, and Santa Clara. The company's recruitment schedule can be found at its web site, at www.sgi.com.

Interviewers at SGI are adamant that "fit" bears importance equal to functional ability. "[There is] one thing that we do here that may be unusual – we hire only people that you wouldn't mind sharing an office with," one interviewer says. "There are plenty of smart people, so get the smart people that have the same type of personality as your group." Says another: "There's a lot of emphasis on selecting people who will fit into the culture in the company." What type of person is the "right kind of person?" Start with SGI's "Purpose and Core Values." SGI's Purpose: "Unleashing the power of human creativity and insight." Its core values: "innovation,

MBA Job Seekers: Receive free e-mailed job postings matching your interests & qualifications! Register at www.VaultReports.com

VAULT REPORTS™

303

www.vaultreports.com

integrity, passion to excel, fairness and respect, breakthrough results." Schmaltzy, and a bit generic, yes, but a start.

OUR SURVEY SAYS

Like many other high-tech companies, SGI is described by its employees as having a company culture that mixes relaxation and high energy, or, as one insider put it, "laid-back frenzy." "Externally, things look relaxed: many if not most people are dressed casually," reports one employee, "most people don't have to be in the office during specific business hours. Internally, though, it's usually quite hectic. Schedules are as tight as they can possibly be." According to another source: "It's a very casual culture, there is no dress code, and everyone can talk to everyone else. There's an open door policy which people take seriously." At the same time, that employee, a longtime worker at SGI, says "it can be a pretty intense working environment in spite of all that. Things happen pretty quickly in Silicon Valley, and there's a fast work pace, lots of things going on."

But the laid-back element is equally as strong. The dress code is based on the notion that "if you are comfortable, then you work more efficiently." "Sales people wear suits, but most everyone else wears casual clothes, all the way down to jeans and T-shirts most days," says an insider at SGI's headquarters. Also, reports one longtime employee currently stationed in Europe: "The work hours are very flexible, and we have many telecommuters." According to a manager at headquarters, "one of my employees comes in at 6:30 a.m., while most of the team comes in between 8 and 9. I arrive between 9 and 9:30 on most days unless I have an early meeting. And in addition to the flexible hours, "every four years you get a six-week paid vacation called a sabbatical when you're supposed to just take time off and 'recharge.'"

Compensation at SGI is described as good but not astounding. "We are very competitive with all the high-tech companies, usually in the top 20 percent of the companies in the Valley," says one employee. The pay is generally a bit higher than comparable companies in the Valley," reports another. According to one insider, however, pay is not the main payoff of working with

SGI: "Don't expect to get rich here, but expect to get some great experience that you'll be able to take anywhere." Tenure does not correlate with compensation at SGI, according to insiders. "A person is measured against specific performance criteria for placement on a particular pay range," explains one employee. As far as perks are concerned: "There's a great cafeteria on (the Mountain View) campus. There are espresso machines in all the buildings." "Benefits are good," says one insider, "including on-site gyms, stock options and a stock purchase plan."

Although employees at SGI are paid relatively well, the mood at Silicon Graphics has been dampened because of poor fiscal results and subsequent layoffs. "The company has recently gone through growing pains where they had to cut almost 10 percent of its workforce," says one glum employee. Says one employee of close to 10 years: "When the company was flying high, we did lots of fun things – huge parties, free screening for the company of *Jurassic Park*, Tag Heuer watches for everyone." Those giddy days, however, have gone the way of dinosaurs: "Now that we are suffering a bit, the company is much more austere." Says another longtime employee, "the culture is changing as we emerge from the small-business mentality into a true internationally large company. Some of the fun is gone, but overall it is still a good place to work." "Think of SGI as a teenager passing through puberty into adulthood," advises one SGI insider. "That's where we are. Lots of changes, but a very worthwhile experience overall."

To order a 10- to 20-page Vault Reports Employer Profile on Silicon Graphics, Inc. call 1-888-JOB-VAULT or visit www.VaultReports.com

The full Employer Profile includes detailed information on SGI's departments, recent developments and transactions, hiring and interview process, plus what employees really think about culture, pay, work hours and more.

MBA Job Seekers: Receive free e-mailed job postings matching your interests & qualifications! Register at www.VaultReports.com

VAULT REPORTS™

305

www.vaultreports.com

Citibank/Citigroup

Commercial Bank

399 Park Avenue
New York, NY 10043
(800) 285-3000
www.citibank.com

CITIBANK◆®

LOCATIONS

New York, NY (HQ)
Other offices across the U.S. and worldwide

DEPARTMENTS

Operations &Technology
Global Consumer Business
Global Corporate Business
Advanced Development Group

THE STATS

Annual Revenues: $34.7 billion (1997)
No. of Employees: 93,700 (U.S.)
No. of Offices: 3,400 (worldwide)
Stock Symbol: CCI
Stock Exchange: NYSE
Chairman: John S. Reed

KEY COMPETITORS

- ◆ American Express
- ◆ BankAmerica
- ◆ Chase Manhattan
- ◆ First Union
- ◆ Wells Fargo

THE BUZZ
What MBAs are saying
about Citibank

- ◆ "Blue chip, merger issues"
- ◆ "Advanced thinking dinosaur"
- ◆ "Bleeding"
- ◆ "Big hitters"

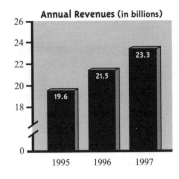

Annual Revenues (in billions)

UPPERS

- Stock purchase plan
- Company gyms at some locations
- Generous vacation time
- Employee activities program

DOWNERS

- Excessive bureaucracy
- Competitive and political atmosphere

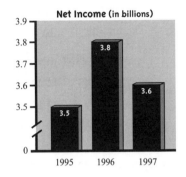

Net Income (in billions)

EMPLOYMENT CONTACT

General Inquiries

3999 Park Avenue
New York, NY 10043
(800) 285-3000

Global Consumer & Global Corporate

Sara E. Ferry
Citibank Global MA Programs
575 Lexington Avenue
New York, NY 10043
Fax: (212) 793-6432

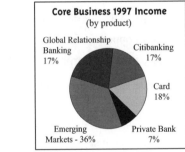
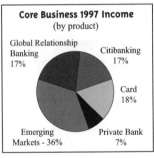

Core Business 1997 Income
(by product)

Global Relationship Banking 17%
Citibanking 17%
Card 18%
Private Bank 7%
Emerging Markets - 36%

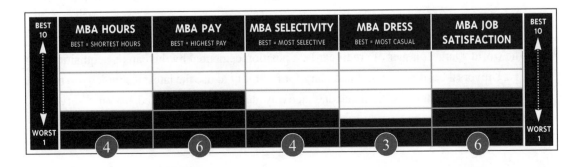

	MBA HOURS BEST = SHORTEST HOURS	MBA PAY BEST = HIGHEST PAY	MBA SELECTIVITY BEST = MOST SELECTIVE	MBA DRESS BEST = MOST CASUAL	MBA JOB SATISFACTION	
	4	6	4	3	6	

THE SCOOP

Founded in 1812 by Samuel Osgood, the first commissioner of the U.S. Treasury, the City Bank of New York began by serving cotton, sugar, metal, and coal merchants and became a pioneer in overseas expansion in the early 20th century. More recently, Citibank became the first commercial bank to make personal loans, the first to provide high-interest, specified-term CDs, and the first to introduce ATMs on a large scale.

In April 1998, Citicorp, Citibank's holding company, stunned the financial world when it announced its plans to merge with Travelers Group to create Citigroup, Inc. The new entity will offer one-stop shopping to its customers, whether they be institutional investors in need of derivatives to hedge bets on the market, or homeowners looking for a mortgage. The U.S. Federal Reserve, anticipating likely changes in federal banking law, gave its conditional approval to the merger in September, and trading of the group's stocks began on October 8, 1998. Citigroup's debut was clouded, however, by reports of huge losses overseas, diminishing the group's net income by more than half the earnings from both companies in the same 1997 quarter. Moreover, news reports in September 1998 indicated that 8000 jobs would be chopped from Citigroup's various operations. The report followed up on August's layoffs at Citicorp's corporate bond-trading department, an area in which Traveler's Salomon Smith Barney is much stronger. The chaos hasn't ceased. Conflicts over the future of Salomon Smith Barney have led to the departure of Wall Street darling Jamie Dimon and Citigroup exec Stephen Black in November 1998, triggering a downgrade of the company by several Wall Street analysts.

Given the scale of the deal, it's clear that fundamental changes are in store for Citibank and other divisions of Citicorp. Nevertheless, it's equally clear that Citibank will remain one of the foremost divisions of Citigroup. The only full-service consumer banking company with a truly global reach, Citibank has over 1200 branches in 97 countries around the world. Citibank is also the world's largest issuer of credit cards, a position cemented by the bank's acquisition of AT&T's Universal Card Services. Legendary for its ability to use the latest technology to make life easier for its customers, Citibank has actively developed web based banking services. Overall, the bank is making good progress toward the mission developed by Citigroup co-CEO

John Reed: to transform the Citibank name into an internationally recognized and trusted brand name like Coca-Cola or Xerox.

GETTING HIRED

MBAs are hired into Citibank in a variety of different groups, such as Citicorp Securities (the corporate finance side of Citibank), various internal consulting groups, and of course, global finance positions, particularly in Latin America and Asia. The normal path to employment with Citibank is an on-campus recruiting session, followed by a Super Saturday all-day affair. MBAs are often recruited into the bank's Global Management Associate Program. However, with a company as large as Citibank, there are many opportunities that can be found by directly contacting the company.

The company offers many summer internships for MBAs, who generally give the programs good reviews. One intern in a real estate group reports a very rewarding experience with group members that were very supportive in terms of explaining the fundamentals of their work. Another, who worked in risk management, reports that attitudes towards the MBAs were positive and cooperative. Says one corporate finance intern: "The corporate culture fostered teamwork, and most of my colleagues were MBAs." Says one with a Citibank strategic consulting group: "They give MBAs lots of latitude and respect your abilities. Also, know that MBAs are wined and dined all summer with numerous cocktail parties and other social events." The summer MBA program in New York is kicked off with a welcome speech by Citigroup co-CEO John Reed; every week talks are given on different areas of the bank by very senior people.

MBA Job Seekers: Receive free e-mailed job postings matching your interests & qualifications! Register at www.VaultReports.com

VAULT REPORTS™
www.vaultreports.com

309

OUR SURVEY SAYS

Employees remark that the defining feature of Citibank's corporate culture is its "international and cosmopolitan" flavor. "If you want to spend your whole life in New Jersey, this may not be the best place for you. But if you're a go-getter and you want to do business in Chile or Singapore, welcome to Citibank," says one branch manager. Another insider agrees, noting that "if you want to make it here, you have to spend some time abroad."

Surveys reveal that associates perceive wide variation between offices around the world, and even between different offices in the same city. One contact even characterizes the differences as "staggering." Nevertheless, some patterns emerge, notably regarding the importance that is placed on a competitive spirit. One contact from the corporate side describes considerable pressure to meet certain goals in equity returns: "it's part of the culture to make sure you meet those targets." Another contact with experience in an office in Africa describes a "high performance culture," where "people wanted to outshine one another. It was very key to be seen as delivering." The same contact warns: "you'll be very challenged because you're looking over your shoulder all the time." Another notes the pressure "always to excel in order to progress – or even just to keep your job." The antidote to competition? "Be nice," advises one insider. "There is so much competition and back-stabbing among staff" that if you plan on making steady advancements through the company hierarchy, "a solid personal network of friends and cronies" is "absolutely essential." Another insider notes that a disadvantage to Citibank's size is "the bureaucracy, and there's politics." When pressed to explain, this contact says: "people are territorial. They stake their claims on certain areas, and want to hold onto those areas." "They're not afraid to reorganize and cut things," this person explains, adding: "you can't freak out every time you hear of a reorganization – that's why it gets political. You want to have a job at the end of the day."

Given Citibank's global reach, it comes as no surprise that the bank gets high marks for the diversity of its people. One contact beams "diversity [at Citibank] is huge. I can't imagine working in a more diverse environment in terms of international." Indeed, contacts frequently describe their colleagues as hailing from all corners of the globe. One insider notes that "we work all over the world, and we want to look like the world." However, one individual who worked on the corporate banking side praises the bank's international diversity, but admits that regarding members of minority groups, the securities business at Citibank "isn't any more diverse than any other investment bank, which is to say, not very diverse at all."

The dress code at Citibank is "generally the corporate type – part of the whole image of a conservative banker you can trust with your money," employees say. However, like perks and corporate culture, the dress code also varies considerably throughout the corporation, and is at its most formal "whenever the slightest client interaction is involved." During the summer months, Citibank maintains a "casual Friday" policy in most of its offices.

To order a 50- to 70-page Vault Reports Employer Profile on Citibank/Citigroup call 1-888-JOB-VAULT or visit www.VaultReports.com

The full Employer Profile includes detailed information on Citibank's departments, recent developments and transactions, hiring and interview process, plus what employees really think about culture, pay, work hours and more.

MBA Job Seekers: Receive free e-mailed job postings matching your interests & qualifications! Register at www.VaultReports.com

VAULT REPORTS™

www.vaultreports.com

311

American Express

Financial Services

World Financial Center
200 Vesey St.
New York, NY 10285
(212) 640-2000
www.americanexpress.com

LOCATIONS

New York, NY (HQ)
Ft. Lauderdale, FL
Greensboro, NC
Minneapolis, MN
Phoenix, AZ
Salt Lake City, UT

SUBSIDIARIES

American Express Bank
American Express Financial Advisors
American Express Travel Related Services

THE STATS

Annual Revenues: $17.8 billion (1997)
No. of Employees: 73,620 (worldwide)
Stock Symbol: AXP (NYSE)
CEO: Harvey Golub

KEY COMPETITORS

- Citibank/Citigroup
- GE Capital
- MasterCard
- MBNA America
- Morgan Stanley Dean Witter
- Visa

THE BUZZ
What MBAs are saying
about Amex

- "Good company, but easy to get a job"
- "Bureaucratic, powerful "
- "Marketing powerhouse"
- "Second-rate financial"

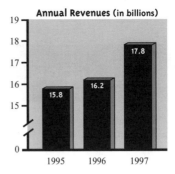

UPPERS

- ◆ Profit sharing
- ◆ Tuition reimbursement
- ◆ Annual bonuses
- ◆ Nationally recognized career enrichment center

DOWNERS

- ◆ Poor inter-department communication
- ◆ Relatively low pay for NY and financial services

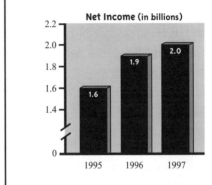

EMPLOYMENT CONTACT

Deborah Hickey
Director of Campus Recruitment
200 Vesey Street
World Financial Center
New York, NY 10285

Fax resumes and cover letters
to 212-619-9770 or submit them online at
www.americanexpress.com/corp/staffing

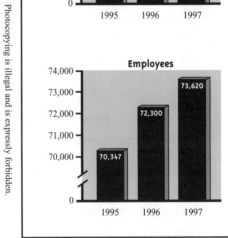

MBA Job Seekers: Receive free e-mailed job postings matching
your interests & qualifications! Register at www.VaultReports.com

VAULT
REPORTS™
313
www.vaultreports.com

THE SCOOP

Henry Wells and his two closest competitors combined delivery services in 1850 and founded American Express. Later in the century, American Express expanded into financial services by offering money orders (1882) and the world's first traveler's checks (1891). The company introduced its famous charge card, which places no credit limits on consumers and requires them to pay off the balance each month, in 1958. The charge card was unprofitable at first, but by the late 1960s American Express boasted more than 2 million cardholders and a total charge volume of $1.1 billion.

Unfortunately, too many customers have been leaving home without their Amex cards during the last ten years. A decade ago, 25 percent of all charges were made with an American Express card; that figure has now fallen to 17 percent. The company has stemmed the tide by reinvigorating Optima, a credit card that it introduced in the 1980s to compete with Visa and MasterCard and by introducing co-branded cards bearing the logos of sports teams like the New York Knicks or corporations like Delta Airlines. The charge cards are part of the company's Travel Related Services division, which also oversees the traveler's checks, a travel agency, and several travel magazines. The other major division, American Express Financial Advisors, sells life insurance, investment funds, and financial advice. American Express spun off its Lehman Brothers investment banking unit in 1994.

The recent economic turmoil in Asia has taken its toll on American Express' banking division, which has extensive holdings in Hong Kong and Indonesia. In the second quarter of 1998, the company reported a $83 million quarterly loss while nonpeforming loans tripled from a year ago to $149 million. As a result, the company enacted a $138 million provision to boost its bank reserves in an attempt to offset any future losses caused by the Asian economic crisis. The action dampened what was a healthy first quarter, when American Express' core charge card and money management business earned record profits.

GETTING HIRED

MBAs are sought primarily for marketing manager positions and strategic planning group consultants, but can also be a source for other positions, including, risk management, human resources, and positions as financial advisors (sort of like financial planners at commercial banks). Insiders say that "Golub is looking to grow Financial Advisors like crazy." The career path for MBAs "is pretty well defined," insiders tell us. After manager comes director, and then vice president. While American Express has moved to eliminate distinctions between these roles, collapsing several managerial levels into one, there are reportedly residual pay grades and levels of responsibility (and offices) within each rank. One MBA criticizes American Express for its hiring methods. "What happens is that you get a general offer at the company, but you don't have that much control over your first initial assignment. It's a matter of what is available at the time." (Summer MBA interns, however, are hired into a specific business unit and function.) While most MBAs are slotted in at the same managerial level, regardless of previous experience, more experienced managers can enter the firm at the director level.

For MBAs applying for a managerial slots, American Express uses a behavioral interviewing method, sometimes (though apparently rarely) interspersed with specific industry questions and marketing "cases." These cases are normally questions that relate to some aspect of American Express' recent business. "The interview process is not too strenuous," says one recent hire. "It goes two rounds, and basically the company wants to make sure that you will be a good fit with the company, there are a lot of behavioral questions." American Express eagerly recruits its summer MBA interns; summer employees report that "MBA interns are treated like princes." According to one intern in the company's consulting division, "they went out of their way to make you happy. MBAs were a priority hire." About 60 percent of the MBA summer hires are invited to return to full-time positions, insiders tell us.

MBA Job Seekers: Receive free e-mailed job postings matching your interests & qualifications! Register at www.VaultReports.com

VAULT REPORTS™
www.vaultreports.com

315

OUR SURVEY SAYS

In some senses, American Express is much like any other gigantic corporation. Employees admit that "the cartoon Dilbert rings true here." One insider's main gripe is that "American Express is such a huge company that there are a lot of office politics and no real sense of belonging or individualism. It's really an issue of being a small fish in a very big pond. But those are issues you would have with any large company." Promotion opportunities are reportedly mixed: Though half of all openings are filled internally, "I have seen many people come from outside the company to take on major responsibilities," says one insider. And insiders say bureaucracy is rampant at American Express. We are told that "there are many levels of approval to get anything done." One employee gives Amex credit for trying to change, saying that "the company is extremely concerned with self-improvement, and has asked me several times how the employment process could be improved." Another Amexer credits his firm as "a great company that is trying to evolve from a sales institution to a bona fide financial planning firm," but says "the problem is that there are too many overpaid management levels." One marketing manager criticizes American Express' tendency to hire few college graduates for its marketing positions. "Basically," says the manager, "you had MBAs doing work that college grads could easily do."

American Express tries to ensure that its employees are fairly compensated. Insiders tell Vault Reports that "pay is competitive with the industry and is kept that way through constant survey. I have never had a complaint." However, in units such as the Strategic Planning Group and for marketing manager positions, "American Express is not as competitive as investment banks and consulting firms as far as attracting top talent, because we simply don't pay as much. We might offer a recent MBA $75,000, whereas they might get an offer for $130,000 from Bain or something." Says a summer MBA intern who was unsure about whether to return to Amex: "If yes, because it's a company that really tries to be fair to employees. If no, it's because for New York, the pay is low." Contacts tell Vault Reports that the company offers "an excellent benefit package." "After one year you can contribute to the 401(k) plan – the company matches up to 3 percent of your contributions and throws in a 1 percent 'gift,'" insiders tell Vault Reports. There is also "a profit sharing plan," which is based on overall company performance and can be up to 7 percent of base pay.

Amex hours are on the "light side" for a financial services company, according to insiders, and the company also offers flexible scheduling, compacted hours, telecommuting and job sharing options. One MBA employee says: "Sometimes I would bring my laptop and work from home on weekends, but it was rare that I actually had to be in the office." If you work at Amex's World Financial Center headquarters, you can leave your Birkenstocks at home. "New York is, by and large, not casual. Other offices vary by times of year and days of week," and "business casual is often the norm," employees tell us. The company appears to be doing fine when it comes to diversity issues. Employees say that "minority recruiting is very proactive, and that American Express has "a large number of women and minorities in upper management positions. The most likely candidate for our next CEO is an African-American [COO Kenneth Chenault]." "I would say that over 50 percent of marketing managers are female," says one former employee. About two-thirds of all Amex employees in the U.S. are women. Two women and two African-American men, including Vernon Jordan (yes, that Vernon Jordan) sit on the company's board of directors.

To order a 50- to 70-page Vault Reports Employer Profile on American Express call 1-888-JOB-VAULT or visit www.VaultReports.com

The full Employer Profile includes detailed information on Amex's departments, recent developments and transactions, hiring and interview process, plus what employees really think about culture, pay, work hours and more.

MBA Job Seekers: Receive free e-mailed job postings matching your interests & qualifications! Register at www.VaultReports.com

VAULT REPORTS™   317

www.vaultreports.com

Bankers Trust

Investment Banking

130 Liberty St.
12th Floor
New York, NY 10006
(212) 250-2500
www.bankerstrust.com

Bankers Trust

LOCATIONS

New York, NY (HQ)
14 other major U.S. offices; Additional offices in more than 50 countries worldwide

DEPARTMENTS

Capital Partners
Corporate Finance
Global Risk Management
Investment Management
Latin America Merchant Bank
Real Estate Investment Bank
Risk Management Service
Technology
Trading & Sales

THE STATS

Annual Revenues: $12.2 billion (1997)
No. of Employees: 18,286 (worldwide)
No. of Offices: 146 (worldwide), 41 (U.S)
Stock Symbol: BT (NYSE)
CEO: Frank N. Newman

KEY COMPETITORS

- BankAmerica
- Citigroup
- JP Morgan
- Merrill Lynch
- Morgan Stanley Dean Witter

THE BUZZ
What MBAs are saying about Bankers Trust

- "Poor management controls"
- "Always changing directions"
- "Risk-taker, aggressive"
- "Trader-like atmosphere"

318
VAULT REPORTS™
www.vaultreports.com
Vault Reports Guide to the Top 50 MBA Employers

UPPERS

- Good support staff
- Entrepreneurial atmosphere

DOWNERS

- Seemingly constant reorganization
- Recent heavy losses

EMPLOYMENT CONTACT

Human Resources
Bankers Trust
130 Liberty St.
12th Floor
New York, NY 10006

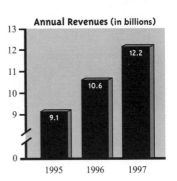

Annual Revenues (in billions)

- 1995: 9.1
- 1996: 10.6
- 1997: 12.2

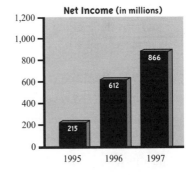

Net Income (in millions)

- 1995: 215
- 1996: 612
- 1997: 866

Employees

- 1995: 14,069
- 1996: 15,228
- 1997: 18,286

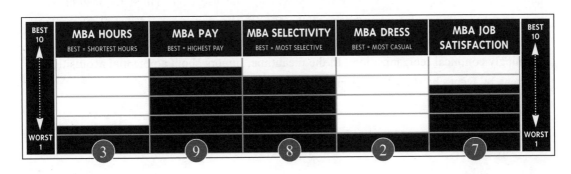

	MBA HOURS BEST = SHORTEST HOURS	MBA PAY BEST = HIGHEST PAY	MBA SELECTIVITY BEST = MOST SELECTIVE	MBA DRESS BEST = MOST CASUAL	MBA JOB SATISFACTION	
BEST 10 ... WORST 1	3	9	8	2	7	BEST 10 ... WORST 1

MBA Job Seekers: Receive free e-mailed job postings matching
your interests & qualifications! Register at www.VaultReports.com

VAULT REPORTS™

319

www.vaultreports.com

THE SCOOP

Founded in 1903, Bankers Trust is an odd animal: half commercial bank, half investment bank. The firm has five major business units: the Global Investment Bank, which manages financing, derivative and advisory capabilities; Global Emerging Markets, which serves East Asia and Latin America; Global Assets, which handles trusts, securities processing, cash management and private banking businesses; Global Investment Management, which manages funds; and Global Markets Proprietary, which oversees proprietary trading and positioning.

In 1989, Bankers Trust decided to expand its investment banking services and formed BT Securities. However, old-timers like Goldman Sachs and Morgan Stanley had already established strong relationships with major corporations, leaving the riskier leveraged buyouts as BT territory. Bankers Trust's propensity for complex risk management deals yielded large profits during the early 1990s, but when interest rates began to rise once again, several of these so-called "derivatives" deals turned bad. In recent years, after settling lawsuits with two of its major clients, Procter & Gamble and Gibson Greetings, Bankers Trust had gradually built back its reputation, focusing on I-banking services for smaller companies in fields such as high tech, telecom and healthcare, and building on its respectable junk bond underwriting practice. In 1996, the firm acquired the M&A boutique firm Wolfensohn (now called BT Wolfensohn). In 1997, BT acquired Alex. Brown – the country's oldest investment bank. Although analysts have called the Wolfensohsn merger something of a bust so far, they agree that the Alex. Brown merger should be a good fit.

However, the firm was pummeled by exposure in emerging markets in 1998. BT reported a $488 million third quarter loss and said it would pull back from emerging markets, where it had aggressively expanded. CEO Frank Newman, who had been hailed for leading BT's turnaround, but began facing criticism as the firm declined, announced that Bankers Trust would reshape its I-banking business. However, industry observers are skeptical about BT's seemingly continual reorganization. In the meantime, rumors about a potential acquisition of the bank by Deutsche Bank have cropped up.

GETTING HIRED

Applicants should direct their applications to the specific division in which they are interested. The firm's employment web page, located at www.bankerstrust.com, has specific addresses and fax numbers for each division, including separate addresses for offices in Los Angeles and London. MBAs are hired as associates and attend the firm's Financial Services Training Program in New York. BT offers summer internships for MBAs as well; the summer associates are asked to perform the work of a first-year associate. MBAs interested in both financial services and consulting may also apply to the Bankers Trust Management Consulting Group (MCG), a full-service consulting organization within BT. BT interviews are a bit offbeat – reportedly, interviewees have been asked to tell jokes during their first round interviews. Make it good!

OUR SURVEY SAYS

Bankers Trust fosters an "entrepreneurial," "dynamic" environment that requires "intense initiative" from employees." Employees appreciate the firm's training program and also claim that Bankers Trust is "more cosmopolitan" and "diverse" than other New York banks: "Bankers Trust does not look for a certain personality type." Part of the reason is BT's relative youth. One insider says: "Some companies are very established, have their formula, and will walk through it. That isn't Bankers Trust." Working at Bankers Trust, though, can be a trying experience. Employees report that "100-hour workweeks are not uncommon." Co-workers range "from very cool to very painful," and tempers can flare out of control. "On occasion the temperature gets too hot and people will yell at you, but they later come back and apologize or take you out for a drink," one insider reports. "But people do occasionally yell – and it isn't pretty."

MBA Job Seekers: Receive free e-mailed job postings matching
your interests & qualifications! Register at www.VaultReports.com

VAULT REPORTS™

321

www.vaultreports.com

On the bright side, the firm's "lean and flat organizational structure" encourages "innovative, aggressive self-starters" and also provides junior-level employees with "abundant" opportunities for contact with upper management. Bankers Trust sports the kind of support staff "that a top-notch firm deserves." Even beginning analysts share secretaries who take their calls. The company also offers "generous vacation time and excellent training," and sponsors "a Christmas party, picnic, beach party, beach volleyball tournament and river rafting." One former employee says "Bankers Trust always treated me fairly and honestly. I genuinely liked the tedium there, even if I realized that I would be much happier doing something else."

To order a 50- to 70-page Vault Reports Employer Profile on Bankers Trust call 1-888-JOB-VAULT or visit www.VaultReports.com

The full Employer Profile includes detailed information on Bankers Trust's departments, recent developments and transactions, hiring and interview process, plus what employees really think about culture, pay, work hours and more.

"On occasion the temperature gets too hot and people will yell at you, but they later come back and apologize or take you out for a drink."

– *BT insider*

Colgate-Palmolive

Consumer Products

300 Park Avenue
New York, NY 10022
(212) 310-2000
www.colgate.com

LOCATIONS

New York, NY (HQ)
Piscataway, NJ; 57 other facilities across the U.S. and more than 250 abroad

DEPARTMENTS

Accounting
Administrative
Computer Finance
Human Resources
Marketing; Research

THE STATS

Annual Revenues: $9.1 billion (1997)
No. of Employees: 37,800
No. of Offices: 280 (worldwide), 60 (U.S)
Stock Symbol: CL (NYSE)
CEO: Reuben Mark

KEY COMPETITORS

- Amway
- Clorox
- Dial
- Gillette
- Lever Brothers
- Procter & Gamble

THE BUZZ
What MBAs are saying
about Colgate

- "International only"
- "9 to 5"
- "Good marketing training "
- "Ho-hum"

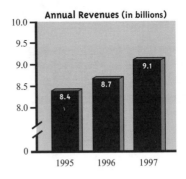

UPPERS

- Profit sharing
- Overseas travel opportunities
- Well-developed training programs for MBAs

DOWNERS

- Recent corporate downsizing
- Extensive overseas work and travel not optional

EMPLOYMENT CONTACT

Human Resources
Colgate-Palmolive
300 Park Avenue
New York, NY 10022

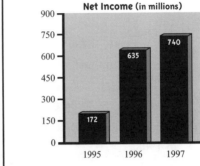

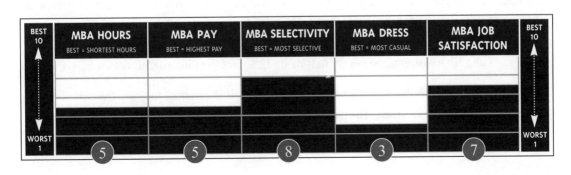

THE SCOOP

In 1806, William Colgate founded the company that bears his name as a maker of starch, soap, and candles. Later in the century, Colgate began to manufacture perfume. It was not until 1877, however, that the company introduced Colgate Dental Cream, the tooth cleansing product for which it is best known today. The company's breakthrough innovation came in 1896, when Colgate presented consumers with the first ever collapsible tube package for its dental cream. Despite its trend-setting dental care delivery system, Colgate might never have risen to its multinational stature, had hygiene not captured the popular imagination at the turn-of-the-century. Riding the wave of sales brought by this newfound infatuation with cleanliness, by 1906 Colgate boasted over 2000 different products – including 160 kinds of toilet soap, 625 varieties of perfume, and a complete line of laundry soap. Colgate went public in 1908.

After a 1928 merger with Kansas City-based Palmolive-Peet, Colgate began an aggressive international expansion campaign. The company first expanded into Europe in the 1930s with the purchase of several French and German soap makers. It expanded into Asia during the 1950s, beating most American companies by a decade. By 1961, foreign sales already accounted for over half of Colgate-Palmolive's revenue. Today the company sells its products in well over 200 countries.

Colgate-Palmolive currently manufactures thousands of brand-name products – including its trademark toothpaste (the world's top-seller), Palmolive liquid soap, and Fab laundry detergent – which it sells in 212 countries. The company is organized along five product lines: Oral Care, Personal Care, Household Surface Care, Fabric Care, and Pet Nutrition. Throughout the 1990s, the company has sought to boost its revenues by purchasing top performers like Mennen, the maker of the country's leading deodorant, as well as several international manufacturers of consumer goods. This expansion was accompanied by domestic downsizing; Colgate-Palmolive restructured nearly half of its U.S. factories in order to cut costs.

To understand Colgate-Palmolive's business operations, it is essential to grasp the extent of the company's international sales. To start with, Colgate sells more than 40 percent of the world's toothpaste – consumers purchase 3 billion tubes of toothpaste with the Colgate name each year.

Non-U.S. sales now account for 70 percent of Colgate's income. Colgate now hopes to diversify sales by refocusing on its sagging domestic market. In early 1998, Colgate introduced Colgate Total, the first toothpaste allowed by the Food and Drug Administration to be advertised as a gum disease fighter. The introduction of Colgate Total has been a total success: the toothpaste grabbed 10.6 percent of total toothpaste sales in the United States by May 1998.

GETTING HIRED

If you have a MBA in Marketing and Management and some professional experience, Colgate's Global Marketing Development Program (GMDP) will allow you to jump headfirst into the company's highly touted brand marketing team. Because the majority of Colgate's sales come from outside the U.S., the program consists of spending 15-18 months rotations in product management and global business development, plus a stint in an international division. GMDP participants also develop their skills in market research, technology advertising, and finance. Upon completion of the program, participants are assigned to a product management team in one of its international operating units where they manage a portion of the company's successful brands.

OUR SURVEY SAYS

Colgate is an excellent opportunity for marketing MBAs who want international business experience. As one Bombay-based employee puts it: "The business school graduates rate Colgate-Palmolive as one of the 'coveted employers.'" The company has very strong, well-structured summer internship programs for MBAs. "There are scheduled breakfasts with middle and upper management to ensure exposure," says one former intern. "The experience

MBA Job Seekers: Receive free e-mailed job postings matching your interests & qualifications! Register at www.VaultReports.com

VAULT REPORTS™
www.vaultreports.com

327

was better than my initial expectations… I was given three different projects that allowed me to dig deeper into specific functional areas."

Those who work at the corporate headquarters describe the atmosphere there as "casual" and "relaxed." Colgate is careful "not to grind employees into the ground," often keeping long hours in check with "half days on Fridays in the summer." "It's a calm place to work when compared to many other companies that I've worked for," reports one employee at company headquarters. Another employee describes the culture as "fast and high pressure, but very rewarding,"

Insiders also say that Colgate is pushing for better representation of women and minorities at higher levels: "Several years ago our CEO, Reuben Mark, made giving opportunities to women and minorities a priority." "I have been promoted twice in five years and I am now a senior manager," according to one woman insider. "They could use a few more women VPs, but I can't feel the glass ceiling." "As for the minority/women situation here, it is very well distributed," says one female marketer. "One good thing that is very good about Colgate as a whole is that they really do a great job with diversity and the success of women in the workforce." Says another employee: "We do not have an on-site daycare facility, as Johnson & Johnson does, but still aim to be fairly progressive, just not cutting edge."

For MBA interns and other management-track employees, senior management has an "open door policy." Employees in marketing and related fields appreciate the opportunity to participate in international business deals, and others enjoy the "teamwork" and "spirited camaraderie" of the company's research facility. As a global company, many policies and norms vary at Colgate-Palmolive, in the sweltering heat of India for instance, dress is formal, but "no jackets unless you want to and can stand it." In New York, dress code is "business – no slouching at the corporate office." On the whole, however, employees say that "as far as corporate culture, dress codes, and special perks, Colgate seems to consciously aim for the middle ground. However, the international assignments can also be a burden. According to one former MBA intern, "you must be willing to work overseas for five to eight years minimum."

To order a 10- to 20-page Vault Reports Employer Profile on Colgate-Palmolive call 1-888-JOB-VAULT or visit www.VaultReports.com

The full Employer Profile includes detailed information on Colgate's departments, recent developments and transactions, hiring and interview process, plus what employees really think about culture, pay, work hours and more.

Levi Strauss

Consumer Products

P.O. Box 7215
San Francisco, CA 94120-6914
(415) 544-6000
www.levi.com

LOCATIONS

San Francisco, CA (HQ)
Atlanta, GA
Dallas, TX
New York, NY
Sales offices across the U.S. and worldwide

DEPARTMENTS

Finance
Information Services
Marketing
Merchandising
Operations
Human Resources
Administrative Support
Legal
Sales
Design
Customer Relations

THE STATS

Annual Revenues: $6.9 billion (1997)
No. of Employees: 37,000
Stock Symbol: Private company
CEO: Robert D. Haas

KEY COMPETITORS

- Calvin Klein
- The Gap
- Guess?
- Tommy Hilfiger
- VF
- The Limited

THE BUZZ

What MBAs are saying
about Levi's

- "Free-spirited"
- "Strong ethics"
- "Unfashionable"
- "More interesting than most
  consumer goods"

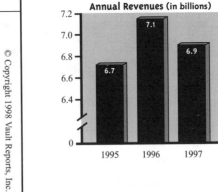

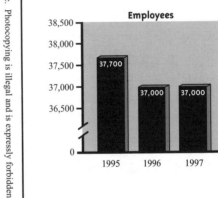

UPPERS

* Wear your (Levi's) jeans to work
* Top-notch pay with bonuses
* Extensive healthcare plan
* Diversity-friendly environment
* Opportunities for advancement
* Relaxed corporate culture
* Stock options

DOWNERS

* Politically correct
* Recent corporate downsizing

EMPLOYMENT CONTACT

ATTN: NETCWEB
Levi Strauss & Co.
1155 Battery Street
P.O. Box 7215
San Francisco, CA 94120-6914

(415) 501-7828 (job hotline)
job@levi.com

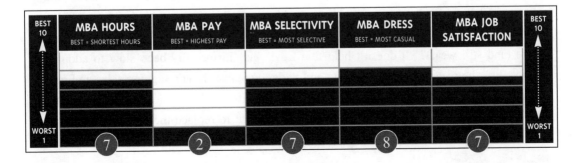

MBA Job Seekers: Receive free e-mailed job postings matching
your interests & qualifications! Register at www.VaultReports.com

VAULT REPORTS™

www.vaultreports.com

331

THE SCOOP

Who would have thought that good old American blue jeans would have its start in Buttenheim, Bavaria? At least, that's where Levi Strauss got his start, way back in 1829. After immigrating to America, Strauss paired up with Jacob Davis, a Reno Nevada tailor, in 1872, and denim jeans were born. The pair's patented process of riveting pants first produced "waist overalls" in 1873. The rivet reinforced the jeans so that miners could more easily stuff them with rocks, tools, or whatever heavy material they chose to carry (gold?). From cattle ranchers to gold-diggers, Westerners were soon clamoring for the one-pocketed denim wonders, inducing Strauss to open several new factories, and assign lot numbers like 501 to the products being manufactured. Over a century later, Levi Strauss & Co. is the leading seller of name-brand apparel in the US, and the number two seller of jeans, just behind the VF Corporation's Wrangler and Lee jeans.

Today, in addition to its famous jeans, the company also manufactures the top-selling Dockers line, as well as Slates, a new line of dress pants. Though Levi went public in 1971, the Haas family returned the company to private status in 1985 due to slumping sales (which, incidentally, made the stock a bargain for a buyout). Still headquartered in San Francisco, Levi-Strauss & Co. remains a private company, run by the now super-rich Haas Company. Current CEO Robert Haas is the founder's great-great-grandnephew.

Known as a loyal, charitable and labor-friendly company, Levis has been hard-pressed to maintain that reputation. The company has struggled to remake its image in the face of fierce competition from younger hipper brands like Tommy Hilfiger, Calvin Klein and the Gap. Levi's overall share of men's and women's jeans fell to 16.9 percent in 1997 from 18.7 percent in 1996. Here is the problem, analysts say: Levi's core baby boomer customer base is getting older, which presents the company with the problem of selling jeans to 16- to 24-year-olds, the fastest growing market in the denim industry. After all, who wants to buy jeans their parents wore (and still wear)? It doesn't help that Levi's has historically been slow to adopt new trends, like the recent craze for bootleg and wide-leg jeans. Levi's sagging sales and market share have forced to company to lay off 34 percent of its North American workforce and shut down one-third of its American plants. Levi's attempt to replace the traditional piecework system, in which one employee repeatedly performs one specialized task, with an integrated teamwork concept has led to fighting and decreased morale.

But company officials aren't about to dump the denim and die. In 1998, Levis launched a massive marketing campaign touting its new, stiff dark indigo denim jeans, which designers believe will be the newest fashion trend. The company also has hired a new advertising agency which created the "(Tommy, Ralph, Calvin) Wore Them" ads in an effort to remind buyers who created the original jeans. Levis also sponsored the successful Lilith Fair summer tour, running ads with stars Sarah McLachlan and Liz Phair wearing the jeans in question.

GETTING HIRED

"The hiring process is fairly basic at Levi's," insiders say. One reports, "The interview process frequently starts with an initial screening interview by a Human Resources person. If the HR person thinks there may be a fit, they pass the candidate on to an interview panel, which usually consists of the hiring manager and several other folks in the business unit (possibly managers or potential co-workers). While the numbers vary, there may be as many as five to six people on the panel." One notes of the initial panel interview: "This could be the final interview or there could be another panel interview, depending on the department and position."

Progressive Levi recruits at both the National Black MBA Association Conference and a recruiting fair hosted by the National Society of Hispanic MBAs. Candidates can submit resumes online at www.levistrauss.com, and can check out job openings at the site. Levi's utilizes a traditional brand management structure with entry as junior brand managers and promotion to the associate brand manager level.

MBA Job Seekers: Receive free e-mailed job postings matching
your interests & qualifications! Register at www.VaultReports.com

VAULT
REPORTS™
www.vaultreports.com

333

OUR SURVEY SAYS

Working at Levi's is as comfy as your favorite pair of worn-in jeans, most employees agree. Insiders deliver nearly unanimous praise for the jeans maker, and say it lives up to the much-trumpeted "corporation with a heart" reputation, in spite of the firm's recent downsizing. One longtime Levi employee says: "I think that you will find that Levi Strauss & Co is a great company because of what it stands for as well as its products. I enjoy the corporate culture and its values. Personally speaking, it's a great place to work." Another insider notes, "There are good reasons for the reputation that this company has regarding its humane values and culture. Although business priorities and focus on core objectives sometimes limit us in doing what we would like to do, creativity is highly valued and people at all levels are listening for good ideas." However, one insider says, "the 'but' is that we are downsizing because competition has forced us to go after the less expensive labor from Central America, the Caribbean, and South America. In the apparel arena, this is a common trend. High overhead has forced the company to cut corporate jobs too." Despite these layoffs, "there is a lot of opportunity to grow within the company."

Insiders deliver high praise for perks and pay at the blue jeans giant. "My experience with compensation has been very satisfying. A yearly raise, profit sharing, long term incentive plans, 50 percent match on 401(k), and the Global Sharing Plan, which pays all employees a bonus equal to their 1996 salary in 2001 if the company meets its financial goals. Levi's is the only company to ever offer this kind of incentive," one contact notes. Another employee reports: "Pay is 3 percent above competitors' wages for the same job, benefits are extremely good, hours are not very bad (40-50 hours/week), the work environment is professional but not hard-core (you can wear jeans to work, for obvious reasons), and they are very minority friendly." In fact, Levi's diversity initiative has won national acclaim. One employee in the San Francisco headquarters reports: "Levi Strauss has numerous organizations which represent minorities in the company." Employees report plentiful opportunities for women as well. One insider says, "Women and minorities are highly valued at all levels. In my division, the head of HR, Finance and President of our exciting new Slates brand are all women." In addition to sample sales, an employee cafeteria, and company events, employees get to wear jeans and Dockers to work. An ego boost never hurts, and Levi Strauss employees say that working for the "leading symbol of American fashion" makes them "the hit of every party."

To order a 10- to 20-page Vault Reports Employer Profile on Levi Strauss call 1-888-JOB-VAULT or visit www.VaultReports.com

The full Employer Profile includes detailed information on Levis' departments, recent developments and transactions, hiring and interview process, plus what employees really think about culture, pay, work hours and more.

MBA Job Seekers: Receive free e-mailed job postings matching your interests & qualifications! Register at www.VaultReports.com

VAULT REPORTS™

335

www.vaultreports.com

NationsBanc Montgomery Securities LLC

Investment Banking

600 Montgomery Street
San Francisco, CA 94111
(415) 627-2000
www.nationsbancmontgomery.com

LOCATIONS

San Francisco, CA (HQ)
Boston, MA
Charlotte, NC
Dallas, TX
Los Angeles, CA
New York, NY
Seattle, WA
London

DEPARTMENTS

Corporate Finance
Correspondent Clearing Services
Equity Derivatives
Prime Brokerage Services
Private Client Department
Research
Sales & Trading

THE STATS

Annual Revenues: $705 million (1996)
No. of Employees: 2,200
(Montgomery division – worldwide)
No. of Offices: 8 (U.S)

NationsBanc Montgomery Securities

NationsBanc Montgomery Securities LLC

Subsidiary of BankAmerica
CEO of Montgomery Division:
Lewis W. Coleman

KEY COMPETITORS

- BT Alex. Brown
- BancBoston Robertson Stephens
- Donaldson, Lufkin & Jenrette
- Hambrecht & Quist
- SG Cowen

THE BUZZ

What MBAs are saying
about NMS

- "Potential to grow brand equity"
- "Aggressive but will disintegrate"
- "Second tier, but good at it"
- "Trying to get to the top"

UPPERS

- Company gym
- Company ski trips
- Generous paid vacation policy
- Lots of parties
- Top pay

DOWNERS

- Lack of support staff
- Long workdays

EMPLOYMENT CONTACT

Sheryl Gee
NationsBanc Montgomery Securities LLP
600 Montgomery Street
San Francisco, CA 94111
(415) 241-3072
jobopps@montgomery.com

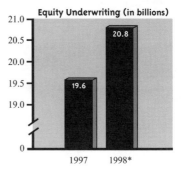

Equity Underwriting (in billions)

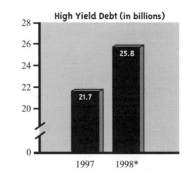

High Yield Debt (in billions)

Mergers & Acquisitions (in billions)

* 1998 figures as of 9/98

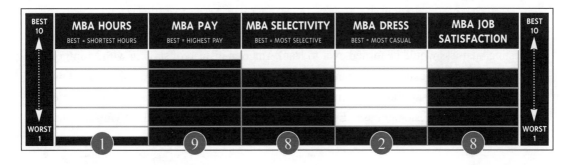

	MBA HOURS BEST = SHORTEST HOURS	MBA PAY BEST = HIGHEST PAY	MBA SELECTIVITY BEST = MOST SELECTIVE	MBA DRESS BEST = MOST CASUAL	MBA JOB SATISFACTION	
	1	9	8	2	8	

MBA Job Seekers: Receive free e-mailed job postings matching
your interests & qualifications! Register at www.VaultReports.com

VAULT REPORTS™   337
www.vaultreports.com

THE SCOOP

Historically, the San Francisco-based investment banking firm of Montgomery Securities has enjoyed success that rivals its New York competitors'. Montgomery Securities' strategy has been to focus on companies in nine industries: financial services, consumer (products, retail and hospitality), media and communications, business services, energy, industrial growth, real estate, and health care. In addition, the company relies upon its ability to integrate its large research department with its trading department, one of the largest outside New York City. Montgomery Security's Private Client Department utilizes the resources of the firm to provide investment services to wealthy individuals and families.

In 1997, the firm was acquired by much larger NationsBank Corporation, the fourth-largest bank in the United States. NationsBank paid a pretty penny for its new subsidiary – the pact cost NationsBank an estimated $1.2 billion in cash and stock. While Montgomery was said to have been searching for a partner to take a minority stake, the overwhelming embrace of NationsBank may have taken the firm by surprise.

More changes are in the works. In early 1998, NationsBank announced a merger with BankAmerica in a deal that created the second-largest commercial bank in the U.S. (trailing only Citibank in size). In September 1998, Montgomery Chairman/CEO Thomas Weisel resigned from his post after close to a year of power struggles with NationsBank. The bank had been extremely aggressive in its efforts to tame the "highly entrepreneurial" securities firm. His exit was not a complete surprise – firm insiders report that Weisel had voiced objections to a number of decisions made by NationsBank concerning its new securities division. For example, though it seemed understood that the Montgomery Securities would control the firms' combined (extremely lucrative) high yield business, NationsBank eventually took control of it – reportedly in preparation for the bank's merger with BankAmerica Corp. The situation was further aggravated when NationsBank announced that the private equity investing business would be turned over to BankAmerica instead of staying with Montgomery. Industry observers expect that bankers loyal to Weisel may follow his lead; however NationsBank execs say most will find it hard to leave a bank with such a wide variety of products and broad customer base. Lewis Coleman, the firm's COO, will fill Weisel's position.

Industry observers say Weisel's departure is probably just the first of many such defections from similar firms acquired by commercial banks in 1997.

GETTING HIRED

NMS conducts on-campus recruiting at select universities. Applicants from schools not visited by Montgomery can send an e-mail to jobopps@montgomery.com for graduate hiring information. Consult the company's Web page www.nationsbancmontgomery.com – for a list of contact names and addresses.

The firm hires MBAs into I-banking as generalists who work across product and industry groups before specializing in either one of the firm's nine industry groups (technology, health care, etc.) or one of its product groups (private equity, etc.). NMS also hires MBAs as as associates into its sales and trading, research, and private client departments. MBAs are hired into all of NMS' offices except Seattle: Boston, Charlotte, Dallas, Los Angeles, London, New York and San Francisco. In addition, business school students can join the firm as a summer associate in San Francisco, but only in I-banking.

OUR SURVEY SAYS

Nationsbanc Montgomery is an "aggressive company" that offers "constant challenges" in a "high-pressure" environment." Employees travel "frequently" and often work "consecutive long days." Those days start early. In the San Francisco office, "traders have to come in around 5 a.m. to be there before the market opens on the East Coast. The rest of us have more reasonable hours." These hours often wear on NMS employees. One employee "was so miserable after working five consecutive days of 15+ hours a day that I almost walked in front

MBA Job Seekers: Receive free e-mailed job postings matching your interests & qualifications! Register at www.VaultReports.com

VAULT REPORTS™

www.vaultreports.com

339

of a car so I wouldn't have to go to work." Another insider says "I lost a lot of friends from working so much." Still, it all comes with the territory, say NMSers. "As an analyst, you have to be prepared to dedicate two years out of your life to the job. There were plenty of times when I had weekend plans that I had to cancel," says a philosophical former employee.

All this toil is not for naught, however. We hear that NMS is "a first class company," where employees " have the most up-to-date computers" and "love working in the Pyramid, the most famous building in San Francisco." And the "golden salaries" provide "superb" compensation for the "rigorous" schedule, and middle management is "eager" to "share their experience" with recently hired employees. In general "the pay is 10-20 percent above average."

Employees report that "quite honestly, the place is very male dominated, like the entire industry," and that "the culture is pretty aggressive – there are many former athletes working here." However, employees "don't see much of a difference in the way men and women are treated. If you work hard and do a good job, you will be rewarded." One associate offers some straightforward advice to prospective employees: "An investment bank is very hierarchical. It's kind of like the army. In order to succeed, you must respect the hierarchy. This sucks as an analyst, because you're at the bottom of the pile. Being responsive to one's superiors, though, definitely gets you noticed." Ambitious employees are pleased that "Montgomery likes to promote from within." After the merger with NationsBank, those possibilities for promotion should multiply, insiders predict: "We have access to a lot more financial products and capital, and can advise our clients on many more ways to raise capital."

To order a 10- to 20-page Vault Reports Employer Profile on NationsBanc Montgomery Securites call 1-888-JOB-VAULT or visit www.VaultReports.com

The full Employer Profile includes detailed information on NMS's departments, recent developments and transactions, hiring and interview process, plus what employees really think about culture, pay, work hours and more.

"I was so miserable after working five consecutive days of 15+ hours a day that I almost walked in front of a car so I wouldn't have to go to work."

– *NMS insider*

MBA Job Seekers: Receive free e-mailed job postings matching your interests & qualifications! Register at www.VaultReports.com

VAULT REPORTS™

341

www.vaultreports.com

Nestlé

Consumer Products

800 North Brand Blvd.
Glendale, CA 91203
(818) 549-6000
Fax: (818) 549-6952
www.Nestlé.com

LOCATIONS

Vevey, Switzerland (World HQ)
Glendale, CA (U.S. HQ)

DIVISIONS

Beverage Division
Chocolate & Confections Division
Culinary Division
Food Services Division
Frozen Food Division
Ice Cream Division
Nutrition Division
PetCare Devision
Sales Division

THE STATS

Annual Revenues: $47.9 billion (1997)
No. of Employees: 225,808
**Locations (offices, manufacturing
facilities, etc.):** 507 (worldwide), 70 (U.S.)
Stock Symbol: NSRGY (OTC)
CEO: Peter Brabeck-Letmathe

KEY COMPETITORS

- Campbell Soup
- ConAgra
- General Mills
- Hershey
- Kraft
- Mars
- Procter & Gamble
- Ralston Purina
- RJR Nabisco
- Quaker
- Unilever

THE BUZZ

What MBAs are saying
about Nestle

- "Finger in every pie"
- "Solid, successful, European"
- "Great brands"
- "Sales-oriented, boring"

UPPERS

- Tuition reimbursement
- Ample advancement opportunities
- Travel opportunities

DOWNERS

- Excessive bureaucracy
- Frequent relocation

EMPLOYMENT CONTACT

ATTN: Strategic Staffing Services
Nestlé USA
800 North Brand Blvd.
Glendale, CA 91203
(818) 549-6000

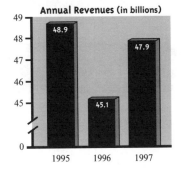

Annual Revenues (in billions)

1995: 48.9
1996: 45.1
1997: 47.9

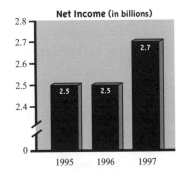

Net Income (in billions)

1995: 2.5
1996: 2.5
1997: 2.7

Employees (in thousands)

1995: 220
1996: 221
1997: 226

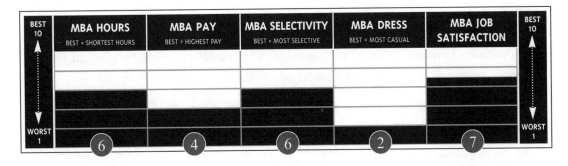

	MBA HOURS BEST = SHORTEST HOURS	MBA PAY BEST = HIGHEST PAY	MBA SELECTIVITY BEST = MOST SELECTIVE	MBA DRESS BEST = MOST CASUAL	MBA JOB SATISFACTION	
BEST 10 ↑ WORST 1	6	4	6	2	7	BEST 10 ↑ WORST 1

MBA Job Seekers: Receive free e-mailed job postings matching
your interests & qualifications! Register at www.VaultReports.com

VAULT REPORTS™

343

www.vaultreports.com

THE SCOOP

Nestlé, the world's leading food company, is so large that it doesn't know exactly how many products it makes. Although the Nestlé name goes on 8500 food, beverage, and pharmaceutical brands, different packaging sizes raise the company's estimated product total to 22,000. Though it may be best known in America for its chocolate Nestlé Crunch bars and Nestlé Quik powder flavoring, the company makes products in nine categories: baby foods and cereals, milk and dairy products, breakfast cereals, desserts, snacks and ice creams, chocolate and an other confectioneries, prepared foods, beverages, and pet care. Nestlé is the leader in mineral water (Perrier) and coffee (Nescafé) sales as well. From its Vevey, Switzerland headquarters, Nestlé feeds the world.

The Nestlé food empire began as a humble attempt to lower infant mortality. Looking for a low-cost, nutritious infant formula for women who could not breast feed their babies, Henri Nestlé, who had recently purchased a company that made rum and nut oils, stumbled onto a lactate-laced gold mine. With the creation of Farine Lactee Nestlé, an innovative combination of cow's milk, wheat flour, and sugar, the Nestlé empire spread throughout Europe. It continued to grow with the purchase of condensed milk, milk chocolate, and powdered soup companies. Nestlé continued to benefit from its ability to adapt to the times: a shortage of milk during WWI forced Nestlé to grow beyond its milk and chocolate business to become the conglomerate of today. Post-war problems in the European market encouraged Nestlé to expand globally into the U.S. market.

Although product advancements – like the 1920 introduction of Nescafé instant coffee – came early, most of Nestlé's expansion came through acquisitions made during the 1970s and 1980s. During this time, Nestlé came under fire for the unethical marketing of infant formula to Third World markets. Activists, claiming that Nestlé was convincing women to forego breast-feeding in favor of the less-healthy infant formula, launched a boycott. Although Nestlé says it now abides by World Health Organization guidelines for the distribution of infant formula, monitoring groups dispute how well Nestlé meets these guidelines.

In 1997, Nestlé was "crunched" when its new product, Nestlé Magic, a chocolate-covered children's toy, was recalled after protests by parental groups and lawmakers. In fact, the combination, which consisted of a toy held in a secure plastic ball and surrounded by chocolate, not only met the FDA's elite safety standards, it exceeded them. The successful opposition was fueled by Nestlé's U.S. competitor, Mars, Inc. Mars had failed recently in their own effort to create a toy/chocolate combination.

Despite the Asian economic crisis, Nestlé still reported a 1998 first half net income of $1.46 billion and a 5.6 percent increase in sales. Company officials said a booming coffee market in Eastern Europe and Russia, which the company plans to continue to aggressively pursue over the next few years, helped offset sales reductions in Asia. Nestlé also announced that the current chair of Credit Suisse Group, Rainer E. Gut, will succeed Helmut Maucher as chairman of the company. But both men plan to retire in 2000, leading analysts to suspect CEO Peter Braneck-Letmathe is being groomed to helm the firm.

GETTING HIRED

As one of the world's largest consumer goods companies, Nestlé is a haven for marketing managers. In the U.S., with its operations based in Glendale, California, the company recruits heavily at top West Coast-based business schools, such as Anderson at UCLA. The company frequently advertises in trade journals and newspapers such as *The Los Angeles Times*. In addition, Nestlé makes use of selected Internet job posting sites. Because of Nestlé's international scope, the company looks for candidates with foreign language proficiency for corporate positions.

Nestlé is most interested in "those with the know-how, energy, leadership, communication skills, and academic excellence," to take part in its plans for ongoing growth. It wants applicants that can not fill the position they're hired for, but "who can grow into future leaders." Most of Nestlé's hires in "marketing are recruited from colleges or come from other companies or internships." An insider reports that "Nestlé has a reputation for attracting and retaining the best qualified people in the industry."

MBA Job Seekers: Receive free e-mailed job postings matching your interests & qualifications! Register at www.VaultReports.com

VAULT REPORTS™

345

www.vaultreports.com

OUR SURVEY SAYS

Nestlé is a very large, global company, and as such, experiences and expectations will vary by office and region. Nestlé's size provides "great opportunity for advancement for those employees who are willing to relocate." Normal hours at Nestlé are "8:30 to 5:00, however in some situations there are flex hours." As for its corporate body "most recent graduates that are hired have MBAs." For those in marketing "the hours are expected to be 10 hours a day" but the "pay is from average to above." While "Nestlé does have sales offices all around the country and some of the sales people even telecommute," the inside scoop is that "all action seems to be in Glendale." (The company also has a major U.S. location in Solon, Ohio, a suburb of Cleveland.) "Most marketing positions will be in that office, as well as finance positions" an insider notes about Glendale. The Glendale office is "very businesslike and professional and yes, they do have a dress code," according to insiders, although the company has business casual Fridays. More specifically, "men must wear coats and ties and women must wear business clothes." As members of the No. 1 food company, employees note: "We are very proud of the products we produce."

Nestlé employees believe that "race, color, gender, creed or any other category has no bearing on the corporate structure at Nestlé," and that "diversity is actually a Nestlé trademark." One insider says: "To put it bluntly, Nestlé doesn't have minorities – just people." Diversity here refers to both ethnicity and gender, with "a lot of women in high-level marketing positions." A reason for this is that with strengths in the Americas, Europe, Africa, India and East Asia, the sun never sets on Nestlé. Nestlé is also "very conscious about its image and therefore has very good history in the HR arena." "The culture is good for everyone and I believe we work well together," one contact says of the environment.

"There are many extra perks such as medical, dental, eye, educational assistance, a wonderful cafeteria at a rate you could not beat, an on-site mail and shipping department, and in-house classes," one contact raves. Employees also enjoy the "constant feedback" that they receive from their superiors. Nestlé also offers entry-level employees "generous tuition benefits" to augment its pay scale. As for insurance, "there is some co-pay involved, but you are offered a choice of various plans."

To put it bluntly, Nestlé doesn't have minorities – just people.

– *Nestlé insider*

Andersen Consulting

Management Consulting

RANKING
47

1345 Avenue of the Americas
New York, NY 10105
(212) 708-4000
Fax :(212) 245-4751
www.ac.com

LOCATIONS

New York, NY (HQ)
The firm has 137 offices in 46 countries

SERVICES

Management Consulting
Technology Consulting

THE STATS

Annual Revenues: $6.6 billion (1997)
No. of Employees: 44,800 (worldwide)
No. of Offices: 137 (worldwide)
A privately-held partnership
CEO: George Sheehan

KEY COMPETITORS

- Arthur Andersen
- Booz•Allen & Hamilton
- Deloitte Consulting
- EDS
- Ernst & Young Consulting
- KPMG Consulting
- McKinsey

THE BUZZ

What MBAs are saying
about Andersen

- "Emerging leader"
- "Androids, techies, strategy wannabes"
- "Army but social"
- "Leading systems consultant"

UPPERS

- Extensive job training
- Free tickets to sporting and cultural events
- Very social firm
- Free meals

DOWNERS

- Long workdays
- Frequent travel
- Chaos of firmwide fission

EMPLOYMENT CONTACT

161 N. Clark
Chicago, Illinois 60601
(312) 693-0161
Fax: (312) 652-2329

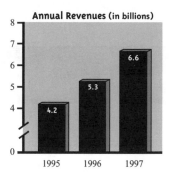

Annual Revenues (in billions)

1995: 4.2
1996: 5.3
1997: 6.6

% of Revenue Growth by Region

Americas 54%
Asia Pacific 10%
Europe, Middle East, Africa and Asia 36%

Employees

1995: 38,027
1996: 44,801
1997: 53,426

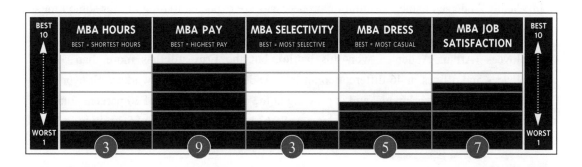

BEST 10	MBA HOURS BEST = SHORTEST HOURS	MBA PAY BEST = HIGHEST PAY	MBA SELECTIVITY BEST = MOST SELECTIVE	MBA DRESS BEST = MOST CASUAL	MBA JOB SATISFACTION	BEST 10
WORST 1	3	9	3	5	7	WORST 1

MBA Job Seekers: Receive free e-mailed job postings matching
your interests & qualifications! Register at www.VaultReports.com

VAULT REPORTS™

349

www.vaultreports.com

THE SCOOP

The younger of the two progeny of Andersen Worldwide (the other being Arthur Andersen), Andersen Consulting is the world's largest management consulting firm. With more than 44,500 consultants and nearly 60,000 employees, Andersen Consulting can draw from a vast array of industrial and technical expertise. Its four competencies (change management, process, strategic services, and technology) work together to design strategies for more than half of the *Fortune* 500 in America, as well as many of the other top corporations worldwide.

Despite its success, Andersen Consulting, led by strong-willed managing director George Sheehan, is unhappy at an inequitable division between the two firms. Under the terms of a 1989 agreement that split Andersen Consulting and Arthur Andersen, Arthur Andersen, the accounting and financial services division, holds a two-thirds majority vote on Andersen Worldwide's board of directors. Arthur Andersen is also entitled to a percentage of the consultancy's profits, despite the fact that Andersen Consulting has become more profitable and faster-growing. Even more galling to Andersen consultants, Arthur Andersen has been setting up its own business and technology consulting services to boost its growth, thus actually competing with Andersen Consulting. In December 1997, Andersen Consulting boldly sought to split off from Andersen Worldwide; George Shaheen announced his intention to take the dispute between the two firms to arbitration at the International Chamber of Commerce in Paris. Under Andersen Worldwide regulations, Andersen Consulting would have to pay compensation of 1.5 times net annual revenues – about $11.5 billion – in order to walk free, but AC plans to argue that Arthur Andersen had nullified the agreement through its internally competitive actions. In January 1998, Arthur Andersen announced that it would seek a $10 billion payment from Andersen Consulting, and also force AC to surrender the invaluable Andersen name. Arbitration proceedings are expected to drag out for some time.

Andersen Consulting seemed to have been in a race with Arthur Andersen to get to 60,000 employees (Arthur Andersen won this battle), but the firm still has more than 59,000 employees and offices in 46 different countries. Andersen Consulting works with over 5000 client organizations worldwide, and is growing at the quick-quick rate of 20 percent annually. Revenue in 1997 for Andersen Consulting was $6.63 billion, compared to $5.3 billion in 1996.

Revenue was up by 68 percent in the energy competency, 56 percent in insurance and 45 percent in high tech. In 1997, revenue grew by 29 percent to $3.7 billion in the Americas, 29 percent in the Americas (outside the U.S.), 23 percent in Europe/Middle East/Africa./India, and by 16 percent in Asia. The currency gyrations in Asia were only a minor setback; they simply caused Andersen to grow by 25 percent instead of 29 percent in 1997. In the United States alone, the largest home country for Andersen Consulting, with 51 offices in 27 states and 25,000 consultants, revenues in 1997 hit $3.4 billion. Andersen Consulting estimates that its revenues have been growing 25 percent a year in the United States. The firm works with 75 percent of *Fortune's* Global 200 largest companies, and "all but one of the 30 most profitable."

GETTING HIRED

Andersen has a very high profile on B-school campuses, but even if you've read this entry, don't ignore Andersen's workshops and recruiting events – attending them can be a competitive advantage for candidates. "Andersen is desperately trying to get top-tier people into the company," says one MBA. "They even flew over people from the London office just to take people to a baseball game. It was ridiculous, because of the time difference; it was about 3 in the morning for them by the time they arrived. The partner I was talking to was falling asleep."

MBAs have two interviews on campus. The first is with one person, the second with two people (normally partners or experienced managers, though you will also interview with a peer). After making it through these screening rounds, there is a day at the nearest office. There are apparently minor differences between offices and campuses; some candidates have had a second round with three managers or partners at an Andersen office. While candidates do have the option to fly out to visit the office of their interest, "it isn't necessary to interview where you want to work, except in the case of San Francisco."

MBAs say Andersen makes its big push "at sell weekend, which is very structured. The first day is in the office and features a series of meetings with the various industry groups. They

MBA Job Seekers: Receive free e-mailed job postings matching your interests & qualifications! Register at www.VaultReports.com

VAULT REPORTS™

351

www.vaultreports.com

provide much more specific information that you get in the recruitment brochures. There is also the opportunity to speak one-on-one with peers, and you go out to wining and dining things and to a Broadway show." Apparently, no one ever mentions Arthur Andersen.

OUR SURVEY SAYS

Employees say that "Andersen Consulting is the place for exciting opportunities and highly visible clients." One employee explains that the firm "is entrepreneurial in the sense that employees can control their own career paths." Consultants travel so frequently that their "home lives often fall into shambles," but they are "rewarded with good salaries." Andersen Consulting is very unusual among consultancies in that "it pays for overtime, and you can be assured that you will work overtime." Know, though that "overtime is straight time, not time and a half." (Strategy consultants don't get overtime pay.) And for most employees, "there are no end-of-year bonuses." Andersen Consulting also offers a plethora of perks – "free flights, great social events, relaxed expense policies, expensed dinners at great restaurants." One outstanding perk – a "concierge service that runs errands for a subsidized rate of $5 an hour. They'll feed your cat, take your car in for service, whatever you need." And the firm is social as well. "We have numerous happy hours, and go on trips together as offices," employees say. "There are also activities like volunteer events, fun runs and corporate sports team playoffs." As for dress, although employees report Friday casual days and sometimes casual dress, depending on clients, they also report that "occasionally, people have been sent home to change if they are dressed inappropriately."

On the client site, says one process consultant, "I arrive at 8 and stay to around 7. Half the time I went back to the hotel and just chilled and ordered room service; the other half of the time I kept working on my laptop – sometimes until midnight." Andersen has a "Friday in the office policy" under which the firm makes an effort to fly back its consultants to their home offices on Thursday night. Says one consultant about Fridays: "I was usually back in the office. Fridays are mostly for administrative stuff – internal development, evaluations, training." Weekend work is "rare but does happen." A business process management consultant agrees with that time assessment. "I work about 55 hours a week and bill 60. The policy is that your work hours are 8:30 to 5:30 and if you go over that you get overtime." Every service line except for strategy gets overtime. "Strategy will bill up to 10 hours a day, but after that they don't bother." But while strategic consultants don't get overtime, they may get "comp time. What happens is that you work like a dog for six months and then you're done. Your manager says, 'It's Wednesday, take Thursday and Friday off.' It's separate from your vacation time, and just gets billed to some random black hole account." In times of crisis, however, the Friday in the office policy shifts." Despite the Friday in the office policy, I have often stayed at the client site five days a week with no trip home. I have heard of some consultants who worked through the weekend at the client with no trip home."

While Andersen Consulting employees are reportedly "a fun-loving, hard-working, thinking group of people" and the scope of work is "global," the hours are "crazy" and the firm itself is "not as prestigious as other consulting firms yet." "The work can be great," says one employee, "but it wears you down after a while. It's tough on personal relationships because you travel so much. You can start to feel like a number sometimes." We hear that "rank is everything. Things aren't as meritocratic as you might expect." One consultant warns that "you need to be flexible and be able to handle a lot of stress." While we're told the strife between Andersen Consulting and Arthur Andersen "hasn't affected day-to-day work or quality of life at ground level yet," everyone is "anxious" and "confused."

To order a 50- to 70-page Vault Reports Employer Profile on Andersen Consulting call 1-888-JOB-VAULT or visit www.VaultReports.com

The full Employer Profile includes detailed information on Andersen's departments, recent developments and transactions, hiring and interview process, plus what employees really think about culture, pay, work hours and more.

MBA Job Seekers: Receive free e-mailed job postings matching
your interests & qualifications! Register at www.VaultReports.com

VAULT
REPORTS™
www.vaultreports.com

353

BIG FIVE FIRMS – 'WE'RE NOT ALL THE SAME'

As Andersen Consulting breaks away from Arthur Andersen, and in the wake of the merger of Price Waterhouse and Coopers & Lybrand, the Big Five firms (Arthur Andersen, Deloitte & Touch, KPMG, Ernst & Young and PricewaterhouseCoopers) are striving to separate themselves from the pack. Here's a look at how the Big Five are scrambling to the top of the heap.

Price Waterhouse and Coopers & Lybrand, if you haven't heard, merged in July 1998 to build a "breakaway" firm – a financial services company of such size (140,000 employees in over 150 countries) that no competitor would be able to stand up to them. Of course, the danger is that such a huge merger might cause a culture clash – and Price Waterhouse and Coopers aimed to ensure that there was no perception of disunity among its clients. The two companies thus rushed to create a new name and logo (spending, according to some insiders, over $1 million in the process), and came up with the name PricewaterhouseCoopers. The new moniker utilized the now-trendy practice in the business world of smooshing two names together to ostensibly appear sleek and modern (witness DaimlerChrysler). The CEOs of Price Waterhouse and Coopers & Lybrand, Nicholas Moore and James Schiro, were reluctant to give up the equity of the Price Waterhouse or Coopers & Lybrand name – and thus PricewaterhouseCoopers was born.

Unfortunately, the ungainliness of the new name was compounded by PricewaterhouseCoopers' insistence on choosing a "playful" jumbled logo – which creates a PricewaterhouseCoopers emblem that looks more like PrIcEwAterHouSeCoOpErs. The new look for the firm has earned mostly disdain from company insiders, industry observers, and the media (London's *Guardian* called the name "cruel"). The joke around PricewaterhouseCoopers goes that "while we may have paid a million dollars for the logo to designers, Andersen paid them two million to screw it up!" Others have quietly suggested that PwC might have been a better choice (and that is, indeed, the nickname used for the company).

Big Five firms, cont'd

Other Big Five firms have turned to the power of advertising to burnish their own brand images. Andersen Consulting, in an effort to differentiate itself both from Arthur Andersen and other Big Fivers, will spend $100 million in 1998 on a marketing blitz that will showcase its own new logo, a large A "raised" to a small c, as with an exponent. Andersen Consulting also considered placing an egg before its name, but this notion was dismissed as too difficult. Industry observers also suggest the new logo is preparation for the possibility that Andersen Consulting might have to forfeit its right to the Andersen name as the consultancy proceeds with its bid to part from Arthur Andersen. Not to be outdone, Arthur Andersen is expected to embark on its own branding advertising spree shortly.

Other Big Five firms are getting into the act too. After the KPMG Peat Marwick/Ernst & Young merger foundered, KPMG opted to shed the "Peat Marwick" from its name, and is in the beginning stages of a $60 million worldwide advertising campaign. The campaign will emphasize the years of experience most KPMG consultants have (13.5 years) and use the tagline "KPMG – It's time for clarity," which also rhymes. And Deloitte & Touche has embarked on its own extensive advertising campaign that gleefully points out that it's the only Big Five firm not distracted by a merger, a failed merger, or internecine strife.

What this means for job seekers, of course, is that these Big Five firms may be more eager than most to accelerate their hiring, at a time when other companies may have reached the saturation point. All those new web sites the Big Five are putting up include slick new recruitment web pages designed to entice new waves of fresh young consultants into their ever-increasing grasp.

For more information on careers in Management Consulting, including actual case interview questions, read the Vault Reports Guide to the Management Consulting.

MBA Job Seekers: Receive free e-mailed job postings matching your interests & qualifications! Register at www.VaultReports.com

VAULT REPORTS™

www.vaultreports.com

355

Kraft

3 Lakes Dr
Northfield, IL 60093-2753
(847) 646-6383
Fax: (847) 646-8960
www.kraftfoods.com

Consumer Products

LOCATIONS

Northfield, IL (HQ)
Rye Brook, NY
(Kraft Foods International HQ)
Don Mills, Ontario, Canada
(Kraft Canada HQ)
97 other North American locations

DEPARTMENTS

Beverages
Cheese
Desserts and Snacks
Enhancers
Coffee
Meals
Oscar Mayer
Post
Food Services

THE STATS

Annual Revenues: $16.8 billion (1997)
No. of Employees: 39,146
No. of Offices: 400+ (worldwide)
Stock Symbol: Subsidiary of Philip Morris
CEO: Bob Eckert

KEY COMPETITORS

- Campbell Soup
- General Mills
- Heinz
- Hormel
- Kellogg
- Nestle
- Procter & Gamble
- RJR Nabisco

THE BUZZ

What MBAs are saying
about Kraft

- "Very hierarchical, great products"
- "Who eats this stuff"
- "Respected"
- "Buttoned-up"

UPPERS

- Free food
- Lavish social events
- Free gyms
- Company stores and credit unions at some locations
- Generous vacation policy

DOWNERS

- Compensation sometimes tied to brand performance
- Association with cigarette manufacturing

EMPLOYMENT CONTACT

Kraft Foods
Attn: Corporate Staffing
Three Lakes Drive
Northfield IL 60093
www.kraftfoods.com/careers

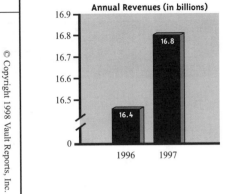

Annual Revenues (in billions)

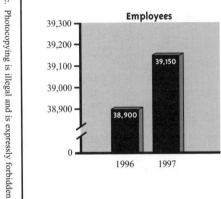

Employees

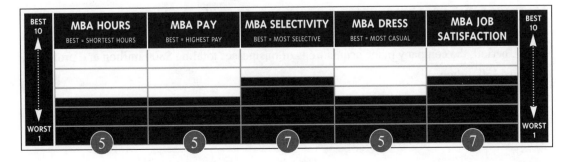

	MBA HOURS	MBA PAY	MBA SELECTIVITY	MBA DRESS	MBA JOB SATISFACTION	
	BEST = SHORTEST HOURS	BEST = HIGHEST PAY	BEST = MOST SELECTIVE	BEST = MOST CASUAL		
	5	5	7	5	7	

MBA Job Seekers: Receive free e-mailed job postings matching your interests & qualifications! Register at www.VaultReports.com

VAULT REPORTS™

357

www.vaultreports.com

THE SCOOP

The largest packaged food company based in the U.S., Kraft Foods has made wiggly Jell-O, Kool-Aid, and the individually wrapped cheese slice staples of the American diet. Kraft traces its history to three of the most successful food entrepreneurs of the late 19th and early 20th centuries: J.L. Kraft, Oscar Mayer and C.W. Post. James L. Kraft and two of his brothers incorporated their business in 1909 and acquired their first cheese factory in 1914. Oscar Mayer and C.W. Posts' companies were founded in the late 1800s. They eventually became part of Philip Morris' General Foods Corporation, and were merged with Kraft upon the cigarette maker's acquisition of Kraft in 1988.

Kraft makes more than 70 major brands, including Kraft cheeses, Oscar Mayer meats, Maxwell House coffee, Post cereals, Tombstone pizza, Stove Top stuffing, and Miracle Whip salad dressing. Four of company's brands (Kraft, Oscar Mayer, Maxwell House and Post) bring in more than $1 billion in annual revenue. The company has suffered through some difficult years recently, and has embarked on a couple of major initiatives designed to help invigorate its brands. In 1995, the company restructured its sales staff to create a 3000-member retail sales force, which is organized into nearly 200 customer business teams. And in the fall of 1998, Kraft launched a $50 million "umbrella" advertising campaign that features several of the the company's products in a documentary-style commercial. The idea behind the plan is to make Kraft a highly recognized brand name in the same way the public recognizes Nike and Walt Disney.

Even as Kraft invests heavily in marketing that promotes its entire business line at once, the company is constantly on the lookout for any advantageous changes to its product line. The company is active in divestitures and acquisitions. Since 1990, Kraft has divested businesses in North America that had annual revenues of about $7.6 billion and earnings of $300 million (including Lenders bagels and CPC International, home of Entenmann's and Boboli). Over the same period, the company made acquisitions of businesses totaling $800 million and profits of about $150 milion.

GETTING HIRED

At Kraft the people are "whip-smart, especially in Marketing." For that division Kraft almost exclusively hires MBAs, but its Marketing Information Department sometimes hires those with "proof that they are working on the degree." One contact notes "We are always searching/recruiting for new talent." Kraft is a young company that "promotes mostly from within," so they are very receptive to hiring prospective employees who seem capable of making a long-term impact on the company. The company recruits at national conferences with an eye toward diversity, such as those sponsored by the National Society of Black MBAs,and the Hispanic MBA Conference.

MBAs also join Kraft in its Finance, Marketing Services, Human Resources, and Operations departments. According to insiders, unlike some other consumer goods companies, Kraft is not run by brand managers – finance officials, for example, have significant pull, and opportunity to move up into general management. Kraft pulls many of its MBAs from "Kellogg (Northwestern), Michigan and especially Chicago. One insider notes, "it's hard to get into Kraft, but easy to move around once you're in."

OUR SURVEY SAYS

Even though Kraft is one of the world's largest food producers, its divisions operate "autonomously" without an "impersonal, big business atmosphere." A "relaxed," "family-oriented" environment predominates throughout its many divisions. The New York and Chicago offices "are located on beautiful, landscaped properties" with ponds and jogging trails.

"Kraft is very interested in retention," and "seems to be constantly looking for ways to assist its employees in their work life." That concern manifests itself in one of the most perk-laden

MBA Job Seekers: Receive free e-mailed job postings matching your interests & qualifications! Register at www.VaultReports.com

VAULT REPORTS™

www.vaultreports.com

359

environments in the corporate world. Besides receiving a "competitive" salary, employees benefit from a "slew of perks" such as a "professionally staffed cafeteria, in-house fitness center, on-site company store, nurse, credit union, cash station, and laundry services," as well as "on-site oil changes and bus service to commuter rail stations." "They'll even match two-for-one any donations you make to charity!" one contact raves. Kraft also features speakers such as Colin Powell, Henry Cisneros and Raul Yzaguirre (President of the National Council of La Raza) and concerts by the likes of country music star Vince Gill and jazz great the Ramsey Lewis Quartet, who have both performed in the Kraft cafeteria.

Kraft functions on flex-time, meaning workdays may begin or end anywhere between 7:30 a.m. and 7:30 p.m. Employees often "spend many hours more" at work than they are asked to. To further assist their employees with time management, Kraft features the Work/Life Balance Program, which "provides information about outside services for almost anything you might need, from a local plumber to child/elder care" as well as many other life issues. There is a dress code of business casual dress in most offices, but "overall the code is rather loose." Almost all employees get "their own phone (three lines), voice mail, computer, e-mail," and "the cubes get bigger and closer to the windows as you move up the ladder." Though the company strives for diversity, and there are awareness classes are taught every year, one insider complains that "that tells you what the environment is like – a class is needed to explain what diversity is."

Kraft employs a "large number of young adults, 21 to 34 years old, probably 45 to 50 percent women" which helps make "it more enjoyable to work on teams or groups" for entering MBAs, who are relieved to find that Kraft is "not really old and stuffy." An internal promotion policy provides current employees with "tremendous promotion opportunities" and even moves them "laterally" to ensure they have the experience that they will need to advance.

People at Kraft are "generally driven, competent at their job function, and upwardly mobile" and yet "not all-consumed with their job." Kraft is broken up into nine divisions and "there are marketing and finance groups for each division," as well as corporate marketing and finance groups for each functional area (sales, operations, logistics, etc.). Within this system "each person is typically responsible for a brand (such as Honeycomb Cereal) and is chartered with growing the brand and typically the category it competes in."

"It's hard to get into Kraft, but easy to move around once you're in."

– *Kraft insider*

Consumer Products

Building 224-1W-02
P.O. Box 33224
St. Paul, MN 55133-3224
(612) 733-1110
www.mmm.com

LOCATIONS

St. Paul, MN (HQ)
Austin, TX
As well more than 200 offices and plants
across the U.S. and around the world

No. of Offices: 200 (worldwide)
Stock Symbol: MMM
Stock Exchange: NYSE
CEO: L. D. DeSimone

DEPARTMENTS

Applications Development
Applied Research
Business Planning
Customer Service
Data Center Operations
Electronic Commerce
Environmental Technology & Services
Industrial Engineering
Process Engineering
Product Development
Staff Operations
Technical Support
Technology Building
Telecommunications

◆ Avery Denison
◆ Baxter Healthcare
◆ Dow
◆ Dupont
◆ Johnson & Johnson
◆ S.C. Johnson

THE BUZZ
What MBAs are saying
about 3M

◆ "Family friendly, entrepreneurial"
◆ "Innovative, risk tolerant"
◆ "Old line, stable"
◆ "Staid, Midwestern"

THE STATS

Annual Revenues: $15 billion (1997)
Income: $2.1 billion (1997)
No. of Employees: 75,639 (worldwide)

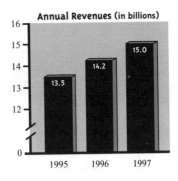

Annual Revenues (in billions)

UPPERS

- ◆ Executive gym
- ◆ Reduced price concert and sports tickets
- ◆ Profit sharing
- ◆ Merchandise discounts
- ◆ Flexible scheduling options

DOWNERS

- ◆ Excessive "red tape"

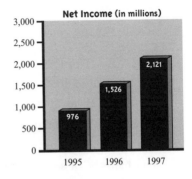

Net Income (in millions)

EMPLOYMENT CONTACT

Human Resources
Building 224-1W-02
P.O. Box 33224
St. Paul, MN 55133-3224
(612) 736-6006
E-mail: careers@mmm.com

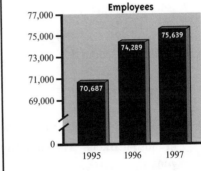

Employees

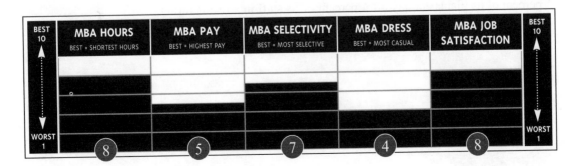

	MBA HOURS	MBA PAY	MBA SELECTIVITY	MBA DRESS	MBA JOB SATISFACTION	
	BEST = SHORTEST HOURS	BEST = HIGHEST PAY	BEST = MOST SELECTIVE	BEST = MOST CASUAL		
	8	5	7	4	8	

THE SCOOP

With a product line totaling more than 50,000 different items, Minnesota Mining & Manufacturing, better known as 3M, has developed a global reputation for technical ingenuity and marketing innovation. Perhaps best-known for consumer products such as Scotch brand tape and Post-it notes, 3M is a global manufacturing giant with operations throughout the U.S. and in over 60 countries. Think you know 3M? Did you know that the company makes highway traffic signs and ceramic dental braces? Yup!

The company's Industrial and Consumer Markets produces Post-it notes and Scotch brand tapes, as well as communication products; the Health Care Markets develops medical and dental supplies; and the Transportation, Safety, and Chemical sector produces reflective sheeting, high performance graphics, automotive parts and industrial breathing filters. More than half of 3M's annual revenue comes from international sales, and the company spends more than a third of its robust research and development budget abroad.

Five Minnesota businessmen founded 3M as a mining business in 1902. The mining venture was not too successful, but the company soon turned to the more profitable venture of sandpaper production. Since then, 3M has capitalized upon innovations such Scotch brand masking tape – introduced in 1925 – and Scotch Magnetic Tape, the market's first commercially acceptable magnetic audio recording tape.

In 1998, the company's profits were hit by weak sales in Asia and Japan as a result of weakness in those markets. The company's stock fell about 20 percent in a one-year period from July 1997 to July 1998. Just under a quarter of the company's earnings came from Asia in 1997. As a result of the recent performance slump, 3M has announced that it will shutter about 10 percent of its plants and lay off 6 percent of its staff in a restructuring.

GETTING HIRED

Known by MBAs as an innovative, family-friendly company, 3M also consistently ranks high as a desirable employer – in 1998, the company again hit *Fortune* magazine's list of 100 best companies to work for. MBAs often come into 3M in the marketing function; for most of the company's marketing positions, 3M will hire only MBAs. Marketing managers are hired into 3M's headquarters in St. Paul and another corporate center in Austin. The company posts job descriptions at its web site, located at www.3M.com. Ever-responsive and friendly 3M responds to resumes within 30 days.

OUR SURVEY SAYS

Although some 3M employees complain about the company's "rigid bureaucracy," most rave about the company's treatment of its employees. "It's an innovative company that tries to provide employees with training and policies to do one's job best," says one insider. "It blends strong business ethics with concern for the well-being of employees and the environment." Says another: "The team concept is very much a part of the 3M culture – rarely, if ever does one person make a major decision." Opines another contact: "Most – maybe 99 percent of the employees you work with – are responsive when you need help." The company's teamwork environment starts with its emphasis on innovation, employees say. For example, all of the company's technical employees are encouraged to spend 15 percent of their time on their own projects. "The company has innovation at its core," reports one 3M contact. "It's employee-oriented and community-minded. They're always inviting employee involvement."

Part of the employee involvement at 3M includes the "3M Club," a program that organizes employees by hobbies and interests. The club is just one of many perks the company offers to help make employees stick. Need tape? "We receive discounts at the company store on 3M products." And "for managers, the stock options are very attractive." Says a longtime

MBA Job Seekers: Receive free e-mailed job postings matching
your interests & qualifications! Register at www.VaultReports.com

VAULT REPORTS™

365

www.vaultreports.com

company employee: "The 3M retirement program is another thing I now consider among the best things about the company. As I approach retirement age, I realize how good the program really is."

"Most – maybe 99 percent of the employees you work with – are responsive when you need help."

– 3M insider

General Mills

Consumer Products

P.O. Box 1113
Minneapolis, MN 55440
(612) 540-2311
Fax: (612) 540-2445
www.genmills.com

General Mills

LOCATIONS

Minneapolis, MN (HQ)
As well as about 25 plants and offices nationwide; major international facilities in England • France • Malaysia • Mexico

DEPARTMENTS

Accounting • Customer Service • Distribution • Engineering • Finance • Human Resources • Information Systems • Manufacturing • Marketing • Marketing Research • Quality Control • R&D • Sales

THE STATS

Annual Revenues: $6.0 billion (1998)
No. of Employees: 10,200 (worldwide)
No. of Offices: 70+ (U.S. & Canada)
Stock Symbol: GIS (NYSE)
CEO: Stephen W. Sanger

KEY COMPETITORS

- Kellogg
- Nestlé
- Philip Morris
- Pillsbury
- Procter & Gamble
- Quaker Oats
- Ralcorp Holdings
- RJR Nabisco

THE BUZZ
What MBAs are saying about General Mills

- "Great people, fun, but low pay"
- "Bland, boring city, family-oriented"
- "Solid marketing, but cereal?"
- "Old-fashioned"

UPPERS

- Family-friendly policies
- Social company
- Special summer hours
- Excellent company for minorities and women

DOWNERS

- Mature industry
- Can be competitive and bureaucratic

EMPLOYMENT CONTACT

Jim Beirne
Director of MBA Recruiting
P.O. Box 1113
Minneapolis, MN 55440-1113

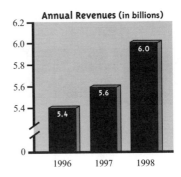

Annual Revenues (in billions)

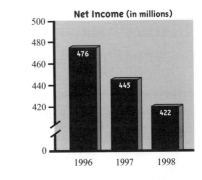

Net Income (in millions)

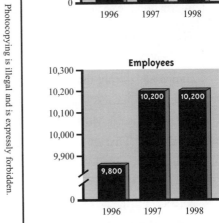

Employees

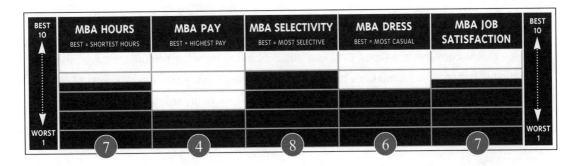

	MBA HOURS	MBA PAY	MBA SELECTIVITY	MBA DRESS	MBA JOB SATISFACTION
	BEST = SHORTEST HOURS	BEST = HIGHEST PAY	BEST = MOST SELECTIVE	BEST = MOST CASUAL	
	7	4	8	6	7

MBA Job Seekers: Receive free e-mailed job postings matching your interests & qualifications! Register at www.VaultReports.com

VAULT REPORTS™

www.vaultreports.com

369

THE SCOOP

The world's second-largest cereal maker, General Mills is home to some of the most recognized brand names in America, such as Betty Crocker, Cheerios and Wheaties. General Mills opened its first flour mill in Minneapolis in 1886, and the company still makes its corporate home there. In 1921 the company began answering the baking questions it received in the mail and gave birth to an American icon by signing the replies "Betty Crocker." The company launched many of the products that have become its mainstay during the two decades that followed, including Wheaties, Cheerios, and Bisquick. More recently, General Mills has refocused its energies on its core businesses by selling off its non-food operations. After a recent damaging price war with rivals Post and Kellogg, General Mills is poised for future growth through the introduction of brand extensions (such as Frosted Cheerios) and international expansion. The company's joint venture with PepsiCo – Snack Ventures Europe – has become the largest snack provider in continental Europe.

General Mills has not experienced the explosive growth enjoyed by many other large companies during the recent boom years. A contractor sprayed an unapproved pesticide on millions of bushels of oats from May of 1993 to June 1994 without the company's knowledge, forcing General Mills to pull 50 million boxes of cereal off the shelves and creating cereal shortages. This sales disaster, combined with plant shutdowns and cleanups, cost General Mills an estimated $147 million. From 1993 to 1995, the company's stock fell from the mid-70s to the high 40s. In 1996, when Post cereals (owned by Philip Morris) cut its prices 20 percent, a price war ensued. General Mills also cut its prices, winning market share from both Post and Kellogg, but it was a pyrrhic victory – the cereal industry overall suffered lower profits. Fiscal 1997 sales in cereal dropped by $100 million.

Today, General Mills is more interested in marketing its current brands and developing new ones than cutting prices. The company recently consolidated several international divisions into a "global convenience-foods business" that includes its yogurt brands, newly launched refrigerated bakery snacks and the Chex cereal line it bought two years ago. General Mills also moved Gold Medal flours into its Betty Crocker division in order to make Betty more competitive with her arch rival: the Pillsbury Doughboy.

GETTING HIRED

MBAs should know that marketing is the heart and soul of General Mills, and its path to the top. The department is organized into brands, and the employees in the brand group are responsible for virtually everything that happens to that brand, from determining how much is produced, to how much it will cost, to giving final approval on the product's packaging. Says one former finance MBA employee: "I left because I didn't want to be at a company that was led by marketing, while I wanted to be in finance." Another echoes: "I looked ahead and saw all the decisions were made by marketing people."

General Mills' extensive employment Web page – located at www.jobs.genmills.com – describes opportunities in each department and provides the company's campus recruiting schedule. For marketing MBAs, GMI administers several written standardized tests. Two are given to applicants between their interview on campus and their interview in Minneapolis; the applicant mails the tests to the company. They are multiple choice, and very, very long. "It took me six hours to do them both," gripes one assistant marketing manager. One of the tests is designed to help recruiters decide if a candidate is a good fit for the position he or she is seeking. The other multiple choice test is shorter but still long. It's used to assemble a psychological profile for the candidate. What is GMI looking for? "A team player, creativity, leadership."

When applicants for AMM positions interview in Minneapolis, they are given a lengthy case question, and a timed creativity test. The latter is a test that employees describe as "very stressful." Does this second test matter? "The ability to generate ideas that the test shows is important," says one recruiter.

MBA Job Seekers: Receive free e-mailed job postings matching your interests & qualifications! Register at www.VaultReports.com

VAULT REPORTS™
www.vaultreports.com

371

OUR SURVEY SAYS

Employees say that GMI has a slender management structure that provides for easy communication between junior and senior managers. "There's a division president, and there's three or so directors, and then three to five marketing managers under them, and then maybe two AMMs under each of them," says one assistant marketing manager. "As far as levels go, there aren't a whole lot of levels. The person I pitch to is the directors, and my managers pitch to the president." But this cozy relationship can sometimes prove suffocating for snarky youngsters. "The senior managers are still committed to their old brands they had when they were junior-level brand people, so they get their hands all over the minor details of the brands. This is often very de-motivating," says one former brand employee. "Little decisions often take forever to make – too many hands in the pot." "The culture is very individual, not that team-oriented," says one former marketing intern. "There's lots of e-mail cc'ing your boss so you are always making sure your boss see what you're doing," says one promotion planner in marketing. "Brown-nosing happens a lot."

Considering the sometimes political atmosphere at General Mills, it is perhaps fitting that the company's campus, located about five miles west of downtown Minneapolis, might as well be its own fiefdom. The company compound has a barber/beauty shop. There's also a variety store that sells gifts, candy, video rentals, and discounted theatre tickets. There's another store that sells discounted General Mills products ("You buy all products for $2"). "We have a full service station on the campus so you can have your car worked on, gassed up and/or washed during the day," reports one employee. "They will shuttle you to and from the employee entrance also so you don't have to walk." There's also a free health club with "weight equipment, treadmills, bikes, Stairmasters, Nordic Track, etc." At the club, employees can even sign up for aerobic classes (though they're charged for that). And there's a health center with a full-time doctor. "You can have your eyes examined, get a physical, see a nurse for a cold," say insiders.

Mills employees are close-knit outside of the office, too. "Not being from Minneapolis, I met most of my friends at work," says one marketing employee. "This happens for most people who have relocated to Mills – at all levels of the company. You get a lot of after-work happy hours, parties and weekends with your co-workers." "There's 30 new employees every year from all over the country, many single" says an assistant marketing manager. "It makes it fun. There's a lot going on." Reports another employee: "People are friendly and the company tries to do things to improve the quality of life." GMI publishes a newsletter that informs employees (they have this thing called the "Employee Club") what's up socially. "For the night scene, there's some pretty great areas." Employees say that many young professionals at GMI join the Minneapolis Sport and Social Club, where they can meet other young professionals from Cargill, Pillsbury and 3M. One employee reports that interoffice romances are actually encouraged. "They have a lot of husbands and wives working here," she says. "They think this helps keep you in Minneapolis. Otherwise, you'd rather leave the whole city, and then they lose you."

Insiders say that GMI carries quite a bit of prestige. "It was head-hunting ground, at least in Minneapolis," reports one former financial analyst who has moved on to another major consumer goods company. "You can't get a better resume booster than General Mills," says one employee, who cites the company's ranking as the most admired food company in the world [according to *Business Week*] as a major prestige plus. Says one AMM: "It's one of the top two brand companies (Procter & Gamble being the other). Talk to a headhunter. Any one will say they want a General Mills person." This belief is widespread: "In the marketing community, General Mills is known as one of the top tier firms along with P&G and maybe Kraft." Why is GMI so prestigious when it comes to marketing? "You are given responsibility from day one," say insiders.

To order a 50- to 70-page Vault Reports Employer Profile on General Mills call 1-888-JOB-VAULT or visit www.VaultReports.com

The full Employer Profile includes detailed information on General Mills' departments, recent developments and transactions, hiring and interview process, plus what employees really think about culture, pay, work hours and more.

MBA Job Seekers: Receive free e-mailed job postings matching your interests & qualifications! Register at www.VaultReports.com

VAULT REPORTS™
www.vaultreports.com

373

VAULT
REPORTS™

The Best of the Rest

American Airlines

Airline

American Airlines

P.O. Box 619616, MD 5105
Dallas/Fort Worth Airport, TX 75261
(817) 963-1234
Fax: (817) 967-4380
www.aa.com

LOCATIONS

Dallas/Fort Worth, TX (HQ)
Chicago, IL
Miami, FL
San Juan, Puerto Rico
Over 170 locations worldwide

DEPARTMENTS

Cargo
Customer Services
Finance
Human Resources Compensation/Benefits
Information Technology
International Planning
Marketing
Purchasing
Revenue Management

THE STATS

Annual Revenues: $18.66 billion (1997)
No. of Employees: 113,900 (worldwide)
Stock Symbol: AMR (NYSE)
CEO: Donald J. Carty
%Minority: 23.8
%Female/%Male: 43/57

KEY COMPETITORS

- America West
- Continental Airlines
- Delta Airlines
- Kiwi Air Lines
- Northwest Airlines
- Southwest Airlines
- TWA
- United Airlines
- US Airways

THE BUZZ
What MBAs are saying
about American Airlines

- "Bus in the air"
- "Arguably the most professional of the airlines"
- "Finance rules; others follow"
- "Bureaucratic; cost-obsessed"

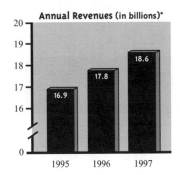

DOWNERS

- Great travel benefits
- Decent hours
- Loosening corporate culture

DOWNERS

- Pay below other industries
- Remnants of old hierarchical culture

EMPLOYMENT CONTACT

American Airlines, Inc.
Human Resources
P.O. Box 619616, MD 5105
D/FW Airport, TX 75261
Fax: (817) 967-4380 or
        (817) 963-5862
aajobs@amrcorp.com

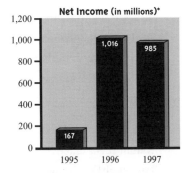

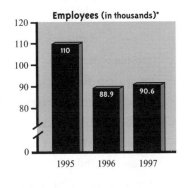

*Figures for AMR Corp.

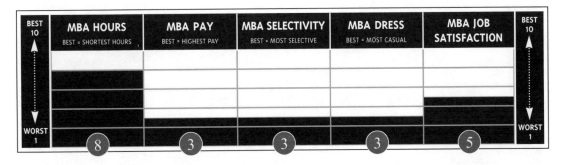

MBA Job Seekers: Receive free e-mailed job postings matching your interests & qualifications! Register at www.VaultReports.com

VAULT REPORTS™
www.vaultreports.com

THE SCOOP

In an effort to consolidate its overwhelming route structure, the New York-based Aviation Corporation (AVCO) founded American Airways in 1930. The company was re-formed as American Airlines in 1934, when new postal regulations compelled AVCO to break up its aircraft-manufacturing and transportation businesses. By the end of the decade, American had beaten out United as the nation's largest airline. In 1964, under the direction of C.R. Smith, the company introduced SABRE, the first automated reservation system in the industry. By using SABRE to track mileage records, American Airlines also became the first in the industry to introduce a frequent flyer program, AAdvantage, in 1981.

The company moved its headquarters from New York to Texas in 1979. In 1989, the company fought off a takeover bid by Donald Trump. Today, American Airlines ranks as the second-largest airline in the world (United has come back to be the leader). The company is owned by parent company AMR and continues to expand through acquisitions and alliances. In July 1998, European Union officials gave preliminary approval to a proposed alliance between American and British Airways that would allow the two companies to control 60 percent of the United States-Great Britain market. Although the EU required the two companies to make provisions to foster competition (such as giving up some airport slots) and the alliance must still pass further review, the two companies are understandably excited by the deal. Also in 1998, American established a relationship with Japan Airlines and joined with British Airways, Canadian Airlines, Cathay Pacific and Qantas to form a "Oneworld" global alliance. Finally in an eventful 1998, Donald J. Carty, a former American Airlines president, replaced Robert Crandall as chairman/CEO.

GETTING HIRED

Top-notch MBAs have the best chances of landing a Finance or Marketing position at American Airline headquarters in Fort Worth, Texas. American recruits extensively from business schools at Top 20 universities and colleges, including Yale, UCLA, Carnegie Mellon, Cornell, Duke, Northwestern, University of North Carolina, Harvard, and the University of Chicago. Universities such as the University of Texas, Vanderbilt, and Texas A&M also have an advantage since American likes to tap local talent. Along with finance and marketing positions, American also recruits MBAs for human resources and commodity manager positions.

The recruiting process for MBAs includes an on-campus interview, during which "a variety of general background questions and questions to determine analytical aptitude" are used. Insiders tell us that for those business school grads at schools to which American does not make recruiting visits, a phone interview will replace the on-campus interview. The screening interview is followed by an on-site interview at American's Fort Worth headquarters, which lasts "a half to three-quarters of a day." This interview schedule will include "both potential managers and peers." Insiders say that airline industry knowledge, though certainly welcome, is less important than analytical aptitude for MBA-level jobs at American.

OUR SURVEY SAYS

With the arrival of new CEO Don Carty, American's traditional coporate culture might be in for a makeover. Carty's predecessor, Robert Crandall, was known as a bit of a party pooper, calling board meetings during the Super Bowl and installing a strict business dress policy (which has relaxed toward the end of his tenure). Reports one employee: "The corporate culture is largely old-line, hierarchical, but it may be changing under the new leadership of

MBA Job Seekers: Receive free e-mailed job postings matching your interests & qualifications! Register at www.VaultReports.com

VAULT REPORTS™

www.vaultreports.com

379

CEO Don Carty." Under Carty, American's headquarters switched to a business casual dress policy in the summer of 1998.

Despite American's heavy marketing, marketers should beware when considering the company. Says one insider: "Due to the high operating leverage in airlines, which gives little room for error, financial types tend to run the company." Whatever the function, MBAs do well at American: "Pay for new MBAs is competitive, but, of course, less than in the hottest areas like top-tier consulting firms." Also, employees report, "all employees receive profit sharing, which in the past few good years has been as high as 12 percent of base pay." And don't forget those famous airline perks. To fly from Fort Worth in coach to either coast costs $10. Raves one insider: "You have unlimited flight benefits where you can fly anywhere we fly for next to nothing. You can fly overseas for less than $100." Employees also have the opportunity to upgrade into Business Class and First Class for a fee. However, one insider cautions about upgrades on the cheap tickets "business travel is also space available and can be an incredible hassle if the flight you need is full of paying passengers."

As for quality of life concerns: "Eighty-hour weeks are uncommon here. A standard workday in finance and planning is 8:15 to 6:15, with a half to one-hour lunch at the cafeteria or your desk." Says one insider: "It isn't uncommon to put in more time, but weekend work is uncommon." Also, the company has a "major diversity effort underway," which involves organized ethnic, religious, and other groups "advising the company on personnel and marketing policies."

"You can fly overseas for less than $100,"

– American Airlines insider

Arthur Andersen LLP

Management Consulting

33 West Monroe
Chicago, Illinois 60603
(312) 580-0033
Fax: (312)507-6748
www.arthurandersen.com

ARTHUR ANDERSEN

LOCATIONS

Chicago (HQ)
Domestic offices in 38 states.
North American offices in Canada (Calgary • Montreal • Ottawa • Quebec • Toronto • Vancouver • Winnipeg), Mexico (Guadalajara • Mexico City • Monterrey) • Bermuda

DEPARTMENTS

Assurance & Business Advisory
Business Consulting
Global Corporate Finance
Tax & Business Advisory

THE STATS

Annual Revenues: $5.2 billion (1997)
No. of Employees: 60,000 (1998)
Private partnership
Worldwide Managing Partner: Jim Wadia
Year founded: 1913

KEY COMPETITORS

- Andersen Consulting
- Deloitte Consulting
- Ernst & Young Consulting
- KPMG Consulting
- PricewaterhouseCoopers

THE BUZZ

What MBAs are saying about AA .

- "Accountants posing as consultants"
- "Accountants getting greedy"
- "Pre-MBA job"
- "Top audit firm"

Arthur Andersen LLP

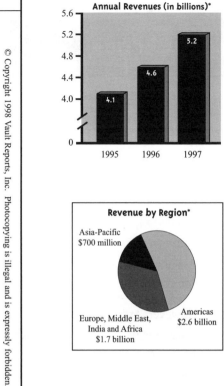

Annual Revenues (in billions)*

*Graphs indicate figures for entire firm

UPPERS

- Stability
- Regenerating company
- Excellent training

DOWNERS

- Uncertainty derived from Andersen Consulting split
- Underpaying company
- Discouraged from bringing lunch

EMPLOYMENT CONTACT

The firm suggests that applicants contact their office of interest. At the firm's headquarters:

33 West Monroe Street
Chicago, IL 60603

careers@arthurandersen.com

	MBA HOURS BEST = SHORTEST HOURS	MBA PAY BEST = HIGHEST PAY	MBA SELECTIVITY BEST = MOST SELECTIVE	MBA DRESS BEST = MOST CASUAL	MBA JOB SATISFACTION	
BEST 10						BEST 10
WORST 1	4	2	4	4	3	WORST 1

MBA Job Seekers: Receive free e-mailed job postings matching your interests & qualifications! Register at www.VaultReports.com

VAULT REPORTS™   383
www.vaultreports.com

THE SCOOP

Ever since 1989, Arthur Andersen has been the stodgier sibling to the sleeker, sexier Andersen Consulting. But now, Arthur Andersen must stand on its own. Arthur Andersen seems to be headed for an inevitable confrontation with Andersen Consulting – once its subsidiary, then a fully fleshed-out sibling, and now an adversary. The roots of the split go back to 1952, when Andersen accountants first helped General Electric install an electrical system. Arthur Andersen's consulting subsidiary continued to grow, until, in 1989, the firm was split into two units – Arthur Andersen, which was expected to concentrate on accounting business, and Andersen Consulting, which would do consulting, especially computer consulting. The agreement contained a proviso that the more profitable side would transfer money to the other.

However, Arthur Andersen soon found that Andersen Consulting was passing up smaller-niche consulting projects, and mobilized its own business consulting units to take advantage of them. Arthur Andersen became more and more adept at consulting – much to the displeasure of Andersen Consulting. The consulting boom of the 1980s had swollen AC's profits beyond those of Arthur Andersen – and the consulting arm was now transferring money to a sibling it viewed as competition. While in 1997 Andersen Consulting was the world's biggest consulting firm (with revenues of $5.7 billion), Arthur Andersen came in as the 14th-largest ($953 million in consulting revenue). In December 1997, Andersen Consulting filed for arbitration, intending to split off from Arthur Andersen. Arthur Andersen has rejoined that Andersen Consulting, under the partnership agreement, must pay $10 billion in penalty fees and a royalty fee for the continued use of the Andersen name. Andersen Consulting claims that, by developing consulting capabilities, Arthur Andersen has voided the 1989 agreement. Today, Arthur Andensen, though hardly puny at a size of 60,000 employees and revenues of $5.2 billion in 1997, is surpassed by its erstwhile subsidiary Andersen Consulting.

In the meantime, Arthur Andersen hasn't been sitting on its hands. The firm, positioning itself as a worldwide financial, consulting and legal services firm, has been making some internal changes. Jim Wadia, the current worldwide managing partner, has appointed Steve Samek as Arthur Andersen's first U.S. managing partner. (Previously, the firm was run by five regional partners working under the head of the Americas practice.) Arthur Andersen has also introduced KnowledgeSpace, a gateway to online business information, tools and resources designed to make the Internet more efficient and productive for business users. Online subscribers receive access to many of the formerly proprietary diagnostic tools and insights from Arthur Andersen's "Global Best Practices" knowledge base as well as many other business performance enhancement tools. In its many overseas offices, Arthur Andersen is rapidly moving into the legal services market. The firm is steadily acquiring law firms in Europe, including the prestigious 300-lawyer London firm Wilde Sapte, in May 1998.

GETTING HIRED

If you're looking for the inside scoop on starting an Arthur Andersen career, you won't find it on the willfully obtuse Arthur Andersen "careers" site. Insiders who've been through the Arthur Andersen interviewing process, on the other hand, say there are a multitude of slots open, from audit to business consulting to financial services. The firm tends to shun hard quant questions, preferring to give behavioral interviews to its prospective consultants and auditors. Typically, Arthur Andersen gives one (sometimes two) screening interviews on campus, conducted by partners. Staff auditors or analysts (depending on whether it is a tax/audit or consultant interview) typically mill around, answering any questions that candidates waiting might have. "They usually don't ask anything stupid," said one recent interviewee.

The firm does two-interview rounds on campus for MBAs. The rounds are either with managers, who have been with the firm for five years, or partners, who have been there at least seven, the junior partners. "By the time you have an office visit you already have an offer," says one insider. MBAs say the firm is assiduously recruiting them for its business consulting practice – "just don't screw up and call them Andersen Consulting by accident."

MBA Job Seekers: Receive free e-mailed job postings matching your interests & qualifications! Register at www.VaultReports.com

VAULT REPORTS™

385

www.vaultreports.com

OUR SURVEY SAYS

Dress is, unsurprisingly for a firm sprung from the loins of accountants, "conservative." "We keep Brooks Brothers in business," opines one consultant. "We can wear "business casual" on Fridays if we are not at a meeting or at a client site. " Some offices have business casual days all summer. Matters of dress "vary office to office, and sometimes floor to floor." Women are allowed to wear pants "at all times if they are part of a pantsuit."

"The travel can be brutal," says a business consultant. "In the interviews they'll tell you three days a week, or four max, but that's just a load of crap. Consultants at every level are very much virtual. If you're thinking of taking a job [at Arthur Andersen], don't even bother to get your own apartment. Just keep your stuff at your partner's and save what you'd pay in rent – you're going to be living out of a suitcase. From what I've seen, people often fly out Sunday night and don't leave the client site until Friday at 5 – and that's if you're staffed at a city with airport connections."

Hours vary, say Arthur insiders. A first-year auditor will "typically have overtime of 100 to 250 hours. A second-year auditor works overtime of between 150 and 300 hours; after that overtime can be 600 hours or more." Usually "great performers" put in the time "because they are so much in demand," though "if working a very large number of hours is incompatible with your goals, it is possible to work in the lower end of the range." Hours for auditors are heaviest "October through April. In the summers you can basically work 40 hours a week."

The culture at Arthur Andersen is said to be "friendly but professional." The audit side of AA "is much more staid, stuffy, conventional and traditional than the business consulting side, which still has plenty of those characteristics." One particularly arcane rule: employees are not permitted to brown-bag their lunches, as it "looks unprofessional." The firm is "very old school, which also means that advocacy of minority and female leadership are kept to a minimum." "As a huge firm governed by a smallish elite of profit-sharing partners, AA can be slow to adapt to prevalent trends in the marketplace," advises one contact. "There is definitely a strong sense of hierarchy. While we pick up on trends and sell them on the revenue generating side, on the operations side it seems we seldom practice what we preach."

All in all, say insiders, "Arthur Andersen is a great place to get a start on your career. You acquire great skills, both technical and interpersonal, and a great name on your resume." "The firm invests a lot in training and education," says another insider, "which means that they value us, and it's something you can take away with you."

To order a 50- to 70-page Vault Reports Employer Profile on Arthur Andersen LLP call 1-888-JOB-VAULT or visit www.VaultReports.com

The full Employer Profile includes detailed information on Arthur Andersen's departments, recent developments and transactions, hiring and interview process, plus what employees really think about culture, pay, work hours and more.

MBA Job Seekers: Receive free e-mailed job postings matching your interests & qualifications! Register at www.VaultReports.com

VAULT REPORTS™

387

www.vaultreports.com

Arthur D. Little

Management Consulting

Acorn Park
Cambridge, MA 02140
(617) 498-5000
Fax: (617) 498-7228
www.adlittle.com

Arthur D Little

LOCATIONS

Cambridge, MA (HQ)
Other offices across the U.S. • Europe • Latin
America • Asia-Pacific

DEPARTMENTS

Strategy
Organization
Information management
Operations management
Technology and innovation management
Technology creation and exploitation
Design and development
Environment, health & safety

THE STATS

Annual Revenues: $589 million (1997)
No. of Employees: 3,500
No. of Offices: 52 (worldwide)
A privately-held company
CEO: Charles LaMantia

KEY COMPETITORS

◆ Andersen Worldwide
◆ Booz•Allen & Hamilton
◆ Boston Consulting Group
◆ Deloitte Consulting
◆ Ernst & Young Consulting
◆ KPMG Consulting
◆ McKinsey

THE BUZZ

What MBAs are saying
about AD Little

◆ "Good brand but weak management"
◆ "Second-tier, interesting work"
◆ "Creative, but everybody's quitting"
◆ "High-tech nerds"

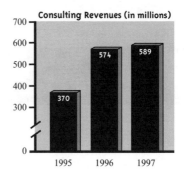

UPPERS

- High pay
- Profit sharing
- Weekly orientations and seminars
- Subsidies for daycare services

DOWNERS

- Few perks for a consulting firm
- Not a party firm
- Grungy HQ

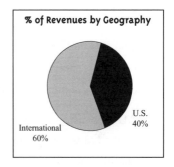

EMPLOYMENT CONTACT

Arthur D. Little
25 Acorn Park
Cambridge, MA 02140
(617) 498-6070
Fax: (617) 498-7140
careers@adlittle.com

	BEST = SHORTEST HOURS	BEST = HIGHEST PAY	BEST = MOST SELECTIVE	BEST = MOST CASUAL	
	MBA HOURS	MBA PAY	MBA SELECTIVITY	MBA DRESS	MBA JOB SATISFACTION
	5	5	6	6	8

BEST 10 — WORST 1

MBA Job Seekers: Receive free e-mailed job postings matching
your interests & qualifications! Register at www.VaultReports.com

VAULT REPORTS™

389

www.vaultreports.com

THE SCOOP

Founded in 1886, Arthur D. Little is the oldest consulting firm in the world, and is still going strong. The firm has more than 3000 staff members based in 30 countries and claims to distinguish itself from its competitors through the breadth and depth of the experience that it offers its clients, as well as a much more solid technological background than most consultancies. Arthur D. Little's technology unit has sponsored numerous useful technological advances over the years, ranging from the development of the first acetate fibers in the early part of the 20th century, to a recent fuel-powered energy cell breakthrough, which should make electric cars more feasible.

ADL's consulting teams are laden with higher-up personnel, and emphasize a "side-by-side" method of working with clients. With its focus on lasting results, Arthur D. Little keeps clients coming back for more – the firm gets 80 percent of its business from repeat customers. The company boasts 16 percent annual revenue growth over the last three years as well as an average stock increase of 17 percent per year. Because all ADL consultants are shareholders, they are driven to continue this record of achievement.

The technology division not only develops innovative products, but sponsors investors and assists them in bringing their creation to market (for half of the proceeds). For example, the U.S. Army asked Arthur D. Little to help them design gloves suited for outdoor wear, rough use and a wide range of hand sizes. ADL's management consulting unit has sixteen industry concentrations (automotive; chemicals; consumer goods; energy; medical products; metals and resources; pharmaceuticals; public sector services; telecommunications; information; media and electronics (TIME); transportation; travel and tourism; and utilities). Arthur D. Little also runs a degree-granting management institute, for which it is seeking accreditation.

GETTING HIRED

"Arthur D. Little has a very positive attitude about MBAs," says one insider. "Traditionally, most of their consultants came out of industry, but direct hire from top MBA schools is an increasingly significant source of talent." The firm expects to hire between 70 to 80 MBAs for full-time positions in 1998-99.

Applicants will go through a "very long, very intense" phone interview before being invited to the recruiting weekends at the firm's offices, where they will have two more interviews. In some cases, ADL gives presentation interviews, for which interviewees prepare and make brief presentations on a case study that Arthur D. Little provides. Presentation interviews are typically administered to management consultants with some experience. In general, the interviews aren't "tricky" – ADL is very concerned with past experience. The case interviews are more like "mini-cases," and focus on recent industry experience. There are no "mind games," according to one recent hire. Offers are made by the end of the weekend for U.S. offices.

MBAs are typically hired into ADL's management consulting area. In the first year, MBAs "problem-solving and technical competencies are intensely tested." The next levels of progression – manager and senior manager – require leading teams and dealing directly with clients. At the level above senior manager, associate director, employees are responsible for rustling up new business. The path from consultant to director generally takes about eight years.

MBA Job Seekers: Receive free e-mailed job postings matching your interests & qualifications! Register at www.VaultReports.com

VAULT REPORTS™

391

www.vaultreports.com

OUR SURVEY SAYS

New hires at Arthur D. Little are paired with senior consultants to encourage "quick, on-the-job learning." Consultants "rapidly" move into positions of "vast responsibility" and are required to travel extensively as part of the firm's "major commitment" to its clients, though you should be prepared to "direct your own career path." Employees comment that Arthur D. Little offers its consultants "flexibility in terms of the type of work that they do" as well as a work schedule that, while demanding, "is slightly lighter than other management consulting firms." Employees say that their "friendly" colleagues make the office atmosphere "egalitarian" and "lively and interactive."

The stripped-down feel of Arthur D. Little continues in the realm of perks. Don't expect lavish frills at sensible ADL. "It's not that perky. We travel coach domestically and business class overseas," says one hammy employee. Fortunately, "the company pays full-fare coach, so most of us can at least grab an upgrade with all our frequent flier miles." Another insider notes that at least "we have free coffee and soda in our office." Our contacts generally think "Arthur D. Little might look more closely at little frills than some other consulting firms, but the benefits and pension plans are great. This is a down-to-earth place." As for pay, it's "not too shabby," though "performance bonuses are given out in a kind of stealthy way."

Employees think that "Arthur D. Little still has a small company feel," and that management "is very approachable in a way that goes beyond the usual 'open door' rhetoric." In general, "people stay a long time at Arthur D. Little, because "they earn a piece of the firm, and they feel comfortable here." You too can join in on the "high" level of satisfaction. Just "have a lot of enthusiasm for technology, or you'll be perceived not to fit in."

The social life at AD Little is "friendly," but "not wild." "I don't think my office is that social, but that's because a lot of people commute and a lot of people are married," says one young insider. Another consultant concurs: "I think, in general, ADL employees may be a bit older than the average, and that means they are less likely to drink themselves ill with their buddies after work." One insider, however, praises the "easy sociability" and "frequent get-togethers" among his co-workers.

Although Arthur D. Little boasts about its Cambridge headquarters, the firm may be overstating the case. "ADL is proud that its Cambridge headquarters was the first corporate campus," say insiders, "but the physical buildings are not nice at all." "I would go as far as to describe the offices as frumpy," one consultant tells Vault Reports. "There is a credit union and a cafeteria, but in general the place looks like an underfunded community college. So maybe that's the campus part."

To order a 50- to 70-page Vault Reports Employer Profile on Arthur D Little call 1-888-JOB-VAULT or visit www.VaultReports.com

The full Employer Profile includes detailed information on A.D. Little's departments, recent developments and transactions, hiring and interview process, plus what employees really think about culture, pay, work hours and more.

MBA Job Seekers: Receive free e-mailed job postings matching
your interests & qualifications! Register at www.VaultReports.com

VAULT REPORTS™

393

www.vaultreports.com

A.T. Kearney

Management Consulting

222 West Adams Street
Chicago, IL 60606
(312) 223-6030
www.atkearney.com

ATKEARNEY

LOCATIONS

Chicago, IL (HQ)

Cleveland, OH • Houston, TX • Los Angeles, CA • Miami, FL • Minneapolis, MN • New York, NY • Phoenix, AZ • San Francisco, CA • Stamford, CT • Washington, D.C.

Amsterdam, Holland • Barcelona, Spain • Berlin, Germany • Brussels, Belgium • Copenhagen, Denmark • Dusseldorf, Germany • London, England • Mexico City, Mexico • Madrid, Spain • Melbourne, Australia • Milan, Italy • Munich, Germany • Moscow, Russia • Paris, France • Singapore • Tokyo, Japan • Toronto, Canada

KEY COMPETITORS

- ◆ American Management Systems
- ◆ Andersen Consulting
- ◆ Booz·Allen & Hamilton
- ◆ McKinsey & Co.
- ◆ Mercer Management Consulting

DEPARTMENTS

Consulting
Financial Institutions

THE BUZZ

What MBAs are saying
about A.T. Kearney

THE STATS

Annual Revenues: $1.1 billion (1997)
No. of Employees: 4,700
No. of Offices: 63
Privately-held company
CEO: Fred G. Steingraber

- ◆ "Implementation shop, laid-back"
- ◆ "Operations focused, mediocre talent"
- ◆ "Analytical, low end"
- ◆ "Average, "EDSee""

UPPERS

- No up-or-out pressure
- Good firm camraderie
- No stereotypical Kearney consultants

DOWNERS

- Strict dress code
- EDS merger knocks down prestige in strategy consulting

EMPLOYMENT CONTACT

A.T. Kearney
Corporate Recruiting
222 West Adams Street
Chicago, IL 60606
(312) 223-6030

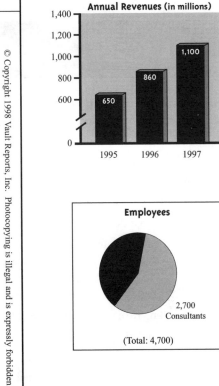

Annual Revenues (in millions)

1995	1996	1997
650	860	1,100

Employees

2,700 Consultants

(Total: 4,700)

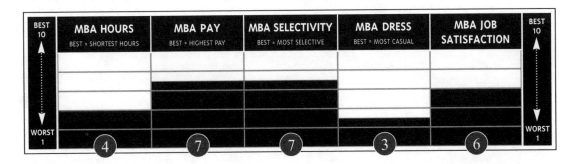

	MBA HOURS BEST = SHORTEST HOURS	MBA PAY BEST = HIGHEST PAY	MBA SELECTIVITY BEST = MOST SELECTIVE	MBA DRESS BEST = MOST CASUAL	MBA JOB SATISFACTION	
BEST 10 ... WORST 1	4	7	7	3	6	BEST 10 ... WORST 1

THE SCOOP

An employee of McKinsey & Co. in the 1930s, Andrew Thomas Kearney split off from that firm in 1939 to start an eponymous firm in Chicago. Solid results with early engagements, including an extensive study of U.S. Steel and a longtime relationship with the supermarket chain Kroger helped put A.T. Kearney on the map. Steady expansion exploded in the 1970s, when then-CEO Ken Block instituted the "Go for Growth" program, doubling the firm's size by 1980. Under the tenure of current CEO Fred Steingraber, A.T. Kearney has entered 26 new countries and doubled revenues every three years. In 1998, A.T. Kearney ranked as the 12th-largest consulting firm in the world, with operations in 30 countries.

A.T. Kearney has been called "the canary that swallowed the cat." In 1995, the 70-year-old consulting firm was acquired by EDS, the gigantic Texas-based computer and information systems giant founded by the ever-interesting Ross Perot. EDS was seeking to shore up its money-losing consulting services; A.T. Kearney CEO Fred Steingraber was attracted to EDS' piles of money and experience in information technology and its implementation – a growing business area for consultancies. EDS merged its consulting service division under A.T. Kearney's name and direction, and the marriage was a resounding success. A.T. Kearney achieved revenues of $870 million in 1996, and hit $1.1 billion in 1997.

Today, Kearney maintains offices across the globe and earns more than two-thirds of its revenues outside the U.S. While Kearney claims expertise in all types of industries, it has particular experience in aerospace, financial institutions, health care, and retail. Unlike some of its competitors, Kearney believes in sticking around to help its clients implement the firm's consulting advice. Implementation has become increasingly important to clients; as a result, Kearney's clients are both satisfied and loyal: more than 75 percent of the firm's business comes from past clients. The firm generally targets companies with at least $2 billion in annual revenue.

GETTING HIRED

MBAs start at Kearney as associates. For MBA hires, Kearney looks for three to five years of full-time business experience, more than the industry average. Kearney values an international perspective: over 55 percent of Kearney employees speak a second language. Insiders also say that Kearney is especially interested in engineering and finance backgrounds. The company's employment web page, located at www.atkearney.com/career.html, provides a list of recruiting contacts. A.T. Kearney also plans to launch a new feature on its web site: an "engagement diary" written by a recently hired consultant that details the recruitment process in more detail. The firm anticipates hiring 230 MBAs for full-time positions in 1998

While, accorrding to A.T. Kearney officials, undergraduate and MBA interviews are similar, MBAs will be expected to add an additional level of insight and analysis to their reasoning. MBAs should "leverage work experience to add industry insights to their responses. "Experience as a summer associate at a consulting firm (whether A.T. Kearney or not) or some time working with clients is a big plus.

The firm has instituted diversity programs to increase diversity in its consulting workforce. The percentage of minority hires was upped in 1998 to 36 percent, while the percentage of women rose to a less-than-impressive 29 percent on the MBA level.

Once hired, associates are involved in all aspects of a project and usually work on only one case for a three to four-month period. MBAs generally remain at the associate level for two to three years, before moving on to a managerial level. After about another three years, managers become principals. The next step up is senior partner. Unlike some of its competitors, Kearney does not follow an "up-or-out" policy.

MBA Job Seekers: Receive free e-mailed job postings matching
your interests & qualifications! Register at www.VaultReports.com

VAULT REPORTS™
397
www.vaultreports.com

OUR SURVEY SAYS

Perhaps even more than other consulting firms, A.T. Kearney considers management consulting a "lifestyle," not just a career. As a result, Kearney employees work "long days and even longer weeks." In addition, Kearney employees report plenty of travel – over 65 percent of Kearney employees have worked on engagements outside their home offices. As part of its "zealous" commitment to quality, Kearney maintains a close eye on employee performance. The firm conducts periodic evaluations to assess the quality of each employee's work. Despite an environment that one employee describes as "intense," Kearney employees get along well with each other, with "plenty of socializing" among project team members. "There are a lot of extracurricular activities," says one consultant. "I pick the ones I want to go to and don't go to the rest, otherwise I'd be doing company stuff seven days a week." Another consultant says: "I find the camaraderie here very appealing, because this industry is somewhat cutthroat and it's good to have that human touch."

Kearney is said to employ "a mix of people including new MBAs, undergrads, and industry experts (especially from the operations and the high-tech industry)." Insiders consistently report that there is "no pressure to conform to any fit type of image." Indeed, unlike the drone-in-a-suit stereotype which permeates other firms, "you will rarely hear about 'the typical Kearney person.'" Despite one insider's assertion that there is "no Kearney prototype," not everybody agrees that the firm's diversity is up to par. "Kearney is not doing anything extraordinary in the diversity department," concedes one. "Kearney's better than most, which is not to say that it's good. About a third of the people I entered with were women. But I didn't see that many non-Caucasians, especially at the top levels. That's probably a function of the fact that this emphasis on diversity is a fairly new thing. Diversity hiring has only been in effect for four to five years and it will probably take another four to five years before we see a difference at the top." Another insider praises Kearney for at least making the effort: "The firm's efforts are genuine, I'm sure. Kearney was a presence at a recent NAACP conference I attended." Nevertheless, Kearney may have "some work to do." Another insider asserts, "the minority numbers here are considerably less than in my business school class."

One employee praises the lack of an "up-or-out" policy. "That kind of policy creates a lot of insecurity. It's survival of the fittest, and I don't know how much teamwork a culture like that would encourage. Kearney doesn't have that policy and it makes it a nicer place to work." Still, don't expect to enjoy the company of your colleagues in a polo shirt and khakis. "Fred Steingraber, the CEO, hates casual dress days and refuses to have them around the office," reports one employee. In general, consultants are "enthused" about the merger with EDS. Not only will joining forces with EDS "help us really compete in the information technology consulting business," but EDS should treat its acquisition kindly, employees predict. "EDS really paid a premium for Kearney," says one consultant, "and they don't want to screw up the name they bought." Since A.T. Kearney bids for EDS business, just like an independent consultancy, "we really got a big client out of them too."

As far as perks are concerned, insiders give kudos to Kearney's "nice, strong salary." One insider claims that the dollars are "higher than average," as well as "a notch above BCG and Bain." In addition, Kearney is reportedly trusting and "very relaxed" about its billing arrangements. "I've worked at other firms where there is a daily allowance or per diem maximum," cites one insider. "There's nothing like that at Kearney. Moreover, nobody asks any questions." Such laxity can lead to the occasional abuse of power – and it does. "People take advantage of the system because it's easy. I know people who put personal dinners on the firm. You can, say, eat an $8 dinner, but write $25 in your travel and expense report since anything under $25 doesn't have to be accounted for."

To order a 50- to 70-page Vault Reports Employer Profile on A.T. Kearney call 1-888-JOB-VAULT or visit www.VaultReports.com

The full Employer Profile includes detailed information on A.T. Kearney's departments, recent developments and transactions, hiring and interview process, plus what employees really think about culture, pay, work hours and more.

MBA Job Seekers: Receive free e-mailed job postings matching your interests & qualifications! Register at www.VaultReports.com

VAULT REPORTS™

399

www.vaultreports.com

CONSULTANTS' TRAVEL: LIFE OUT OF A SUITCASE

If investment banks are famous for their infinitely long hours, consulting firms are known for perpetual travel. But will all consultancies park you on a plane the moment you set foot in the door? Vault Reports turned to our insiders to find out.

In general, consultants can indeed expect to travel a lot – but there are no guarantees. Some consultants report "being on a project in our consulting firm's home city, where the most travel I did was catching a taxi every morning," while another young consultant says: "I started work on Monday. Tuesday, I was shipped off on a six-month project in Canada which actually ended up being 18 months."

Then, there's the commuting. Many consultants complain that in their field "the hours are already 60 hours plus, and then there is all the damn airplane time. The travel is the worst, just the worst." A typical consulting firm tells its consultants to "expect to be out of the office several days each month during your first year and two to three days each week in subsequent years." Many consultants would say that's on the low side. "Travel can take up to 80 percent of your time," say consultants, and many note that they are "required to be available for travel 100 percent of the time." In general, say consultants, "travel is the rule."

This doesn't mean that travel is all that bad. Some consultants actually think that "the extensive travel" is "a big perk." One consultant gloats: "If you want frequent flyer miles, you got 'em!" Some consulting firms try to make travel fun; one offers "free business class airfare for employees and their spouses when flying to international locations." A former consultant raves about his travel experiences, citing "the unbelievable opportunities to travel around the world and enjoy yourself in style. Things I did because of my consulting job: flew the Concord, went to the winter Olympics, took a cruise from Miami to the Bahamas, gambled in Monte Carlo, opera at Covent Garden, dinner in the Eiffel Tower, a summer afternoon at a topless beach in Nice, and the list goes on." Some consultants feel in control because of the travel; one says: "As a consultant, you work very independently, always traveling around the country, so in effect you are your own boss."

Life out of a suitcase, cont'd

Despite its initial novelty, for many consultants travel becomes wearisome. Many consultants feel that the "travel stops being a perk after the first three or six months, and then becomes a royal pain." Others caveat that "if you're travelling – which is about half the time – you're away from home a lot more than this. There is some flexibility to when you schedule your work. Generally weekends are free if you want them to be – but not always." Consulting firms realize this, and most try to strike some kind of "balance between work and personal life." Many firms now offer a "Fridays in the office" policy to ensure that employees spend their weekends at home (or at least, at their home office). Others have telecommuting options that permit consultants to spend some days at home. Still, many consultants say the job "is best for those who are unattached" since "you're rarely home."

For more information on careers in Management Consulting, including actual case interview questions, read the **Vault Reports Guide to Management Consulting.**

MBA Job Seekers: Receive free e-mailed job postings matching your interests & qualifications! Register at www.VaultReports.com

VAULT REPORTS™ 401
www.vaultreports.com

Atlantic Richfield (ARCO)

Energy

515 S. Flower St.
Los Angeles, CA 90071
(213) 486-3511
www.arco.com

ARCO ◆

LOCATIONS

Los Angeles, CA (HQ)
Ancorage, AK
Dallas, TX
Houston, TX

DEPARTMENTS

Capital Investing
Engineering
Finance
Human Resources
Performance
Planning
Research

THE STATS

Annual Revenues: $18.7 billion (1997)
No. of Employees: 24,000 (worldwide)
Stock Symbol: ARCO (ARC: NYSE)
CEO (ARCO): Mike R. Bowlin

KEY COMPETITORS

- Amerada Hess
- Amoco
- Chevron
- Exxon
- Mobil
- Royal Dutch/Shell
- Texaco

THE BUZZ

What MBAs are saying about ARCO

- "Progressive for industry"
- "Takeover bait"
- "Boring industry"
- "Global, entrenched"

UPPERS

- Flexible work schedules
- Emergency childcare
- Ample advancement opportunities
- Company gyms at some sites
- Retirement planning software

DOWNERS

- Frequent layoffs
- Volatile industry

EMPLOYMENT CONTACT

ARCO
MBA Recruiting Coordinator
515 South Flower Street
Los Angeles, CA 90071

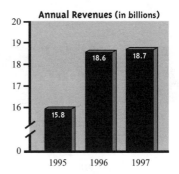

Annual Revenues (in billions)

1995	1996	1997
15.8	18.6	18.7

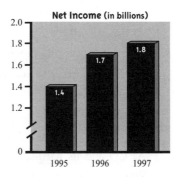

Net Income (in billions)

1995	1996	1997
1.4	1.7	1.8

Employees

1995	1996	1997
22,000	22,800	24,000

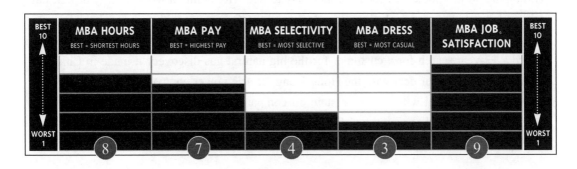

	MBA HOURS BEST = SHORTEST HOURS	MBA PAY BEST = HIGHEST PAY	MBA SELECTIVITY BEST = MOST SELECTIVE	MBA DRESS BEST = MOST CASUAL	MBA JOB SATISFACTION	
BEST 10 / WORST 1	8	7	4	3	9	BEST 10 / WORST 1

THE SCOOP

The beginning of ARCO, some 130-plus years ago, wasn't particularly noteworthy. Charles Lockhart and his partners founded the Atlantic Petroleum Storage Company in 1865 to store and transport crude and refined oils. In 1870, the company expanded into processing oil, but John D. Rockefeller's Standard Oil swallowed the company in 1874. Rockefeller's monopoly was dissolved via Supreme Court case in 1911, leaving undistinguished Atlantic on its own, with no crude oil, pipelines, or tankers. Yet, fueled by key discoveries in the American Southwest, Atlantic amassed a fleet of tankers, and set up service stations throughout the eastern part of the United States. In 1963, Atlantic merged with the Richfield Oil Corporation, a leading West Coast gasoline marketer which owned many refineries and production properties. Thus, the Atlantic Richfield Company – or ARCO – was born. Five years later, ARCO and its partner Exxon, struck oil – and lots of it. Drilling into Prudhoe Bay's North Slope, ARCO discovered the largest oil deposit in the Western hemisphere. The steady supply of "black gold" lubricated ARCO's aggressive expansion; the firm bought many smaller outfits. Today, ARCO is the seventh-largest oil company in the world.

ARCO's operations are primarily in the Western half of North America. The company has also established a range of businesses apart from its core operations, most prominent of which is a chain of gas stations called Prestige Stations, which runs the AM/PM convenience store chain. ARCO has more than 1,700 ARCO gas stations in Arizona, California, Nevada, Oregon, and Washington. However, the company has recently divested some of its major non-oil businesses: it sold an 82 percent interest in ARCO Chemical also sold its coal mining operations.

Hitting the oil jackpot at Alaska's Prudhoe Bay turned ARCO into a world energy power, but other oil strikes have been elusive. For decades, ARCO has met with failure when trying to discover new, reliable fuel sources. Since 1996, ARCO has turned a corner. In 1996, ARCO ended a 13-year search for a customer for the big natural gas discovery it made in China by entering into a 20-year deal with the Hong Kong electric power company. The company has also completed a deal with Algeria's state oil company for production from the Rhourde El Baguel field and made several significant natural gas discoveries in Indonesia. ARCO also became a player in the former Soviet Union with two large deals. The good news continued into 1997. ARCO announced in September that a natural gas field that it jointly owns with the Indonesian government is one of the world's biggest finds of its nature this decade. ARCO recently announced a plan to develop a new oil oilfield named Alpine on the Alaska North Slope. ARCO expects this field to yield 250 to 300 million barrels of oil over its lifetime.

Despite its turnaround and heady optimism, ARCO, like the rest of the oil industry, engaged in sizeable layoffs during the last few years. In 1997, the company laid off 3700 employees, including 1300 from its Dallas office. Due to slumping worldwide energy prices, the company announced it will again cut its workforce by an unspecified number by the end of 1998 in order to slash its operating costs. William Wade, ARCO's president, also announced that he will be retiring, after less than a year on the job.

GETTING HIRED

An MBA may enter ARCO as a Strategic Planning Analyst, Treasury Financial Analyst, Performance Analyst, or as a Marketing Analyst in either the Corporate Finance group or in one of the operating company finance groups. The most common locations for MBAs are in Los Angeles (corporate headquarters), Anchorage (oil and gas), Houston (oil and gas), and London (oil and gas). But from those common starting points, career paths vary. Careers often "cross functional, operating unit, and corporate lines," insiders say.

ARCO has a three-tiered interview process, according to insiders. Candidates interview with HR, the management of the group applied to, and potential colleagues. The three groups get together to discuss the potential candidates. For MBAs, ARCO hires about 20 full-time employees and 20 summer interns. The buzzword around ARCO is creativity, so "if you can present or discuss anything innovative you may have done which falls into the 'bright ideas' category then this will be a strong plus in your favor," insiders report. The reviews for the summer MBA intern program are laudatory. "Outstanding," one participant says. "A great summer experience," says another. One participant notes that ARCO was "dynamic" and that

MBA Job Seekers: Receive free e-mailed job postings matching your interests & qualifications! Register at www.VaultReports.com

VAULT REPORTS™

www.vaultreports.com

405

there were "lots of transfers and opportunities for advancement." ARCO uses the summer MBA students for corporate planning, finance/planning, and into all of its operating companies.

OUR SURVEY SAYS

Perhaps it's the California sunshine that puts everybody in a good mood, but whatever the reason, workers at ARCO are extremely pleased with their company. Employees find that ARCO is "people-oriented," "sensitive," and "a great company to work for." Why all the raves? For starters, ARCO "is a very flat, open organization and a friendly place to work." To illustrate that point, insiders report that junior employers are encouraged to interact with top-level managers. "The CEO of (spin-off company) Vastar and an Executive Vice-President of Atlantic Richfield work in my building, and I stand in line and chat with them every day in the lunch room," one such employee reports. Insiders also like that ARCO is fostering a risk-taking environment. "ARCO is trying to encourage people to take risks, be adventurous and creative with no fear of blame if it doesn't work out: one senior manager once said, 'If you're not making mistakes, you're not trying hard enough," a source says.

In a winning pro-worker morale strategy, ARCO offers superb pay and benefits, with reasonable hours. "ARCO has always been a pay-and-benefit leader, subscribing to the theory that this practice attracts strong people. In recent years we have broadened the band, but I think we are still in the top quartile of other exploration and production (E&P) companies," an insider says. Echoing this comment, one insider says: "We have excellent medical and dental benefits, and we have a 401(k) plan that is the envy of my friends in other companies." ARCO also offers a 9/80 schedule, which means workers can opt to work 80 hours over 9 days so they can take every other Friday off. "We have a very relaxed easy-going work environment," a contact reports. The company recently adopted a casual dress code at its Los Angeles headquarters.

To order a 10- to 20-page Vault Reports Employer Profile on Atlantic Richfield (ARCO) call 1-888-JOB-VAULT or visit www.VaultReports.com

The full Employer Profile includes detailed information on ARCO's departments, recent developments and transactions, hiring and interview process, plus what employees really think about culture, pay, work hours and more.

AT&T

Telecommunications

32 Avenue of the Americas
New York, NY 10013-2412
(212) 387-5400
www.att.com

LOCATIONS

New York, NY (HQ)
Locations in all 50 states and in every country in the world

DEPARTMENTS

Accounting & Finance
Applied Engineering
Information Systems
International Business
Marketing & Sales
Research & Development
Software Development
Wireless Communications

THE STATS

Annual Revenues: $51.3 billion (1997)
No. of Employees: 113,000 (worldwide)
Stock Symbol: T (NYSE)
CEO: Michael Armstrong

KEY COMPETITORS

- America Online
- Ameritech
- British Telecom
- Deutsche Telekom
- GTE
- MCI WorldCom
- Sprint

THE BUZZ

What MBAs are saying
about AT&T

- "Too big, too immobile for the industry"
- "Stodgy and slow"
- "Still on top of the telecom world"
- "Coming or going?"

UPPERS

- Flexible work schedules
- Telecommuting
- Access to latest technology

DOWNERS

- Excessive bureaucracy
- Overwhelming size

EMPLOYMENT CONTACT

AT&T Resume Scanning Center
1200 Peachtree Street
Promenade I, Room 7075
Atlanta, GA 30309
(212) 387-5400
attjobs@hrdiv.att.com

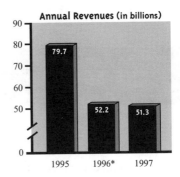

Annual Revenues (in billions)

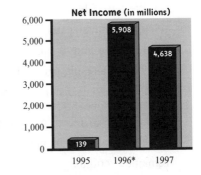

Net Income (in millions)

Employees (in thousands)

* Reflects spin-offs

	MBA HOURS BEST = SHORTEST HOURS	MBA PAY BEST = HIGHEST PAY	MBA SELECTIVITY BEST = MOST SELECTIVE	MBA DRESS BEST = MOST CASUAL	MBA JOB SATISFACTION	
BEST 10 ↑ ⋮ WORST 1	6	4	4	7	7	BEST 10 ↑ ⋮ WORST 1

VAULT REPORTS™

THE SCOOP

In 1876, Alexander Graham Bell announced his revolutionary invention with the words, "Mr. Watson, come here, I want you!" American Telephone and Telegraph – first known as American Bell – has been making the world a smaller place ever since. The company scooped-up Western Electric, the largest U.S. maker of electrical equipment, and dominated the telephone industry until 1968, when the FCC broke up its monopoly to allow competitors like MCI into the long-distance arena. Anti-trust litigation forced the company's historic break-up in 1984; as a result, seven "Baby Bells" were established, while AT&T was allowed to keep its hold on the long-distance market.

In the wake of recent market deregulation, AT&T once again split up in 1996, this time into three separate companies: AT&T, NCR, and Lucent Technologies. This move allows the remaining company – AT&T – to concentrate on new communications opportunies such as cellular phone services, Internet access (through the company's WorldNet service), and personal communications operations like e-mail.

In June 1998, AT&T took its biggest step towards universal telecommunications service (just like the old days) by purchasing the Colorado-based Tele-Communications Inc., the nation's largest cable television provider for $48 billion ($37.3 billion in cash and stock and the assumption of $11 billion in debt). Even though critics have suggested that AT&T overpaid and that it will take years for both companies to implement the necessary technology, AT&T is hoping to transmit local and long-distance telephone service, high-speed Internet access, and cable television over a superefficient network based on TCI's existing infrastructure. Also, the merger paves the way for AT&T to move more aggressively into providing local phone service. The company – and others who want into the local markets – have complained that despite the 1996 Telecommunications Act, which was supposed to open local service to competition, local companies have not cooperated in leasing it facilities needed to provide services. Now, AT&T can use TCI's cable facilities – which may be good news for both itself and consumers.

GETTING HIRED

AT&T hires MBAs into marketing, product management, finance, treasury, strategic planning and operations management. The tracks for business school grads are somewhat confusing, especially since the company continually reorganizes. One insider points out that a couple of years ago, when she participated in the Global Leadership Development Program (GLDP): "It's somewhat concerning that AT&T has six "fast track" programs." It's also somewhat confusing that AT&T is comprised of many different organizations, such as its long distance arm, its on-line services. However, insiders also note that most of these organizations are eager to hire and promote MBAs. Says one insider: "the organization needs MBA skills. There's lots of opportunity to advance." Says another MBA insider, who spent an internship as a regional marketing manager: "It was definitely a real project, plus there was an interest in injecting some MBA perspective into the organization."

MBAs report generally casual interviews. "The interview was informal, mainly about my work experience and its applicability, and my thoughts about the industry" says one recent summer hire. Says one MBA who went through two rounds (including one on-campus): "Both were informal and casual, asking about prior experiences, assignments and my interests."

OUR SURVEY SAYS

AT&T is described as having a casual and relaxed atmosphere that stresses teamwork. "It was very informal, with an open door policy." Says another: "The people are for the most part genuinely friendly and willing to help out with a problem, even if it's not their problem." This informal atmosphere extends to a generally casual dress code, flexible hours, and great telecommuting options. Reports one insider about the dress code: "I would say 99 percent of the locations have casual business dress on Fridays. At about 75 percent of the locations, you have business casual every day, unless you have a special meeting." Flexible hours? "You can

MBA Job Seekers: Receive free e-mailed job postings matching your interests & qualifications! Register at www.VaultReports.com

VAULT REPORTS™

411

www.vaultreports.com

come in anytime between 7 and 9:30. They also have a compressed workweek program where you work 40 hours in four hours in four days and get a day off every week, or work 80 hours in 9 days and get a day off every two weeks." And as for telecommuting, more than 28,000 of the company's employees telecommute regularly.

But make no mistake about it – AT&T is a big company. Just because people are willing to help doesn't mean the system speeds things along, insiders tell us. "It's very bureaucratic," says one insider. "It's hard to get to do what you really want to do." Says a former employee: "It took forever to make a decision." And with the big-company culture comes some politics. "There is some resentment of young hires by others because it is perceived that we are on the 'fast track' and get more perks. I'm not sure that that's untrue, but I don't think that they need to resent us for it."

Perks at AT&T are plentiful. Of course, there's the free long distance. One former employee reports receiving the first $35 per month free, and a 50/50 split with the company for the next $65. Another reports discounts up to $67.50 a month. The company also sponsors a stock purchase plan that lets employees buy its stock at "15 percent below the market." Pay is considered above average, "but consulting and I-banking salaries you won't draw. On the other hand, you won't be working those crazy hours either."

Insiders report that the MBA summer AT&T experience allows plenty of opportunity to reach out and touch senior managers. Says one: "There was lots of contact. There were several sessions with senior management." Reports another: "There was lots of expsosure to vice presidents and above, and access to division-level managers." And another: "There were frequent meetings with senior management and opportunities to initiate new sales and marketing programs."

"It's very bureaucratic. It's hard to get to do what you really want to do."

– AT&T insider

MBA Job Seekers: Receive free e-mailed job postings matching
your interests & qualifications! Register at www.VaultReports.com

VAULT
REPORTS™

413

www.vaultreports.com

BankAmerica Corp.

Banking

401 N. Tryon Street
Charlotte, NC 28255
www.bankamerica.com
(704) 386-5000

LOCATIONS

Charlotte, NC (HQ)
More than 4800 branches in 22 states
and the District of Columbia

DEPARTMENTS

Corporate Finance
Finance and Accounting
Information Technology
Investment Banking
Operations
Public Finance

THE STATS

Total Assets: $572 billion (1998)
No. of Employees: 200,000 (worldwide)
No. of Offices: 1,965 (U.S)
Stock Symbol: BAC (NYSE)
CEO: Hugh McColl

KEY COMPETITORS

- American Express
- Chase Manhattan
- Citibank/Citigroup
- First Union
- J.P. Morgan
- Wells Fargo

 THE BUZZ
What MBAs are saying
about BankAmerica

- "Mammoth"
- "Aggressive, acquisitive"
- "Not high-profile on campus"
- "Read NationsBank"

VAULT
REPORTS™
www.vaultreports.com

UPPERS

+ Free accounts
+ Bonus checks for innovation
+ NationsBank histroical culture has been un-bureaucratic

DOWNERS

+ Bigger doesn't mean nicer
+ Uncertainty and restructuring because of merger

EMPLOYMENT CONTACT

For NationsBank:

NationsBank Recruiting
401 N. Tryton St.
Charlotte, NC 28255

For BankAmerica:

Recruiting Scanning Operations # 10583
P.O. Box 37000
San Francisco, CA 94137

KEY STATISTICS	
Customer Households	30 million
Business Customers	2 million
U.S. Locations	22 states and DC
U.S. Banking Centers	4,.854
ATMs	Nearly 14,000
International Scope (do business in)	190 countries
Total assets	$572 billion

* Figures at the time NationsBank/
  Bank of America merger

	MBA HOURS BEST = SHORTEST HOURS	MBA PAY BEST = HIGHEST PAY	MBA SELECTIVITY BEST = MOST SELECTIVE	MBA DRESS BEST = MOST CASUAL	MBA JOB SATISFACTION	
BEST 10						BEST 10
WORST 1						WORST 1
	6	4	4	4	4	

THE SCOOP

BankAmerica Corp. is finally living up to its name. Formed by the $43 billion merger of the already large Bank of America and NationsBank, has close to 5000 branches in 22 states and the District of Columbia, the bank is looking to become an even bigger giant through more acquisitions. Before the merger, which was completed in September 1998, Bank of America was the third-largest commercial bank, based in San Francisco and with its major presence in the West. NationsBank, based in North Carolina had a strong presence in the Southeast.

The combined bank is now looking to poke its nose into New England and the eastern Midwest. Officially, NationsBank acquired Bank of America – the combined bank has its headquarters in NationsBank's digs in Charlotte, North Carolina. With 8.1 percent of U.S. bank deposits, and 29 million households it can count on as customers, bank is the second-largest in the nation. However, the merger hasn't been a smooth one. In October 1998, former BankAmerica CEO David Coulter (and then-President of the merged bank) resigned amid a power sturggle with CEO Hugh McColl (who was the former CEO of NationsBank).

Both sides of the banking merger grew through aggressive mergers and acquisitions in the last decade. In the early 1990s, BankAmerica bought out Security Pacific, and made forays into the mortgage origination business, through acquisitions of Minnesota's United Mortgage and New York's Arbor National Holdings. In the fifteen years below the merger, NationsBank had metastasized from a smallish Charlotte-based bank with assets of $12.8 billion to a major player with over $300 billion in assets and operations in 16 states (and the District of Columbia).

Both banks had also been looking to boost their investment banking operations previous to the merger. Bank of America had acquired high-tech I-banking stalwart Robertson Stephens & Company, although the company sold the bank affectionately known as Robbie to BankBoston after the announcement of the merger with NationsBank. In a deal that mirrored Bank of America's, NationsBank had acquired Robertson Stephens competitor Montgomery Securities.

GETTING HIRED

With the merger between NationsBank and Bank of America only being approved by its shareholders in September 1998, the hiring process of the two banks is expected to be run separately for the '98-'99 academic year.

At NationsBank, MBA-level associates are recruited directly by department. One former employee cautions: "Here's a tip. You can't always choose your city. NationsBank will try, but for example if you want to work in high yield bonds, you aren't going to be working in San Francisco."

NationsBank, unsurprisingly, tends to recruit at Southeastern schools, especially at UNC/Chapel Hill and Duke. "Our core schools on the MBA level are Wharton, Chicago, Michigan, Darden and Duke, but we will read a resume from anywhere," says one insider. NationsBank reportedly has "a very disorganized recruitment structure. The on-campus recruiting events are poorly advertised and attended. The recruiters don't seem to follow up. If you want to get hired by NationsBank, you should make a strong independent effort," says one former employee.

MBA-level candidates have two interviews on campus, back to back, then a third interview day in Charlotte. The last day of interviews is the most extensive and stressful, with four to seven interviews in one day, including an HR interview, and time out for lunch. While undergraduates will likely be interviewed by their potential managers, MBA-level associates talk to their potential co-workers and peers. "The interviews are not meant to be stressful," says one recent interviewee. "What they are looking for is the usual stuff, intelligence, leadership and mental horsepower, but also a good personality fit and a real interest in NationsBank."

MBA Job Seekers: Receive free e-mailed job postings matching your interests & qualifications! Register at www.VaultReports.com

VAULT REPORTS™

417

www.vaultreports.com

OUR SURVEY SAYS

BankAmerica Corp. employees who worked for the San Francisco-based Bank of America before the merger with NationsBank have nothing but praise for the bank's on-site job training but caution those looking for a kinder, gentler company. "This used to be an organization where we felt like family," says a manager, but no longer. The company is now "an extremely large retail bank with an extremely large retail bank culture." This shift in the corporate atmosphere has nevertheless fostered an "entrepreneurial" environment in which new employees receive "immediate exposure to clients, upper management, and other bank groups." While some feel that the recent changes have been detrimental to employee morale, others approve of "a new aggressive attitude with an emphasis on teamwork."

NationsBank insiders concur that the culture of NationsBank reflects the personality of hard-charging yet caring ex-Marine CEO Hugh McColl. "NationsBank is very aggressive, and, because the bank is growing so quickly, offers plenty of opportunities. The exposure to top management is gratifying," says one associate. "You can truly feel the 'growth' feeling of NB," echoes a loan officer. "NationsBank culture involves team work, working hard and playing hard. You will not find many jerks in the organization, as they get culled fast," comments one insider. "NationsBank, much more than other banks, is a really go-getter kind of a place. There isn't a lot of bureaucratic bullshit. We are a lean organization." McColl himself promotes this attitude; anyone who saves the bank money will receive a check for 10 percent of the amount saved, delivered by the CEO himself. "People now and again will have Hugh McColl show up on their doorstep with a check for $10,000," one employee says. Employees seem proud of their gruff, rough-and-ready CEO. Many praise "the good senior leadership, especially the CEO" and "our grenade thrower Hugh McColl." "Every year, the senior management, including McColl, goes around to five or six cities and does a presentation where they say how the company is doing and give out the crystal grenade awards."

To order a 50- to 70-page Vault Reports Employer Profile on BankAmerica call 1-888-JOB-VAULT or visit www.VaultReports.com

The full Employer Profile includes detailed information on BankAmerica's departments, recent developments and transactions, hiring and interview process, plus what employees really think about culture, pay, work hours and more.

MBA Job Seekers: Receive free e-mailed job postings matching your interests & qualifications! Register at www.VaultReports.com

VAULT REPORTS™   419

www.vaultreports.com

Cargill

15407 McGinty Rd.
Minnetonka, MN 55440-5625
(612) 742-6000

Consumer Products

LOCATIONS

Minneapolis, MN (HQ)
Nearly 1,000 locations in more than 65 countries worldwide

DEPARTMENTS

Commodity Trading and Processing
Industrial
Financial
    Futures Brokerage
    Global Financial Markets Trading
    Money Market and Foreign Exchange
Trading
    Risk Management Services
    Trade and Structured Finance
    Value Investing

THE STATS

Annual Revenues: $51 billion (1998)
No. of Employees: 80,600 (worldwide)
No. of Offices: 1,000 (worldwide)
A privately-held company
CEO: Ernest S. Micek

KEY COMPETITORS

- Archer Daniels Midland
- ConAgra
- Continental Grain
- Monsanto

THE BUZZ
What MBAs are saying
about Cargill

- "Great firm, no one knows about them"
- "Great company, boring products"
- "Family controlled, career limitations"
- "Secretive"

UPPERS

- High job security
- Friendly Midwestern environment
- Promote-from-within culture
- Strong ethics

DOWNERS

- Not too many perks
- Conservative company culture

EMPLOYMENT CONTACT

Cargill
Human Resources
15407 McGinty Rd.
Minnetonka, MN 55440-5625
(800) 741-7431 (job hotline)

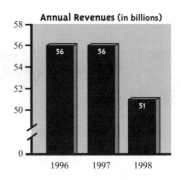

Annual Revenues (in billions)

1996	1997	1998
56	56	51

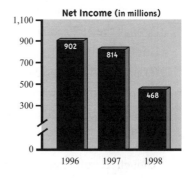

Net Income (in millions)

1996	1997	1998
902	814	468

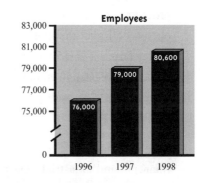

Employees

1996	1997	1998
76,000	79,000	80,600

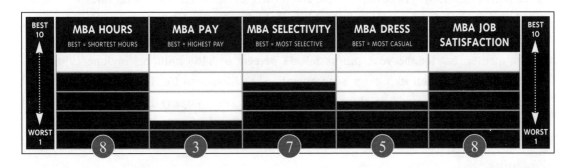

	MBA HOURS BEST = SHORTEST HOURS	MBA PAY BEST = HIGHEST PAY	MBA SELECTIVITY BEST = MOST SELECTIVE	MBA DRESS BEST = MOST CASUAL	MBA JOB SATISFACTION	
BEST 10 ... WORST 1	8	3	7	5	8	BEST 10 ... WORST 1

MBA Job Seekers: Receive free e-mailed job postings matching
your interests & qualifications! Register at www.VaultReports.com

VAULT REPORTS™

www.vaultreports.com

421

THE SCOOP

Going public may be popular with washed-up celebs booked on morning talk shows and ambitious Internet wizards in garage-based startups. But Cargill, the ninth-largest corporation in the United States and the third-largest food company in the world, prefers to keep things private – it's been privately owned for over 130 years. The bull market muscling its way through the 1990s makes an initial public offering extremely tempting, true, and many Cargill heirs are mindful of that fact – and eager to cash in. But cooler management heads have thus far prevailed, and the Minnesota-based conglomerate has yet to emerge into the light of public scrutiny and investment. However, in July 1998, the company embarked on a name and image-recognition campaign, hiring a Minneapolis ad agency to launch television and print ads in 1999.

Though Cargill may lack a stock exchange listing, it's got plenty of other assets. The company's annual sales top $50 billion, drawn from its businesses as an international marketer, processor and distributor of agricultural, food, financial and industrial products. The company operates all over the globe, with major facilities in Asia, Europe, and Latin America. From turkey farming to steel, Minneapolis-based Cargill is the "biggest company you've never heard of." For prospective employees who have found their way to low-profile Cargill, the company offers a stable and self-consciously ethical alternative to the sometimes volatile and cutthroat dealings of the rest of corporate America.

Cargill divides its operations into three major groups: commodity trading and processing, financial, and industrial. Despite extremely volatile commodities prices, Cargill posted three consecutive record profits from 1994 to 1996 ($571 million in 1994, $671 million in 1995 and $902 million in 1996). However, revenue and profits leveled off in 1997, with sales stalling at $56 billion and profits dropping to $814 million. And in the first half of 1998, profits dropped precipitously, falling 74 percent from 1997 first-half earnings. The company rebounded in the fourth quarter, but for the year, profits fell 43 percent to $468 million. In June 1998, the company agreed to sell its foreign seed operations to Monsanto Co. for $1.4 billion. Still, Cargill retains a commanding share of its markets. The company handles 25 percent of America's grain exports, one-fifth of the country's corn-milling capacity and one-fifth of the nation's cattle slaughtering. Moo!

GETTING HIRED

MBAs have three major career paths to choose from in Cargill: Strategy & Business Development (SBD), Financial Markets Group (FMG) or Cargill Foods marketing management. All three of these programs have career tracks that lead into general management. But, insiders say, "SBD is clearly a fast-track program." SBD also accepts "high-potential managers within Cargill (who do not have an MBA)" employees report, but "does not hire undergraduates as a general rule of thumb." Cargill hires from one to three MBAs each year into FMG. SBD hires about 10 MBAs a year, according to insiders. Cargill Foods hires MBAs for specific functional needs.

Most MBAs go through a screening interview (either on-campus or by phone) and then are brought to Minnesota for an all-day affair. SBD candidates participate in a "Super Saturday"; the Friday evening before, they are taken to a fancy restaurant in Minneapolis to schmooze with company execs. Cargill has summer internships in most of its departments. However, these are mostly aimed at college students, not MBAs, because Cargill has specific training and career track programs for recently graduated MBAs.

OUR SURVEY SAYS

SBD hires start on one year field assignments to give them a hands-on feel for one of the company's businesses. After that comes a two-year tenure as business analyst, which involves working on financial strategy projects, such as one of Cargill's frequent M&A targets. Afterwards, analysts are promoted to project team leader. At the end of the program, SBD

MBA Job Seekers: Receive free e-mailed job postings matching your interests & qualifications! Register at www.VaultReports.com

VAULT REPORTS™
www.vaultreports.com

423

graduates get placed into management positions on the basis of a placement search. Says one employee in the program: "The pace of work at SBD can be intense, but so is the learning and the skill development."

Cargill is "not for everyone," its employees report. "It's a Midwestern culture, very much interested in working smart and working hard." "I would describe the culture as very conservative and old-fashioned at times," says one employee. "There are certain areas of business that Cargill has allowed itself to fall behind in, like human resources and technology." For those who can deal with a less modern approach, there are benefits. Insiders say that "the company has always emphasized the importance of maintaining a strong code of ethics. The company is very loyal to its employees." This loyalty translates to a very real benefit: "Layoff is a word that is not even in Cargill's vocabulary." Loyalty runs both ways: job satisfaction at Cargill runs high. One employee has worked there "for almost eight years and I can tell you that since the start there has never been a boring moment. Things are so flexible that at any time there will be something new and interesting to do."

Despite its large size, employees say "the company is like one big family." "Everyone is addressed on a first-name basis," says one insider. Some employees appreciate the mix of Midwest friendliness with a dose of seriousness: "It's very down to earth," says one FMG employee. Current employees, however, say that "Cargill's not really a perks-based company." Perks for Cargill employees seem to have more to do with work than money or objects: "For me the perks are all of the opportunities that exist," rationalizes one employee. And, for a $56 billion company, "the pay's not great." Employee estimates run from "industry standard" to "below industry standard," or the more tactful "competitive for Minneapolis." Employees aren't bitter, claiming that "the job security more than makes up for it." While the pay may not be "astronomical," neither are the hours "too bad." One employee says, "You are expected to put in 40 hours a week." Another says it is "closer to 55." The average appears to be somewhere in the range of "40 to 50 hours per week." One employee with FMG, however, reports that you should "get ready to work your ass off – no less than 10 hours a day." But overall, insiders say, "No one at Cargill is killing himself like someone on Wall Street. It's a lot more relaxed."

To order a 50- to 70-page Vault Reports Employer Profile on Cargill call 1-888-JOB-VAULT or visit www.VaultReports.com

The full Employer Profile includes detailed information on Cargill's departments, recent developments and transactions, hiring and interview process, plus what employees really think about culture, pay, work hours and more.

MBA Job Seekers: Receive free e-mailed job postings matching your interests & qualifications! Register at www.VaultReports.com

VAULT REPORTS™
www.vaultreports.com

425

Chase Manhattan

Commercial Bank

270 Park Avenue
New York, NY 10017-2798
(212) 270-6000
www.chase.com/on-campus

LOCATIONS

New York, NY (HQ)
Other offices in 39 states and 50 countries

BUSINESSES

Global Inv. Banking and Corporate Lending
Global Asset Mngmnt and Private Banking]
Global Markets
Middle Markets
Chase Capital Partners
Chase Bank of Texas
Credit Cards
National Consumer Finance
Retail Payments of Investments
Mortgage Banking
Community Development
Global Services
Information Technology and Operations

THE STATS

Annual Revenues: $30.4 billion (1997)
No. of Employees: 69,000 (worldwide)
Stock Symbol: CMB (NYSE)
CEO: Walter V. Shipley

KEY COMPETITORS

- BankAmerica
- Citigroup
- J.P. Morgan
- Merrill Lynch

THE BUZZ
What MBAs are saying about Chase

- "My ATM card bank"
- "Wannabe I-bank"
- "Behemoth"
- "Leader in bank debt"

UPPERS

- Stock options
- Company gyms
- Incentive bonuses
- Tuition reimbursement
- Extensive training program
- On-site back-up child care

DOWNERS

- Low pay for finance
- Trouble building I-banking businesses

EMPLOYMENT CONTACT

University & Student Relations
One Chase Manhattan Plaza
27th Floor
New York, NY 10081
Fax: (212) 552-4884

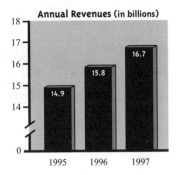

Annual Revenues (in billions)

1995: 14.9
1996: 15.8
1997: 16.7

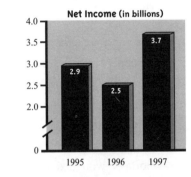

Net Income (in billions)

1995: 2.9
1996: 2.5
1997: 3.7

Employees

1995: 72,696
1996: 67,785
1997: 69,033

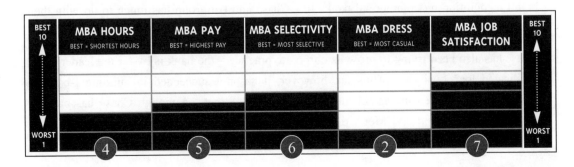

	MBA HOURS BEST = SHORTEST HOURS	MBA PAY BEST = HIGHEST PAY	MBA SELECTIVITY BEST = MOST SELECTIVE	MBA DRESS BEST = MOST CASUAL	MBA JOB SATISFACTION	
	4	5	6	2	7	

BEST 10 — WORST 1

THE SCOOP

Today's Chase Manhattan was formed in 1996 through the merger of two financial giants: Chemical Bank and the "old" Chase Manhattan. The merger makes the new company the largest banking institution in the U.S. with over $350 billion in assets and clients in more than 180 countries around the world.

The earliest Chase predecessor was The Manhattan Company, a private firm chartered in 1799 to supply water to New York City. A clause in the bill which created the water company, which Aaron Burr had the New York State legislature, led to the establishment of the Bank of The Manhattan Company. Burr, an anti-Federalist, saw his bank as a rival of the New York City office of Alexander Hamilton's powerful Bank of the United States. The antagonism of these two early financiers raged until 1804, when Burr challenged Hamilton to a duel. Hamilton was mortally wounded in the duel, and Burr's reputation and political career were effectively destroyed. Happily, the pistols in the duel were perserved – and are part of Chase's historical collection.

By 1930, Chase had become the world's largest bank thanks to a close relationship to the Rockefeller family. Chase's latest partner, Chemical Bank, became the third-largest bank in the U.S. through its 1992 merger with Manufacturers Hanover. While the Chemical-Hanover merger was a rocky one, the company learned its lesson. The more recent Chase-Chemical marriage has had a relatively smooth transition period.

Chase is trying to build its brand name to build stronger bonds with customers as it competes with Citigroup for worldwide name recognition. In 1997, Chase spent more than $60 million on an advertising campaign which touted it was "The Relationship Bank." The emphasis on brand recognition by commercial banks like Chase and Citigroup has much to do with their strategies of offering one-stop supermarket-style services for consumers.

Chase has also been trying to grow its corporate practice – the bank is by far the leader in the syndicated loan business. Thus far, however, it has not succeeded in building I-banking practices that threaten the established banks on Wall Street. Although Chase has built up respectable junk bond and M&A practices, it has lagged in stock underwriting and equity research.

GETTING HIRED

Chase Manhattan launched an extensive web site for career opportunities in the fall of 1998, – located at www.chase.com/on-campus. Applicants should consult the web site to obtain the regular mail or e-mail address of the proper recruiter. Prospective employees can also post their resumes online. Chase also conducts on-campus recruiting throughout the U.S. The company offers programs for MBAs in Global Investment Banking, Global Markets and Consumer Banking, and has been among the most active banks (I-banking or commercial) in recruiting and hiring business school students in the last couple of years.

Although the company recruits at major business schools, one insider from a top-tier school advises that you "call the bank and set up an appointment to meet with someone informally." That source continues: "The people are very open. And just to simply get placed on the interview schedule, a great deal has to do with who knows your name, do they remember you, have you shown a sincere interest in the bank." Another insider says that "unfortunately, the banking industry requires networking and schmoozing. One really has to go to the information sessions and find opportunities to sell oneself wherever possible."

OUR SURVEY SAYS

From employee contests to a variety of social and charitable events, "there is always something going on at Chase," says one employee. This includes tickets to events such as the U.S. Open and the NIT college basketball tournament. The bank's perks don't stop with events – there's dinner and taxi service for those who stay after 8 p.m., and free breakfast and snacks during a 10-week training period for new hires. Also, the company's headquarters provides perks like a company gym. Pay is described as "adequate, but probably not as high as salaries available to financial managers in industrial companies."

MBA Job Seekers: Receive free e-mailed job postings matching your interests & qualifications! Register at www.VaultReports.com

VAULT REPORTS™
www.vaultreports.com

429

The company's international scope helps it to assemble "one of the most diverse workforces anywhere, let alone in the banking industry." Chase Manhattan has also introduced "flextime," a scheduling option that "helps a lot when it comes to having two small children," according to one working mother. (The firm also provides on-site back-up child care.) One insider notes that "statistically, white males still hold a large majority of the management positions. But there are so many positions that numerically there are many women and minorities in management."

Employees are satisfied at Chase. One financial analyst remarks it's a "good experience without completely insane hours." "For it's size, there is little to no back stabbing. Everyone is busy and doing their job. There is some politics, but it is really not bad," says one insider who joined Chase from a bulge-bracket I-banking firm. At Chase headquarters at 270 Park Avenue in New York, it's business dress always; other locations have business casual codes. Says one MBA intern: "It's a friendly culture, with generalist training for new people." Everyone at the company appreciates the "unparalleled reputation" that the Chase name carries to "the far corners of the earth."

To order a 50- to 70-page Vault Reports Employer Profile on Chase Manhattan call 1-888-JOB-VAULT or visit www.VaultReports.com

The full Employer Profile includes detailed information on Chase's departments, recent developments and transactions, hiring and interview process, plus what employees really think about culture, pay, work hours and more.

"Just to simply get placed on the interview schedule, a great deal has to do with who knows your name, do they remember you, have you shown a sincere interest in the bank."

– Chase insider

Clorox

Consumer Products

P.O. Box 24305
Oakland, CA 94623
(510) 271-7000
Fax: (510) 208-2673
www.clorox.com

LOCATIONS

Oakland, CA (HQ)
Pleasanton, CA
As well as 18 U.S. manufacturing locations
and 24 foreign manufacturing locations

DEPARTMENTS

Brand Management
Finance & Accounting
Information Services
Marketing Research
Product Supply
Purchasing
Research and Development

THE STATS

Annual Revenues: $2.7 billion (1998)
No. of Employees: 6,600
Year Founded: 1913, Oakland
Stock Symbol: CLX (NYSE)
CEO: G. Craig Sullivan

KEY COMPETITORS

- Amway
- Colgate-Palmolive
- Lever Brothers
- Procter & Gamble
- S.C. Johnson

 THE BUZZ
What MBAs are saying
about Clorox

- "Cool people, but dull products"
- "It's OK if you want to sell bleach"
- "Good for marketing majors"
- "Nerdy, solid training in marketing"

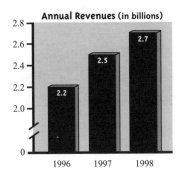

Annual Revenues (in billions)

UPPERS

- Profit sharing
- Philanthropic company
- Good opportunities for women and minorities

DOWNERS

- Conservative corporate culture
- Up-or-out pressure in brand management

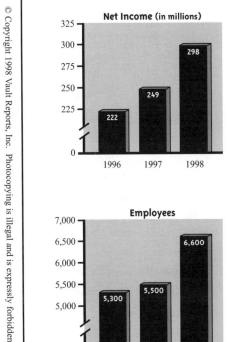

Net Income (in millions)

EMPLOYMENT CONTACT

The Clorox Company
Attn: Corporate Staffing, Dept. INJCM
P.O. Box 24305
Oakland, CA 94623
Fax: (510) 208-2673

Employees

	MBA HOURS BEST = SHORTEST HOURS	MBA PAY BEST = HIGHEST PAY	MBA SELECTIVITY BEST = MOST SELECTIVE	MBA DRESS BEST = MOST CASUAL	MBA JOB SATISFACTION	
	6	6	8	6	7	

MBA Job Seekers: Receive free e-mailed job postings matching
your interests & qualifications! Register at www.VaultReports.com

VAULT REPORTS™
www.vaultreports.com

433

THE SCOOP

In 1913, five California entrepreneurs invested $100 apiece to make bleach using water from the salt ponds around San Francisco Bay. The next year, the company acquired a plant in Oakland, a diamond-shaped logo, and a corporate name derived from the words "chlorine" and "sodium hydroxide." While Clorox's bleach and diamond logo are still the company's best-known assets, capturing 62 percent of the U.S. market, the company has been acquiring other well-known cleaners and insecticides since the late 1960s. Pine-Sol, Soft Scrub, S.O.S Pads, Liquid-Plumr, and Black Flag are all Clorox brands – as are products as diverse as Kingsford charcoal briquets, Fresh Step cat litter, and Hidden Valley salad dressing. With more than 40 well-known brand names, brand management is crucial for Clorox, which has lately emphasized growth in its laundry, household cleaning, and insecticide businesses. The company also makets Brita water filtration systems, a product that has enjoyed rapidly increasing sales over the last few years. Part of Clorox's strategy for the 1990s has been expansion overseas, especially in Latin America and Asia. International sales now make up 18 percent of Clorox's total revenue. And the firm continues to churn out new products: in its 1998 fiscal year, Clorox shot out 41 new ones.

Financially, Clorox has also pleased shareholders in recent years, Clorox profits have consistently exceeded analyst's expectations, a happy state of financial affairs that has driven Clorox's stock price skyward. In its 1998 fiscal year, the company posted sales of $2.7 billion, up 8 percent from 1997. Earnings, at close to $300 million, jumped 19 percent. Clorox has an internal measure of performance called the Clorox Value Measure, adopted in 1993 to correlate with stockholder value. That measure grew 20 percent in 1996, and a still-not-bad 10 percent in 1997. Without much hype, Clorox has steadily risen through the ranks of the *Fortune* 1000, by nurturing its flagship brand and acquiring companies that complement its core competencies. German consumer products giant Henkel has paid attention to Clorox's healthy earnings since 1974. Henkel now owns 30 percent of Clorox stock, and the two firms share research efforts and R&D knowledge.

GETTING HIRED

Those looking to find positions as associate marketing managers with a Clorox brand unit, beware of stiff competition: "The brand management program generally only recruits MBA's from top business schools," says one insider. "I am aware of only a couple of instances in my nine years at Clorox that we have hired undergraduates into brand." One summer brand intern remarks that the brand personnel "are all intelligent, highly motivated individuals from top MBA schools." Another contact says that although senior management in the company continues to be male-heavy, "I would say we hire more women than men in marketing these days by a slight margin."

Clorox lists its recruiting schedule on its web site, located at www.clorox.com. The company's extensive career web pages also allow applicants to e-mail resumes, and sift through job opportunities by department and qualifications. Says one brand employee: "During the interview, marketing questions will definitely be asked to launch new hypothetical products." An insider says that the interview process begins with a two-hour interview with a senior brand manager. "If you pass that interview, it will be recommended in the senior marketing ranks that the candidate be re-invited for a whole day interview among different marketing folks."

OUR SURVEY SAYS

Insiders describe Clorox's culture as driven by specific goals, and, as such, more constrained and less freewheeling than some of its West Coast counterparts. "We are a very analytical organization, and pride ourselves in knowing just about everything there is to know about our business from a quantitative numbers standpoint," reports one employee. "It is an atmosphere of strong direction and purpose," says an insider in research and development. "We are results oriented – hitting the number – but we are willing to take appropriate business risks," says another. One marketing insider puts it more bluntly: "Either you make your numbers on a

MBA Job Seekers: Receive free e-mailed job postings matching
your interests & qualifications! Register at www.VaultReports.com

VAULT
REPORTS™
www.vaultreports.com

435

fairly consistent basis, or you should start looking for employment elsewhere." This insider says there is "something of an up-or-out policy" in brand. With respect to this emphasis on goals, "a lot of people in the industry have compared our culture to that of P&G," says one insider. Those familiar with Procter & Gamble's notoriously bureaucratic and professional culture will know that being compared to P&G isn't exactly like winning a beauty contest: "The work culture is very conservative – not very dynamic but still interesting," notes one marketing insider. Says one insider, "I think Clorox is a satisfying place if you can adapt to the somewhat East Coast style of management." And yet another reports that "as with most corporations, Clorox has its issues with respect to bureaucracy, particularly with respect to getting appropriate sign-off on special projects and other brand management decisions."

Although Clorox may have an "East Coast" style of management and culture, it is West Coast progressive in certain aspects. "There's very good representation of both women and minorities," says one insider in a function with close contact with brand employees. "Half of my brand manager counterparts are women, with about the same proportion in junior marketing roles. Half of my brand manager counterparts are members of ethnic minorities." "We had an African-American vice president who left the company in the past year to head up another company," another insider remarks. "I think we have room for improvement when it comes to ethnic minorities, but we have ample representation from which to draw." "We're a pretty diverse group of people, with many women and minorities in key positions," says one R&D worker. One marketing insider remarks that the company has "great female role models." "I know several women in management positions and we now have a woman on the Clorox board," says another employee. "She got huge applause at the yearly meeting."

Employees are also proud of the company's community involvement. "Clorox is very active in community affairs," boasts one. "During the annual United Way fund raising drives that occur late each year, Clorox has ranked No. 1 in total contributions the last five years of all Bay Area companies. I think that says something about our company and its people." "They encourage community service and participation in outside activities," says another. "They want you to have a life outside of work." "It's almost an expectation that Clorox people will personally get involved in some non-profit venture (schools, churches, community activities, etc.)," says one employee. "I think that's one of the most important things about us that really sets us apart from most other organizations."

Clorox is also trying to instill a more entrepreneurial atmosphere. "We tend to give people significant levels of responsibility at relatively early points in their career," says one insider. "There is a strong push for creativity. Creativity meetings, programs and incentives are in place rewarding unusual or creative thinking. Activities like off-site team-building and creativity seminars are common." Summing up the mix of old-business and forward-looking culture, one employee says that "you have to consider that Clorox is working from a very conservative background. That being said, it is my perception that our current management is very open-minded about evolving the company into something that is successful and sustainable into the next decade."

To order a 10- to 20-page Vault Reports Employer Profile on Clorox call 1-888-JOB-VAULT or visit www.VaultReports.com

The full Employer Profile includes detailed information on Clorox's departments, recent developments and transactions, hiring and interview process, plus what employees really think about culture, pay, work hours and more.

MBA Job Seekers: Receive free e-mailed job postings matching your interests & qualifications! Register at www.VaultReports.com

VAULT REPORTS™

437

www.vaultreports.com

Deloitte Consulting

Management Consulting

1633 Broadway
New York, NY 10019
(212) 492-4000
www.dtcg.com

**Deloitte &
Touche LLP**

LOCATIONS

New York, NY (HQ)

Atlanta, GA • Boston, MA • Chicago, IL •
Detroit, MI • East Brunswick, NJ • Kansas
City, MO • Los Angeles, CA • Minneapolis,
Minnesota • Parsipanny, NJ • Philadelphia,
PA • Pittsburgh, PA • Phoenix, AZ • Orange
County, CA • Sacramento, CA • San
Francisco, CA • Seattle, WA • San Francisco,
CA • Texas (several offices) • Washington, DC
Numerous offices overseas

KEY COMPETITORS

- Andersen Consulting
- Arthur Andersen
- A.T. Kearney
- Ernst & Young Consulting
- KPMG Consulting
- PricewaterhouseCoopers

MAJOR SERVICES

Strategy Transformation
Process Transformation
Technology Transformation
People Transformation

THE STATS

Annual Revenues: $2.3 billion (1997)
No. of Employees: 2,900
A privately-held company
CEO: J. Michael Cook

THE BUZZ

What MBAs are saying
about Deloitte

- "Good workplace, getting there"
- "Touchy-feely"
- "Unclear mission, unpolished people"
- "Basic"

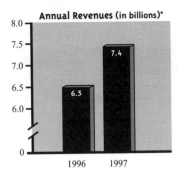

UPPERS

- Unpretentious
- Saturday child care in some locations
- Women's initiative has improved opportunities for women

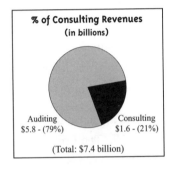

DOWNERS

- Poor treatment by some partners

EMPLOYMENT CONTACT

John Worth
National Director of MBA Recruiting
First Union Capital Center
Suite 1800
Raleigh, NC 27601
Fax: 919-833-3276

*Graphs indicate figures for entire firm

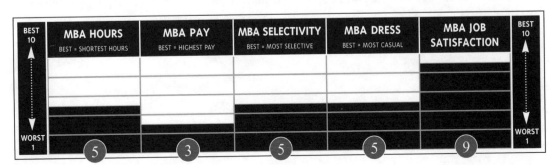

	MBA HOURS	MBA PAY	MBA SELECTIVITY	MBA DRESS	MBA JOB SATISFACTION	
	5	3	5	5	9	

MBA Job Seekers: Receive free e-mailed job postings matching
your interests & qualifications! Register at www.VaultReports.com

VAULT REPORTS™

www.vaultreports.com

439

THE SCOOP

Deloitte & Touche (D&T), one of the Big Five professional services firms, is the American branch of Deloitte Touche Tohmatsu, a global leader in professional services with 59,000 employees in 126 countries. The firm's consulting arm, Deloitte Consulting, has 2900 employees in the U.S. and ranks as one of the largest consulting practices in the industry, exploits the firm's expertise in international business and its global resources. Deloitte Consulting complements its parent company's other competencies, and emphasizes the building long and lasting relationships with its clients; more than 75 percent of its business comes from repeat customers.

D&T's consulting group has grown rapidly in recent years, doubling its revenues from 1995 to 1997. The firm is considered a leader in certain fields such as systems integration consulting. Relationships with software and systems companies like Oracle, AutoTester and SAS Management only enhance D&T's techno-savvy. A recent *ComputerWorld* survey ranked Deloitte Consulting highest among all management consulting firms for systems consulting; its customer relationships and efficiency were praised by respondents. In 1997, about half of Deloitte Consulting's revenues came from management consulting business; half was information technology revenue. The firm expects that its consulting revenues will break $3 billion in 1999.

In 1998, D&T set aside $25 million in an aggressive advertising campaign designed to differentiate it and its consulting arm from the rest of the Big Five. The ads target Andersen as "distracted by infighting," and portray PricewaterhouseCoopers and KPMG as part of an undifferentiated mass. The firm already has a reputation as a nicer place to work than the other Big Five – the firm earned the No. 14 spot in *Fortune* magazine's 1998 100 Best companies to Work for in America list, and was the only Big Five firm to make the list.

GETTING HIRED

Interested MBA applicants should contact the career services offices at their schools for contact information, resume deadlines, interview dates, and recruitment schedules. MBAs can also submit resumes to the firm's human resources department and indicate their department of interest. MBAs with prior experience join the firm as senior consultants. Deloitte Consulting's web site, located at www.dtcg.com, provides instructions on how to go about submitting a resume, as well as recruiting contacts.

MBA applicants should have at least three to five years of relevant business experience. Applicants to Deloitte's management consulting department should have some accounting or business background. Deloitte is growing rapidly and has stepped up its on-campus recruiting efforts; last year, the firm hired 200 MBAs. That process consists of three rounds, as well as a social event at which interviewers observe the candidates in a more relaxed setting.

D&T also offers a summer program for MBAs to work with senior consultants (in 1997, the firm hired more than 100 summer associates). Summer associates report enjoying a "high degree of autonomy" and "immediate project management responsibility."

OUR SURVEY SAYS

Deloitte Consulting likes to emphasize that "experience teaches better than training." The lack of ego is also refreshing, say employees: "People don't go around bragging about where they went to school. The jerk is the exception." While most consultants acknowledge that "we aren't a McKinsey or Andersen," they feel "we are well known." Even though consultants work "intensely demanding schedules," they say that the firm has an "extremely flexible" approach to the ways in which employees structure their time. Deloitte, one employee comments, "respects personal commitments and fosters a better life-work balance than many

MBA Job Seekers: Receive free e-mailed job postings matching your interests & qualifications! Register at www.VaultReports.com

VAULT REPORTS™

441

www.vaultreports.com

of its competitors." Contributing to this balance is Deloitte's "3-4-5" policy: Employees spend three nights on the road, fly back on the fourth day, and spend their fifth day at the home office, ensuring a weekend at home (or at least, in the home city).

Despite this enticing flexibility, "sooner or later, the bureaucracy gets to you," insiders report. One consultant complains that "Deloitte's corporate culture is great, but I don't know where it comes from, because the partners are not a great lot at all. I've worked for a few who are decent, but overall they don't know what you're doing as far as human resources go." Turnover is about 16 percent a year, and "only a few people stay a decade." Workweeks can be "ominously long," and the dress code is "suits, suits, suits all around," except for Fridays, "which are business casual, though not beach bum casual." However, Deloitte Consulting is making a valiant effort in the field of gender diversity. Its "Women's Initiative" has "immensely improved" career prospects for women, as "Deloitte Consulting has become very sensitive to gender and life-style issues." Ethnic diversity is less impressive; one employee comments that "until Deloitte comes up with a Minority Initiative like its Women's Initiative, nothing is going to change." Be that as it may, the firm was named the company of the year by the National Association of Black Management Consultants.

To order a 50- to 70-page Vault Reports Employer Profile on Deloitte Consulting call 1-888-JOB-VAULT or visit www.VaultReports.com

The full Employer Profile includes detailed information on Deloitte's departments, recent developments and transactions, hiring and interview process, plus what employees really think about culture, pay, work hours and more.

"People don't go around
bragging about where
they went to school.
The jerk is the exception."

– *D&T insider*

VAULT
REPORTS™

Ernst & Young Consulting

Management Consulting

787 Seventh Avenue
New York, NY 10019
(212) 773-3000
Fax: (212) 773-6504
www.ey.com

ERNST & YOUNG LLP

LOCATIONS

New York, NY (HQ)
Cleveland, OH
Houston, TX
San Francisco, CA
Washington, DC
As well as over 100 offices nationwide,
and 650 around the world

DEPARTMENTS

Consulting
Financial Advisory Services
Health Care Consulting
People Effectiveness
Performance Improvement
Mergers & Acquisitions

THE STATS

Annual Revenues: $2.7 billion (1997)
No. of Employees: 80,000 (worldwide)
No. of Offices: 678 (worldwide)
A privately held company
Chairman: Philip A. Laskaway

KEY COMPETITORS

- Arthur Andersen
- Andersen Consulting
- Deloitte Consulting
- KPMG Consulting
- PricewaterhouseCoopers

THE BUZZ

What MBAs are saying
about Ernst & Young

- "Technically good"
- "Mid-tier consulting"
- "Plodding"
- "Dime a dozen"

UPPERS

- Training's a blast
- 16 weeks of family leave available to parents
- Daycare facilities
- Tuition reimbursement
- Generous vacation

DOWNERS

- Long work days
- Below average pay
- No private work space

EMPLOYMENT CONTACT

Jeanine Paolicelli
730 Seventh Avenue
New York, NY 10019
(212) 773-1007
Fax: (212) 773-1118

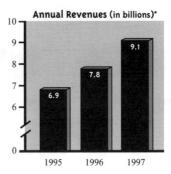

Annual Revenues (in billions)*

% of Revenues by Geography (in billions)

International $4.7 - (52%)   U.S. $4.4 - (48%)

(Total: $9.1 billion)

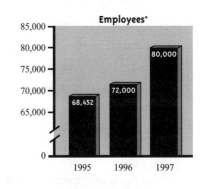

Employees*

*Graphs indicate figures for entire firm

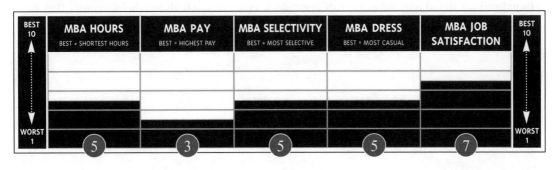

	MBA HOURS BEST = SHORTEST HOURS	MBA PAY BEST = HIGHEST PAY	MBA SELECTIVITY BEST = MOST SELECTIVE	MBA DRESS BEST = MOST CASUAL	MBA JOB SATISFACTION	
BEST 10 / WORST 1	5	3	5	5	7	BEST 10 / WORST 1

VAULT REPORTS™

www.vaultreports.com

THE SCOOP

If you like big firms, you should feel warmly about Ernst & Young. The firm is more than a century old, and is the product of a succession of mergers that started in the 1950s. The current incarnation of Ernst & Young was created from a 1989 merger of two members of what used to be called the Big Eight professional services firms – Arthur Young and Ernst & Whinney. In 1998, Ernst & Young had 82,000 employees in 132 countries around the world.

Ernst & Young currently ranks as the second-largest largest integrated professional services firm in the U.S. Ernst & Young Consulting is a big part of this prominence, with 10,500 professionals. (Total U.S. employment is 29,000.) In the past two years, growth at Ernst & Young Consulting has far outstripped that of the consulting industry as a whole – the consultancy has enjoyed a 35 percent increase in revenue per year for the last few years. In 1996, management consulting revenue exceeded $2 billion.

No doubt this strong growth is influenced by innovations like "Ernie," a popular on-line consulting service for small businesses. Ernie members pay a membership fee, and then can submit their queries to official Ernst & Young consultants via email. Ernst & Young draws on its consulting expertise, and Ernie-users soon get a reasoned and usable answer. Ernst & Young Consulting also uses Ernie to feature "Trend Watch," a survey of most common concerns and questions. Another of E&Y's consulting innovations is the Ernst & Young Entrepreneurial Consulting group. While most of Ernst and Young's clients are big bruisers that earn over $100 million yearly, Entrepreneurial Consulting takes on smaller businesses hungry to grow.

Ernst & Young tried to grow bigger in 1998 by merging with its competitor KPMG Peat Marwick (as it was then called), another Big Six firm. The planned merger, however, foundered on the shoals of European regulatory concerns. (It didn't help matters that the mergers of competitors Price Waterhouse and Coopers & Lybrand was also pending at the time.)

GETTING HIRED

Ernst & Young sets its hiring goals in April of each year, organizing its strategic planning and forming "school teams." Each campus has a Campus Ambassador and Campus Captain. Beginning in 1998, each campus team has been assigned its own budget.

The firm has identified about eight "mega competencies," which include leadership, communication, technology, flexibility and teamwork. Each interviewer focuses on one of two of these competencies. The typical format to identify these skills goes as follows – "Tell me about a situation where you used your (competency) skill. What was your role? What did you do? What happened? What did you learn from this experience?" The candidate is also taken to lunch and evaluated during the meal on cultural fit and interest in Ernst & Young.

In Ernst & Young's consulting competency, case interviews are used on in the Strategic Advisory Services Group. Neither brainteasers nor guesstimates are employed, insiders tell us.

Some offices have "sell days" for MBAs, including the New York and Philadephia offices. At these sell days, the firm "discusses the Accelerated Solutions Environment, our unique approach to decision making." The attendees are taking through exercises where they discuss the sort of workplace they want to be. After a tour of E&Y, at the end of the day, comes the "breakthrough decision," when candidates learn how to break a wooden board with their hand, "meant to mirror their breakthrough career decision, that they should work at Ernst & Young." Firm-wide, about half of offerees opt to work at Ernst.

OUR SURVEY SAYS

Ernst & Young's size brings both advantages and disadvantages. On the less positive side, some consultants indicate that Ernst possesses a conservative culture. "I think it's a very conservative firm in terms of the way management acts, in the way projects are handled," says

MBA Job Seekers: Receive free e-mailed job postings matching your interests & qualifications! Register at www.VaultReports.com

VAULT REPORTS™
www.vaultreports.com

447

one consultant disapprovingly. Another contact notes: "It's a large firm, and if you're ambitious, it can be tough sometimes." The same contact continues: "[Ernst is] great if you want to settle down, but if you want to be making the most money of anyone your age, or if you want to do everything that interests you, you might get frustrated. It's more structured. You get assigned to something and that's your project – hopefully you'll like it, 'Cause that's what you'll be doing for a while." Note however, that the rigid structure reported by those working in U.S. offices doesn't necessarily exist in other countries. "In Canada, people do a mix of everything," says one insider, who adds: "In general, U.S. people are much more segmented."

E&Y insiders tend also to comment on the firm's increasing international outlook and encouraging attitudes towards going abroad. One contact notes that 30-40 percent of his office actively chose international assignments, and explains: "It's really encouraged, I guess because of globalization, and they know that a lot of these people would just leave if they couldn't go abroad. It's very easy to transfer between countries." One contact marvels: "On my first business trip ever, I went to Rio!" Another contact on the consulting side recalls an extraordinary assignment: "I went all over the world – you name it, I was there."

Pay doesn't seem to be one of E&Y's strong suits. "As for compensation," one contact tells us, "the general pattern is that you make a fair salary, but nothing spectacular." The same individual notes however, that the pay is "good lifestyle money," and that "you'll never have to beg on the floor of a car dealership for a loan." One former E&Y consultant, however, notes that "to get a big jump in pay, it just would have taken too long." Another ex-consultant says: "The pay was not going to do it for me." Note that, in consulting, there is no overtime and working all night "comes straight out of your salary."

E&Y seems to be taking steps to increase its compensation package. One of our contacts from the financial services side mentions that Ernst & Young plans to institute a better bonus system to lure candidates away from bonus happy jobs in investment banking and elsewhere. Another contact reminds us: "[E&Y is] recruiting at the top business schools, so they must be willing to pay more."

If anything, working at Ernst & Young means a sociable work environment. One contact explains: "In many cases, you've got a huge room of 25 cubicles, and everyone is between the ages of 23 and 29." "It's where I met my boyfriend!" chimes another. Insiders report frequent lunches, and regular soirees with colleagues.

When asked about firm-organized activities, one consultant responds with a rather unsettling comparison: "There aren't as many as Andersen. I've talked to people there, and it almost seems like they want to make their employees a bunch of alcoholics." While perhaps more subdued than its competitors, Ernst & Young has its debauched spots. "There's the training and that's a blast," reports one consultant who elaborates: "Every division has their own form of training. Basically you try and stay awake all day during some kind of class, and then you go out and drink all night."

One source of complaints from consultants is the firm's "utilization" goals, targets that require consultants to bill 80 percent of all hours to clients. The goals are particularly pertinent for individuals at the lower levels, who focus more on project work and less on business development. While not as rigid or demanding as billable hours targets at law firms, consultants still feel the pressure. "They want you to bill those hours!" gripes one consultant. Another consultant levels particular criticism at the utilization goals: "If you're in consulting, when you're working on projects, there's a lot of down time, and then there's the recruiting and other non-chargeable time. Basically, the expectation is that you'll bill out eight hours a day and then do all the other stuff later, and the fact is that the people with the highest utilizations get noticed."

To order a 50- to 70-page Vault Reports Employer Profile on Ernst & Young call 1-888-JOB-VAULT or visit www.VaultReports.com

The full Employer Profile includes detailed information on Ernst & Young's departments, recent developments and transactions, hiring and interview process, plus what employees really think about culture, pay, work hours and more.

MBA Job Seekers: Receive free e-mailed job postings matching your interests & qualifications! Register at www.VaultReports.com

VAULT REPORTS™

449

www.vaultreports.com

Ford Motor

Automotive; Financial Services

The American Road, Room 49
Dearborn, MI 48121
(313)-322-3000
www.ford.com

LOCATIONS

Dearborn, MI (HQ)
Hundreds of other facilities across the U.S.,
many in IL • KY • MI • MO • OH

DEPARTMENTS

Finance • Human Resources • Manufacturing
• Marketing & Sales • Product Engineering •
Process Leadership/Systems • Purchasing •
Research • Environmental/Safety Engineering

THE STATS

Annual Revenues: $153.6 billion (1997)
No. of Employees: 363,900 (worldwide),
189,800 (U.S.)
Stock Symbol: F (NYSE)
CEO: Alex Trotman
% Minority: 22 (in U.S.)
%Male/%Female: 81/19 (in U.S.)

KEY COMPETITORS

- DaimlerChrysler
- General Motors
- Honda
- Hyundai
- Toyota
- Volvo

THE BUZZ

What MBAs are saying
about Ford

- "Best of Detroit"
- "Bad location, bureaucratic"
- "Leading brand name"
- "Good firm, but boring industry"

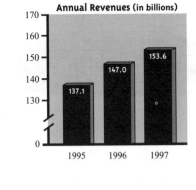

Annual Revenues (in billions)

UPPERS

- Excellent prestige, especially in finance
- Hugely profitable company
- Vroom-vroom!

DOWNERS

- Hierarchical management structure
- Headquarters in depressed area

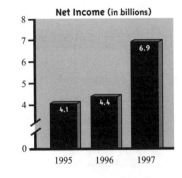

Net Income (in billions)

EMPLOYMENT CONTACT

Malcolm Macdonald
The American Road, Room 49
11th Floor-East Wing
Dearborn, MI 48121
(313)-323-0850

Employees (in thousands)

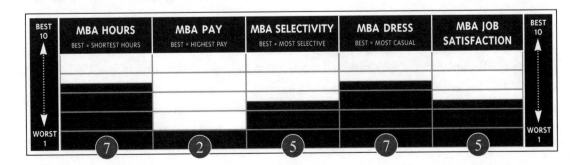

	MBA HOURS BEST = SHORTEST HOURS	MBA PAY BEST = HIGHEST PAY	MBA SELECTIVITY BEST = MOST SELECTIVE	MBA DRESS BEST = MOST CASUAL	MBA JOB SATISFACTION	
BEST 10 ↑ WORST 1	7	2	5	7	5	BEST 10 ↑ WORST 1

VAULT
REPORTS™
www.vaultreports.com

THE SCOOP

Nearly a century ago, Henry Ford invented mass production and forever changed the way we live. As the industrial century awaits the new millenium, the company he founded is continuing to churn out cars: In 1996, the Ford Motor Company celebrated its 250-millionth vehicle. If you put all the Ford vehicles ever produced bumper to bumper, they'd circle the globe 30 times.

Ford's road to prominence hasn't been without its potholes. The company suffered down years in the 1970s and 1980s, when strategic mistakes, indifferent cars and Japanese competition caused sales at Ford (and the other two big American car companies, General Motors and Chrysler) to drop precipitously. But Ford has steadily driven its way back to the top with its successful Taurus and Escort models, and its mainstay F-series pickup. In December 1994, the company announced Ford 2000, a plan to consolidate the company's operations, and thus cut costs and boost profits. The plan took effect January 1995, when Ford's North American and European operations were consolidated. Ford 2000 will ultimately bring the Ford global organization under one operational umbrella, which, company officials say, will eliminate duplication in product development, and create savings by permitting parts to be used interchangeably between models.

Ford is also using computing might to cut its development costs. In 1985, the cost of a crash simulation in 1985 was $60,000. In 1996, the cost, thanks to more sophisticated computer programs, had fallen to $200. By 2001, the company predicts it will cost $10 or less for each simulation. During initial car design, creating clay models used to take twelve people twelve weeks. Now, a single designer can take an idea to computer-animated fruition in just three weeks. Prototype part development time has been slashed from weeks to hours, and costs from $20,000 to $20. As part of Ford 2000, the company is seeking to cut overall development time from 33 months to 24 months.

When Ford first began slogging through the early stages of the Ford 2000 reorganization, company officials said that they expected the program to begin to bear fruit in late 1997, 1998 and 1999. For once, a company forecast was correct. By the end of 1997, Ford was already enjoying record revenues. Vigilant Ford finance officials will try to cut another $1 billion in costs in 1998, all toward the goal of cutting $11 billion in operating costs by the year 2000. Wall Street bankers and shareholders are happy, but Ford knows it must also keep customers and employees satisfied. Ford's cost-cutting has caused resentment among many workers. Business trips to Europe came under careful scrutiny, longtime employees were implored to take early retirements and voluntary buyouts. Ford officials are currently drafting a generous employee buyout plan that will prevent prized talent from leaving the company while targeting for eliminiation underpeforming/mediocre employees who have little chance of advancing within the corporation.

Ford recently announced a new leadership team to succeed Alex Trotman once the chairman/CEO/president leaves in 2000. William Clay Ford, the great-grandson of Henry Ford will serve as non-executive chairman while Jacques Nasser will take over as president and CEO. Industry analysts say Ford's clear line of succession will give the company a competitive edge over its rivals by ensuring future stability and a smooth transition once Trotman retires.

The company is also looking into potentially lucrative emerging markets, particularly Asia. Ford entered Asia in earnest in 1994, targeting markets in China, India, Thailand, Vietnam and Indonesia. Ford sells about 320,000 vehicles in the Asia-Pacific market annually – accounting for only 2 percent of the region's 13.5 million sales. Ford and other U.S. automakers merely dabbled in those markets during the last 20 years, preferring to concentrate on keeping their domestic market shares strong. But with growing Asian middle classes and (until recently) booming Asian economies as enticement, all of the Big Three have plunged into the marketplaces of Asia. GM and Ford both intend to have 10 percent of the market by 2005 – no small boast in a market currently dominated by Japanese companies (which currently have a combined 90 percent market share). Ford also has witnessed a resurgence in its European operations after years of disappointing sales and profits. Company officials estimate European sales will pass $1 billion a year by 1998.

MBA Job Seekers: Receive free e-mailed job postings matching your interests & qualifications! Register at www.VaultReports.com

VAULT REPORTS™

453

www.vaultreports.com

GETTING HIRED

For MBAs, Ford hires primarily into a Financial Analyst program and the Marketing Leadership Program. Both programs hire about 10 to 15 full-time employees a year, insiders say. MBA candidates usually go through a couple of on-campus screening interviews, before being taken to Ford for a "Super Saturday" type all-day affair with all the other applicants. The recruiting process includes a presentation in the fall (marked by Ford's bringing of "cool cars" like Mustangs onto campus lawns), and on-campus interviews in the winter. In the finance function, the company offers a "Ford Finance Test Drive," which allows prospective hires to shadow a recent MBA hire.

Full-time hires who are recruited on-campus generally have two interviews at their school, usually with current members of the program to which they are applying, and sometimes with HR personnel. Those who make that cut are then taken to Dearborn for a few days for an all day interview with senior managers. "They put you up in a hotel, let you tour headquarters, tour a plant, feed you well, give you drinks, basically butter you up," reports one employee. During the Super Saturday, interviewees are split into groups of about five and matched up with a group of interviewers. Each interviewer in the group then interviews each interviewee. Here's the catch: interviewers are told they can only hire two from their group (maybe three if there's an exceptionally strong group), insiders say, so interviewees are directly competing against each other. "It's sort of brutal," says one employee. Aside from that form of brutality, Ford's interviewing process is reportedly easygoing. "It was pretty chatty," says a financial analyst. "I didn't get any finance-related questions. They want to kind of pick your brain and know you're really interested in the job."

For MBAs, Ford also offers finance and marketing summer internships. Those applying for Ford's summer program generally go through two interviews on campus, one with a recent MBA graduate, and one with a senior manager. Says one intern: "My interviewer was the No. 3 finance person in all of Ford. The company makes full-time offers based on the performance of the project; for those who don't receive offers, Ford gives evaluations that are "pretty candid."

Most MBA interns give good reviews of their summers. "There was excellent access to senior management," says one marketing intern. "The projects that we do are presented to all the Vice Presidents at the end of the summer." "Interns get to choose from a number of projects which have been developed well in advance," says another intern in marketing. "The projects deal with topics of significance to Ford and senior management." Financial analyst interns also report "very substantive" projects. "We presented our final report to various upper level managers – great exposure," says one. "I was given a lot of responsibility and exposure to upper management," says another. However, shy CEO Alex Trotman reportedly does not meet the interns.

OUR SURVEY SAYS

While Henry Ford's organizational genius sped up automobile production beyond anything imaginable at the turn of the century, his company has become something of a clunker as it approaches the milennium, according to employees. "There's a lot of e-mails, a huge approval chain," says one financial analyst. "You've got to get literally 15 to 20 people to sign of on one thing. It's ridiculous." "I would have to say it's pretty slow-moving and conservative," says a marketing employee. "I'm sure you could find pockets of rogue managers within the company that would be different, but for the most part, managers have been working at Ford since they left college (in some cases high school) and they do not have any knowledge of other industries."

One woman employee in marketing is slighty pessimistic when speaking of advancement opportunities at Ford: "I think advancement possibilities exist for women, but are they good? I would have to say that they probably would be better elsewhere." She elaborates: "Within the marketing area, there are several women who hold senior positions and I would say that your chances for advancement are pretty good. However, in the finance area, there are very few women in management positions and I would say that your chances are not as good." On the plus side, Ford employees have access to privately-owned childcare and elder care facilities on Ford land properties. As of 1997, the company had also endowed $6.4 million in

MBA Job Seekers: Receive free e-mailed job postings matching
your interests & qualifications! Register at www.VaultReports.com

VAULT
REPORTS™
www.vaultreports.com

455

scholarships for women and minorities in technical fields at 42 colleges. And reports one insider, during the recent major management restructuring as part of Ford 2000, "women were treated pretty favorably" because the company was "acutely aware of a paucity" at the top.

If you're considering Ford and have your eye on a corporate-level job in Dearborn, don't expect a cosmopolitan, or even nice, place to call home. "It's a morgue," reports one employee. "The Detroit area is decaying. Ford is a good company, but is impacted greatly by the local culture." "To be quite frank," says another, "the area that Ford is located in is fairly nasty." As far as social opportunities are concerned: "If you're young there and single, there's not a whole lot to choose from. It's pretty dead."

With the history of the 'whiz kids' backing them up, Ford has a great reputation when it comes to training its financial employees. "Ford Finance has a reputation as one of the top three financial programs around. It is telling that only two or three years after working in Ford Finance, many people go on to be controllers and CFOs of smaller companies," says one MBA intern. A financial analyst agrees, to an extent: "If you're looking at I-banking, most investment banks will say that Ford's a really good place to learn corporate banking. On the flip side, they still have a bias to hire from those who have experience in I-banking." However, because of the way the company is structured, Ford's marketing department is less highly regarded. "The marketing people have very little power in that company," according to one financial analyst. A former MBA marketing intern reports: "The finance people definitely take the lead in the company."

To order a 50- to 70-page Vault Reports Employer Profile on Ford Motor call 1-888-JOB-VAULT or visit www.VaultReports.com

The full Employer Profile includes detailed information on Ford's departments, recent developments and transactions, hiring and interview process, plus what employees really think about culture, pay, work hours and more.

HEADACHE CHOOSING AN INTERNSHIP? WHY NOT SPLIT 'EM?

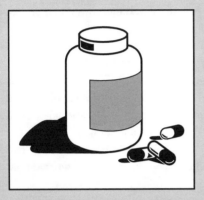

Getting summer internships, especially in business school, is incredibly competitive, and the MBA who has two or more tempting internships to choose between is lucky indeed. Most students feel they must choose one over the other, but there is another option. Vault Reports estimates that about one in ten MBAs split their summer internships – that is, intern at more than one company. In the vast majority of cases, internships are split between companies in different industries, for example consulting and investment banking.

While split summers are still relatively uncommon, the question has arisen often enough for many top firms to establish policies designed to stamp out internship excess, whether these policies be informal or formal. But in many cases, with enough effort, it is still possible to spend your summer doing two separate internships. You won't get any time off during the summer, however – most firms will ask for a minimum of 8 or 9 weeks, and many will require you spend at least 10 or 12 weeks at the company. Since many business schools have summers lasting only 16-18 weeks, splitting your summer may even require you to take a couple of weeks off from school, either during finals week, the first week or two of your second year, or both. In general, smaller firms and firms in less formal industries, like high tech, will be more open to fitting you in at a time convenient for you, while at most investment banks and consulting firms, the time limitations are likely to be more stringent and the internship programs themselves less flexible.

The Pros and Cons of Splitting

Let's weigh the pros and cons: On the one hand, splitting your summer will allow you an inside look at two different companies or industries, and you'll have two valuable names on your resume. However, remember that internships are, in part, designed to reflect your deep and abiding interest in a particular firm or industry when you go looking for a full-time offer. Splitting your summer may suggest that you lack commitment – not a good sign to hold up to companies who want to make sure that you'll stay with them. You'll also have to show up late to at least one of your internships which "never looks good, and then you'll have to explain to everyone where you were the first half of the summer," one MBA tells Vault

MBA Job Seekers: Receive free e-mailed job postings matching your interests & qualifications! Register at www.VaultReports.com

VAULT REPORTS™   457
www.vaultreports.com

Why not split 'em?, cont'd

Reports. In addition "you run the risk of pissing off the companies who've offered you the internship," says one MBA student. "So, if you think you might definitely want to work for one of the companies, you should take that into account." A quantitatively-inclined MBA student who split his summer advises: "You shouldn't split your summer if you are only 5 or 10 percent curious about what it might be like in another industry. Your minimum curiosity level should be around 25 percent." In general, says one MBA grad, "it makes more sense to split your summer if you're interested in the two industries involved, but perhaps not the firms in particular. Remember that summer internships are normally much more difficult to get than permanent employment, so you may be able to trade up to better firms during full-time job interviews. In other words, if you split a summer interning at two places you're not interested in for permanent employment, you don't have to worry about what the firms think."

Structuring a Split Summer:

According to insiders who've done it, here are some useful strategies for structuring a split summer internship. First of all, never let on that you intend to split your summer during your interviews. Express full enthusiasm for corporate finance, or strategy consulting, or whatever you're interviewing for… you can bring up a split summer if you get a job offer. Secondly, decide which internship is your priority internship, and put that one at the beginning of your summer. That way, you'll enter with the rest of the intern class, and your leaving early will excite less notice than your arriving late. Thirdly, know that there are some summer opportunities that fit into the "second stage" of a split summer more easily.

For example, consulting internships and some investment banking internships are a poor fit for a split summer because they are normally quite structured, with set dates for orientation, performance reviews and training sessions. However, sales and trading internships on Wall Street tend to be quite flexible, largely because the internships themselves are entirely unstructured. "You're assigned one general 'desk' and given a small project at the beginning of the internship, but that's about it," says a former sales & trading intern. "You have no other assigned duties, no assigned place to sit, no phone number. If there's no one out that day, you have to pull up a chair and sit between desks. I even took a couple of days off and no one noticed. They figured I must be on another floor that day." High tech firms also tend to be more flexible in their internship requirements, though not to the degree of sales & trading jobs, say insiders. The more unstructured the internship, the better a split summer will work.

Why not split 'em?, cont'd

After you've gotten the summer offers (not before, mind you), you'll have to broach the subject of a split summer with your employers. First, identify your first priority firm' if one or the other is recalcitrant, you may have to make a choice after all. One MBA grad says: "Sometimes telling your first choice straight-up that you want to split your summer, but that you'll drop your other internship if they have a problem with it, is enough. I had already accepted an internship with a consulting firm when I got a chance at another internship at a Wall Street firm that normally does not allow split summers. I told them that I had already accepted the consulting internship, but if they wanted I would ditch it in their favor in a second. They met about it and then told me that since I had been willing to give up the other internship, and had already accepted another offer, they would go against their policy and let me split the summer."

One excuse to use when asking to split the summer: Tell them that you need to keep your options open in another city. This tactic, of course, works only if one of your potential internships doesn't have an office in the city where your other internship is based. One unscrupulous MBA advises: "Just say that you don't know where your fiancée will be working, and you want to explore your city options. The company can't really fault you for this, because they'll want to be family-sensitive. You don't even need to actually have a fiancée!"

And if all those techniques fail, it's always possible to split a summer secretly (albeit less than ethically). One MBA student explains: "I just called up one of my summer internships and told them I couldn't start until late June. They asked why, because it was unusual to start that late. I said I was traveling in California, which was kind of true, because I had an internship there."

MBA Job Seekers: Receive free e-mailed job postings matching your interests & qualifications! Register at www.VaultReports.com

VAULT REPORTS™

459

www.vaultreports.com

KPMG Consulting

Management Consulting

Three Chestnut Ridge Road
Montvale, NJ 07645
(201) 307-7000
www.kpmg.com

LOCATIONS

Montvale, NJ (HQ)
Offices in 1,100 offices in over 150 countries

DEPARTMENTS

Consulting

THE STATS

Annual Revenues: $3.8 billion (1998)
No. of Offices: 1,100 (worldwide)
No. of Employees: 83,500 (worldwide)
Employer Type: Private Company
CEO: Stephen Butler

KEY COMPETITORS

- Andersen Consulting
- Arthur Andersen
- Deloitte Consulting
- Ernst & Young Consulting
- PricewaterhouseCoopers

THE BUZZ
What MBAs are saying
about KPMG

- "Generic, Big Five"
- "Growing fast"
- "Civic-minded"
- "Failed merger set it back"

UPPERS

- Aggressive in promoting diversity
- Sporting event and theater tickets
- Day care assistance
- Flexible hours
- Community involvement assistance
- Four weeks vacation

DOWNERS

- High turnover
- Starting pay below competing
  Big Five firms

EMPLOYMENT CONTACT

Susan Tillman
KPMG
Three Chestnut Ridge Road
Montvale, NJ 07645

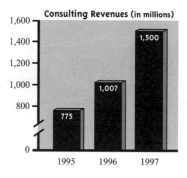

Consulting Revenues (in millions)

- 1995: 775
- 1996: 1,007
- 1997: 1,500

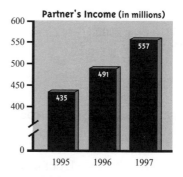

Partner's Income (in millions)

- 1995: 435
- 1996: 491
- 1997: 557

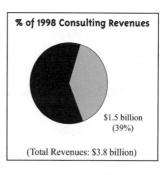

% of 1998 Consulting Revenues

$1.5 billion
(39%)

(Total Revenues: $3.8 billion)

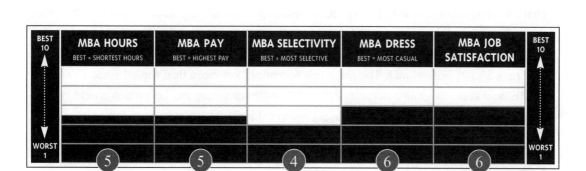

	MBA HOURS BEST = SHORTEST HOURS	MBA PAY BEST = HIGHEST PAY	MBA SELECTIVITY BEST = MOST SELECTIVE	MBA DRESS BEST = MOST CASUAL	MBA JOB SATISFACTION	
BEST 10 ↑ WORST 1	5	5	4	6	6	BEST 10 ↑ WORST 1

MBA Job Seekers: Receive free e-mailed job postings matching
your interests & qualifications! Register at www.VaultReports.com

VAULT REPORTS™
www.vaultreports.com
461

THE SCOOP

After scratching plans to join forces with fellow Big Five professional services firm Ernst & Young, KPMG still stands alone. But KPMG (formerly called KPMG Peat Marwick in the United States) is hardly in need of any sympathy. The professional services firm has been adding business steadily, figure that the firm aggressively plans to increase to $6 billion by the year 2000. The consulting arm has risen dramatically in recent days, earning $1.5 billion in the U.S last year, up a staggering 50 percent over 1996. KPMG refuses to stand pat, however, and is launching an ambitious $60 million promotional campaign aimed at bolstering its already considerable name recognition. And a proposed plan to go public with part of the consulting business could spell even more big bucks for the firm and its employees. Truly, in more ways than one, KPMG is a firm on the move.

KPMG has a lot of dizzying numbers attached to its name. The humongous firm has 85,291 employees (of which 59,663 are professionals) in 155 countries worldwide. In North America, the firm has 25,167 employees scattered about hundreds of offices (KPMG is the only Big Five firm that has larger operations in Europe than in North America). KPMG services 44 percent of top 500 banks and 46 percent of the largest 100 insurance firms. Despite all these big numbers, KPMG's new philosophy, proclaimed from the mount (i.e., by CEO Stephen Butler) rests on a very small number – the campaign is called "The Power of One." This transcendent "guiding vision" has three major components: becoming number one in the marketplace, functioning as a unified firm, and involving all KPMG employees in the firm's success. "The only acceptable position for this firm," proclaims KPMG, "is to be number one in all of the businesses in which we choose to compete."

That's a rather ambitious aim, for KPMG Consulting is a relatively young branch of the firm. Yet it already totals more than 5000 consulting professionals. But the first time, in 1998 the consulting division surpassed assurance in terms of U.S. revenue, grossing $1.511 billion of the firm's $3.801 billion total. The practice's revenues have more than tripled since 1994, and KPMG now seeks to retain 5 percent of the worldwide consulting market (which would be 400 percent more that the consultancy's current market share).

GETTING HIRED

"Working for any investment banks or [like] monetary groups" is a distinct advantage. KPMG likes those with a history of leadership or sports" as well. But although "intelligence and [academic or professional] qualifications are more important," personality does count for something. KPMG "is more laid back than other consulting firms," says an insider. It is therefore important to be "good natured and good humored."

KPMG puts a premium on interactive, non-stressful interviews, so prepare to answer several questions with a somewhat lighter tone than you might expect. But this doesn't mean that KPMG isn't serious. Because KPMG tends to hire consultants with significant industry or technical experience, the firm hardly ever uses case interviews to evaluate its consulting applicants, instead directing questions about work experience and computer expertise. Recalls one veteran of the interview process, "[they asked] what I had done in my internships and what I was interested in." Audit and tax interviewees, similarly, should be prepared to fully discuss their work experience and background, and why they feel they would be a good fit with KPMG.

According to insiders, "most people apply to a specific group," and will interview only with members of that group. That does not necessarily mean that the number of interviews will be limited, however. One current KPMG employee reports coming in for "a full day, from nine to six, with interviews with 15 people [total; some meetings were with two or three people]. It was exhausting." Again, the process seems to be "more laid back" than at other firms. Job offers are delivered promptly, usually in about a week. An agreement is typically reached quickly as well, since there is "not much room for negotiation."

MBA Job Seekers: Receive free e-mailed job postings matching
your interests & qualifications! Register at www.VaultReports.com

VAULT REPORTS™

463

www.vaultreports.com

OUR SURVEY SAYS

It's unsurprising that at a firm as large as KPMG, employees have many different takes on the corporate culture. One employee praised the "open door" atmosphere, where "managers are able to answer questions and provide guidance." Another employee had a slightly different take. "It's nurturing for newbies. This means you find a manager you are compatible with and become a sponge." We're told that KPMGers should "prepare your psyche for high turnover. Since I came to the firm six months ago, four people I worked with closely have left. Two defected to another Big Five firm, one went over to industry, and one transferred to another KPMG office."

As for atmosphere, "Culture varies somewhat between offices. In DC, for example, there's a Gay/Lesbian support group, but Raleigh is very stuffy and "old-boy." In general, the smaller offices tend to be more rigid and controlling." Now's the time to sign up for your frequent flyer card. "Consultants travel, on average, about 70 percent of the time. We try to stay regional in our business, but when the client has offices all over the country, sometimes it is necessary to work at all those offices." As for the employees themselves, they are "fairly young, with most large projects staffed by people in the 25-35 year old range."

At KPMG, "community involvement is encouraged and you are paid for four workday hours per month to perform volunteer work, provided that you match these hours with volunteer hours on your own time." One tax consultant reported that "Some offices have flex time. For example, I work 10 to 7 to avoid rush hour traffic." Additionally, "continuing education opportunities abound and usually involve travel, with KPMG picking up the tab." Employees say that "when you start with the firm, KPMG gives you a new laptop, supplies and briefcase with the firm logo," and that the firm offers "5 weeks of vacation." Well, not exactly one insider comments that "KPMG is a bit unusual in that it combines vacation time with sick leave, so it's great if you're young and healthy, maybe not so great if you're sickly." Be forewarned that "some perks vary from office to office, or partner to partner, or even manager to manager."

In consulting, "The hours are officially 8:30 to 5:30, expecting that you'll take an hour for lunch. Sometimes I do leave at 5:30, other days [I stay] until 7:30." Another consultant concurs that "10 or 11 hours a day is typical." At times, "hours can be very long [for consultants], with late nights spent compiling and analyzing data, or preparing a presentation for a project meeting or board meeting."

To order a 50- to 70-page Vault Reports Employer Profile on KPMG Consulting call 1-888-JOB-VAULT or visit www.VaultReports.com

The full Employer Profile includes detailed information on KPMG's departments, recent developments and transactions, hiring and interview process, plus what employees really think about culture, pay, work hours and more.

MBA Job Seekers: Receive free e-mailed job postings matching your interests & qualifications! Register at www.VaultReports.com

VAULT REPORTS™

465

www.vaultreports.com

Nortel Networks

Telecommunications

8200 Dixie Road Suite 100
Brampton, Ontario L6T 5P6
(905) 863-0000
Fax: (905) 863-8408
www.nortelnetworks.com

NORTEL
NETWORKS™

LOCATIONS

Main U.S. offices in Richardson, TX,
and Research Triangle Park, NC
Other offices and facilities in North America
• Europe • Asia/Pacific • Caribbean • Latin
America • the Middle East • Africa

KEY COMPETITORS

- Alcatel
- Ascend Communications
- Cisco Systems
- Lucent Technologies
- Motorola

DEPARTMENTS

Carrier Packet Solutions
Carrier Solutions
Enterprise Data Solutions
Enterprise Solutions
Wireless Solutions

THE STATS

Annual Revenues: $18 billion (1997)
Income: $957 million (1997)
No. of Employees: 80,000 (U.S.)
Stock Symbol: NT
Stock Exchange: NYSE
CEO: John Roth

THE BUZZ
What MBAs are saying
about Nortel

- "Big, Canada, bureaucracy"
- "Stale"
- "Potential"
- "Nothing happening"

UPPERS

- Laid back atmosphere
- Casual dress
- Emphasis on training and development
- Recognition of hard work

DOWNERS

- Recent corporate downsizing
- Hiring freeze
- Workaholic atmostphere in some departments

EMPLOYMENT CONTACT

Nortel Networks
P.O. Box 3511 Station C
Ottawa, Ontario K1Y 4H7
Fax: (613) 763-7277
cur@nortel.ca

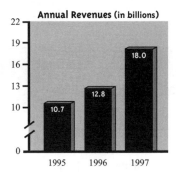

Annual Revenues (in billions)

1995: 10.7
1996: 12.8
1997: 18.0

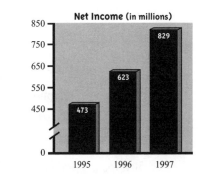

Net Income (in millions)

1995: 473
1996: 623
1997: 829

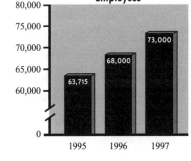

Employees

1995: 63,715
1996: 68,000
1997: 73,000

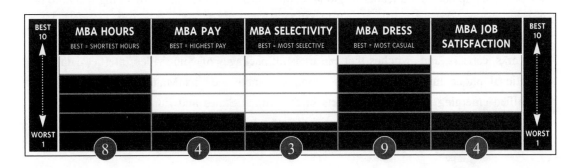

	MBA HOURS BEST = SHORTEST HOURS	MBA PAY BEST = HIGHEST PAY	MBA SELECTIVITY BEST = MOST SELECTIVE	MBA DRESS BEST = MOST CASUAL	MBA JOB SATISFACTION	
BEST 10 ↕ WORST 1	8	4	3	9	4	BEST 10 ↕ WORST 1

THE SCOOP

Leave it to an arcane 19th century Canadian patent law and an untimely death to lead to one of the world's largest providers of telecommunications products and global communications networks. Nortel's story begins north of the border in 1881 when Charles Fleetford Sise, a New England sea captain, arrived in Montreal to start The Bell Telephone Company of Canda. Sise got off to a rocky start: his domestic equipment supply was cut off when James Cowherd, operator of the world's first telephone manufacturing plant, died of tuberculosis. Worried that he would not find another supplier and would thus lose his Canadian patent rights, Sise decided to make his own telephone equipment. A year later, the Manufacturing Branch of The Bell Telephone Company of Canada was born, eventually becoming the Northern Electric and Manufacturing Company Limited in 1895.

For fifty years, Northern Electric primarily made telephone equipment for Bell Canada, not to mention a few television sets, radios, and police call boxes. With the introduction of the electronic telephone switch during the 1960s, Northern Electric and Bell Canada decided to combine their research and development divisions in order to get a jump start on the rapidly changing telecommunications market. The new R&D entity, now called Northern Telecom, developed its first electronic switch, the SG-1 in 1972 and went on to sell some 6000 units during the next three years. But the electronic switch quickly became outdated with the arrival of digital technology. Northern Telecom sold its first digital switch in 1977. With the breakup of AT&T five years later, the company witnessed a decade of explosive growth. The company is now called Nortel Networks.

Throughout much of the 1990s, Nortel has sought to reinvent itself as not merely a maker of telephone equipment but a leader in global communications and data networking technology. Take advantage of the deregulation of the telecommunications industry in 1996, Nortel, along with rival Lucent Techonologies, have sought to supply telephone companies with intergrated networks, carriers, and switches that can transmit packages of voice/video/Internet data over traditional phone lines. In 1993, the company announced its Magellan portfolio which identified emerging multimedia markets in the United States and Europe. Today, the U.S. accounts for 60 percent of Nortel's sales. Like other high-tech and telecom companies, Nortel is actively pursuing markets in Asia and Latin America.

Realizing the need to compete more effectively with Lucent and Cisco Systems, Nortel recently formed a strategic alliance with Microsoft Corporation to jointly market high-speed Internet modems. Nortel also purchased Aptis Communications, which specializes in remote-access Internet and telephone switches. In June 1998, Nortel bought Bay Networks, Inc. in a highly publicized $7.68 billion deal. By acquiring Bay Networks, the company hopes to provide corporate customers with data management equipment such as Intranet servers. However, some people have questioned the move because Bay Networks, itself the product of a difficult merger, has struggled to turn a profit and has little experience in the fast growing public carrier market, an area some analysts say Nortel should be paying attention to. Despite lower than expected growth in 1998, Nortel officials insist they will make the merger work. The company recently announced that it will cut 3500 jobs worldwide and restructure its operations. Under the plan, Nortel is dividing its data networking business into two units: one that deals with telephone companies and the other with corporate customers.

GETTING HIRED

In recent years, Nortel has hosted a three-year program for MBAs called the Leadership Development Program, but the program is in some disarray because of the company's recent financial troubles. The program hires business school grads into finance, marketing, human resources and operations for both the summer and full-time positions. "They're all separate programs," explains one insider. "For example, you would come in as a marketing leadership program, and wouldn't do rotations in other functions." MBAs in the program, however, rotate through different business lines every nine to 12 months. (For example, from wireless solutions to carrier packet solutions.)

However, because of staffing cutbacks company-wide, Nortel discontinued the program in 1998 – although insiders expect it to be resurrected. Now, individual business lines pursue their own MBA programs. "Originally, you were supposed to be able to switch business lines," explains one insider. "The way the new program is, you stay within your line of business.

MBA Job Seekers: Receive free e-mailed job postings matching your interests & qualifications! Register at www.VaultReports.com

VAULT REPORTS™

469

www.vaultreports.com

That's definitely a downside, because you're locked in. You can definitely move in the company, but not through the program."

Because of its major presences in Texas and North Carolina, Nortel draws heavily from MBA programs at "Purdue, the University of Texas, Emory, UNC, and Fuqua (Duke)." Despite the company's tech-heavy businesses, "there were no technical questions at all," reports one recent interviewee. "A lot of it's probably learning on the job, there are definitely some training options you could go to, but the company's so different in different areas, I don't know how much good that would do."

OUR SURVEY SAYS

Nortel is often ranked among MBAs as a desirable employer because of its relatively soothing lifestyle. "It's very laid-back," says one insider. "It's the dress code, number one, and number two, the hours are very flexible, people come in at all different times." How laid back is the dress code? "It's shorts, T-shirts. I mean it's really taking business casual to an extreme." Also, Nortel is not as regimented as other top employers. "It's a very open door policy. It's a cube city, there's no offices. They do have cube-offices, where they put doors on high-walled cubes, but that's about it." Says one recent MBA hire: "Access to executives is definitely key – if you want access to senior-level executives, you have great opportunity at Nortel." However, say insiders "[Nortel is] definitely a technical-oriented company. There's not that many generalists there. I don't know if they're committed to (MBAs) yet." Notes that contact: "Pay is probably on the lower end for telecom."

Perks range from a generous 401(k) plan, health club memberships, and the ability to work at home. Employees also praise the company's emphasis on training and the recognition of hard work. "People come first," gushes one employee. "As employees, we get every tools we need to do our work. Nortel encourages everyone to continue training and learning. Nortel is also a company that rewards employees who peform beyond expectations." Adds another insider, "Nortel has great training and training is taken very seriously. So your personal and professional development are quite assured." Says one recent MBA summer intern about that program: "We had a three-day training program, where they flew us out to Texas, in Richardson, outside of Dallas. It was a three-day training seminar, an educational type of thing – this is Nortel. And then there were a couple of activities outside of work, like we went to this racetrack place with go-carts."

Nortel's treatment of women and minorities also receive high marks, although few are represented in upper management. "Looking at the corporate officers will show a staff of mostly white men," observes an insider. "On the other hand, we do have women and racial minorities quite well represented throughout the ranks." The company recently sponsored a Diversity Day sponsored by a senior VP. Employees were bused to the event and were treated to "food, ethnic music and dance, and booths offering supporting information especially for women, minorities, gays, and our keynote speaker was Coretta Scott King."

MBA Job Seekers: Receive free e-mailed job postings matching
your interests & qualifications! Register at www.VaultReports.com

VAULT
REPORTS™
www.vaultreports.com

471

PricewaterhouseCoopers

1301 Avenue of the Americas
New York, NY 10019
(212) 596-7000
Fax: (212) 790 6620
www.pwcglobal.com

Management Consulting

PRICEWATERHOUSECOOPERS ℞

LOCATIONS

PricewaterhouseCoopers has offices in 152 countries. It is headquartered in New York City and London.

SERVICE LINES

Strategic Change
Process Improvement
Technology Solutions

THE STATS

Annual Revenues: $15 billion (1998), $3.8 billion (consulting)
No. of Consultants: 31,000 (1998)
No. of Offices: 867 (worldwide)
CEO: Scott Hartz
Year Founded: 1998

KEY COMPETITORS

- American Management Systems
- Andersen Consulting
- Deloitte Consulting
- Ernst & Young
- KPMG Consulting

 THE BUZZ
What MBAs are saying
about PwC

- "East Side marries Harlem"
- "Strong potential, need more focus"
- "Disgruntled employees"
- "Mouthful of a name"

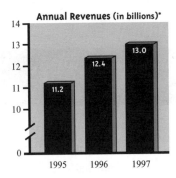

UPPERS

- Hiring like mad
- Huge company = wide choice of locations and opportunities
- Solid benefits; nifty laptops

DOWNERS

- Gigantic and confusing
- Hideous logo
- Nifty laptops needed due to extensive travel

EMPLOYMENT CONTACT

Human Resources
1301 Avenue of the Americas
New York, NY 10019
(212) 259-2100
Fax: (212) 259-1907

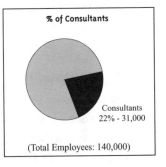

% of Consultants

Consultants
22% - 31,000

(Total Employees: 140,000)

*Graphs indicate figures for entire firm

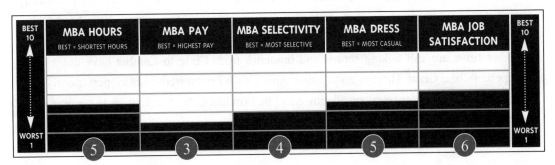

	MBA HOURS BEST = SHORTEST HOURS	MBA PAY BEST = HIGHEST PAY	MBA SELECTIVITY BEST = MOST SELECTIVE	MBA DRESS BEST = MOST CASUAL	MBA JOB SATISFACTION	
	5	3	4	5	6	

MBA Job Seekers: Receive free e-mailed job postings matching
your interests & qualifications! Register at www.VaultReports.com

VAULT REPORTS™

www.vaultreports.com

473

THE SCOOP

Those of you who thought the Big Six financial services firms were due to become the Giant Four are half-right. While the planned merger of KPMG and Ernst & Young fell by the wayside, Price Waterhouse – the smallest and perhaps most prestigious of the Big Six – and Coopers & Lybrand managed to put one and one together. On July 1, 1998, the awkwardly named PricewaterhouseCoopers was born. To celebrate, employees in Los Angeles supped "Merger Beer," brewed especially for the occasion.

The joke around PwC is that the companies paid a design firm $10 million to create its new logo and look – upon which Andersen Consulting paid that designer $20 million to screw it up. But no one's going to mess with PricewaterhouseCoopers right away – this is a daunting firm. PwC has 140,000 employees and 9000 partners around the globe, with projected annual revenues of $15 billion yearly. Consulting revenues, if the firm had been combined in 1997, would have been $3.23 billion (that's just a jot behind number one Andersen Consulting). More than 30,000 PricewaterhouseCoopers employees currently work as consultants. Despite its jaw-dropping size, PricewaterhouseCoopers would like to convey the message that it is no faceless monolith. The firm plans a huge advertising drive to begin in September 1998, mostly black and white photos of staff members, in order to promote the "human face" of gigantic PricewaterhouseCoopers.

Pricewaterhouse Coopers plans to use its new size to truly bring about a globally integrated firm. Roughly 90 percent of its revenues will be generated within the integrated organization, though some practices, such as those in Japan and Korea, will not be integrated for some time (owing to regulatory and cultural concerns). The leaders of PwC believe that the bigger a firm is, the faster it grows, and that the new bulk of PwC will create an inexorable "breakaway firm." Competitors point out that skills also matter. Already, competitors have been taking advantage of the changes at PwC to steal away its "network" firms. Five percent of PwC member firms are still talking terms, and branches from Chile to Zambia have defected to competitors like Grant Thorton and Arthur Andersen. PricewaterhouseCoopers clearly sees these defections as short-term considerations. The firm has stated that it plans to become a $30 billion firm by the year 2005.

Post-merger, PricewaterhouseCoopers has become a true giant; in a time when every company that has ever made an international call touts itself as having an international presence, PwC is truly a globalized firm with a presence in 152 countries and 867 offices worldwide.

GETTING HIRED

The first recruiting season for PricewaterhouseCoopers is kicking off, and there are a few changes. "They are trying to involve the professional staff a lot more," says one insider. "They have incentives every quarter from bringing in people who are hired as professional staff, from entry-level folks to very senior people." The firm also has very nice incentives for bringing them in, including stuff like cash bonuses and "a trip to France." This means that qualified, experienced hires, or anyone interested in the idea of working with PricewaterhouseCoopers, might do well to approach someone already working at the firm.

Current students might take a slightly different approach. PricewaterhouseCoopers is going with an approach that Coopers & Lybrand used to good effect last year. "First, we will do presentations on campus," confides one insider. "We will tell people who are interested to apply online. Then, we use the online applications to screen through the on-campus applicants and make up our recruitment schedules. So it's really not possible to sneak into the interviewing schedule." The online application will be tweaked this year, muses one contact: "I don't think we have a writing sample section like we did last year." Candidates will be notified by phone (and also online, if they're enterprising enough to check). Interviews are given on campus by a partner or senior manager. Those brought back to the office are interviewed by three or four partners and managers. Two associates or analysts will take the candidate out to lunch in the middle as a de-stresser. Still, "it's a long day."

MBA Job Seekers: Receive free e-mailed job postings matching your interests & qualifications! Register at www.VaultReports.com

VAULT REPORTS™

www.vaultreports.com

475

OUR SURVEY SAYS

PwC insiders enjoy their culture. "The people here are young – between 24 and 35. It is a relaxed atmosphere, and people feel very comfortable about going out for a drink together after work. It is a very social place if that is what you choose, but you are never made to feel guilty for not participating in any activities or parties." Speaking of parties, "there are usually lots of them going on – mostly going away parties. Big Five firms are notorious for high turnover. That's not a reflection on the company, just the nature of the beast." "The people here are friendly and fun. There is always lots of work to do, and you also have lots of freedom to do whatever you have to in your personal life outside of work, even during work hours." On-site dress for consultants vaies according to the client's specifications, "though we always try to dress a bit better than the client employees," while at the office, it's professional Monday through Thursday, and business casual Friday and all summer."

What do insiders say about the massive merger? Most are cautiously optimistic. "With the merger, we are expected to gain more experience from the increased clientele base that we already have as the merged firm," suggests one consultant. Another points out that "since the merger our benefits have increased. We now get three weeks vacation, healthcare and a 401(k) (the firm matches 20 percent). PwC employees have 10 paid holidays, plus 15 vacation days to start (and 22 vacation days after two years)." Another consultant speculates about the PwC kulturkampf. "Coopers was known to be the most laidback of the Big Six firms in terms of things like dress code and workplace environment. The merger with the more conservative Price Waterhouse presents interesting questions regarding clashing cultures. There is no way to know what type of personality the combined firm will take on, particularly at this early stage, when most offices haven't even been combined yet. Both firms were huge and the combination results in a sort of a colossus."

Like most consulting firms, PwC offers its people long hours. For most, "work hours are what you make them. If you become a workaholic, like many do, then you can work all the time. If you're disciplined enough, you can work 8 to 5, Monday to Friday. No one gets overtime – you just work until the job gets done." A business consultant complains: "The hours suck. I won't lie. You will have to work an average of 50 to 60 hours a week." Much of this long workweek involves travel – though consultants say that the "traveling policies are nice. When traveling, you "have a very nice laptop," and "stay at nice hotels and have enough money to eat well. Most people are on the road during the week, leaving on Monday and returning Thursday evening."

Though Big Five firms aren't known for their generous pay, "I feel that the pay is competitive," says one consultant. "The truth is that three years ago the pay was very low, but the firm has taken strides in improving that." "An organization as big as PwC will need everyone it can get," says one insider, and befittingly, PricewaterhouseCoopers has already shown marked signs of flexibility. "The firm would rather see you stay part time than leave because of their inflexibility. While the truth is that there are few female partners, that seems to be changing." "I know a woman," says one consultant, "who was recently promoted to partner while working part-time." Ethnicity and race seems to be "no consideration whatever, though a firm with 140,000 employees is bound to have one or two bad apples. But only one or two!"

To order a 50- to 70-page Vault Reports Employer Profile on PricewaterhouseCoopers call 1-888-JOB-VAULT or visit www.VaultReports.com

The full Employer Profile includes detailed information on PwC's departments, recent developments and transactions, hiring and interview process, plus what employees really think about culture, pay, work hours and more.

MBA Job Seekers: Receive free e-mailed job postings matching your interests & qualifications! Register at www.VaultReports.com

VAULT REPORTS™

477

www.vaultreports.com

Sprint

Telecommunications

2330 Shawnee Mission Pkwy.
Westwood, KS 66205
(913) 624-3000
Fax: (913) 624-3281
www.sprint.com

LOCATIONS

Westwood, KS (HQ)
Offices throughout United States and Europe

DEPARTMENTS

Customer Service
Distribution
Engineering
Field Sales
Finance
Information Systems Software
Marketing
Operations
Publishing and Advertising
Technical Applications

THE STATS

Annual Revenues: $15 billion (1997)
No. of Employees: 52,200 (worldwide)
Stock Symbol: FON (NYSE)
CEO: William T. Esrey

KEY COMPETITORS

- AT&T
- Bell Atlantic
- GTE
- MCI WorldCom

THE BUZZ

What MBAs are saying
about Sprint

- "Happening, but Midwest"
- "Good management programs"
- "Nimble, aggressive"
- "Also-ran"

UPPERS

- Spiffy new HQ
- Excellent training programs for MBAs

DOWNERS

- Some tensions between different company groups
- Slow town for young people

EMPLOYMENT CONTACT

Human Resources
2330 Shawnee Mission Pkwy.
Westwood, KS 66205
(913) 624-3000
Fax: (913) 624-3281

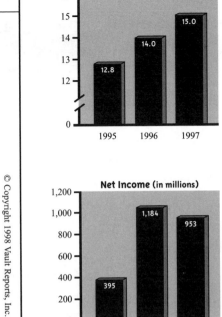

Annual Revenues (in billions)

Year	Value
1995	12.8
1996	14.0
1997	15.0

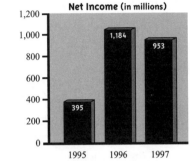

Net Income (in millions)

Year	Value
1995	395
1996	1,184
1997	953

Employees

Year	Value
1995	48,265
1996	48,000
1997	51,000

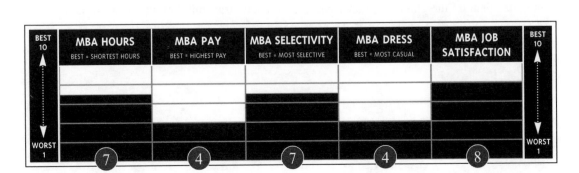

	BEST 10 ↑ WORST 1	MBA HOURS BEST = SHORTEST HOURS	MBA PAY BEST = HIGHEST PAY	MBA SELECTIVITY BEST = MOST SELECTIVE	MBA DRESS BEST = MOST CASUAL	MBA JOB SATISFACTION	BEST 10 ↑ WORST 1
		7	4	7	4	8	

MBA Job Seekers: Receive free e-mailed job postings matching your interests & qualifications! Register at www.VaultReports.com

VAULT REPORTS™
www.vaultreports.com

479

THE SCOOP

Sprint, perhaps best recognized for its ubiquitous "Pin Drop" and Candice Bergen commercials, would prefer to be known as your provider of all your telecommunications needs. But Kansas City-based Sprint is already known by management-minded folk as a top employer with outstanding training programs and a reputation for being a jumping board to high-level positions in the telecommunications industry. Sprint was ranked as one of the top 50 companies to work for in a 1997 *Fortune* magazine survey of American and Canadian MBA students.

While Sprint, valued at $18 billion, is constantly the subject of takeover rumors, the firm prefers to remain in control of its own telecommunications destiny. Sprint's betting on cutting-edge technology to keep it independent and ahead of the pack. The first company to create an all-fiber optic network in the 1980s, Sprint currently plans to be the first telecommunications firm to create digitized wireless networks. Such a wireless network would allow the firm to offer a 21st century-esque integrated personal communication service (PCS).

Faced with increasing competition from a recently deregulated telecommunications industry, Sprint is embarking on a bold strategy to remake itself as more than just a long distance carrier. And Sprint has raised the stakes in the booming telecommunications market by announcing plans for a new, more efficient high speed communications system. Called Sprint ION, the new network consists of advanced switching and data routing technology that will integrate phone/Internet/video service into one existing line. For example, customers will be able to make phone calls, transmit videos and surf the Net at the same time. With this new network, Sprint will charge customers by the amount of data transmitted rather than by the number of minutes spent on the phone. A meter will measure data transmission, in much the same way an electric utility tracks how much electricity is consumed in one month. Sprint plans to start selling the new network by 2000.

GETTING HIRED

In 1992, Sprint created the Staff Associate Program, a three-year executive development program that is a "fast track to management." Almost all associates are based at the company's world headquarters, and rotate through different functions based on personal objectives. The program is designed to familiarize associates with industry issues and operations and prepare them for supervisory positions. According to one former intern, "the SAP is [CEO William Esrey's] idea and pet project." Insiders also report that Sprint is exploring the construction of an MBA track more similar to traditional brand management, although that is not yet underway.

With only about 15 staff associates per class, admission into the program is very competitive. "They bring 50 or 60 people out in January," says one associate. "I think they'll make 20 or 30 offers." Full-time staff associate candidates interview twice on their campuses, and, if they go on to the next round, have a full day of interviews in Kansas City. The interviews on campus are performed by human resources staff and staff associates. The interviews in Kansas are usually with three or four high-ranking managers, sometimes presidents of divisions or senior VPs. Also, associates report that Sprint uses panel interviews during which several candidates are interviewed at the same time. The summer internship program for MBAs is a feeder into the Staff Associate Program, although only about half to two-thirds of the 20 or so interns a year receive offers, according to insiders. Summer MBA interns have one round of back-to-back one-on-one interviews with company execs.

OUR SURVEY SAYS

Employees say that Sprint management is markedly decentralized, even within Sprint's Kansas City headquarters, meaning that different departments may have disparate environments. "The Multimedia Group, where I most recently had responsibilities, was a very unstructured, self-

MBA Job Seekers: Receive free e-mailed job postings matching
your interests & qualifications! Register at www.VaultReports.com

VAULT REPORTS™

www.vaultreports.com

481

motivated environment," says one longtime Sprint employee, "whereas others are more rigid and structured. And, according to one insider, "there are cultural tensions between the mature and more entrepreneurial groups within the company." "The company is very decentralized when it comes to implementation of policies – they are left up to local management," another contact says. "Corporate culture? Well, it varies from location to location. Sprint's a big place and there's more than one 'culture,'" sums up another employee. "It depends on where you're working, what you're doing and who you're working for. Here in the Kansas City area, there are at least 35 to 40 separate places to work." However, the company states that "with the completion of the new corporate campus in Kansas City and a new management focus on 'One Sprint,' the culture is shifting out of 'silo' mentality rapidly."

While Sprint may be unconnected culturally from division to division, many employees say the company offers a decent social life with "picnics, awards dinners, pep rallies and parties outside of work." "I'd say there is definitely a social atmosphere to the company," says one insider. "There is always something going on outside the office, be it happy hours, golf tournaments, or what," says another. Several contacts note that "Sprint is a fun place to work."

Among Sprint's extras are what one employee calls "phenomenal health goodies." "They pay a large portion of your insurance and that can mean extra money in your pocket. If you price how much you pay as compared to any other company you will see very fast how much Sprint pays," says one employee. "Also there are many different options depending on what your preferences are on how much you can afford and how much flexibility you need on where you have your doctor or hospital." "I am paying around $6 a week for insurance – both medical and dental – for myself, my wife and our 8 month old baby," reports one insider.

"The company is in middle America, and the lifestyle is kinder and gentler than in Manhattan, but my peers were as smart and savvy as anywhere else," says one former summer associate. Sprint employees heap praise on their co-workers. "One of the things that always impresses me is the quality of the people that work here," says one insider. A recently hired staff associate concurs: "I think it's pretty competitive. They only recruit from the top schools." "Sprint is very selective – you should have general management aspirations," says another insider in the staff associate program. "We are also looking for more experience. An associate's experience prior to business school is usually more than four years."

With the high selectivity comes prestige for the staff associate program. "People are contacted by headhunters all the time," reports one staff associate. Another associate explains that once those in the SAP program become directors they can either advance to an assistant vice president position "or you take your credentials elsewhere. They'll get hired away by a start-up, made a VP in a year or two." Why are the associates so highly sought? "We have a very strong training program, they give you a lot of responsibility, and we are doing well in the marketplace."

To order a 50- to 70-page Vault Reports Employer Profile on Sprint call 1-888-JOB-VAULT or visit www.VaultReports.com

The full Employer Profile includes detailed information on Sprint's departments, recent developments and transactions, hiring and interview process, plus what employees really think about culture, pay, work hours and more.

MBA Job Seekers: Receive free e-mailed job postings matching your interests & qualifications! Register at www.VaultReports.com

VAULT REPORTS™

483

www.vaultreports.com

United Airlines

Airline

1200 E. Algonquin Rd.
Elk Grove Township, IL 60007
(847) 700-4000
Fax: (847) 700-5229
www.ual.com

LOCATIONS

Chicago, IL (HQ)
Denver, CO • San Francisco, CA • Washington, D.C. • London, United Kingdom • Tokyo, Japan

DEPARTMENTS

Accounting
Clerical
Customer Service
Data Entry
Flight Attendant
Ramp Service
Reservation Sales
Secretarial
Ticketing

THE STATS

Annual Revenues: $17.4 billion (1997)
Income: $949 million (1997)
No. of Employees: 91,700 (worldwide)
No. of Offices: 150 (worldwide)
Stock Symbol: UAL
Stock Exchange: NYSE
CEO: Gerald Greenwald

KEY COMPETITORS

◆ AMR (American Airlines)
◆ British Airways
◆ Continental Airlines
◆ Delta
◆ Northwest Airlines
◆ TWA
◆ US Airways
◆ Virgin Group

THE BUZZ

What MBAs are saying about United Airlines

◆ "Employee controlled"
◆ "Faceless"
◆ "Potential for the future"
◆ "Stodgy, low profit"

UPPERS

+ Travel discounts
+ Stock options
+ Corporate culture is becoming looser

DOWNERS

+ Unsexy industry
+ Travel perks cut into pay

EMPLOYMENT CONTACT

Jim Rynott
P.O. Box 66100
Chicago, IL 60666
(706) 952-4000

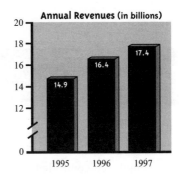

Annual Revenues (in billions)

- 1995: 14.9
- 1996: 16.4
- 1997: 17.4

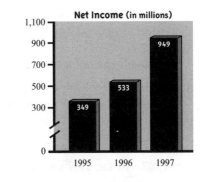

Net Income (in millions)

- 1995: 349
- 1996: 533
- 1997: 949

Employees

- 1995: 83,929
- 1996: 87,628
- 1997: 91,700

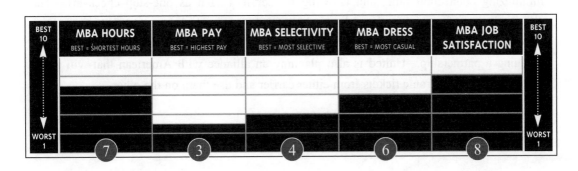

	MBA HOURS BEST = SHORTEST HOURS	MBA PAY BEST = HIGHEST PAY	MBA SELECTIVITY BEST = MOST SELECTIVE	MBA DRESS BEST = MOST CASUAL	MBA JOB SATISFACTION	
	7	3	4	6	8	

MBA Job Seekers: Receive free e-mailed job postings matching
your interests & qualifications! Register at www.VaultReports.com

VAULT REPORTS™

www.vaultreports.com

485

THE SCOOP

The world's second largest airline (and America's largest), United is also the world's largest employee-controlled corporation. Employees currently own 55 percent of the corporation, and since United's employee buyout in 1993, the company has revived profits and recorded unprecedented sales. United's recent success as an airline, however, comes after years of bitter union battles and failed forays into the hospitality business.

Originally part of a conglomerate that included Boeing and Pratt and Whitney, United Airlines split from these industrial divisions in 1934. Slow to offer jet service, United nevertheless became the number one airline in the world by 1961. United bought Westin Hotel in 1970, Hertz Rent-A-Car in 1985, and Hilton International in 1987 as part of its effort to become a travel conglomerate. A shareholder revolt forced United to sell its non-airline operations in 1987. In the 1990s several failed attempts to lower costs through labor concessions led to layoffs and bitter labor disputes instead – an impasse that led to the 1994 plan that ceded 55 percent of the company to employees in exchange for $4.8 billion in wage concession and work rule revisions.

Profitable again, United is turning its attention to forming profitable partnerships with competitors. The company has signed an agreement with several international carriers to share profits and resources on several flight routes. In 1998, the airline announced a marketing alliance with the U.S.'s third-largest carrier, Delta. As the first step in this strategy, the two airlines linked their frequent-flier plans, lumping together United's 30 million members with Delta's 23 million. United and Delta also plan to begin code sharing (allowing one airline to put its two-letter ID code on the flights of another airline to coordinate schedules, thus minimizing connection time, and allowing for services such as one-stop check-in). The alliance is one of several in the airline industry – American Airlines and US Airways have announced a plan to link frequent flier plans and codes, and Northwest and Continental are also pursuing a partnership. United is also planning an alliance with American that will allow travelers to buy electronic tickets from either carrier and use them on the other.

GETTING HIRED

United hires MBAs for finance, marketing, and operations functions; most business school hires have two to three years of work experience. New recruits – about a dozen a year – are brought into the company's Finance Planning & Analysis division. The MBAs spend one year serving as internal consultants to senior management, before moving to another division. In the first year, each MBA is assigned to a team that focuses on one particular aspect of United's operations: performance analysis, operating budget, capital planning, or financial analysis. MBAs progress from staff analyst to senior staff analyst to manager and then director.

OUR SURVEY SAYS

United Airlines' employees boast of their "soaring morale" now that they are part owners of the friendly skies. "We're the largest employee-owned company in the world. Since our employee stock option plan several years ago, we have definitely become more people and customer oriented," reports one contact. "Years ago we were very conservative with a traditional corporate environment, but that has all pretty much changed. No more stuffy suits and ties." Says another insider: "The culture is excellent, with a lot of team decisions and a relaxed, dress-down atmosphere."

United is MBA-happy. "It may take a while to get established with only an undergrad degree," says one insider. On the other hand, "MBAs can do quite well." All United employees, however, enjoy the "generous flight allowances" that enable them to "make each vacation count." The travel benefits may not be such a hot deal, since "pay is considered to be at a discount because the travel benefits are valued highly by many – one could expect to make from 10 percent to 25 percent less than at a company with standard benefits." On the bright side, as befits a company that literally works all over the world, employees term the workforce

MBA Job Seekers: Receive free e-mailed job postings matching your interests & qualifications! Register at www.VaultReports.com

VAULT REPORTS™
www.vaultreports.com

487

"multinational and multicultural." Says one minority insider: "The company is really great in promoting equality in opportunities and goes to great lengths to make sure that things are fair and above board."

"Years ago we were very conservative with a traditional corporate environment, but that has all pretty much changed. No more stuffy suits and ties."

– United insider

Appendix

ALPHABETIZED INDEX OF MBA EMPLOYERS

VAULT
REPORTS™
www.vaultreports.com

INDEX OF MBA EMPLOYERS BY INDUSTRY

INVESTMENT BANKING

MANAGEMENT CONSULTING

MBA Job Seekers: Receive free e-mailed job postings matching
your interests & qualifications! Register at www.VaultReports.com

VAULT REPORTS™
www.vaultreports.com
495

HIGH TECH

MBA Job Seekers: Receive free e-mailed job postings matching
your interests & qualifications! Register at www.VaultReports.com

VAULT
REPORTS™
497
www.vaultreports.com

INDEX OF MBA EMPLOYERS BY HQ LOCATION

MBA Job Seekers: Receive free e-mailed job postings matching
your interests & qualifications! Register at www.VaultReports.com

499

www.vaultreports.com

NEW YORK

OHIO

OREGON

VAULT REPORTS™
www.vaultreports.com

TEXAS

WASHINGTON

ONTARIO, CANADA

MBA Job Seekers: Receive free e-mailed job postings matching
your interests & qualifications! Register at www.VaultReports.com

501

www.vaultreports.com

H.S. (Sam) Hamadeh: H.S. Hamadeh is co-founder and managing director of Vault Reports. He holds a BA in economics from UCLA and a JD/MBA from the Wharton School of Business and the University of Pennsylvania Law School, where was an editor on Law Review. He has worked at the law firms Cravath Swaine & Moore and Skadden Arps and at the investment banks Goldman Sachs and Morgan Stanley. He has authored three books on career-related subjects.

Marcy Lerner: Marcy is executive editor of Vault Reports. She graduated from the University of Virginia with a BA in history and holds an MA in history from Yale University.

Ed Shen: Ed is managing editor of Vault Reports. He graduated from Harvard University with a BA in English. Previously, he was a reporter with *The Advocate* of Stamford, CT.

Doug Cantor: Doug is an associate at Vault Reports. He graduated from Vanderbilt University and is the editor of the online magazine, therumpus.com.

Andrew T. Gillies: Andrew is an associate at Vault Reports. He graduated from Brown University with a BA in History and holds an MA in French from Middlebury College.

Chandra Prasad: Chandra is an associate at Vault Reports. She graduated from Yale University in 1997 with a degree in English, with a concentration in Women's Literature. She joined Vault Reports after confusing it with a club in New York with a similar name.

Nikki Scott: Nikki is an associate at Vault Reports. She graduated from Amherst College in 1997 with a degree in English Literature, with a concentration in Caribbean Literature. After a brief stint in the advertising world, Nikki joined Vault Reports.

MBA JOB SEEKERS:

Have MBA job and internship openings that match your criteria e-mailed to you!

VAULTMATCH™

FROM VAULT REPORTS

VAULT REPORTS™

A free service for MBA job seekers!

Vault Reports will e-mail you job and internship postings that match your interests and qualifications. This is a free service from Vault Reports. Here's how it works:

1 You visit www.VaultReports.com and fill out an online questionnaire, indicating your qualifications and the types of positions you want.

2 Companies contact Vault Reports with job openings.

3 Vault Reports sends you an e-mail about each position which matches your qualifications and interests.

4 For each position that interests you, simply reply to the e-mail and attach your resume.

5 Vault Reports laser prints your resume on top-quality resume paper and sends it to the company's hiring manager within 5 days.

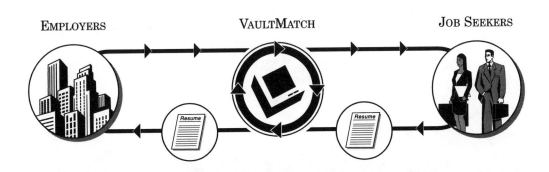

EMPLOYERS   VAULTMATCH   JOB SEEKERS

EMPLOYERS: PUT VAULTMATCH TO WORK FOR YOU. CONTACT VAULT REPORTS AT 888-562-8285.

www.VaultReports.com

JOB INTERVIEWS ARE COMING!

Your competition is prepared...are you?

Vault Reports Employer Profiles are 50- to 70-page reports on leading employers designed to help you ace your job interviews. **Vault Reports Industry Guides** are 100- to 400-page guides providing in-depth information on leading industries, including industry trends, sample interview questions, and snapshots of the top firms. Filled with "insider" details, the Profiles and Industry Guides provide the hard-to-get company info that no recruiting brochure would dare reveal. Profiles are available on hundreds of leading companies.

> **Price: $25 per Employer Profile***
> **$35 per Industry Guide***

As Featured In
Newsweek
& The Wall
Street Journal

EMPLOYER PROFILES

American Express	KPMG
American Management Systems	Lehman Brothers
Andersen Consulting	McKinsey & Co.
Arthur Andersen	Mercer
Arthur D. Little	Merrill Lynch
AT Kearney	Microsoft
Bain & Co.	Mitchell Madison
Bankers Trust	Monitor
Bear Stearns	Morgan Stanley Dean Witter
Booz Allen & Hamilton	Oracle
Boston Consulting Group	PricewaterhouseCoopers
Cargill	Procter & Gamble
Chase	Salomon Smith Barney
Citicorp/Citibank	Sprint
Coca-Cola	Walt Disney
Credit Suisse First Boston	
Deloitte & Touche	.......100s more!
Deutsche Bank	
Donaldson Lufkin & Jenrette	
Enron	### INDUSTRY GUIDES
Ernst & Young	
Fidelity Investments	Advertising
Ford Motor	Brand Management
Gemini	Fashion
General Mills	Healthcare
Goldman Sachs	High Tech
Hewlett Packard	Internet and New Media
Intel	Investment Banking
JP Morgan	Management Consulting
	MBA Employers
	Media and Entertainment

To order call 1-888-JOB-VAULT or order online at www.VaultReports.com

The first career guides of their kind, Vault Reports' Industry Guides offer detailed evaluations of America's leading employers. Enriched with responses from thousands of insider surveys and interviews, these guides tell it like it is – the good and the bad – about the companies everyone is talking about. Each guide includes a complete industry overview as well as information on the industry's job opportunities, career paths, hiring procedures, culture, pay, and commonly asked interview questions..

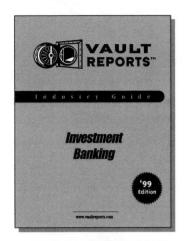

Each employer entry includes:

 The Scoop: the juicy details on each company's past, present, and future.

 Getting Hired: insider advice on what it takes to get that job offer.

 Our Survey Says: thousands of employees speak their mind on company culture, satisfaction, pay, prestige, and more.

PRICE: $35 PER GUIDE

GUIDE TO ADVERTISING™

Reviews America's top employers in the advertising industry, including Bozell Worldwide, Grey Advertising, Leo Burnett, Ogilvy & Mather, TBWAChiat/Day, and many more!

100pp.

GUIDE TO FASHION™

Reviews America's top employers in the fashion industry, including Calvin Klein, Donna Karan, Estee Lauder, The Gap, J. Crew, IMG Models, and many more!

100pp.

GUIDE TO HEALTHCARE™

Reviews America's top employers in the healthcare industry, including Amgen, Eli Lilly, Johnson & Johnson, Oxford, Pfizer, Schering-Plough, and many more!

120pp.

GUIDE TO HIGH TECH™

Reviews America's top employers in the high tech industry, including Broderbund, Cisco Systems, Hewlett-Packard, Intel, Microsoft, Sun Microsystems, and many more!

400pp.

GUIDE TO INTERNET AND NEW MEDIA™

Reviews America's top employers in the Internet and new media industry, including Amazon.com, CDNow, DoubleClick, Excite, Netscape, Yahoo!, and many more!

130pp.

GUIDE TO INVESTMENT BANKING™

Reviews America's top employers in the investment banking industry, including Bankers Trust, Goldman Sachs, JP Morgan, Morgan Stanley, and many more!

400pp.

GUIDE TO MANAGEMENT CONSULTING™

Reviews America's top employers in the management consulting industry, including Andersen Consulting, Boston Consulting Group, McKinsey, PricewaterhouseCoopers, and many more!

400pp.

GUIDE TO MARKETING AND BRAND MANAGEMENT™

Reviews America's top employers in the marketing and brand management industry, including General Mills, Procter & Gamble, Nike, Coca-Cola, and many more!

150pp.

GUIDE TO MBA EMPLOYERS™

Reviews America's top employers for MBAs, including Fortune 500 corporations, management consulting firms, investment banks, venture capital and LBO firms, commercial banks, and hedge funds.

500pp.

GUIDE TO MEDIA AND ENTERTAINMENT™

Reviews America's top employers in the media and entertainment industry, including AOL, Blockbuster, CNN, Dreamworks, Gannett, National Public Radio, Time Warner, and many more!

400pp.

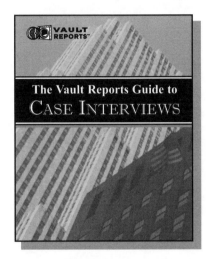

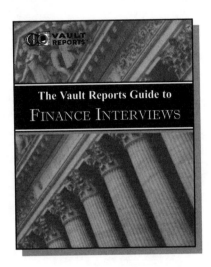

austere culture